1977

Linguistics, English,
and the Language Arts

Linguistics, English,
and the Language Arts

CARL A. LEFEVRE
Temple University

ALLYN and BACON, Inc.
BOSTON

#79457

For Helen

Contents

Contents

List of Illustrations

Foreword

In the quest for excellence in education, the English teacher, especially the elementary teacher who is the first teacher of formalized instruction in the English language — skills, attitudes, and content — is often asked to operate from a base that is tragically lacking in understanding of the history and structure of the English language.

Carl Lefevre, in *Linguistics, English, and the Language Arts,* has attempted, and succeeded admirably in my opinion, in closing the gap between what teachers know and what they need to know about language in order to use the new materials in helping young learners reach their highest linguistic potential. What the linguists and psycholinguists have been able to contribute to modern teaching materials and method is nothing short of miraculous; children's interest in, and ability to understand, the history of our language and the phonemic, morphemic and syntactical patterns of English amazes and delights the scholars; but teachers trained in a different era find themselves submerged in a sea of confusion and frustration which often leads to uncertainty and rejection of new ideas and materials.

It is no longer a question of new English or old. Today no single grammar suffices to explain and describe language; every competent teacher should have some basic understanding of what each of the grammars has to contribute. It is its synthesis of traditional, structural, transformational or generative grammars, its treatment of the phonemic, morphemic and syntactical structuring of utterance, its insistence upon the importance of the spoken word, thoughtfully spoken and thoughtfully listened to, and its appreciation of the place of literature in the school curriculum that makes this volume unique.

MIRIAM E. WILT
TEMPLE UNIVERSITY

Preface

This is a book for teachers, written by a teacher.

The teachers for whom it is written comprise three principal audiences:

1. College students, both undergraduate and graduate, preparing themselves for teaching English or the language arts.

2. Classroom teachers, with their years of rich experience.

3. College teachers of English and language arts methods — including teachers interested but not expert in linguistics, who are willing to share their own learning experiences with their students.

To teach and learn from this book it is not necessary to be an authority in linguistics; all that is necessary is to approach it in a spirit of exploration and discovery.

Inquiry is the fundamental method advocated throughout.

This book can serve an inquiring student or teacher as an introduction to linguistics. At the same time, without attempting to outline a detailed curriculum, it does offer an extended presentation of English linguistics applied to the teaching of English and the language arts, grades N–12, with Notes and Selected References for each chapter. Thus it may also serve as a reference text in a teacher's professional library.

The three divisions of the book serve different but related purposes. Part One (three chapters) is concerned with values and perspective in the teaching of English and the language arts; with the breadth and depth and scope of language study; and with the centrality of language in human life and culture. Part One is designed to give a humane orientation and a sense of the magnitude of the subject as a whole. Part Two (seven chapters) is the main body of the book: the direct exposition of linguistic information, coupled with teaching methods; the order of chapters proceeds from the smallest units, sounds and letters, through increasingly larger elements of language, words and sentences, to intonation, and finally to literature.

The chapter on literature is suggestive rather than exhaustive; moreover, it does not treat all aspects of literature that may be taught, but only those that fall within the province of the previous discussion. Part Three presents two overviews: Chapter 11 is a brief survey of grammars considered as teaching devices; Chapter 12, taking an N–12 perspective view of Parts One and Two, is designed to be the capstone of the book. The organization of the entire text is highlighted for the reader by outlines of headings and subheadings at intervals throughout the chapters.

Within a short space, Chapter 11 surveys the various grammars in existence today, and evaluates them in terms of their classroom utility. In common with the book as a whole, this discussion is integral with and rests upon the author's broad theoretical position, which may be outlined somewhat as follows.

The ultimate aims of instruction in English and the language arts are governed by such fundamental assumptions as these (which may also determine the educational outcomes):

1. Language and language learning are the most important of all learnings — to the individual, to his speech community, to the larger society, and to the world.

2. These learnings involve fundamental human and philosophical values; the degree of success (or failure) in acquiring them will be reflected in the relative success or failure of each person, not only as a learner but as a human being.

3. Language and language learning, understood in these terms, underlie and to a large degree determine the measure of success or failure in the basic skills of literacy — reading and writing — and in the mastery of the higher language skills and the other subjects that are dependent upon them.

4. Thus, the broad aims of school instruction in English and the language arts, briefly stated, are: (a) to implant and cultivate appreciation of the central importance of language (oral/written) and literature in both the private and the social life of man; (b) to develop ease and fluency in all the varied uses of language, oral and written, listened to and read; and (c) to cultivate the ability to experience literature directly and to enjoy the experience.

Some operational assumptions that follow from these fundamental assumptions may be stated in this way:

1. Normative prescriptivism in instruction in all aspects of English and the language arts, no matter what philosophical or

descriptive view underlies and pervades it, is a principal cause of disabilities and failures in several skills and various dimensions of language learning and appreciation.

2. It is not an aim of school instruction to make grammarians or junior linguists out of the students, nor to make them over into precocious literary critics; it is a serious but common mistake to try to do one or both.

3. Although no teacher is in danger of knowing too much about language and linguistics, many try to teach (or simply to tell) their students altogether too much of whatever they do know.

4. Our present knowledge of language and language learning is still in its infancy; we are involved in an interdisciplinary and open-ended enterprise.

5. Nevertheless, teachers must teach, using their best insights and informed by the best values that present knowledge, experience, and professional judgment can provide; the best teaching approach is that of intellectual inquiry, expressed in a willingness to explore and discover with their students, and to accept the students' findings along with their own, share and share alike.

6. As to compulsory grammar instruction specifically: in the elementary school, the technical content should be a spiral treatment of what may be described as pregrammar, through repeated exposure, imitation, and manipulation by the children, with only a necessary minimum of terminology learned by association rather than verbal definition; in the secondary school, optional instruction in several grammars as disciplines should be offered in elective courses, without pressure, for interested and motivated students; in the junior high school, transitional learning units in linguistics and grammar would be appropriate as part of the larger program.

In sum, what is set forth in this book is the carefully considered opinion of the author. While this position is intellectual in its linguistic rigor, and philosophical in its concern with human values, it is not supposed to be sicklied o'er with the pale cast of thought. The basic position is humanistic, and is deeply rooted in human experience: in personal, immediate, observed experience, and in the vicarious experience of the scholar. Language is deeply felt to be the central attribute of man, and by far his most distinctive attainment. As to language learning, language teaching, and the uses of language generally, it is essential not to forget that man is the only talking animal — that language is the respect in which man differs qualitatively from all other animals on earth. Despite his kinship with his fellow creatures, with all forms of life, man must never be confused with the parrot, the pigeon, the chicken, the chimpanzee — not even with the communicative dolphin, attractive as that bright creature may be. Nor should man be confused with any kind of machine; linguistic and other comparisons of men with machines can distort and dwarf the essential image of man. All this seems perfectly and completely obvious to the author, and perhaps to others. But today it seems that such an explicit humanistic view must be clearly and firmly stated, lest by default humane teaching of language, even in the preschool years, give way to the methods of carrot-and-stick conditioners of babes and sucklings, or the methods of other teaching mechanics. If this be a partisan position, then so be it; it is deliberately partisan in the good old cause — the cause of man.

Linguistics is inherently no more difficult than several other subjects successfully studied by undergraduate students, including majors in elementary education. Linguistics is, after all, the systematic modern study of language in all its dimensions; in its narrower dimensions, linguistics can be rigorously precise, scientific, like mathematics, say, or science, or music. But it is no more difficult.

What may make linguistics seem more difficult to learn is the embeddedness of the native language in the consciousness and personality of the learner. Because he is a native speaker of his language, he is literally unconscious of many complexities of the language which in his everyday life works so fluently, so automatically, for him. The inner workings of his language tend to remain inaccessible to him, because he is normally inclined to take it all for granted, much as he does his sectarian religious beliefs, or his partisan political loyalties. His language and his naive opinions about it are not open to rational discussion, much less rigorous examination or criticism; in fact, disagreements on points of grammar and usage often share with disputes over politics and religion the same manner and tone of voice: noisy, heated, muddled, inconclusive. No one ever changes his mind. Successful study and teaching of linguistics — especially as applied to the speaker's native language — means trying to achieve a degree of linguistic consciousness conducive to developing an objective view, first of all, of the native tongue, then of language generally, and finally of language learning.

The linguistic autobiography project at the end of Chapter 1 can be highly profitable to anyone willing to do the work it requires; one of its special values is to help develop and enhance linguistic consciousness. Teachers of beginning students using this book may choose to limit their assignments to the text itself; in some courses it may be appropriate to assign individual students to report on a chapter or section not assigned to the whole class. For advanced and graduate students, however, the Notes to each chapter (included in the back matter), and Selected References at the ends of chapters, provide a substantial variety of materials for study going well beyond the text proper. Thus, the discussion of both language and methods throughout this book can provide an adequate foundation for teaching completely language-centered courses; yet by selecting particular sections for emphasis a teacher may fashion the methods course that suits him best. Students who have access to classrooms may try out one or more of the **Teaching Suggestions** to be found throughout the text; many of them are quite adaptable to microteaching. These **Suggestions** are also intended to stimulate further and deeper study of particular linguistic topics.

Acknowledgments

First, I would like to express my sense of an incalculable debt to those linguists, scientists, philosophers, creative writers, and scholars of humane letters whose works I have studied, and which have formed the matrix of my education. The Notes and Selected References for each chapter are a form of recognition of the linguists especially. I gratefully acknowledge also the formative influence of my own teachers, professors, and colleagues; and the help of my students, many of them classroom teachers, who have contributed qualitatively to my understanding of the teaching of language and literature, and of the applications of linguistics as part of that teaching.

My professional work is not identified exclusively with any single discipline, and much less with any special "school" within a discipline. In so far as I am identified as a linguist, I associate myself with the broad descriptive tradition that begins with Aristotle rather than with Plato; this tradition is just as much concerned with philosophy as the introspective neo-Platonic movement in linguistics, although their values and methods are quite different. In our own century in America, this tradition includes the work of such men as Boas, Sapir, Bloomfield, Fries, Gleason, Hill, Hockett, Joos, Nida, Pike, Smith, Trager, and Whitehall; this is a representative but not exhaustive list. The descriptive linguistic tradition is characterized by an objective view of language, and sets a high premium on empirical data and replicable studies as bases for interpretations and conclusions; it is also characterized by a cultural-anthropological view of language and human society that I find thoroughly compatible with humanistic philosophy and scholarship. It must be emphasized, however, that the views set forth in this book are my own; I take full responsibility for them.

Grateful acknowledgment is herewith made to The National NDEA Institute for Advanced Study in Teaching Disadvantaged Youth for permission to use material in Chapter 1 that was published in part in *Report Three*, June, 1968, with other papers from a seminar directed by Dr. Miriam Wilt, Professor of English Education at

Temple University and to the NCTE for generous permission to quote, paraphrase, or otherwise use my own articles published in *Elementary English*, in appropriate places in the book.

Parts of Chapter 9 were first written at the invitation of a joint committee of the National Council of Teachers of English and the International Reading Association, for publication in a projected volume of articles on linguistics and reading; a few copies of a mimeographed version were distributed, bearing my copyright notice. Similarly, a part of Chapter 11 was first presented during a symposium and later published in a book (with my copyright notice and permission) entitled *The Psycholinguistic Nature of the Reading Process* (Detroit, Michigan: Wayne State University Press, 1968).

Part One

The Nature of Language and Communication

Chapter 1

Values in the Teaching of
English and the Language Arts

Let me begin with a space-age fable.

Once upon a time, an *ad hoc* committee of reading specialists, with an NDEA grant and a hoist from NASA, blasted me off to another galaxy to lecture on linguistics and the teaching of reading. The lectures were in real time, but the space travel out and back was in light-years. I became the first space-age Rip Van Winkle.

Upon my return, remarkable progress had been made in the study of language and language learning, and in teaching the arts and skills of English. This progress was all the more remarkable because it now included reading, which was fruitfully associating with the other English language arts; all were harmoniously language-centered. Although characterized by a variety of multi-media learning materials and instructional practices, the field of English, reading, and the language arts had become a single, unified discipline.

It was called simply "English."

No dividing lines cut across the N–12 continuum; school and community interacted busily and occasionally merged. In college and university the immemorial Balkan subdivision into warring principalities had given way to a loose confederacy; borders between academic states were no longer fortified, and some had virtually disappeared. A few professors moved about freely within the confederacy, and some enjoyed full citizenship in two or more states. A liberal

3

student visa policy permitted students to cross state boundaries, study for a time, and return without loss of face; exchange rates favored the students. Wars between the states had become so boring that only an occasional centenarian sounded ancient alarms; there were no more armed truces. Town and Gown were already redeveloping their original educational park. Halcyon day!

Perhaps such a multidisciplinary approach is light-years removed from present concerns with the inviolable territorial rights of isolated departments and colleges, and with the jurisdictional security they try to maintain by fortifying and patrolling the boundaries that divide them. If so we may as well gaze into interstellar space and await what may transpire with the passage of time. A professional solution, however, can be reached in our lifetime, provided we are ready to consider our problems in the light of the values we seek in English education.

What values do we seek in our teaching of English and the language arts? We Americans are supposed to be great at know-how, the practical means of getting the job done; but we are sometimes contemptuous of theory, which could sharpen perspective on what we are doing. Adequate theory might also help us discover jobs we should be doing but are neglecting Solving our professional problems requires more than know-*how;* it requires know-*what* and know-*why.* These questions relate to developing a theory of English teaching.

The great question is, "What is the essential nature of language, what is its true role in human cultures and sub-cultures?" (I am not fond of the term *sub-culture,* but if we take it to mean simply a smaller culture embedded in a larger culture — an embedded culture coextensive with a speech community — perhaps *sub-culture* need not have a pejorative tone.)

We also need to ask other questions: What is English? Why teach English? Can we develop a theory of English teaching? What is the nature of the English teacher's role? What should the English teacher do? What should the English teacher not do? What is the professional identity of the English teacher?

These questions are suggestive. In the following exploratory discussion, some of them will be directly confronted; others will be approached obliquely. The intent of such questions is to stimulate serious consideration of the profession of teaching English and the language arts.

Let us turn now to a brief consideration of the nature of language, and of linguistics in relation to it. In its largest sense, linguistics is simply the modern study of language, a spacious subject. As an objective way of looking at the central and most characteristic achievement of mankind — language and the uses of language — modern linguistics originated in and emerged from anthropology. The study of language and its uses is the most comprehensive of the humanities; moreover, language study is fundamental to other humane studies. It is language that makes man human, language that offers a basis for hope that human life can indeed become human, that human societies may become worthy of man's promise.

Every English teacher should deeply understand the centrality of language in human life and human culture. Insights contributing to this understanding may come from anthropological linguistics, biolinguistics, philosophical linguistics, psycholinguistics, sociolinguistics, from applied English linguistics — from life itself, including the interpersonal relationship of student and teacher, which can be a means of studying language by exploration. Those of us who teach English and the language arts must concern ourselves with the attainment of these insights. The study of language is the most interdisciplinary of all studies; it is in fact multidisciplinary.

The remainder of this chapter is presented as six subtopics, as follows:

Developmental Causes and Effects

A Model of English as a General Field: Know-what, Know-how, Know-why

The Professional Identity of the English Teacher

The English Teacher: Martyr or Monster?

Nurturing Growth of Language

A Linguistic Autobiography Project

Developmental Causes and Effects

Some understanding of the physiological equipment used in speech is helpful in appreciating *the developmental nature of language in human growth and development.* This topic is part of the special study of *biolinguistics.*

All human beings the world over use the same biological organs to produce all the sounds of thousands of languages; but there are no "speech organs" used either primarily or exclusively for the production of speech sounds. Quite the contrary. Every one of the so-called speech organs must first be developed through its use in fundamental biological functions before it is capable of playing its part in the production of language. The human infant and child must first learn how to cry, cough, suck, bite, chew, swallow, and burp before he can produce the consonant and vowel sounds of language; before he can control the vibrations of his vocal folds, or initiate and terminate the speech stream; before he can learn how to impart rhythm to his speech; before he can speak in the native melodies and tunes.

If we isolate their limited functions in language, the "speech organs" have some resemblance to the various parts of a musical wind instrument. The breathing system as a whole contains and controls the stream of air that emerges from the oral and nasal openings as speech. At one end of this wind instrument lies the diaphragm, a powerful layer of tendon and muscle separating the abdominal and chest cavities; although most of its action is involuntary, the diaphragm can be controlled in speech, in concert with the musculature of the rib cage, to act as a bellows. As we learn to speak English, this "bellows" is developed through practice to impart a stress-timed rhythm to our speech; this rhythm, like all other specific linguistic symbols, is not instinctive but learned. (Stress-timed rhythm is discussed more fully in Chapter 9. American English Intonation.)

Above the diaphragm and within the rib cage, the lungs supply the column of air that becomes the speech stream, and with the bronchial tubes, trachea, larynx, pharynx, oral and nasal openings, form the resonating chambers that give individuality to the voice. The larynx houses the vocal folds that vibrate, somewhat like a double reed in a bassoon, to produce the air waves that carry the sound of the human voice to the listening ear. This sound is given specific linguistic overtones by the action of the tongue, lips, teeth, and inner surfaces of the mouth to produce speech, a communicative system of vocal symbols. (See Figure 1.1.)

In his first months of life, along with developing the fundamental biological functions of the organs later to be used in talking, the infant normally experiments with prelinguistic intonation (cooing, crowing, crying, lallation, murmuring, singing, whimpering), and with a variety of prelinguistic sounds that resemble vowels and consonants. These are prelinguistic because they are not part of any

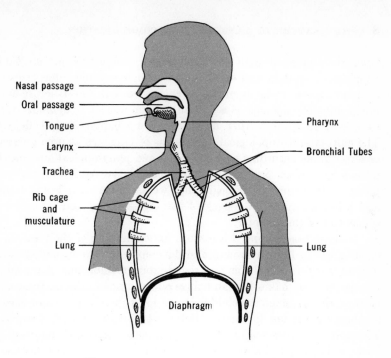

*Figure 1.1 Human organs used in speech.**

language system but are produced with only minimal linguistic consciousness or control; they are of extraordinary importance, however, as the raw linguistic materials out of which the child will fashion, by selection and rejection, a specific system of vocal symbols for communication with members of his speech community. Generally between the ages of six months and one year, the human infant begins to make the conversion from the various vocal noises made by all normal human babies to the intricate and very specific structural components of the language he was born to.

This developmental process is studied further in the special fields of *psycholinguistics* and *sociolinguistics*. We are only now beginning to map some of the intricate psycholinguistic processes involved in the acquisition and use of language. In essence, the term *psycholinguistics* suggests the merging, or better, the marriage, of psychology and linguistics — two distinct but closely related disciplines dealing with specialized areas of human behavior. To state the matter somewhat narrowly and oversimply, psychology of lan-

* Original drawing by Richard R. Smith.

guage is concerned with the internalized, subjective processes of language in thought and emotion, self-expression, and interpersonal communication; while linguistics is concerned with the structure and functioning of language as a system of communicative symbols in a total culture. (For further discussion, see Chapter 3, pp. 60–61.) The cultural-anthropological dimensions of language assume greater or lesser value according to one's social and philosophical outlook; I myself have been profoundly impressed by the American anthropological tradition whose beginnings we associate with Franz Boas and Edward Sapir. For suggested readings, see Selected References at the end of this chapter.

English teachers need a mature understanding of the vital role of language in human growth and development; in personality and individuality; in social role and social-group membership. Language is what in time makes human beings out of human infants. In every culture, the language the child is born to is a specific system of vocal symbols that is not instinctive but must be painstakingly learned. Through the processes of acquiring language, every human being becomes intimately linked with his speech community, with his self-image and his social role, with his sense of his own identity and of belonging. These linkages are emotional and intellectual, neurological and physiological, familial above all, and are inextricably enmeshed with his value system; his faith and beliefs, his hopes and fears, his affections and hatreds, his dreams and his nightmares — all are deeply interwoven with his language to become the living tissue of his life. In short, *the individual's language is the essential socio-psychological bond that makes him one with his culture;* similarly, a child born into a subculture feels, thinks, and speaks as a part of that subculture.

The specific variety of language spoken in any culture or subculture is its dialect; a dialect may have special characteristics associated with a geographical region, a social class, or the national origin of its native speakers. The word *dialect* does not carry pejorative overtones, but is a neutral technical term in the study of language. All native-born Americans speak one or another dialect of American English. And that dialect is very important to us.

Anyone who attacks or appears to attack an individual's dialect is immediately understood to be attacking the person himself, attacking him and his very way of life; this is doubly true if the attacker is a teacher, a powerful official who may represent an alien, even a threatening way of life. A teacher who peremptorily undertakes to alter deeply ingrained language habits can inflict irreparable damage, especially a teacher who does not have linguistic insights and knowledge, or who lacks strong bonds of empathy with the student. Such inept efforts, no matter whether well meant, constitute a direct threat and will be so taken. The professional teacher's understanding of the meaning of language to each individual will preclude such threatening behavior.

It sometimes happens that a well-meaning teacher confuses reading instruction with corrective speech, or even with teaching the student to speak a different dialect; under the guise of teaching phonics, she tries to give him a new set of speech sounds and in more general reading instruction, she tries to teach him a new set of noun and verb endings. Yet all over the world, adult speakers of diverse English dialects read the sounds of their own speech from standard printed English: dialects of England, Scotland, Ireland, Wales, South Africa, Australia, New Zealand, and a dozen or so regional dialects of North America. The student's natural dialect, unchanged, can be his immediate bridge to the skills of literacy; the teacher should not bewilder him in his initial approach to literacy by attempting to force him to learn a new dialect as a prerequisite. *The two linguistic processes, learning to read and write, and learning to speak a new dialect, cannot be combined without serious danger that both will be jeopardized.*

Language learning is voluntary learning. If dialect change is to be effected, each individual speaker must first volunteer to make the change himself. No captive audience in an American classroom, no captive people in a conquered land, have ever been forced to change their language without their consent; language change must be motivated, because it cannot be forced. If the student cannot be persuaded to volunteer, it is unlikely that he will ever consent to change his dialect, and nothing can be done about it. He must volunteer or else.

There is another way to look at dialect change. First and foremost, such a change need not involve "elimination" of any dialect; rather, it should involve mastering a second dialect without sacrificing the first. The essential differences will be in sentence structure and noun and verb endings, rather than in basic sounds, although a few differences in basic sounds may be significant. The persuasive argument for bidialectism, for being able to use both "school talk" and "country talk," for learning standard English as a second language — aside from the convenience of being able to talk out of either side of one's mouth to suit the occasion — is an entirely different argument. The gist of this argument is that every American child should be helped to gain access to that universe of knowledge and experience expressed in a special dialect, standard *written* English, the only key that can unlock the doors of libraries and the accumulating heritage of human culture and experience embodied in all forms of printed English. Standard *spoken* English is another matter entirely, even if we could all agree on a firm definition of it.

It remains an open question whether widespread dialect changes should be attempted anyway, beyond offering suitable instruction to students who volunteer for it, because this would mean fundamental alterations in a speaker's natural way of talking. An appealing and less expensive alternative would be to rid ourselves of prejudice toward dialects that differ from our own, and to look more deeply into language, man, and society.

Besides, the case for onward and upward mobility is not necessarily convincing to everyone, perhaps especially not to the black child in the urban ghetto. Upward mobility may not strike him as a possibility — *for him.* Or striving mightily to move up the socio-economic ladder into the dominant white world simply may not appeal to him, at least not early enough in his life for him to make a substantial dialect change. The rationale of upward mobility for all Americans does seem to ignore basic socio-economic realities: such as the actual number of presently available jobs, *regardless of dialect;* and the hair-raising prospect of ever-increasing automation, with its threat of *reducing* the number of jobs to the point where work of any kind may become a rare privilege. Moreover, the black child may not believe that his dialect is all that sentences him to life in the ghetto; he may rather think his color lies at the bottom of his troubles. Does anyone seriously believe that the elimination of ghetto dialects could really cause the ghettos themselves to disappear?

Standard written English is a special English, organized for visual presentation — prose — to be found in books of all kinds, including textbooks, and in magazines and newspapers; in even more specialized forms it is the visual medium of poetry (see Chapter 10). Learning to write standard English can help in learning to read it; the two processes, writing and reading, can be presented and discussed so as to emphasize their interaction and thus reinforce the learning of both. Moreover, the learner can begin painlessly to acquire new spoken language patterns by reading standard written English and his own compositions aloud; the helpful effect of both reinforcing processes can be further enhanced by attentive work with a tape recorder. In any case, the learner of a second dialect must first be persuaded to volunteer.

Sooner or later most of us do learn to speak several variants of English by adapting to the varied persons and situations we encounter in life, and according to changing motivations, self-images, and goals. But a prestige dialect, treated prescriptively (that is, snobbishly or sadistically), is "superior" to every other ("inferior") dialect: that is the point of a prestige dialect. This constraint applies to the non-standard dialect spoken by many a white Anglo-Saxon Protestant child in suburbia just as it does to the speech of the slum child deep in the inner-city ghetto; the difference is one of degree. As a segregating device, shibboleth is very ancient, and as hateful as Cain.

A Model of English as a General Field:
Know-what, Know-how, Know-why

It is fashionable to construct elaborate diagrammatic models of psychological processes on the analogy of the electronic computer, with flow-chart visualization of input, output, scanning, feedback, and cybernetic data processing; often this is solemnly intended to be taken literally. The model of English presented in Figures 1.2 to 1.5 is more in the nature of a metaphor suggesting some of the complex interrelationships among the know-what, know-how and know-why of English teaching and learning.

Under know-what (Figure 1.2), we may visualize language, literature, and rhetoric (composition and speech) as a triangle, with language as the base. These components are related to know-how, but in school programs, only rhetoric qualifies as an outright how-to-do-it study; rhetoric should include both oral and written composition, and at least two modes of presentation, exposition and persuasion. In the modern world, language and literature are more substantive than rhetoric, yet classical rhetoric (oratory) encompassed the complete education of a prince or statesman.

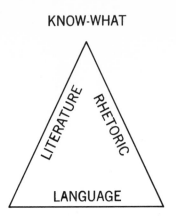

KNOW-WHAT

LITERATURE · RHETORIC

LANGUAGE

Figure 1.2 *

Under know-how (Figure 1.3), we may visualize as a square the four communicative arts and skills of speaking, listening, reading and writing; the audio-lingual processes, listening and speaking, are the top and bottom sides; the visual-manual processes, reading and writing, are the left and right sides. These four communicative processes may also be thought of as two *sending* operations, *speaking* and *writing;* and two *receiving* operations, *listening* and *reading.*

KNOW-HOW

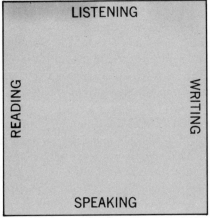

LISTENING

READING · WRITING

SPEAKING

Figure 1.3

* Original drawings for Figures 1.2–1.5 by Warren H. Groff.

Figure 1.4

Know-why (Figure 1.4) involves the full range of cognitive and affective processes within the individual, teacher and student alike; we may designate these processes as intellect and emotion, or as brain and heart, without being too literal-minded about it. We may regard intellect and emotion as polar attributes, as antipodes, but they are better understood as interacting processes than as static positions. In English as elsewhere in life, intellect and emotion blend imperceptibly into one another. We may visualize their polarity and the continuum between extremes as an ellipse with intellect (brain) at one end, and emotion (heart) at the other; intellectual and emotional processes contribute to conceptual thought, esthetic enjoyment, and creative experience. The suggestion is that in English, such complex arts and skills as appreciation, creativity, criticism, and performance combine both kinds of processes, the intellective and the affective. We may visualize these high level arts and skills as a circle within the ellipse that here represents the continuum of intellectual and emotional processes.

Expression of intellect in a nearly pure form may be illustrated by the clear linking-verb sentences used by mathematicians and scientists:

$$x^2 + y^2 = z^2 \qquad \text{or} \qquad e = mc^2.$$

As linguistic expressions, such equations are essentially uncolored by emotion, although they may give a measure of esthetic enjoyment.

Emotion, or heart, may be illustrated by those intense moments in poems that we sometimes call pure poetry, the best evidence being the chill that tingles down the spine of the reader. Much of Blake's "The Tiger" affects some readers in this way.

> Tiger! Tiger! burning bright
> In the forests of the night.
> What immortal hand or eye
> Could frame thy fearful symmetry?
>
> In what distant deeps or skies
> Burnt the fire of thine eyes?
> On what wings dare he aspire?
> What the hand dare seize the fire?
>
> And what shoulder and what art
> Could twist the sinews of thy heart?
> And, when thy heart began to beat,
> What dread hand? and what dread feet?

What the hammer? what the chain?
In what furnace was thy brain?
What the anvil? what dread grasp
Dare its deadly terrors clasp?

When the stars threw down their spears
And watered heaven with their tears,
Did he smile his work to see?
Did he who made the Lamb make thee?

Tiger! Tiger! burning bright
In the forests of the night.
What immortal hand or eye
Dare frame thy fearful symmetry?

No poem is all pure poetry; other literary modes, although emotionally moving, have relatively less intense emotional coloring than poetry.

English teaching and learning is a variable mix of the three *know-s:* know-why, know-what, and know-how. In Figure 1.5 is a complete metaphorical model; think of it as a complex of processes, interrelated and interacting.

The Professional Identity of the English Teacher

To play his role with optimum success, the English teacher should cultivate an integral set of mature attainments, personal and professional:

Compassionate understanding of what language means in human life and culture.

Appreciation of the developmental processes of language learning from cradle to college.

Understanding that exploration is a valid approach to language and literature.

Knowledge of the history and structure of the English language; of the history and development of dictionaries; of the teaching values (if any) of English grammars.

Appreciation that great literary works embody great intellect, great emotion, and great language, incorporated in permanent

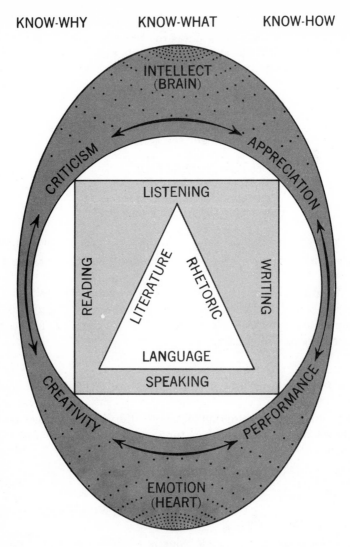

KNOW-WHY   KNOW-WHAT   KNOW-HOW

Figure 1.5

forms; and that all literary works of merit, including children's literature, partake of these qualities in some degree.

Personal experience in arts and skills of communication, including advanced work in composition and rhetoric; acting, oral reading, and interpretation; wide critical reading in literature, both children's and adult.

A vocation for teaching English.

Professional commitment to teaching English.

Perhaps only a super teacher could possess all these attainments in superlative degree, but every English teacher can try.

The remainder of this topic — *The Professional Identity of the English Teacher* — is presented under six subtitles as follows:

UNRECONSTRUCTED NATIVE SPEAKERS OF ENGLISH AS TEACHERS
UNDERSTANDING THE INTERPLAY OF SPEECH, READING, AND WRITING
GENERAL RESPONSIBILITIES OF THE ENGLISH TEACHER
SPECIFIC RESPONSIBILITIES OF THE ENGLISH TEACHER
RESPONSIBILITIES OUTSIDE THE CLASSROOM

UNRECONSTRUCTED NATIVE SPEAKERS OF ENGLISH AS TEACHERS.   A major problem of English teaching is that teachers are frequently unreconstructed native speakers of English. That is, many are largely unconscious of the internalized, automatic language processes acquired before they went to kindergarten; largely unconscious of deep-seated attitudes and "rules" that govern their personal, communicative use of English, as well as the how, what, and why of their teaching of English. This problem is about the same as that presented by teachers of other subjects in their approach to English: the fallacy that any native speaker of a language without special training is qualified to teach it seems to be quite generally believed. Yet what could be further from the truth?

Every English teacher needs to go through a discipline akin to that of the linguist, in order to become sharply conscious of his intuitive language behavior, whose controls lie well below the threshold of consciousness. The English teacher needs to become a *conscious* native speaker, with two parallel tracks in his consciousness and use of English: (1) skillful, direct communication by means of the arts and skills of his native tongue, a living model for his students;

(2) sophisticated consciousness of his own language system and its contrasts with those of his students so that he can relate successfully to them as their teacher. This is no mean assignment, but completing it satisfactorily is an important part of the English teacher's commitment to his teaching field and his lifelong personal involvement with students; without this discipline, he is blind on one side. A "linguistic autobiography" project, designed to help develop this sophisticated consciousness, is described at the end of this chapter.

UNDERSTANDING THE INTERPLAY OF SPEECH, READING, AND WRITING. Most of us, English teachers and laymen alike, need also to overcome a visual bias toward language that afflicts us all in some degree, probably as an outcome of formal education. The negative effect of this visual bias is a tendency to regard the standards of written English — prose — as normative for speech as well as writing; this leads in turn to self-defeating prescriptivism in all the arts and skills of English, and sets the teacher at odds with his students. It is especially important that the English teacher overcome this bias; he should master the concept and grasp the profound consequences of the fact that handwriting and print comprise a secondary symbol system — a system of incalculable importance — but nevertheless one based upon and derived from speech. He should deeply understand the complex interplay between spoken language on one side, and its graphic counterparts and derivative graphic forms on the other. Appreciation of the interplay of the two symbol systems is fundamental to the development of skills in both rhetoric and reading.

GENERAL RESPONSIBILITIES OF THE ENGLISH TEACHER. The English teacher is responsible for organizing and directing developmental learning experiences in language, literature, and rhetoric — content, forms, media, and techniques. He is also responsible for providing original and continuing stimuli for experiences that contribute to the student's overall development of all the arts and skills of communication — reading, writing, speaking, listening, appreciation, creativity, criticism, performance. He should try to keep abreast of learning theory and be familiar with multi-media learning materials and instructional programs. To be able to organize and direct developmental experiences in English for his students, the teacher himself should have enjoyed his own successes (perhaps modest) in similar experiences of his own.

Ideally, the English teacher would embody the attainments of a Renaissance man.

SPECIFIC RESPONSIBILITIES OF THE ENGLISH TEACHER. The English teacher is called upon to develop students' abilities to read, write, spell, listen, and speak both formally and informally; he should be able to motivate students to work as self-starters. He must make assignments, evaluate work in progress, judge completed work both in its own terms and in developmental terms. He must be able to initiate projects undertaken by individuals and groups, to keep them moving, and bring them to an appropriate conclusion; he should know how to stimulate activity without controlling it, lead discussion without dominating it, explain without telling all. The classroom English teacher should learn to play the creative, constructive role of day-to-day consultant, helping students toward successful performance of what he initially motivated them to attempt. Sometimes a teacher, always a model, he must be able to lecture when appropriate, chair a meeting, summarize, define, read aloud, interpret orally, compose a variety of communications in both speech and writing.

RESPONSIBILITIES OUTSIDE THE CLASSROOM. The English teacher should "keep up with his profession" by participating in professional activities locally, in his city and state, and nationally. He should belong to professional societies, attend their meetings as often as he can, and read professional journals pertinent to his field. He should help to recommend subscriptions to journals and purchases of books and other learning materials to his school librarian and the director of the audio-visual center. See Selected References at the end of this chapter.

The English Teacher: Martyr or Monster?

An old hand at English teaching, I have repeatedly been depressed and deeply chagrined by the ritual shock reaction of my fellow American when he learns that I teach English. He and I, friendly strangers, together on a plane or bus, or in any casual meeting, have been having a pleasant chat. But sooner or later my hail-fellow-well-met asks the ceremonial American question, "What are you in?" or "What's your racket?"

When he realizes that he has been caught having a relaxed conversation with an English teacher, a heavy gloom darkens our day. He mutters, "I never did know much grammar." His face falls; muscles twitch; latent tics spring to life; he grimaces autistically. He yields up only the bare legal minimum of heavily guarded language, in the hollow tone reserved for funerals. He gets lost.

In the same impasse, the teenager, bright-eyed and bushy tailed, and smarting from formal skirmishes with the English enemy in the classroom (privileged sanctuary), literally covers his mouth with both hands. He blurts, "I'd better not say anything," and gets in the wind. He's gone.

This ghoulish reputation — this dread image of the language censor — is something English teaching and the teaching profession must answer for. By our works we have earned it. This image is created by the incessant interruption and correction of students in the middle of their sentences, when they are reciting in class or participating in a discussion. Not all teachers do this, of course, but too many do; for some unlucky children, this rude practice may begin in the first grade and never stop.

Is it any wonder that so many students prefer silence to speech? That so many prefer blank paper, or no paper at all, to writing, in view of the slashed and bleeding compositions returned by some teachers? Altogether too many have learned a profoundly simple lesson: whenever they speak or write, they are wrong, dead wrong. And some of the worst English teachers, in this respect, are teachers trained in other subjects — shop, gym, science, social science, music. Any other subject. It makes no difference.

The remainder of this topic is presented under the following subtitles:

MISS FIDDITCH AND MR. PRINGLE
PURITANICAL SYNDROME
MISSPELLING: A CARDINAL SIN
DRILL, DRILL, DRILL
A REGRETTABLE EXERCISE
EMOTIONAL VIOLENCE ASSOCIATED WITH ENGLISH
PHYSICAL VIOLENCE ASSOCIATED WITH ENGLISH

MISS FIDDITCH AND MR. PRINGLE. Miss Fidditch and Mr. Pringle personify the image of the teacher as the censor of living language, the fiend for "correct English," who ceaselessly interrupts every child who dares open his mouth in the classroom; who vigilantly "corrects" every child who risks putting pen to paper for the teacher's inspection. English teachers should rid themselves of the sadistic mania for "correctness" in spelling, handwriting, and writing mechanics; and for "complete sentences" and other oddities and quiddities in classroom conversation and recitation, when in fact the complete sentences of language organized for visual presentation — prose — are almost never uttered in conversations outside the classroom or in real life anywhere.

By renouncing their example, even fledgling English teachers can take revenge on all the Miss Fidditches and Mr. Pringles under whom they and their friends have suffered in English classrooms. Miss Fidditch and Mr. Pringle are locked in the neurotic grip of a cleansing, disinfecting syndrome; using caustics and acids, applied with steel wool and stiff brushes, their program is to scrub the oral and written English of all their young charges within an inch of their lives. These two avenging furies have souls of New England granite; their mortality rate is criminally low.

PURITANICAL SYNDROME. Teachers, but English and language arts teachers especially, often play the role of guardians of public morality in so-called correctness in English grammar and usage. There must be some ancestral puritanical rigidity in this black-and-white syndrome of correct and incorrect English. To provide classroom authority and a source of ceremonial rites and penances, there is a musty old generic book of so-called rules, disregarded outside the classroom, that a social compulsion demands be enforced. According to my students, the old rule book just goes on and on, through an inexhaustible list of hoary old wrong-headed proscriptions. All the examples to follow came from linguistic autobiographies of good students; many had notebooks and other records attesting to the accuracy of their examples.

One such rule forbids the use of the prevalent "It is me." Another commands the speaker or writer never to use *who* instead of *whom*. Still another clarifies a point of usage thus: "*But* means but except when it means *except*." *And* never use a conjunction to start a sentence, nor a preposition to end a sentence *with*. During World War II, Winston Churchill's radio addresses were checked against possible security leaks by an official reader; when this official undertook to rearrange a sentence to conform to this mistaken rule,

Churchill asserted himself as follows: "This is the kind of arrant nonsense *up with which I will not put!*"

MISSPELLING: A CARDINAL SIN. Misspelling was once an upper class shibboleth; today it is a cardinal sin. The puritanical code of correct English dictates a stern insistence at all times on the correct spelling of all words, beginning with the first grade. Too often lists of mysterious words must be studied, completely out of context, with no immediate function for the child. In some classrooms, unhappy pupils are drilled on false, illogical, and misleading rules or precepts by which they are apparently expected to spell words correctly by deduction.

Much of this kind of instruction confuses and confounds the separate processes of (a) spelling individual words, (b) writing compositions, and (c) reading.

For example, "When two vowels go a-walking, the first one does the talking." This ridiculous rule may be further clarified by the teacher's explanation that the first vowel "says its name," or "pronounces its long sound." Let us pass over certain facts of language, such as that sounds are sounds, and letters are letters; and conversely, letters are not sounds and do not make sounds. Taking the rule at its face value — ignoring its high level of abstraction, ignoring its use of the literary device of personification — this so-called rule is just plain nonsense.

Consider such lists of common words as those in which the letters *a* and *i* go a-walking: *rain, again, plaid, aisle;* or those in which the letter *e* says its name in the *ea* sequence: *read* (present tense), *read* (past tense), *great, earth, hearth* and *heart;* or those in which the letter *o* pronounces its long sound in the *oa* sequence: *road, broad, boa, oasis;* or those in which *e* and *i* go a-walking, in that order: *receive, rein, stein, sleight;* or those in which the letter *o* says its name in the *ou* sequence: *soul, soup, sound;* and those in which other letters go a-walking and behave oddly together: *people, yeoman, laugh, gauge, neuter, canoe, amoeba.* Such lists can be extended *ad nauseum.*

What shall we say of that old bromide learned in school at the turn of the century, *"I* before *e,* except after *c,* and when pronounced *a,* as in *neighbor* and *weigh."* Consider this list of common words spelled with the *ei* digraph: *either, heifer, leisure, neither, seize, sleight, weird;* and there is *financier,* with a *c* before *i.* One ingenious teacher, along with rigorous drill on the lovable old *i* before *e* rule, required memorization of the following sentence full of exceptions: "Neither had the leisure to seize the weird financier." This does not account for all the exceptions, but it does increase the excitement.

Another rule purports to account for plural spellings of nouns ending in *f* or *fe.* This entertaining rule is really two separate rules: Rule 1 — form the plurals of *some* nouns ending in *f* or *fe* by changing *f* or *fe* to *ve* and adding *s;* Rule 2 — form the plurals of *other* nouns ending in *f* or *fe* by adding only *s.* What could be clearer than that? The writer simply guesses whether any given word ending in *f* or *fe* belongs with *some* nouns (*leaf, life*) or with *other* nouns (*muff, safe*).

Still another precept governs the spelling of words ending in silent *e* when a suffix is added. This rule states that a word ending in silent *e* drops the final *e* before adding a suffix beginning with a vowel. But there are exceptions, of course: Exception 1 — *ce* and *ge* do not drop the silent *e* but keep it before the suffixes *–able* and *–ous;* Exception 2 — words that may be confused or mispronounced do not drop the silent *e* before adding a suffix beginning with a vowel.

Sorrowfully I report that much of the foregoing spelling instruction is presented as reading instruction.

DRILL, DRILL, DRILL. Many students are dulled by incessant "seatwork" drills on grammar and points of usage. One sharp example will serve as a symbol for the experiences of many. In her linguistic autobiography, a graduate student, an in-service teacher, writes:

> How I detested those endless pages of writing in the correct word from the given pair. Whatever teacher I had, when we began to work on *lie* and *lay,* told us they are difficult and troublesome. I always felt I might not have had trouble with these verbs if the idea had not been suggested to me so many times. To this day I consciously avoid using either *lie* or *lay.* Instead, I *set* the table, *stretch out* for a nap; *place* a dish on the table; or use any other verb I can think of in place of *lay* or *lie.*

One little exercise will exemplify hundreds equally dull in English grammar workbooks. In this example, the student is asked to discover three incorrect words, one in each of three pairs, all in a single sentence:

(*Who's/Whose*) *dog got* (*lose/loose*) *from* (*it's/its*) *collar?*

Aside from its dullness, this exercise deliberately presents three errors in written form, a possible source of lifelong confusion. A satirical development of this exercise follows.

A REGRETTABLE EXERCISE. Here is a classical example, slightly exaggerated, of a breed of English exercise that should become extinct immediately, if not sooner.

> **TO THE STUDENT**: Below are eight sentences containing three common errors in English. You probably make these same mistakes yourself, through carelessness or ignorance, every time you write a theme.
>
> There are three danger spots, as follows:
>
> > (1) *who's*   *whose*
> > (2) *lose*   *loose*
> > (3) *it's*   *its*
>
> Only one sentence is correct in all three spots!
>
> Place an X in the space provided before the one correct sentence. Be careful!
>
> ( ) 1. **Who's dog got lose from it's collar?**
> ( ) 2. **Who's dog got lose from its collar?**
> ( ) 3. **Who's dog got loose from it's collar?**
> ( ) 4. **Whose dog got lose from it's collar?**
> ( ) 5. **Who's dog got loose from its collar?**
> ( ) 6. **Whose dog got lose from its collar?**
> ( ) 7. **Whose dog got loose from it's collar?**
> ( ) 8. **Whose dog got loose from its collar?**
>
> **TO THE TEACHER**: The first principle of this kind of exercise is to present correct and incorrect forms together, *placing the incorrect form first.* If the student has never seen the incorrect form before, he will be more likely to remember it. Then the exercise itself must ring all the variations on combinations of errors before presenting the combined correct forms. This technique takes the guesswork out of it, and reduces the statistical chances of the student's making the right choice through random luck.
>
> **TEACHER'S KEY**:   (X) 8. (No. 8 is the answer.)

Dull and wrongheaded as so many of such exercises are, it is not simply the drill on wrongheaded rules that is wrong; one can easily imagine a teacher full of the most up-to-date linguistics making the same profound mistake, drilling away day in and day out on modern certitudes. The real mistake here lies in the antiseptic spirit of the teaching, in the puritanical passion for attacking on sight every conceivable sin against the language, great or small, real or imagined. Before the learner has a chance to make his own mistakes in normal channels of communication, any number of undreamed-of errors are presented to him to worry about as seatwork. He is asked to study handbooks of possible errors in grammar and usage. By the time a student has completed high school, he probably will have systematically studied n times the number of English "errors" he ever could encounter in the normal course of his life. And the Fidditch-Pringle spirit of the teaching embodies a cleansing and purifying zeal armed with disinfectants and germicides. No one's language could possibly thrive in this environment.

EMOTIONAL VIOLENCE ASSOCIATED WITH ENGLISH. It is distressing to learn how many adults carry scars inflicted by emotionally immature and unstable teachers in connection with learning the arts and skills of their native language. Again I dip into linguistic autobiographies written by some of my best students. Here is a typical example of an undergraduate student's experience with one of his high school teachers, told in the third person.

> The boy was assigned to a teacher he could not tolerate. How he hated her, her impossible work loads, her unreasonable attitude, her rantings and ravings of "tossing pearls before swine." She obviously had problems. After this traumatic experience, he was fortunate to be transferred to another school.

But how the memory lingers on.

Following is a summary of the accumulated feelings of a brilliant, gifted young woman, now married and a successful teacher of English, as she recalls them when she was in the upper elementary years. She had had severe problems with spelling and phonics, but here she talks of her bouts with English grammar.

> Grammar was the real bane of her existence. She saw no logical organization to it. When they made her learn a list of pronouns, she found that they function either as nouns or as adjectives. When she learned

that adverbs end in *-ly,* the teacher yelled at her for giving the word *friendly* as an example.

The result of these and similar frustrations was a girl who was afraid to express herself on paper for fear of making spelling errors or grammatical mistakes. She cried before writing each theme because she was so tied up worrying about errors that she could not transmit the ideas in her head to paper.

Language was becoming cancerous for this girl. Every time she tried, she was criticized, and criticism was not something she took to readily. As a result of many traumas, she began to dislike school. She expended little or no energy on learning.

PHYSICAL VIOLENCE ASSOCIATED WITH ENGLISH.   Clausewitz, the great Prussian military stategist, once wrote, "War is the extension of politics by other means." Linguistic autobiographies of many of my best students have convinced me that more teachers than I would like to think carry their campaign to educate children into the realm of corporal punishment, some of it extremely cruel and sadistic. Two illustrations will suffice as reminders of a matter too serious to pass unnoticed.

An in-service teacher in a graduate class, a young woman from a warm and stable home, in her language autobiography wrote of her school experience as follows:

> Two teachers held my progress in check. They were greatly feared by most of the pupils, for their tempers were often violent and their sarcasm no less wounding. Years later, one of them seriously injured a boy and was dismissed from her position because of it. She had banged his head against the chalkboard. In my time, actual physical injuries were slight, but the fear engendered by these teachers was enough to scatter my wits. These experiences left a soft scar, not yet healed today.

One of the cruelest stories of this kind submitted to me is related by a young man, now succeeding as an in-service teacher, whose early school experiences connected with learning language and the skills of literacy contributed significantly to his eventual need of psychiatric help. In a quiet, low key, he tells his tale about a teacher he had in both first and second grades.

> She was a large, powerful woman; her method was intimidation. The outstanding thing I remember about her was a tapered yellow pointer with a thick red handle. She showed it to me often before using it on me.

On one particular occasion she broke it while beating my knuckles. Other incidents I remember are being picked up, shaken, and having my ears twisted; also having my hands slapped with a ruler until I cried. I vaguely remember being instructed by this teacher that if I told my parents I was unjustly punished, that would be a lie and I would receive more punishment from them.

This is all actual fact. If anything, for the sake of discretion, I have watered down the above incidents and omitted others. I also recognize that I probably needed correction for many of the things I did, but I hardly think they warranted such methods.

Nurturing Growth of Language

What is the meaning of the language-learning experience sketched in the foregoing discussion?

Despite the fine work of the best English teachers, the Fidditch-Pringle image, varying somewhat in intensity, has been created by too many teachers in too many classrooms. This image should be erased by a new generation of professional English teachers; teachers who will encourage comfortable, fluent everyday speech in their classrooms in place of stubborn silence or stilted, miserable "recitation"; teachers who will encourage lively, natural writing in place of dwarfish, dispirited compositions. Unless some such sea-change comes about in the emotional impact of English teaching as a direct result of teachers' attitudes, it will matter very little which grammar or which "English," new or old, comes to dominate the curriculum. The malevolent alchemy of Fidditch-Pringle transforms all the elements of English, even the most benign, into caustic and acid.

In English and the language arts — language and language-centered studies — linguistic sensibilities and humane attitudes in the teacher are equal in importance to all the academic learning in the world; they may indeed be of greater importance. The successful English teacher must deeply understand language and all its potential values. He must practice more than preach.

A Linguistic Autobiography Project

A language autobiography — *linguistic autobiography* — is a piecing together of an individual's language growth and development from his earliest memories to his present age.

It is not an autobiography of one's life, but an autobiography of the writer's linguistic development. It tells this story from infancy, with as much relevant detail as possible. It is an autobiography only in this strictly linguistic sense; the language autobiographer must first have studied the structure of American English as an objective entity. Otherwise he will not know what he is looking for in his language growth. The attentive reader of this book will find between these covers an adequate basis for writing his own linguistic autobiography.

In preparation, the linguistic autobiographer may call upon the memories of friends and relatives, tape recordings, baby books and pictures, scrapbooks, school papers, notebooks, and the like; *but the main use of these helps is to revive his own buried early memories.* The writing of a true language autobiography can only be the outcome of a deep inner searching into the roots of his personal learning of the mother tongue. Preparing to write a language autobiography resembles self-directed therapy and self-analysis in its general searching for the traces of language growth in its totality, both root and branch. But of course writing a language autobiography does not imply ill health or neurosis.

Remember that, once acquired, our speech becomes automatic; the processes of acquisition are forgotten; the methods of producing and controlling language become habitual and drop below the threshold of consciousness, submerged with lost memories. The essence of a language autobiography is peeling away the scales of custom and habit, penetrating layers of unconsciousness that conceal the traces of early language memories. The process of learning one's language — if it can become partially conscious again — is a rich mine of language-learning lore. A conscientious effort to reconstruct the process he went through in creating his own individual version of American English can sharpen a teacher's consciousness of what every single human being must do, every American specifically, when he learns to talk. This consciousness yields knowledge, sympathy, and insight into the nature and processes of learning that every parent and teacher needs if he is to bend the twig the way it should grow, and not into some twisted form that can never regain its normal shape.

Everyone who talks has a theory of language — a grammar — whether he is conscious of it or not; his grammar is a set of internalized rules, attitudes, and beliefs about his language; it has become unconscious and works automatically. If he did not have such a theory, he would not be able to talk. This is true even if he "don't know no grammar." Whether conscious or not, the language theory held by a teacher has a profound and pervasive influence on the children who live with him in his classroom. Every teacher, not just teachers of reading, English, and the language arts, wields a strong influence over the language development of children. Children deserve teachers who have a language theory better than that of the man in the street. Writing a linguistic autobiography is one means of developing a more conscious theory.

One method of developing a complete language autobiography is to write a series of five short expository papers at intervals of two weeks, that will be the basis for an extended exposition, ten to twenty pages long, or even longer. In this method, each short paper is a summary of one important topic to be covered in the final paper itself; a complete language autobiography, however, should cover much more than these five topics. These short papers, or summaries, are to be regarded as source papers for the language autobiography; they are neither sections nor first drafts of sections of the final paper.

An alternative to writing a complete linguistic autobiography is to write papers on one or more of the topics suggested below, or on related topics.

SUGGESTED TOPICS FOR SUMMARY PAPERS.   The papers would not necessarily be written in this order:

1. Childhood development of phonemes and morphemes.
2. Childhood development of syntax and intonation.
3. Speech communities (by neighborhood, ethnic group, age, sex, hobby, job, etc.).
4. Special influences upon, and interests in, language.
5. Influences of individual teachers on language skills (reading, writing, speaking, listening — *thinking*).

Each of these five short papers should summarize information on the assigned topic that is applicable to the individual student's language development, his idiolect. Each paper should be sharply focused: as a rule of thumb, it should offer at least one specific example in support of every general statement. Each paper should begin with a short paragraph tailored to fit the student's idiolect;

this opening statement should outline what he is going to say in the paper as a whole. The paper itself will then develop according to this opening commitment. The student's purposes will not be served if he writes a general essay on the topic, or even if he writes generalities that do apply to his idiolect but are not supported by specific examples.

BASIC PRINCIPLES. Following is an outline of basic principles for writing a complete linguistic autobiography (or for writing one or more shorter papers).

1. Your language autobiography focuses more on your language than on your autobiography. It tells, in as much relevant detail as possible, the life story of your language from birth to the present.

2. Your purpose is to become conscious of the entire process of your own individual creation of your personal version of American English: your idiolect.

3. Your process of learning your language, if you can gain access to it, is a mine of language-learning lore.

4. As a teacher, you will need all the knowledge, sympathy, and insight you can acquire as to the nature and processes of language learning.

5. In reconstructing in detail the process you went through in creating your idiolect, you will become conscious of what every human being must do, generally, and every American specifically. This consciousness is the ultimate value of working up your language autobiography — to you, as a teacher.

6. Although you are a unique person, in many respects speaking a unique version of American English, you have mastered the language system as a native speaker.

7. Your language resembles the language of other Americans more than it differs from it. Most American college students have the main features of the system in common. Significant individual differences are mainly outside the system, not inside.

   If you naturally speak a divergent dialect, however, close attention to comparative contrastive features of that dialect and standard forms will be an important part of your linguistic autobiography.

TEACHING SUGGESTION : Variants of this linguistic auto-biography project are interesting and useful at any grade level, from pre-school to graduate school.

Selected References

GENERAL LANGUAGE: INTRODUCTORY

Joseph H. Friend, *An Introduction to English Linguistics* (Cleveland: World, 1967).

Charles C. Fries, *American English Grammar* (New York: Appleton-Century-Crofts, 1940).

———, *The Teaching of English* (Ann Arbor, Michigan: Wahr, 1949).

Robert A. Hall, Jr., *Introductory Linguistics* (Philadelphia: Chilton, 1964).

Baxter Hathaway, *A Transformational Syntax: The Grammar of Modern English* (New York: Ronald Press, 1967).

Charlton Laird, *The Miracle of Language* (Greenwich, Conn.: Fawcett, 1963).

William G. Moulton, *A Linguistic Guide to Language Learning* (New York: Modern Language Association, 1966).

Norman C. Stageborg, *An Introductory English Grammar; with a chapter on Transformational Grammar by Ralph Goodman* (New York: Holt, Rinehart and Winston, 1966).

George L. Trager, *Language and Languages* (San Francisco: Chandler, 1969).

Harry R. Warfel, *Language: a Science of Human Behavior* (Cleveland: Howard Allen, 1962).

GENERAL LANGUAGE: ADVANCED

Harold B. Allen, ed., *Readings in Applied English Linguistics*, 2nd ed. (New York: Appleton-Century-Crofts, 1964).

Francis P. Dinneen, *An Introduction to General Linguistics* (New York: Holt, Rinehart and Winston, 1967).

W. Nelson Francis, *The English Language: An Introduction* (New York: Harcourt, Brace and World, 1965).

H. A. Gleason, Jr., *An Introduction to Descriptive Linguistics*, rev. ed. (New York: Holt, Rinehart and Winston, 1961).

———, *Linguistics and English Grammar* (New York: Holt, Rinehart and Winston, 1965).

Charles F. Hockett, *The State of the Art* (The Hague: Mouton, 1968).

R. H. Robins, *General Linguistics: an Introductory Survey* (Bloomington: Indiana University Press, 1966).

BIOLINGUISTICS AND PSYCHOLINGUISTICS

John P. DeCecco, ed., *The Psychology of Language, Thought, and Instruction: Readings* (New York: Holt, Rinehart and Winston, 1967).

Eric H. Lenneberg, *New Directions in the Study of Language* (Cambridge, Mass.: M.I.T. Press, 1964).

Charles E. Osgood and Thomas A. Sebeok, *Psycholinguistics: A Survey of Theory and Research Problems;* with *A Survey of Psycholinguistic Research,* 1954–1964, by A. Richard Diebold; and *The Psycholinguists,* by George A. Miller (Bloomington: Indiana University Press, 1965).

Sol Saporta, assisted by Jarvis R. Bastian, *Psycholinguistics: a Book of Readings* (New York: Holt, Rinehart and Winston, 1961).

Theodore W. Walters, S.J., *The Georgetown Bibliography of Studies Contributing to the Psycholinguistics of Language Learning* (Washington, D.C.: Georgetown University Press, 1965).

George Kingsley Zipf, *The Psycho-Biology of Language: an Introduction to Dynamic Philology,* Intro., George A. Miller (Cambridge, Mass.: M.I.T. Press, 1965). (A reprint of the first edition, Houghton Mifflin, 1935.)

For references on Language, Thought, and Culture, turn to pp. 77–78.

General Bibliographies

Harold B. Allen, ed., *Linguistics and English Linguistics,* in Goldentree Bibliographies (New York: Appleton-Century-Crofts, 1966).

James Broz, Jr. and Alfred S. Hayes, *Linguistics and Reading: a Selective Annotated Bibliography for Teachers of Reading* (Washington, D.C.: Center for Applied Linguistics, 1966).

Robert W. DeLancey, *Linguistics and Teaching: a Manual of Classroom Practices* (Syracuse, N.Y.: New York State English Council, 1965).

Linguistic Bibliography for the Teacher of English, compiled by Committee on Curriculum, Minnesota Council of Teachers of English, 1966.

BROAD PROFESSIONAL RESOURCES

"Annual Review of Research in English and Language Arts," *Elementary English.*

"Annual Review of Research in English and Language Arts," *The English Journal.*

John Dixon, *Growth Through English* (Champaign, Illinois: National Council of Teachers of English, 1968).

Freedom and Discipline in English: Report of the Commission on English (Princeton, N.J.: College Entrance Examination Board, 1965).

Inventory of Projects and Activities in Reading and English, a series beginning February, 1966 (Washington, D.C.: Center for Applied Linguistics, 1966–).

Language Research in Progress, a series beginning June, 1965 (Washington, D.C.: Center for Applied Linguistics, 1965–).

Herbert J. Muller, *The Uses of English* (Champaign, Illinois: National Council of Teachers of English, 1968).

The National Interest and the Teaching of English (Champaign, Illinois: National Council of Teachers of English, 1961).

Research Reports: A Series of Research Reports Sponsored by the NCTE Committee in Research (Champaign, Illinois: National Council of Teachers of English, 1962–).

Michael F. Shugrue, MLA, and Eldonna L. Evertts, NCTE, eds., "Guidelines for the Preparation of Teachers of English — An Explanation," *English Journal*, April, 1968, *57*, No. 4, pp. 475–554.

AMERICAN ENGLISH-DIALECTS: GENERAL

Eldonna Evertts, ed., *Dimensions of Dialect* (Champaign, Illinois: National Council of Teachers of English, 1967).

J. Vernon Jensen, *Effects of Childhood Bilingualism* (Champaign, Illinois: National Council of Teachers of English, 1962).

Hans Kurath, *A Word Geography of the Eastern United States* (Ann Arbor: University of Michigan Press, 1949).

Jean Malmstrom and Annabel Ashley, *Dialects USA* (Champaign, Illinois: National Council of Teachers of English, 1963).

Carroll E. Reed, *Dialects of American English*, foreword by Raven I. McDavid (Cleveland: World, 1967).

Roger W. Shuy, *Discovering American Dialects* (Champaign, Illinois: National Council of Teachers of English, 1967).

AMERICAN ENGLISH-DIALECTS:
SOCIAL, NONSTANDARD, DISADVANTAGED

Board of Education of the City of New York, *Nonstandard Dialect* (Champaign, Illinois: National Council of Teachers of English, 1968).

Edward R. Fagan, ed., *English and the Disadvantaged* (Scranton, Pa.: International Textbook Co., 1967).

Improving English Skills of Culturally Different Youth (Washington, D.C.: U.S. Dept. of H.E.W. Office of Education, OE–30012 Bulletin No. 5, 1964).

Herbert R. Kohl, *Teaching the "Unteachable,"* intro. by John Holt (New York: The New York Review, 1967).

——, *36 Children* (New York: New American Library, 1967).

William Labov, *The Social Stratification of English in New York City* (Washington, D.C.: Center for Applied Linguistics, 1964).

——, *The Study of Non-Standard English* (Washington D.C.: Center for Applied Linguistics, 1969).

Language Programs for the Disadvantaged: Report of the NCTE Task Force on Teaching English to the Disadvantaged (Champaign, Illinois: National Council of Teachers of English, 1965).

Review of Educational Research: Education for Socially Disadvantaged Children, American Educational Research, December, 1965, *XXXV,* No. 5, pp. 373–442.

Roger W. Shuy, ed., *Social Dialects and Language Learning* (Champaign, Illinois: National Council of Teachers of English, 1964).

——, "A Selective Bibliography on Social Dialects," *The Linguistic Reporter, 10,* No. 3, June, 1968. pp. 1–5.

——, *Social Dialects and Language Learning* (Proceedings of the Bloomington, Indiana, Conference, 1964) National Council of Teachers of English.

William A. Stewart, ed., *Non-Standard Speech and the Teaching of English* (Washington, D.C.: Center for Applied Linguistics, 1964).

NONSTANDARD AMERICAN ENGLISH:

GENERAL SOURCES OF INFORMATION

Clearing House for Social Dialect Studies
Center for Applied Linguistics (CAL)
1717 Massachusetts Ave., N.W.
Washington, D.C., 20036

Information Retrieval Center on the Disadvantaged (ERIC)
Ferkauf Graduate School of Education
Yeshiva University
55 Fifth Avenue
New York, New York, 10003

IRCD Bulletin, A Bi-monthly publication from the Information Retrieval Center on the Disadvantaged
Graduate School of Education
Yeshiva University
150 West 56th Street
New York, New York, 10019 (Bibliographies, *Passim.*)

Linguistic Reporter
CAL Newsletter (Same address as above)

M.I.T. Press Catalog
50 Ames Street
Cambridge, Massachsetts, 02142

Materials Center
Modern Language Association of America
62 Fifth Avenue
New York, New York, 10011

National Council of Teachers of English (NCTE)
508 South Sixth Street
Champaign, Illinois, 61820

Occasional Papers
Publication of the American Language Institute
1 Washington Square North
New York, New York, 10003

Project English
Center for Curriculum Development
University of Minnesota
Minneapolis, Minnesota

Publications Section
Center for Applied Linguistics (CAL)
(Same address as above)

Journals

The Catholic Educational Review

College English (NCTE)

Elementary English (NCTE)

English Journal (NCTE)

English Language Teaching

Harvard Educational Review

The Journal of Negro Education

Language Learning

Language

Modern Language Journal

Publications of the Modern Language Association (PMLA)

TESOL (Quarterly) Teaching of English as a Second or Other Language
James E. Alatis
Institute of Languages and Linguistics
Georgetown University
Washington, D.C.

Chapter 2

Communication, Language, American English

This chapter is a short introduction to important aspects of language study that should be reflected in various ways in the teaching of English and the language arts. The sensitive teacher is the best judge of just what these various ways will be.

The discussion is presented in three main sections:

Communication in Man and Animals: Kinesics and Paralanguage
The Child's Acquisition of Language
The Development of American English

Communication in Man and Animals: Kinesics and Paralanguage

The Expression of Emotion in Man and Animals, published by Charles Darwin in 1872, was the first modern study of animal communication. A new science of animal communication has since developed, notably since about 1960. Like Darwin, modern investigators compare and contrast communicative behavior of man with analogues in animal behavior. They seek to understand more fully the nature and development of language itself, which all agree is uniquely human; and of kinesics and paralanguage, shared to some extent by man and animals.

36

The remainder of this section is presented under seven subtopics, as follows:

MAN'S COMMUNICATIVE AND EXPRESSIVE MOVEMENTS: KINESICS. *Kinesics* is a term used by many investigators to designate the whole range of communicative and expressive movements of the human body or parts of the body; whole-body stances: slouch, defensive crouch, lax or rigid body, "on tiptoe"; lesser bodily stances: "set" of the head, cocked head, head erect, stiff neck, arms akimbo, legs spread; gestures of arm, leg, hand, foot, finger, thumb (too numerous to mention); and facial movements, gestures, and expressions: comic or tragic "mask," mealy mouth, sourpuss, wink, smirk, sneer, smile, frown, twinkle in the eye, and so on.

Some of these movements may be conventional signs; that is, they are always intended and understood within a given social group to have a definite meaning in specific situations: head movements for "yes" and "no," hand gestures for "stop" and "go," a welcoming handshake, waving goodbye, for example. Other kinesic movements are simply expressive of emotions or attitudes suiting individuals in specific situations. To some extent, animals share analogous kinesic movements with man, as signs of referents and as expressions of emotion.

A comment may be in order on the special meanings of the terms *referent, sign,* and *symbol* in this discussion of language and communication. The root of *referent* is *refer:* a referent is an object or event occurring in space/time, to which a sign or symbol refers. A referent may be observed and referred to; both signs and symbols may refer to referents. The essential difference between *sign* and *symbol* as used here is that a sign must be made in the presence of the referent, or close enough to it in time so that the reference is immediately apparent. A dog for example may warn by barking as a thief approaches, while he is present, or after he has escaped; the dog's bark is a sign, not a symbol. This comment also applies to the human signs noted in the previous paragraph. A symbol, on the other hand, can refer to its referent at any time — past, present, future; and in any place — close proximity or great distance. Especially pertinent here is the fact that language is a complex system of vocal symbols; writing and print comprise a system of graphic symbols ultimately derived from and representative of that vocal symbol system. See pages 41–42 in this chapter; see also the comment of the psychologist Vendryes on page 61.

Although in human behavior kinesics may go so far as extended pantomime (charades, for example, or a performance by Marcel Marceau), in a linguistic discussion the term usually designates physical movements that are a part of, or a visible accompaniment of, communication by speech. These physical signs may be more than reinforcers of speech: they sometimes replace spoken symbols. Anyone who owns a pet or other domestic animal, or who has observed wild animals closely, can recall instances of "animal kinesics" analogous to human. This similarity may in part explain the secret of the fascination animals have for man.

TEACHING SUGGESTION: Open a discussion of kinesics with your students. Let them demonstrate with examples from life, literature, movies, television. Classwork may lead to carefully prepared performances.

EXAMPLES OF ANIMAL COMMUNICATION: "CALLS." Many animal species — birds, insects, fish, animals — have mating calls or other vocal symbols of sexual attraction. Not only do individuals within species communicate with each other, but men master these calls and lure unsuspecting victims to their death. Hunters stalking moose imitate the cow's call to lure the bull within rifle range; turkey hunters imitate a hen calling to mislead gobblers within gunshot. The lore of game calling is a lifelong study in itself.

TEACHING SUGGESTION: Open a discussion of animal "calls." Perhaps some of your students can give prepared demonstrations at a later class meeting.

EXAMPLES OF ANIMAL COMMUNICATION: KINESICS. Bees return to the hive and perform ritual dances to communicate the direction and distance of nectar sources to other bees; they may supplement these dances with meaningful sounds, and even carry samples of the flowers' scent. Gorillas use bodily stances, gestures, and near-human facial expressions to communicate with each other and to maintain social order within the group; gorillas also achieve a sort of fraternal communion by various vocal noises and gestures, including touching each other. Rhesus monkeys use special gestures to distinguish between the desire to play at fighting in contrast to gestures signaling intent to fight in earnest.

I have a beagle who, in a fast-running game of tag, will repeatedly risk being tagged while he desperately avoids it, near-miss after near-miss. Yet the moment I assume a relaxed stance indicating I am no longer playing, my hound also relaxes, wags his tail, comes within easy reach and lies down at my feet. We both know the game is over. This is kinesic communication between master and dog without speech or other vocal sign.

TEACHING SUGGESTION : Discuss animal communication by movements with your class. As a follow-up, perhaps some students can do animal pantomimes. This activity can be coordinated with a visit to a farm, a fair, or a zoo.

PHATIC COMMUNION IN MAN AND ANIMALS. Speaking precisely, phatic communion is a function of human speech, yet animals share with man various forms of vocal communication that serve largely to maintain sociability and a sense of group security; this is the essence of phatic communion. Again, the close observer of insects, birds, or animals — domestic or wild — can call to mind many examples. These vocal sounds are neither signs nor symbols of referents in any strict linguistic sense; they may signify mere presence, well being, or friendly interest. Phatic communion is the earliest communicative speech function acquired by babes in arms; it persists throughout life in greetings, farewells, chit-chat, small talk — ritual verbal activity that preserves sociability while communicating virtually no specific linguistic message. Phatic communion is of basic importance in both animal and human communication.

TEACHING SUGGESTION : Students may enjoy doing short dialogues or skits showing the uses of small talk in human communication, after adequate time to prepare.

A SIMPLE COMMUNICATION MODEL. A communication model usually specifies a minimum of four elements: a sender, a receiver, a message, and a channel. The message is conveyed by a code; thus we refer to the sender as the encoder, the receiver as the decoder. In speech and writing, the speaker/writer encodes the message, the listener/reader decodes it. In speech, both encoder and decoder are generally present (of course some people talk to themselves, and many talk to recording devices for future listening); in writing, the purpose generally is to preserve the communication for decoding later. (See Table 2.1)

TABLE 2.1

Skeletal Communication Models

Sender (encoder)	Message (encoded)	Channel (transmission)	Receiver (decoder)
Speaker	Spoken language	Air waves	Listener (Auditory reception)
Writer	Written language	Light waves	Reader (Visual reception)

In speaking-listening, the speaker encodes his message in the audio-lingual code of speech; the channel is the air carrying the vibrating, pulsating stream of audio-lingual symbols from the speaker's mouth to the listener's ear. In writing-reading, the message is reduced to handwriting or print on paper; the channel is light waves carrying an impression of the manual-visual symbols to the eyes of the reader.

But even when the encoder and decoder use the same dialect, spoken or written, the channel carries some irrelevant "noise," tending to jam the signal; noise is any distracting element not essential to the "pure" form of the communication. Individual differences of experience associated with elements of the message, permanent differences of feeling, attitude, or mental set, even transient differences of mood or physical well-being — all such subjective conditions may color the communication at either end of the channel, the origin or the destination. Thus messages are subject to disorientation and misinterpretation by both sender and receiver.

TEACHING SUGGESTION : Discuss disorientation and misinterpretation of messages with your class. Students may enjoy demonstrating in short dialogues and skits. Adequate preparation is important, after discussion.

ANIMAL COMMUNICATION, YES; LANGUAGE, NO. It is clear that animals communicate with each other and with man, and that man communicates with animals, even with language. My dog Bucko — because he has been rewarded for obedience with a tidbit plus a congratulatory "good dog" — associates "good dog" in that special tone of voice with "snack for me." As his master, I must avoid giving that vocal sign of approval except in the obedience-reward situation, because whenever the dog hears it, he signals his joy and expectation by watching me eagerly, eyes bright, by "grinning," by dancing and leaping. He just can't wait. He reads my signal and I read his. This is a good example of communication between man and animal.

Please note that the vocal sounds and physical movements of animal communication differ from human speech in major ways.

1. If we agree that a *sign* of a referent is used only in the immediate physical situation or in close proximity to the referent, but that a *symbol* may be used at other times and in other places to designate the referent, then we may conclude that *the sounds and physical movements of animal communication are signs rather than symbols*. Linguistic symbols may be used at any time and in any place, far removed from the referent; writing may be studied or even translated by later generations.

2. The simple signs of animal communications are somewhat like single lexical items (words), the referent often being an entire situation. In sharp contrast, the complex symbolism of human speech relies heavily on intonation and syntax, lexical items, structure words, grammatical inflections, and derivational affixes. Languages

enable human beings to create and interpret original sentences and longer constructs, never before spoken or heard.

3. Animal signs are limited to vocal sounds and physical movements as signs (leaving aside scents and trails as not important to this discussion). Language, on the other hand, may be supplemented by movements (kinesics), occasionally replaced by kinesics, as well as fleshed out by paralanguage, or tone of voice. Tone of voice — whining, laughing, crying, rasping, hollowness, overloudness, oversoftness — is somewhat analogous to qualities of vocal sounds in animal communication.

Thus we see that other animals have a system, or systems, of communication but do not have language or anything qualitatively resembling language. Man is the only animal that talks. A so-called talking bird can be taught to say, "Birds don't talk."

TEACHING SUGGESTION: Open a discussion of language, kinesics, and paralanguage (not necessarily using these terms). Have students develop pantomimes and skits to illustrate the superiority of language (or language plus the others) over nonlanguage.

A NOTE ON THE ORIGIN OF LANGUAGE. We have no scientific evidence to account for the origin of language (or languages). Speech is by nature gone with the wind, leaving only impermanent traces in the fickle memories of men; even the immediate predecessors of modern languages, thriving mere thousands of years ago, can be studied only in the few, sparse written records that have been preserved. Everything surrounding the ancient beginnings and early development of language is lost in the impenetrable prehistory of man.

Apparently all languages are equally old, but no one knows how old. In structure, all languages are equally sophisticated; there are no "primitive" languages. All languages are viable means of communication among the peoples who speak them; all can express what the people need to express. All languages are equally difficult or equally easy to acquire *as first languages;* all over the world, normal children learn to speak their native tongues fluently by the age of six. We know many such facts about language, but we have no inkling as to its origin.

It seems reasonable, however, to suppose that before man invented language, he communicated by signs similar to those used by animals. A point of intense interest in the study of animal communication is the distant hope of developing a hypothesis that may help to explain the origin of man's most remarkable invention, language.

The Child's Acquisition of Language

Since man alone on this planet has the ability to acquire language, it seems possible that during a very long period of mutually reinforcing development, going back into prehistory, speech and thought became inextricably intertwined with each other. Empirical evidence fails to support the philosophical dichotomy of "mind" and "body." Nothing but confusion will result from attempting to separate language from man's neurophysiological ability to acquire it, or to isolate human intellect (in the form of "mind" or "innate ideas") from the biological organism of which intellect is a part, and without which human thought has never been known to exist.

The remarkable creative properties of language have excited some investigators to the pitch of asserting that mere infants obviously cannot possibly learn natural human languages. Some mathematicians seem to feel that language is the highest form of mathematics; logicians, that it is an exalted form of symbolic logic. How then dare babes and sucklings, barely out of their diapers, presume to grasp the principles of a creative symbol system that requires many years of post-graduate study by the most brilliant minds of our time? In their excitement, some of these gentlemen tend to lose their perspective and exaggerate the case.

The acquisition of language is a lifelong developmental task, beginning with the birth cry and continuing steadily during *the slow maturing of the whole personality*. It is true that the normal child about the age of six has acquired the basic principles and operations of his language; but he is still a child: he thinks like a child and he talks like a child. *The child's language is the language of a child*. No matter how well-formed his sentences are (and they are not always so), they remain the sentences of a child.

Even when a child speaks a sentence identical in linguistic form with one spoken by a forty-year-old symbolic logician, the two "messages" are not at all the same; they are qualitatively different because the two speakers are qualitatively different, as both source and destination. This is a brief reference to an essential point about language development, a point that must be firmly grasped by those who teach children and young adults, and by those who undertake the humbling task of teaching the teachers. The normal six-year-old has a very long way to go before he will have developed, even to minimal levels, all the arts and skills that English instruction is committed to try to teach.

TEACHING SUGGESTION: Open a class discussion of the different meanings brought by children and adults to the same sentence, or to a series of sentences in a paragraph. Some students may enjoy preparing and giving demonstration-discussions. This topic is suitable for elementary as well as secondary school.

The remainder of this section — *The Child's Acquisition of Language* — is presented under the following four subheadings:

VOCAL NOISE VERSUS VOCAL SYMBOLS
DEVELOPMENTAL STAGES: INTONATION AND PHATIC COMMUNION
DEVELOPMENTAL STAGES: BASIC SOUNDS, "WORDS," SENTENCES
DEVELOPMENTAL STAGES: SYNTAX AND WORD-FORM CHANGES

VOCAL NOISE VERSUS VOCAL SYMBOLS. In considering the actual process of the child's acquisition of his first language — a viable, consistent, and highly complex system of audio-lingual symbols — we must observe a qualitative distinction between his early random production of vocal noise and his emergent conscious use of vocal symbols. Every baby produces a great deal of vocal noise having no linguistic significance other than giving him practice in articulating sounds from which he will later select (and also reject) specific items to form his repertoire of language patterns to be used systematically in speech for communicative purposes; items that he selects and rejects include not only phones and phonemes, but melodic and rhythmic patterns of speech — intonation, in short. This distinction is qualitative because it involves (a) the infant's consciousness, to the point of imitation and creative manipulation, of language patterns he hears, as well as (b) an infantile attempt to communicate with others, going beyond simple egocentric expression. We must not look for minutely accurate production of patterns nor a comprehensive grasp of meaning while he is still in the cradle: all things in due time.

There is striking evidence suggesting the primacy of large, over-riding general patterns in the early language learning of infants and young children. These patterns are sentences and sentence-like structures, shaped by and associated with basic English patterns of rhythm and tune. Even the child's single-word utterances and his predicates without subjects conform to linguistic descriptions of stress patterns with concurrent pitch contours in English sentences. The same may be said of questions and commands. And while these fundamental *structural* patterns of intonation may be accompanied by *expressive* features that are entirely optional, this fact should not obscure the systematic use of the underlying patterns, which are not only of fundamental importance in adult language structure, but of prior occurrence in the native language learning process.

Intonation apparently precedes the development of the phonemic repertoire and the formation of vocabulary: indeed, nursery and even primary school children often cannot single out so-called words from longer utterances. Publications by Lewis,[1] Grewel,[2] Weir,[3] Braine,[4] Huttenlocher,[5] and Lieberman,[6] to mention only a very few, support these observations. They can also be checked independently by any-one who will make careful observations of the uses of intonation by babies and young children.

TEACHING SUGGESTION : Invite students to recall, or make fresh observations of, young children's uses of intonation. Some may enjoy preparing a demonstration-discussion for the class.

Lieberman, a sort of physiolinguist, investigated intonation with a view to supporting claims of innate language universals that prescribe the form of any human language. He believes that the typical cry of the infant, beginning shortly after birth, is innately determined, and specifically that the rising-falling pitch contour of this cry provides the lifelong basis for "breath groups" that he asserts segment language into sentences.[7] Whether or not one chooses to go all the way in this search for "language universals" that are innate rather than learned or conditioned, there is little doubt that human speech begins with the first cry of the newborn child. But so does respiration begin then, the very breath of life itself. Does anyone question that the infant's tendency to live and breathe is innately determined? Not I.

DEVELOPMENTAL STAGES: INTONATION AND PHATIC COMMUNION. We have noted that the first intonation pattern of a newborn child is his birth cry. Very shortly, however, a healthy baby begins experimenting with other rhythms and tunes, "singing" and "cooing" as we say, with interludes of self-indulgent babbling, gurgling, and lallation. At first he sings by himself, without much regard for anyone else; but soon in response to vocal signs of attention from his mother and the family, he begins to enjoy phatic communion with them. Much of it is egocentric self-expression, but gradually it acquires social dimensions. This first two-way vocal communication with the human race opens a critically important stage for the baby's emotional development as well as for his continued growth in language. The infant is entering the first stage of complex linguistic interactions, involving spontaneous vocal expressions mingled with the responsive and the imitative; he experiments creatively with pattern variations and manipulations of many kinds, laying a foundation for the fundamental language skills he will master within two or three years.

DEVELOPMENTAL STAGES: BASIC SOUNDS, "WORDS," SENTENCES. In the first few months of his life, every normal baby experiments playfully with all the basic speech sounds within his rather remarkable capabilities; this may mean producing most of the sounds adults use in all languages. These baby sounds do not combine to form a language system, and the baby does not "mean" anything by them; he simply produces them as random sounds, not as phonemes of an established language. He tosses them out as experimental embellishments of his intonation patterns while he continues his communion with the people around him and begins to realize that he is one of them.

Generally, between the ages of six months and one year, the baby begins to sound as though he is going to be a native speaker of a particular language. His intonation patterns increasingly make sense to the native ear, his vocal sounds of all nations take on the distinctive qualities of his specific language; soon he says recognizable "words," many of them actually *sentences as defined by intonation and by what the baby intends them to mean.* He becomes prolific of commands and questions, while remaining almost barren of declarative statements and philosophical generalizations of the "Birds sing" type (kernels).

At this stage *mama* and *dada* (or their equivalents in local babytalk), are by no means proper nouns, nor is *mook* a common noun (adult, *milk*). When the baby says *mook,* he means *give me my bottle;* if he doesn't get it, he may cry, or threaten to. By *mama* he means simply *do whatever it is I want done right now;* for example, *pick me up, sing to me, feed me, change me. Up* is often a simple command for *pick me up. Dada* may mean, *I want him, where is he?* or *there he is.* These early sentences, using only intonation patterns and single referent words, communicate fairly effectively in the total situation; they resemble the communicative signs of animals, but the great difference is the baby's human brain, neural system and musculature, and his socially inherited language that, taken all together, give him incomparable potential for linguistic development.

Babies at this stage and even later like to use rhythmic tunes of greater length than they can fill with "words." Children up to the age of two or two and one half years often ask questions, give orders, make statements, or just plain wheedle, using intelligible intonation patterns almost devoid of "words." The very concept, word, may in fact have to be carefully taught in connection with the first attempts at reading and writing.

DEVELOPMENTAL STAGES: SYNTAX AND WORD-FORM CHANGES. While still using "nouns" as sentences (*ball, bike, sand, car*), the child will progress to "verbs" (*eat, drink, ride, swing*). Predicates without subjects also begin to serve as sentences: *eat candy, drink milk, ride bike.* These sentences will usually have (a) the falling intonation of statements or the rising intonation of yes-no questions, along with (b) a portion of normal sentence order; these appear to be the child's first two elements of syntax, in that order.

As his sentences become more mature and his syntax more complete, the child generalizes rules governing the operations he has mastered; about the same time, he begins to generalize other rules for noun singular and plural forms, for agreement of noun and verb forms, and for adverb and adjective inflections (*nicely, badly; bigger, biggest*); he may also begin to understand simple derivational prefixes such as *un–* and *mis–* (*untie, mislay*), and suffixes such as *–er* and *–y* (*runner, curly*). Similarly, the child will internalize the rules for the use of pronouns that are practiced in his family and larger speech community. But these rules are far from the direct gift of Nature; the child will not acquire any grammatical "rules" that are not practiced by the people around him; in fact, he may acquire a whole system of rules that conflict in an orderly, consistent, systematic way with the rules of standard written English. There is no case on record of a child's internalizing "rules" transcending those operating in the dialect spoken in his immediate vicinity.

The foregoing is only a broad sketch of salient points in the child's mastery of his dialect from birth to the age of three or four years, when nursery school may challenge him with opportunities for greater enrichment and rewards. Thorough study of the acquisition of language is a specialized discipline in itself.

TEACHING SUGGESTION: Open a discussion with your class of preschool language, either their own or that of children they can observe. Some students may enjoy preparing demonstration-discussions. This interest knows no age or grade limits.

The foregoing section briefly describes the child's acquisition of language according to my present understanding. This discussion carries implicit references to a controversial neo-Platonic view of language as being not learned but innate — a view emphatically asserted by Noam Chomsky in *Cartesian Linguistics* (1966). This view I believe to be profoundly mistaken. Because of Chomsky's influence in the schools as the linguistic source and support of Paul Roberts' textbooks, among others, his view of the child's acquisition of language is cited here as a matter of professional interest as well as linguistic scholarship. And as he himself never tires of saying, *the consequences of Chomsky's philosophical position should be deeply pondered by those who are interested in his work.*[8] For a more extended discussion of Chomskyan transformational linguistics in the schools, please refer to Chapter 11.

The Development of American English

Whatever language or dialect is spoken by an American, it has a fascinating history. This section outlines that history briefly, from its ancient beginnings to the present, under the following seven subtitles:

ENGLISH, A GERMANIC LANGUAGE
OLD ENGLISH, OR ANGLO-SAXON
MIDDLE ENGLISH, THE LANGUAGE OF CHAUCER
STANDARDIZED ENGLISH SPELLING
ENGLISH BORROWING FROM OTHER LANGUAGES
EARLY CONTACT OF ENGLISH WITH INDIAN, AFRICAN, DUTCH, FRENCH, SPANISH
THE THREE MAJOR PERIODS OF AMERICAN IMMIGRATION AND SETTLEMENT

ENGLISH, A GERMANIC LANGUAGE. Historical scholarship has traced the modern languages of Europe and the Middle East back to a hypothetical reconstructed ancestor, proto Indo-European. Unlike as they now are, modern Germanic and Romance languages descended from this common ancestor. English belongs to the Germanic group including Danish, Dutch, German, Norwegian, Swedish, and Yiddish; Latin is the parent of the Romance group including French, Italian, Portuguese, Romanian, and Spanish. English is a Germanic language, not a Romance language.

OLD ENGLISH, OR ANGLO-SAXON. In the fifth century A.D. the ancestors of the English people came to England from Europe: the Angles from Denmark, the Saxons from Schleswig and Holstein, and the Jutes from Jutland. Eventually the languages of these invaders became the English language and developed several different dialects. The dialect of London eventually became the ruling dialect. The Christianizing of England in the sixth and seventh centuries brought the nation into contact with Latin and the international community that used Latin. At this time English began to borrow words from Latin, often changing them to suit English needs. For about five hundred years, until the successful conquest by the Norman French in 1066, Old English, or Anglo-Saxon, was the language of England. What was it like?

Old English, like Latin, was a *synthetic* language; that is, Old English depended heavily upon an involved inflectional system — a complex set of endings that could be added to word bases — to express grammatical and syntactical relationships. This inflectional system included forms for grammatical gender of nouns and adjectives; eight different noun cases; forms for tenses, modes, and aspects of verbs, as well as forms for singular and plural; and a system of derivational prefixes and suffixes that could convert one part of speech to another, or alter the meaning of the base form, or both. Old English also had beginnings of the basic English sentence, the actor-action-goal pattern that has become dominant in English structure today. Out of this whole complex synthetic apparatus, all that remains today are a few noun and verb inflections, pronouns, some of the derivational affixes, and the *-ly* suffix for adjectives and adverbs. Modern English is an *analytic* language; that is, in place of its former synthetic inflectional system, English now depends upon sentence patterns, word order, and structure words (or function words); intonation is also of great importance in English syntax.

TEACHING SUGGESTION : A high school student might like to look up the Lord's Prayer in Anglo-Saxon and compare it with a modern version, for an oral or written report.

MIDDLE ENGLISH, THE LANGUAGE OF CHAUCER. While the structural changes were taking place that led first to Middle English and then to Modern English, there were several periods of heavy borrowing of words from many languages. We have already noted the first period of direct borrowing from Latin, often with English modifications, during the sixth and seventh centuries; these borrowings of course did not affect the *structure* of the language. Following the Norman conquest, the official language of England was Norman French, but the common people continued to speak Old English; by about 1200 the primacy of English had reasserted itself, and something like a marriage of Norman French and Old English was consummated, coincident with structural changes that characterized

Middle English. The great period of borrowing from French was during the eleventh and twelfth centuries, approximately two hundred years before the death of Chaucer in 1400. His works, written in the latter part of the fourteenth century, remain a monument of Middle English language and literature.

TEACHING SUGGESTION: High school students may enjoy comparing and contrasting a passage from Chaucer in the original with a modernized version. Nevill Coghill's is exceptionally good; parts of it have been broadcast by BBC and are available on discs.

STANDARDIZED ENGLISH SPELLING. For many reasons, English spelling became relatively fixed about 1400, despite the existence of several dialects at the time, and even though significant sound changes occurred afterward. Our spelling is not generally regarded as a satisfactory guide to the sounds of English words today; but we tend to overlook the fact of a multiplicity of English dialects, having a great variety of basic sounds. Our standard English spellings do have one overriding advantage: they allow English speakers of all dialects all over the globe to read and write down the sounds of their own speech in identical forms, irrespective of dialect. No spelling reform can ever duplicate that advantage, because it would have to relate to a single dialect and ignore the others.

ENGLISH BORROWING FROM OTHER LANGUAGES. During the sixteenth century, English borrowed heavily from Latin, sometimes as part of a nationalistic "scholarly" effort to rewrite etymologies that had too much French influence to suit English sensibilities. During the nineteenth and twentieth centuries, English vocabulary reflected vast technological changes in the outright invention of new words and the importation of word elements from Greek and Latin to be used in new ways. And all down the years, the seafaring British and Americans have brought back words from all over the world, along with fruits of commerce, to enrich our great English word hoard.

North American English has its special wealth of words originating in many American Indian nations, from several frontiers,

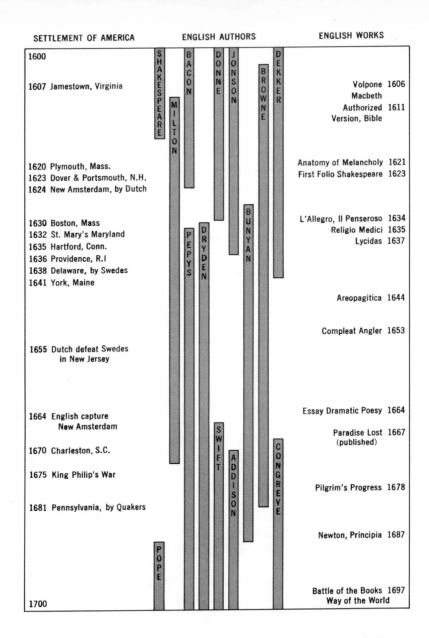

Figure 2.1 Important dates in the settlement of America and English literary history. *

* From *American English*, by Albert H. Marckwardt. Copyright © 1958 by Oxford University Press, Inc. Reprinted by permission.

from Mexico, and through the direct influence of French and Spanish cultures in our early history. A presentation here of this rich topic can be no more than an introductory sketch; interested students may consult Selected References at the end of the chapter.

TEACHING SUGGESTION : Students of all ages, but in high school especially, can profit by studying and reporting on specific, limited parts of the vast borrowing that characterizes English.

EARLY CONTACT OF ENGLISH WITH INDIAN, AFRICAN, DUTCH, FRENCH, SPANISH. The original British colonists brought with them to America the English spoken by Shakespeare, Spenser, Jonson, Donne, Milton, Bunyan, Dryden, and Newton (Figure 2.1). This English came into intimate contact with a variety of languages spoken by native Indians, Negro slaves from West Africa, and Dutch, French, and Spanish settlers who had arrived earlier.

Around 1600, about a million Indians lived in America. While they spoke a variety of languages and dialects, the most influential was that of the Algonquian tribes who inhabited the coastal areas first settled by the colonists. Close contact with Algonquian and the languages cited above resulted in the borrowing of many words for plants, animals, foods, human activities, geographical features.

Following are representative examples of distinctive American English borrowings during the colonial period:

Indian: *catalpa, chipmunk, hickory, hooch, mackinaw, mugwump, muskellunge, pecan, persimmon, podunk, powwow, skunk, squash, succotash, woodchuck*

African: *banjo, chigger* and *jigger, cooter* (turtle), *goober* (peanut), *gumbo, hoodoo* and *voodoo, jazz* and *juke, zombi*

Dutch: *cole slaw, boss, bowery, caboose, dingus, dope, dumb* (stupid), *pot cheese, poppycock, Santa Claus, sleigh, spook, stoop* (porch), *waffle, Yankee*

French: (largely via Canada): *buccaneer, calumet, caribou, cent* (coin), *chowder, depot, levee, portage, pumpkin, prairie, rotisserie, sashay, toboggan, voyageur*

Spanish: *adobe, alfalfa, alligator, bonanza, buckaroo, calaboose,*
chile con carne, cockroach, corral, desperado, lasso,
marijuana, mosquito, palomino, patio, poncho, stam-
pede, stevedore, tamale

This list of early American English loanwords merely suggests their great interest; no effort has been made to suggest many other borrowings that have become distinctive of American English, nor the ingenious coinages that characterize our language from colonial times to the present.

TEACHING SUGGESTION : Investigations of loanwords and coinages can be very profitable to students of almost any age, from elementary to graduate school; the depth and extent of any project depends only upon the student's ability, interest, and motivation.

THE THREE MAJOR PERIODS OF AMERICAN IMMIGRATION AND SETTLE-MENT. (1) From approximately 1600 to 1800, the American colonists were mainly British; they brought with them the English of their time (see Figure 2.1); and established the general form American speech has followed. About 1800, at the end of the first great wave of immigration, ninety per cent of the population of four million had come from the British Isles; ninety-five per cent of them lived east of the Appalachian Mountains. Among these settlers were the owners of substantial numbers of Negro slaves, the progenitors of the teeming ghettos of today.

(2) During the sixty years from 1800 to the Civil War, the slave trade continued while the original thirteen colonies expanded in a dramatic sweep, first to the South and the Old Northwest (Upper Midwest today), and then all across the continent to the Pacific. About three million immigrants, half of them Irish, the other half German, settled in the Midwest, in addition to pioneers of British ancestry moving from the East. The Irish and German immigrants were refugees: the Irish from the potato famine that began in 1845, the Germans from the consequences of the abortive revolution of 1848. Thousands of Negro slaves labored as field hands and domestics, but many fled north and east and into Canada.

(3) From the Civil War to the present, millions of immigrants have come to America, from Scandinavia, Southern Europe, Central Europe and the Slavic countries, Asia, South America and Puerto Rico — all bringing their own languages and cultures with them.

Today, America has a population of more than two hundred million people speaking a number of regional dialects; because of high mobility and the mingling of dialects, and exposure to the common language of radio, television, and film, regional dialects are more and more homogenized. Regional dialects persist, however, and are still being studied by linguistic geographers and dialectologists. (See Figures 2.2 and 2.3.) The study of inner-city black English speech is of intense concern to linguists and educators working in our large urban centers.

TEACHING SUGGESTION : Projects on regional dialects and the special vocabulary of local speech communities (ethnic, vocational, recreational) can be carried out successfully by students of all ages, by direct investigation. One good format is the compilation of a dictionary; further activities include stories or a newspaper using the special vocabularies of the dictionaries.

Since World War II, for a variety of reasons, Southern blacks in great numbers have emigrated northward. Today, about twenty-five million Americans are black, the majority of them barely subsisting in the urban ghettos of the larger cities of the North and East. This segregation has created tragic educational problems; it has raised a dialect barrier between the ghetto and the affluent world of spoken and printed English reflecting the middle-class values of white America. Some of the greatest teaching challenges, to young teachers especially, are to be found in these ghettos; nothing less than rigorous professional study and wholehearted dedication to the task can meet these challenges successfully.

TEACHING SUGGESTION : High school students can profit by studying linguistic investigations of ghetto dialects. This is a serious topic, appropriate for a major report or a term paper.

*Figure 2.2 Progress of the American atlases.**

* Prepared by Mrs. Raven I. McDavid for *The Structure of American English*, by W. Nelson Francis. Copyright © 1958. The Ronald Press Company, New York.

Figure 2.3 Dialect Areas of the United States. *

* Atlantic Seaboard Areas (after Kurath). Tentative Dialect Boundaries.
Arrows indicate direction of migrations.

THE NORTH

1. Northeastern New England
2. Southeastern New England
3. Southwestern New England
4. Inland North (Western Vermont, Upstate New York & derivatives)
5. The Hudson Valley
6. Metropolitan New York

THE MIDLAND

North Midland

7. Delaware Valley (Philadelphia)
8. Susquehanna Valley
10. Upper Ohio Valley (Pittsburgh)
11. Northern West Virginia

South Midland

9. Upper Potomac & Shenandoah
12. Southern West Virginia & Eastern Kentucky
13. Western Carolina & Eastern Tennessee

THE SOUTH

14. Delmarva (Eastern Shore)
15. The Virginia Piedmont
16. Northeastern North Carolina (Albermarle Sound & Neuse Valley)
17. Cape Fear & Peedee Valleys
18. The South Carolina Low Country (Charleston)

* Prepared by Mrs. Raven I. McDavid for *The Structure of American English*, by W. Nelson Francis. Copyright © 1958. The Ronald Press Company, New York.

Selected References

Margaret M. Bryant, second ed., *Modern English and Its Heritage* (New York: Macmillan, 1962).

Rémy Chauvin, tr. George Ordish, *Animal Societies: from the Bee to the Gorilla* (New York: Hill and Wang, 1968).

Otto Jespersen, ninth ed., *Growth and Structure of the English Language* (New York: Doubleday, 1955).

Albert H. Marckwardt, *American English* (New York: Oxford University Press, 1958).

L. M. Myers, *The Roots of Modern English* (Boston: Little, Brown, 1966).

Thomas Pyles, *The Origins and Development of the English Language* (New York: Harcourt, Brace and World, 1964).

Margaret Schlauch, *The English Language in Modern Times (since 1400)* (London: Oxford University Press, 1964).

Thomas A. Sebeok, *Animal Communication: Techniques of Study and Results of Research* (Bloomington: Indiana University Press, 1968).

E. H. Sturtevant, *Linguistic Change: an Introduction to the Historical Study of Language*, intro. by Eric P. Hamp, 1962 ed. (Chicago: University of Chicago Press, 1917).

Chapter 3

Teaching American English as Language

So far we have briefly surveyed (a) questions of value in teaching English and the language arts, (b) elements of communication in man and animals, (c) salient points in the child's acquisition of language, and (d) the development of American English. Against that broad background, this chapter poses key questions about how to apply linguistics to teaching American English to native speakers, including speakers of divergent dialects. The suggested answers to these questions are necessarily broad, and are often stated as *principles*.

The optimum use of this chapter is twofold: first, as an immediate introduction to Part Two. Teaching Applications of American English Linguistics; and second, as an essential cross reference to each of the seven chapters in Part Two. For although every chapter does discuss teaching principles and does present Teaching Applications, every element of language cannot be related to every teaching principle and method at every point in the presentation. A chapter like this is needed as a general source of supplementary teaching principles and methods.

What linguistic principles and what principles of native language teaching and learning should guide the teacher of English and the language arts? What competence in linguistics is required of this teacher?

What language learning goals can be reached by direct teaching of formal grammar? By indirect teaching? What goals can be reached by direct teaching about language generally? Indirect teaching? What grammatical terminology is needed by the learner? How should he learn it?

How can the teacher helpfully discuss usage, "correctness," and style in spoken and written English? In order to develop skills and appreciation, is it helpful to adopt a descriptive rather than a prescriptive approach to the English language? Is it effective methodology to teach English and the language arts by inductive, exploratory, and experimental approaches? If so, how can this be done?

What are some of the major traps and pitfalls to be avoided?

These are some key questions to bear in mind as we consider basic principles of teaching the arts and skills of English. The following discussion is presented in four main sections and a concluding section, as follows:

Basic Approach to Language, Thought, Meaning
The Teacher's Knowledge of Language Structure
Basic Teaching Principles
Basic Principles Applied
A Capsule Statement of Teaching Methods

Basic Approach to Language, Thought, Meaning

Educators need to develop a multidisciplinary view of language and literacy. Linguistics, narrowly defined, can describe language as a hierarchical structural system of interrelated parts, or constituents — language as a code. Psychology, via learning theory, can describe language as a system of habits relating symbols to behavior; and via information theory and communication models, can describe language as a means of transmitting "information" by both speech and writing. Comprehending oral and written language requires auditory and visual perception, respectively, both within the domain of psychology. But *perception alone is not enough:* in both listening and reading, entire meaning-bearing language patterns must be not simply decoded but *interpreted* and *evaluated.* Interpretation and evaluation must take into account, as part of the "information" in the message, its emotional, volitional, denotative, and connotative content. Moreover, social and cultural dimensions often must be considered: regional, class, and standard dialects, for example; and the many forms of extended discourse, including the forms of literature.

Interpretation and evaluation of meaning-bearing language patterns thus lead into a consideration of relationships between language and thought, however we choose to define "thought." This brings us into the traditional realm of philosophy. Every major philosopher beginning with Plato has made the study of language an important part of his work; the influence of philosophy is strong today in attitudes and assumptions brought to language study.

The view we take of language and thought is basic to our understanding of meaning. Let us turn our attention briefly to some important relationships among *language, thought,* and *meaning.* Whatever the precise relationship, and whatever the inner mechanism or process of the relationship may be, human thought and linguistic operations and patterns appear to be so closely interrelated as to be inseparable. The following discussion is not intended to be a survey of this major topic, but rather a presentation of a few seminal ideas.

Of the specific nature of linguistic symbols, the French psychologist, Joseph Vendryes, in a book published in translation in 1925, said this: "Psychologically, the original linguistic act consists in giving to a sign a symbolic value. This psychological process distinguishes the language of man from that of animals." [1] Animals and birds can go no further than to use signs in close proximity to the referents of their signs; they cannot use signs symbolically, specifically not at other times or in other places (see pp. 41–42). But signs given symbolic value enable man to communicate with others, both directly and immediately, and at times and in places far removed from the situations or events symbolized in his language structures; *linguistic symbols also enable man to think, silently or aloud.*

In a famous work first published in 1921, Edward Sapir, arguing that language is primarily a pre-rational function, wrote: "At best language can but be the outward facet of thought on the highest, most generalized level of symbolic expression." [2] He believed that "language is an instrument originally put to uses lower than the conceptual plane" and that "thought arises as a refined interpretation of its content." [3] Granting that thought and speech may be separate and apart, he noted that speech nevertheless seems to be the only road we know of that leads to thought. It is a road that goes both ways. "We see this complex process of the interaction of language and thought actually taking place under our eyes," he wrote. "The instrument makes possible the product, the product refines the instrument." [4] *Language* is the instrument, *thought* the product. Sapir regarded thinking as "an abbreviation of the speech process." [5] He insisted that "Auditory imagery and the correlated motor imagery leading to articulation are, by whatever devious ways we follow the process, the historic fountainhead of all speech and all thinking." [6] In summation, he returned to his original symbolism: "Language, as a structure, is on its inner face the mold of thought." [7]

It is fascinating to note similarities between the insights of Sapir and the Soviet psychologist, Vygotsky, incorporated in a monograph published in 1934. "Thought is not expressed in words, but comes into existence through them," wrote Vygotsky. [8] "Thought, as it turns into speech, undergoes numerous changes. It does not simply find its expression in words; it finds its reality and form." [9] Regarding the nature of words, he said, "The meaning of a word represents such a close unity of thinking and speech that it is not possible to say whether it is a phenomenon of speech or a phenomenon of thinking. . . . It [meaning] is the word itself looked at from within." [10] Vygotsky was deeply impressed by the dynamic quality of the relationship of language and thought: "The bond between thought and words is a living process: thought is brought forth in words. The word, deprived of thought, is a dead word." [11] His investigations eventually led him to a consideration not only of thought, but of consciousness itself: ". . . thinking and speech are the key for understanding the nature of human consciousness," he concluded. "Words play a central part not only in the development of thought but in consciousness as a whole." [12]

Although much of what Vygotsky had to say about language and thought has deep significance for advanced skills of literacy, he did not comment on them explicitly. Sapir did, however, and what he said is of special interest to us.

> The most important of all visual speech symbolisms is . . . that of the written or printed word . . . The written forms are secondary symbols of the spoken ones — symbols of symbols — yet so close is the correspondence that they may, not only in theory, but in the actual

practice of certain eye-readers and, possibly, in certain types of thinking, be entirely substituted for the spoken ones. Yet the auditory-
motor associations are probably always latent at the least, that is,
they are unconsciously brought into play. Even those who read and
think without the slightest use of sound imagery are, in the last analysis,
dependent on it. They are merely handling the circulating medium,
the money, of visual symbols as a convenient substitute for the economic
goods and services of the fundamental auditory symbols.[13]

This statement is rich with implications for teachers of English and
the language arts.

If the foregoing sketch suggests the multidisciplinary dimensions
of language, thought, meaning, and the arts and skills of literacy,
it has accomplished its purpose. A new synthesis of approaches to
these interrelated processes is needed and is in the making; but it
must not be an eclectic agglomeration of elements, nor should it exaggerate out of its due proportion any single element. Such a synthesis
should simply reflect the multidisciplinary dimensions of the subject
itself.

The Teacher's Knowledge of Language Structure

It may be useful here to summarize my view of the basic knowledge
of language structure needed by all teachers of English and the
language arts. This summary will forecast information that is given
more detailed development in Parts Two and Three; it will also supplement the presentation of the linguistic autobiography project in
Chapter 1 (pp. 27–31).

Adequate knowledge of English structure must begin with basic
syntax — the practical analysis of sentences; sentences and elements
of sentences are the basic building blocks of English. An understanding of basic sentence patterns and their variations can be helpful in
both oral and written composition; this understanding is crucial to
the development of sentence sense, which in turn is fundamental
to successful writing and to reading comprehension.

Basic syntax, or the practical analysis of sentences, may be
helpfully discussed in terms of four subsystems:

1. INTONATION: the systematic rhythms and melodies of English.
   (Chapter 9)

2. SENTENCE PATTERNS: the order and arrangement of sentence parts; word order. (Chapter 7)
3. STRUCTURE WORDS (or function words): about three hundred words that have more to do with syntax (structural relationships within sentences) than with the "real" world outside language to which language refers. (Chapter 8)
4. WORD-FORM CHANGES: grammatical inflections of the four word classes: noun, verb, adjective, adverb (Chapter 5); derivational prefixes and suffixes (Chapter 6).

An adequate teaching knowledge of English structure also includes some acquaintance with phonemes, the smallest sound units; phonemes do not occur singly, but patterned in groups as words, word bases, or affixes. The relationship of phonemes to spelling is a subtle matter, since the sounds of "words" in the flowing stream of speech vary considerably according to rate, stress, and their relationships to sounds going before and coming after them. It can also be argued, however, that for spelling purposes words are removed from the speech stream, which strongly delimits the effects of intonation, stress, and rate; but words pronounced in this unnatural way should not be confused with their counterparts in normal speech. A knowledge of phonemics can be helpful in teaching phonics when that is what is needed, and also in knowing when it is not needed. The main point is that phonics instruction should deal as simply and effectively as possible with the relationships between spellings and sounds (graphemes and phonemes) — and should never stray off into remedial speech (Chapter 4).

INTONATION. Intonation is an important part of the English structural system, involving both obligatory and optional (or interpretive) features. Intonation is what makes native speech sound like native speech; faulty intonation is an unmistakable mark of non-native speech. Intonation can be a specialized study, but any teacher, especially one equipped with a tape recorder, can rely on his intuitive command of it for many practical applications in reading and writing.

The fade-fall and fade-rise terminals are the two basic intonation features for English teaching, particularly for reading and writing. The fade-fall is the dropping of the voice that marks the end of most sentences, as well as many questions; in sentence-level utterances it signifies finality. The fade-rise terminal is the "rising inflection" that marks the end of certain questions; it also may occur within sentences at points marked by commas in writing, where it signals the end of one syntactical element and suggests that another is coming.

Optional or interpretive intonation (tone of voice) is what gives individual quality and variety to oral reading and interpretation; many linguists call it *paralanguage*. Paralanguage and kinesics — the non-lingual, visible accompaniment of speech, such as bodily movements, nods, shrugs, gestures of all kinds, winks, "mugging" and so forth — underlie the art of acting. Kinesics is the basis of pantomime, and of the dance as a performing art. Both paralanguage and kinesics have a bearing on the study of literature (see Chapters 9 and 10).

SENTENCE PATTERNS. Despite their differences, linguists agree that the English sentence in all its variety is a meaning-bearing language pattern; they agree that it can be described. It is also agreed that syntax deals with basic sentence patterns, propositions, or kernel sentences, that are capable of infinite variation by means of inversions, expansions, substitutions, and transformations of several kinds. The chief difference between the structuralists and the transformationalists — *as analysts of language structure* — is that structuralists tend to limit themselves as closely as possible to language as meaning-bearing code, with descriptive emphasis on the objective code as code; whereas transformationalists are concerned more with the formulization of "rules" to produce grammatical statements of subjective messages. Their reliance on meaning rather than language system to explain linguistic structures gives them a remarkable resemblance to traditional grammarians. The explicit assumptions of the structuralists are those of empirical science in general, of behavioral science in particular. For a more extended treatment of these topics, refer to Chapter 11.

It is helpful for English teachers to understand that only about ten basic sentence patterns are needed for teaching students to generate a great variety of sentences, both oral and written. These correspond to the declarative sentences of school grammar; many of them have inversions or passive transformations as counterparts; other major patterns are questions, requests, and commands. All these patterns are capable of virtually infinite variation by means of four operations: *transformation, relocation, elimination,* and *expansion* (see Chapter 7).

STRUCTURE WORDS. English has a subsystem of about three hundred words whose primary function is to serve as joints or glue between syntactical elements; although relatively few, these words occur with very high frequency in speech and writing. The most important for teaching are five sets of markers:

1. **noun markers** (articles and all other words that fill the positions of articles)
2. **verb markers** (auxiliaries and other words that function in the same positions)
3. **phrase markers** (prepositions, singly and in groups)
4. **clause markers** (two kinds, so-called coordinating and subordinating conjunctions, and all words that fill the same positions)
5. **question markers** (such words as *who, why,* and *how,* when those words initiate question patterns).

Structure words are of great importance in both reading and writing; detailed knowledge of and experience with them can be invaluable to the English teacher (see Chapter 7).

WORD-FORMS AND WORD-FORM CHANGES. Grammatical inflections and derivational affixes are the two kinds of word-form changes. Grammatical inflections include noun singular, plural, and genitive forms; the parts of verbs; and the forms for the comparison of adjectives and adverbs. This residue of an elaborate Old English inflectional system is the basis of many differences between standard English and divergent dialects; so, of course, are the forms of pronouns. Derivational affixes comprise the remarkable system of English prefixes and suffixes; generally, suffixes added to word bases (roots) change the word from one form class (part of speech) to another, and prefixes change the meaning of a word without changing its class; but there are enough exceptions to "prove" this rule many times over: it is not a rule but a statement of common occurrence. Just as with the subsystem of structure words, a detailed knowledge of affixing is invaluable to the English teacher (see Chapters 5 and 6).

PHONEMES AND GRAPHEMES. Phonemes are the basic sounds of language which combine in larger patterns; phonemes do not occur singly, in isolation. (The noun marker *a* as in *a man,* is a word, or morpheme, not a single phoneme functioning alone *as a phoneme*.) Graphemes are the letters and combinations of letters that represent phonemes in standard spellings. Study of phonemes and graphemes is of great utility in spelling, and has the same relevance to reading that spelling has. In thinking about phonemes, an English teacher would do well to consider the linguistic phenomenon that Pike calls "smearing" or "slurring." This insight might help avoid the egregious error of asking students to "pronounce all the letters in every word."

Phonemes are the smallest structural units of language. For clarity in his own mind, and for the sake of good English instruction, the English teacher should take the trouble to understand the difference between phonemics and phonetics. **Phonemics** deals with the smallest distinctive and significant classes of sounds in the language system. **Phonetics** is the scientific study of speech sounds of all kinds, with no necessary concern with phonemes at all. Phonemes are basic *structural* units of a language or a dialect; in descriptions of phonemes, phonetics can deal with non-distinctive variants of phonemes, *allophones;* allophones are the members of the significant and distinctive classes of sounds collectively designated as phonemes. The native speaker automatically disregards the non-distinctive, non-significant variants of phonemes; he has learned to group them all together into classes of sounds which he unconsciously treats as identical. For the communicative purposes of the language system, they *are* identical: that is what the term *phoneme* means.

Clarity on these distinctions is essential to good English teaching. See Chapter 4 for a detailed explanation.

Basic Teaching Principles

Successful teaching of English language arts coordinates and clarifies the interrelationships of all components and processes of English as a general field — *speaking, listening, writing, reading, thinking* (see pp. 11–15). In the kindergarten-primary years, components and processes are appropriately simple; as students mature toward high school graduation and college, interrelationships become increasingly sophisticated. But varying the complexity of materials presented does not change the fundamental nature of English: the field is implicitly and explicitly unified. A tragic flaw of poor teaching is the mistaken effort to fragment English into unrelated segments for instruction.

The best English teachers base their work on fundamental principles that counteract this unnatural fragmentation of language topics, skills, arts, and appreciations. The prime task of the schools is to help each learner attain the highest possible standards of literacy. Ideally, every kindergarten-primary child would master essential linguistic concepts and operations before going on to higher levels; in practice, some students graduate from high school far short of any such mastery. This is why teachers at all levels must keep fundamental principles in mind; some of these principles are presented in the remainder of this section.

English is an intellectual discipline. Beginning in preschool and continuing without let or hindrance through the senior year of high school, excellent teaching of English and the language arts should challenge students *intellectually.* As native speakers of English, of one or more of many dialects, they have considerable linguistic skill; moreover, they inherit a great legacy of language and literature. Professional English teachers seek ways of tapping the rich language lore and know-how of all normal children and young adults — ways of helping them gain access to their linguistic birthright. They encourage the student's natural curiosity about language and his natural spirit of play in language learning; conversely, they avoid doing anything to stifle the student's innate curiosity and sense of the fun of language. The successful teacher of the arts and skills of English avoids even the appearance of condescension and patronage; deeply aware that the student's language and dialect are closer to him than his skin of whatever color, he treats the student with respect and dignity.

Readiness and performance in both writing and reading are closely related. Instruction can be strengthened by coordinated lessons that handle writing and reading in explicit relation to speaking and listening, with the reminder, appropriately phrased at grade level, that thinking is the great coordinator of all. Concretely, lessons incorporate as many elements as possible in closely connected instruction: through speaking, writing, dictation, copying from dictation, and analysis of word and sentence patterns in spoken and written language. Not *every* lesson can do all this simultaneously, but many can; the point is to aim at this objective consistently, in order to score the maximum number of hits.

Talk can be written down and printed; writing and print can "talk." A student is *conceptually* ready to write as soon as he understands that his own talk can be reduced to writing and that he can read it back to himself: "talk can be written down." This is the excellent point of the experience chart method in kindergarten-primary instruction; and the more individualized the "chart," the better. *This method may also be extended into individual remedial writing and reading projects at all grade levels, by using as subject matter whatever the student already has some interest in and knowledge of.* The language is that of the student, especially at first; later the teacher may introduce language patterns from standard written English, but not at the very beginning. The next stage is conceptual readiness for reading what others have written: talk written down can be read off the printed page — "print talks"; the printed page is specifically designed to talk to the reader, to tell him something (and it had better be something he wants to hear!). There are high school graduates whose thoughts are quite fuzzy about these basic facts of literacy.

Writing and reading can be enjoyable. As a by-product of various pre-reading and reading-like experiences, especially hearing stories read aloud by parents, siblings, and relatives, some students begin to read and write before they come to school. Such experiences can be duplicated in the classroom by the teacher's own oral reading, supplemented by prepared tapes and discs, and by current radio and TV programs. Whatever his age or grade, the student is emotionally ready to read and write — stimulated and motivated — when his personal experiences associated with reading and writing are happy and successful. He has a strong desire to read and write — by and for himself. This principle holds for the high school functional illiterate as well as for the kindergarten prereader.

TEACHING SUGGESTION: Ask students to tell about their earliest experiences with reading and writing in class. The discussion may suggest specific topics for oral and written reports.

It is wise to have an occasional unit on linguistic fun in every grade (linguistic jokes, word plays, puns, conundrums, spoonerisms, bloopers, double-entendres, riddles, limericks, nonsense verse, word games); but whenever suitable, similar items should also be laced throughout the teaching of other topics — as examples, illustrations, highlights, and sometimes just for the fun of it.

TEACHING SUGGESTION: Organize a linguistic fun session, the only requirement being that the point of the humor must depend on a point of language.

Similarly, the principle of linguistic contrasts can be illustrated and pointed up as a normal part of the development of units in all grades: contrasts of language elements, both structural and lexical (or semantic); contrasts of two or more dialects; contrasts of two or more speech communities (defined by neighborhood, ethnic group, age, sex, occupation, hobby, sport, for example). Such activities as linguistic fun, linguistic contrasts, language games, and others that may occur to you, reinforce specific linguistic principles and understandings; they are also living demonstrations that language and language study can provide lively and interesting things for students to do.

TEACHING SUGGESTION: As a basis for class discussion, ask students to discuss speech communities that they, their friends, or members of their families belong to. One outcome might be the preparations of "dictionaries" (glossaries of special vocabularies used in various speech communities).

How MUCH FORMAL INSTRUCTION IN GRAMMAR? The teacher of English and the language arts cannot know too much about the English language and the grammars available today. But that same teacher can all too easily attempt to teach too much of this knowledge directly in the classroom. It is not an objective of English teaching to make grammarians of the students. It can be cogently argued that *direct teaching of grammar as formal subject matter — to be mastered for its own sake as a discipline — should be limited to a specific course or courses offered in high school; or to specific units of instruction possibly in junior high school.*

Little evidence supports the belief that formal instruction in grammar in that sense directly improves ability to read and write; there is in fact evidence to the contrary. The reason for this may well be in part that such instruction is usually prescriptive, and negatively prescriptive at that. Negative prescription does not even tell *what to do;* it tells *what not to do:* "Thou shalt not, not, not . . ." engraved in stone. *This kind of teaching has never worked.* Instruction in English and the language arts should be language-centered but not grammar-centered in the formal sense. However, inductive and exploratory teaching of grammar can be related to developments of the skills of literacy, informally and indirectly.

GENERAL APPROACH. The best English teaching is centered upon language: the nature of language, the history of language, the structure and functioning of language, the manifold uses of language. A direct attack may be made on many of these and related topics; uses of language include composition and rhetoric, speech and speaking, literature, oral interpretation, dramatics — all the practical, social, creative uses and forms of language. A variety of classroom activities can be interwoven with the subject matter of lessons at all grade levels; a variety of methods can also be used, including deduction, induction, exposition by the teacher, and the approach through inquiry. A spirit of inquiry permeates and informs the working English classroom.

TEACHING THE LANGUAGE SYSTEM: A SYNTHESIS OF GRAMMARS. The English language system, or grammar, is a changing thing; so, to an even greater extent, is the description (or descriptions) of it. This means that language study is an open rather than a closed subject; but it also means that language study has a rationale, a set of guiding principles, and is no mere hodge-podge of purely personal piffle.

In applying English linguistics to serve educational ends, we may think in terms of a synthesis of grammars, including sound and useful features of school grammar, traditional or classical grammar, descriptive and structural grammar, and transformational grammar.

At the same time, we must avoid the trap of subjective eclecticism, which is likely to mean a conglomeration of inconsistent personal whims. Those features of the various grammars that best serve a descriptive rather than a prescriptive approach are the most useful in the English classroom. This concept of a synthesis of grammars for classroom teaching is illustrated throughout Part Two and explained further in Chapter 11.

Basic Principles Applied

In English and language arts instruction, many lessons and units must deal with specific knowledge, facts, information; or with specific skills of literacy to be developed, practiced, reinforced. Following is a brief outline of principles that can be clearly and concretely applied in lessons dealing with such specifics. While these principles do have some relevance to lessons that develop concepts, deepen understandings, and sharpen appreciation, they are more applicable to lessons dealing with specific points of language structure and with specific applications and skills.

CLEAR REALIZATION OF THE SPECIFIC UNDERSTANDING, GENERALIZATION, APPLICATION, SKILL TO BE DEVELOPED THROUGH THE LESSON. Clear realization in the first place *by the teacher* as an aim, or an objective to be reached; secondly, achievement *by the student* as the principal outcome of the lesson. So far as possible, students should be patiently led to find out for themselves — to discover — the desired outcomes of each lesson; at the same time, teachers should recognize that students cannot actually discover everything for themselves, and that the process of discovery can be speeded up by judicious help from the teacher. In some lessons, the *sense of discovery* is the end to be sought; this sense may be developed in many ways by inventive teachers. Chapters 4–11 give examples of ways in which the sense of discovery can be developed through instruction; they also present information to challenge the wit and ingenuity of the teacher.

CAREFULLY DESIGNED, CONTROLLED, AND SUCCESSFUL PRACTICE BY STUDENTS. The purpose of practice lessons is not only drill and reinforcement, but *successful manipulation* of the language patterns and constituents offered for practice. It is of the greatest importance that students experience *success* in their work with language, not once but time after time. Thus it is desirable to present lessons that are both interesting and error-proof, so far as possible. For example, instead of offering the student his choice of finding the right item or making a "mistake," give him a model that is right to begin with and ask him to imitate it; it is also possible to present material selected so that arranging it or rearranging it is a genuine problem for the student, yet a problem he can hardly reach a wrong answer to: the material won't go together wrong and still make sense to him. For example, the following scrambled words, rearranged, make an old proverb:

never but liars lie can figure figures

Figures never lie, but liars can figure.

This kind of problem is pertinent to the study of sentence patterns and structure.

INDIVIDUAL APPLICATIONS BY THE STUDENT. *The best proof of the student's learning is his ability to apply what he has studied in some productive activity that is unmistakably his own;* learning that is essentially rote memory of verbal formulations given by a teacher or a textbook cannot be applied creatively to new projects. Rote verbal memory is the proper function of a parrot, or a tape recorder; neither can do anything except repeat, word for word. Successful teachers devise interesting applications to be made by their students, or used by students as launching pads into their own orbits. So far as possible, projects should be individual; the students themselves can contribute suggestions that are personal and individual.

It is good practice to provide for three "levels" or areas within most classes: slow, average, and advanced; this sort of provision can be made, however, without loss of individualization. Enrichment projects may also be devised, not only for advanced or gifted individuals, but for any student who is interested or who can be motivated. Successful projects of either immediate application or enrichment may extend far beyond class time; they may lead to field trips, excursions, library investigations, personal interviews, collections, exhibits, bulletin board displays, panel and group discussions, individual oral and written reports. The trick is to interest and motivate the student.

APPRECIATION AND DISCOVERY. Lessons created to develop the student's appreciation and deeper understanding of the nature and uses of language will not always provide "carefully designed, controlled, and successful practice"; nor will they always permit "individual applications" that can be objectively measured or even evaluated reliably by any known standards. But it would be unwise to allow such considerations to rule out the development of language lessons or entire projects that may have deep and lasting value for the students but cannot be measured at all in pragmatic terms.

Examples of such lessons or units might be those dealing with the nature of language, animal communication, human communication, wordless communication and pantomime, sign languages, braille, communication by various systems of non-verbal signals and signs, the development of the alphabet, structural elements of literary style, and selected topics under English language structure itself. But every lesson or unit should be made accessible to the student in terms as concrete and specific as possible — terms within his grasp if not always entirely within his previous experience. *Many lessons should lead to experience*, significant experience that the student might never have had without the lesson; in these lessons, *the new experience generated is in itself a discovery made by the student*. Such important experiences will not necessarily take place during the prescribed time for the lesson, but may unfold in a series of "double takes," possibly over many years. The concept of the spiral shape of each individual's learning is especially pertinent to these experiences; in providing them, the teacher needs all the insight and imagination he can command.

The importance of discovery experiences in appreciation and deeper understanding of the nature and uses of language cannot be overestimated. Not only are they of great intrinsic value as humanizing experiences; they can also round out and give a three-dimensional shape to narrower, more precise learnings that otherwise might seem static and flat to the students.

The foregoing suggestions are intended to give aid and comfort to the teacher who is trying to live up to the professional demands of English and the language arts on several levels and in many dimensions. *The essential teaching principle is to relate the nature of every topic closely to the nature of the learner and his lifelong develop-*

ment of the arts and skills of language through experience. Through his own experience the student can begin to see language as both individual and social behavior, and gradually he can acquire a sense of the multidisciplinary nature of man's greatest invention — language.

A Capsule Statement of Methodology

The most important principle of this methodology is that it is language-centered. That is, language itself, in all its aspects and all its uses, provides a large share of the material presented to the student for direct observation, study, and practice.

Teachers today know that students in elementary as well as secondary schools can deal intelligently — *in their own terms* — with concepts in science and mathematics that formerly were not presented until students entered college or university. The "new" math and the "new" science demonstrated this; something similar is happening in English and the language arts. Modern knowledge of language (linguistics) and modern psychological knowledge of the way children learn to use their language (psycholinguistics) combine to build the foundation for a new approach to both subject matter and methods. The new emphasis upon language requires a modern point of view toward language and language learning, and corresponding teaching methods.

Point of view and method together determine the form and content of the actual lessons, in practical classroom terms for teacher and student alike. So far as possible, the student should experience his English lessons directly, through *inductive processes of discovery,* and then express his experience in his own language; conversely, he should never be asked to memorize definitions and other purely verbal formulations that lie outside his experience. Thus, teachers try to realize an overall aim: the student's learning should be *concrete* and *operational,* rather than *verbal* and *abstract.* This method avoids the serious pitfall of verbalism, a curse of our schools. The student's language learning in school should parallel his early childhood method of learning to speak his native tongue — playfully, through delighted experiences of *discovery* — through repeated *exposure* to language forms and patterns, by creative *imitation* and *manipulation,* and by personal trial and error, with kindly (and not too much) correction from adults.

This teaching method is designed for a *descriptive* rather than *prescriptive* treatment of language and language learning. Differences in the lessons at various grade levels, differences in the oral and written work expected of the student, should reflect the spiral concept of his development through *direct experience with language* — both in school and out. This spiral method of presentation at different levels means a minimum of drill, drill, drill until the point loses its point; it means reliance upon repeated discovery and rediscovery, repeated exposure, repeated chances for creative manipulation in successive lessons and in successive school years. *This is the secret of the powerful influence of the child's language experience outside the school upon his whole language development; teachers of English and the language arts should make use of this secret.* Prescriptive, abstractly verbal methods and materials cannot match the power of this natural process of discovery, exposure, and creative manipulation of language in "real life," which we all know means outside the English classroom. This method also avoids the serious trap of "coverage," so that the student is freed from the burden of trying to learn every new thing "permanently," once and for all. A minimum of grammatical terminology is used, and the student learns primarily by association of terms with referents rather than by verbal definitions.

Teachers can learn to tailor their lessons to attract the student's attention to *language as language*, to *American English as language* — to its breadth and depth of dimensions, historical, social, cultural — as well as to many of the specifics of American English structure itself. The student is encouraged to acquire these learnings gradually, without nagging, through experiences suited to his ever-changing age and growth. To require him at any age to repeat, parrot-like, our ancient verbal rules and definitions, to mimic our formal statements about English — this is empty *verbalism:* it cannot help him or teach him anything worth knowing. No, the emergent human being is entitled to form his own concepts, in his own way and in his own terms, as he develops and modifies them continually, while he grows older, and we hope, wiser. This is really the way people learn; indeed, we cannot learn in any other way. Eventual mastery can be the outcome of an upward spiral development toward maturity, in lesson after lesson and grade after grade.

The term *spiral* means a number of things. Differences between grade levels are differences in complexity of language structure, including differences in the amount and the kind of derivational

affixing; differences in control of the syntactical operations of transformation, relocation, elimination, and expansion; differences in
difficulty of vocabulary and concepts represented by vocabulary; differences in assumed maturity in all respects; differences in oral and
written assignments; differences in independent reading; and so on.
The term *spiral* also means revisiting previously taught concepts in
later years in new and more sophisticated ways.

Most students will not be required to develop concepts completely unknown to them. What normal students need initially is
to develop consciousness of language structures and operations they
are familiar with in everyday conversations, reinforced by helpful
practice in writing and reading structures they already know operationally in audio-lingual form; this consciousness can become their
most direct bridge to literacy.

Spiral instruction also means that in addition to making students
conscious of language structures and operations they already know
and use, teachers should introduce them to patterns and structures
that they might otherwise never encounter in understandable terms.
Among other things, this means structural analysis of poems and
other literary forms, as well as similar analysis of exposition and other
modes and styles, both oral and written, that are not a part of
"real life" outside of school. This obligation, over the entire N–12
school career, is probably more important than simply stimulating
consciousness of language forms and operations the students already
know and use without a teacher's assistance.

Selected References

Franz Boas, *Race, Language and Culture* (New York: Macmillan, 1940).

Roger Brown, *Words and Things* (Glencoe, Illinois: The Free Press, 1958).

Jerome S. Bruner, *On Knowing: Essays for the Left Hand* (Cambridge: Harvard University Press, 1962).

———, *The Process of Education* (Cambridge: Harvard University Press,
1963).

Jerome S. Bruner, ed., *Learning about Learning: a Conference Report*
(Washington: U.S. Government Printing Office, 1966).

John B. Carroll, *The Study of Language* (Cambridge, Mass.: Harvard University Press, 1959).

Edward T. Hall, *The Silent Language* (a Premier Book) (Greenwich, Conn.: Fawcett, 1959).

Herbert Landar, *Language and Culture* (New York: Oxford University Press, 1966).

Jean Malmstrom, *Language in Society* (New York: Hayden, 1965).

Edwin A. Sapir, *Language: An Introduction to the Study of Speech* (New York: Harcourt, Brace, 1921, 1949).

L. S. Vigotsky, "Thought and Speech," Chapter VII of *Language and Thought*, tr. Helen Kogan, Eugenia Hanfmann, and Jacob Kasanin, in *Psycholinguistics: a Book of Readings*, ed. Sol Saporta (New York: Holt, Rinehart and Winston, 1961), pp. 509–537.

See also Biolinguistics and Psycholinguistics, p. 32.

Part Two

Teaching Applications of American English Linguistics

Chapter 4

Sounds and Letters

To most teachers, **phonics** is an innocent term suggesting methods and materials for teaching the relationships of sounds and letters as a basis for elementary instruction in reading, writing, and spelling; phonics is also associated with remedial programs at all levels, and with "sounding out unknown words." Until quite recently, the informational content of phonics was simply devoid of linguistic influence, particularly data from scientific phonetics. A good share of phonics was handed down by word of mouth, supplemented by simplistic commercial programs, all having a remarkable family likeness; audio-visual aids, including records for individual and choral drill, were developed to reinforce the teaching of phonics. The subject was complete, narrow, closed.

FUNDAMENTAL ERRORS OF PHONICS. In reality, phonics is a snarl of complex linguistic and instructional matters about which a useful and rather long book perhaps should be written. The limited material set forth in this chapter is the minimum required to enable a teacher (a) to make truthful statements about American English sounds and letters, and (b) to avoid the most serious mistakes of phonics. Let's begin by noting contradictions and discrepancies. Phonics methods and materials often perpetuate one or more of the following fundamental errors:

1. Blurring the basic distinction between sounds and letters: far from observing this distinction, *phonics attributes the sounds to*

the letters. Children are asked "to learn the sounds the letters make," and in oral reading, "to sound all the letters in every word." It is a common school practice to have children recite a singsong list of the vowels as *"a, e, i, o, u,* and sometimes *y"* — disregarding the fact that *vowels are sounds,* and that in recitation *a, e, i, o, u,* and *y* are simply *names of letters.* This ritual blurring of a fundamental distinction can lead to profound confusion and misunderstanding.

2. Confusing the way syllables are divided by typographer's rules with the way syllables sound in speech (which requires accurate phonological analysis); so-called double consonants (letters) that represent single sounds are a major point of confusion, as in *fellow, follow, funny, humming, letter,* etc.

3. Converting the dubious practice of "sounding out the letters," one by one, into remedial speech instruction: "teaching the sounds," as though normal children must go to school to learn how to make the basic sounds of their native language.

4. Confounding the child's early inability to relate isolated speech sounds to particular letters with his ability to discriminate the sounds of speech: the child is often incorrectly judged to be lacking in auditory discrimination. If he can speak and respond appropriately to speech (that is, carry on a conversation), he thereby demonstrates his possession of the requisite auditory discrimination; the teaching problem is to relate this discrimination to spelling, reading, and writing, which involve a totally different category of symbols (graphic and visual) from the vocal symbols of speech.

5. Propagation of false and misleading spelling rules (see pp. 22–23).

6. Confusing spelling with the very different processes of reading and writing.

Small wonder that Leonard Bloomfield derided phonics as "the hiss and groan method" of teaching sound-spelling relationships.

DIFFERENTIATING SPELLING FROM READING AND WRITING. Sometimes it seems that we virtually equate spelling with reading and writing, though we surely know better. Correct spelling tends to become a shibboleth; even in the very beginning stages of reading and writing, it receives a disproportionate and often harmful emphasis. Let's note some comparative-contrastive distinctions among the language-related processes of spelling, reading, and writing; all these processes are *active* in that they involve direct, effective participation, but the kind and degree of activity vary greatly. Clarity on these distinctions can deeply affect the teacher's implicit as well as explicit influence upon the child's learning.

As linguistic operations, both spelling and writing, though quite different, are *productive* in a sense that reading is not; spelling requires discriminating and producing single letters in single words, sequentially, one letter at a time; writing, however, requires above all the creation of original meaning-bearing language patterns — sentences fashioned out of words — and arranging them in combinations and series as the basic building-blocks of compositions. The basic unit of spelling, the letter, is remote from the basic unit of composition, the sentence; the word, visually and manually produced by the spelling process suggested here, is a unit less than halfway between the letter and the sentence. It seems clear that writing, or composition, is the linguistic process actively concerned with communication; spelling is little more than a copy-editing operation within this larger process.

Now consider reading, the all-important key to the many worlds locked within printed English. Although it is an active process in other ways, reading requires no *production* of letters, words, and sentences at all; what reading requires is not pronouncing all the letters in every word, not naming all the words in list order, but recognition and comprehension of graphic representations of entire sentences taken as unitary meaning-bearing patterns. Sentence comprehension — sentence sense — is the beginning of reading comprehension as well as of the ability to write compositions. These considerations can serve as broad guidelines for evaluating the roles of sounds and letters in teaching the arts and skills of literacy.

All the letters in all the words, all the words laid end to end, line after line and page after page, must reach not from here to eternity in the student's eyes; the words must first pattern themselves into sentences, *comprehended sentences*. With patience and skill, sentences may indeed be put together skillfully in interesting serial arrangements, with references forward, backward and across, to compose all the larger language constructs — not in the primary grades, but by spiral and sequential development through all the grades, out of high school and into college, and beyond. This is a learning that never ends, unless it is nipped in the bud.

Following are the three main topics to be discussed in the remainder of this chapter:

Language, Writing, and the Alphabet
Phonetics, Phonemics, Graphics
Phoneme-Grapheme Relationships

Language, Writing, and the Alphabet

A lot of ink has been spilled in speculation about the origin of language, but no empirical data exists to base any conclusions on. No one knows how language began, nor how long ago this remarkable invention was made. All we know for sure is that language is very ancient in origin. At least five hundred thousand years ago, men knew how to make primitive weapons, tools, and utensils of stone and wood. It seems reasonable to suppose that language preceded, or coexisted with, early man's ability to hand down well-developed crafts and skills from generation to generation: mixing, shaping, and firing a clay pot, for example, or making stylized pictures on wood, stone, animal skin, and bone, with various applicators and pigments designed for this purpose.

The remainder of this section is discussed under three subtitles:

FIVE STAGES IN THE DEVELOPMENT OF ALPHABETICAL WRITING
THE IMPORTANCE OF THE ALPHABET
CONCEPTS AND UNDERSTANDINGS TO BE DEVELOPED

FIVE STAGES IN THE DEVELOPMENT OF ALPHABETICAL WRITING. On the walls of caves in France and Spain, paintings believed to be forty to fifty thousand years old have been preserved to this day. Man was a graphic artist before he became a writer. The development of the alphabetical principle and of alphabets cannot be traced precisely, but the general outline is reasonably clear. Five main stages are often specified in the long development from the painting of pictures to alphabetical writing. These stages were not separately sequential, however, but overlapping and mixed, up to the invention of a genuine alphabet with letters representing the basic sounds of spoken language.

1. **Thing-pictures:** direct representational drawings, usually stylized or schematic, as in the representation of human figures by stick drawings. A sequence of pictures could tell a story of a hunt, a

migration, or a battle; the same sequence might also foretell an event, or outline a plan. This kind of "writing" is not related to any specific language.

2. **Idea-pictures:** symbolic drawings, or ideographs, such as a circle with rays representing the sun. A sequence of ideographs might be used in much the same way as thing-pictures in the example above, but the difference is that these symbols comprise a formal system for communication rather than a loose method of directly representational pictures. Like thing-pictures, idea-pictures are not related to any specific language; that is, the sun symbol could represent the word for sun in any language.

3. **Word-sound pictures:** rebuses in which graphic symbols represent specific words in a given language. Complete sentences in a given language can be represented by this kind of rebus; for example, three successive drawings of an eye, a can, the sea, and a ewe, would give a rebus for *I can see you.*

4. **Syllable-sound pictures:** rebuses in which graphic symbols represent syllables of words in a given language. Complete sentences in a given language can also be represented by syllable rebuses; for example, successive drawings of a spring and a field (*Springfield*); a can and a knot (*cannot*); a bee (*be*); two gates and a head (*Gateshead*): *Springfield cannot be Gateshead.* Both word rebuses and syllable rebuses depend on an accurate analysis of a specific language; entire formal syllabaries have been developed for writing certain languages; through time, the symbols become less representational and increasingly stylized.

5. **Letter-sound pictures:** alphabetical writing, the principle being that each picture or symbol represents a single phoneme, an ideal that cannot be realized in many languages, for a variety of reasons. In English, the sound system of the language changed substantially after the spellings became fixed; moreover, the English language at any time is a congeries of dialects having different phonemes, but all represented by the same alphabet.

TEACHING SUGGESTIONS: Early elementary school children can enjoy working with thing-picture stories, and can learn the limitations of this kind of writing in contrast to alphabetical writing; idea-picture writing requires a formal stylized set of

picture symbols. Nearly everyone can enjoy working with rebuses as puzzles. For example:

(a) I C U R Y Y 4 me   is a rebus for *I see you are too
wise for me.*

(b) stand   took   write   taking
     I   he   to   this

is a rebus for *I understand he undertook to underwrite
this undertaking.*

See the Selected References at the end of the chapter for
sources of material and ideas.

THE IMPORTANCE OF THE ALPHABET. If language itself is man's
greatest invention, then alphabetical writing is a close second. Com-
pared with the great antiquity of language, writing is a brash new-
comer: the clear-cut principle of one symbol for one sound apparently
was first applied systematically by the Phoenicians about three
thousand years ago. The history of alphabets is a history of adapta-
tions of one alphabet to match the needs and circumstances of many
peoples speaking many tongues. Every educated person should enjoy
a keen appreciation of the importance of alphabets and alphabetical
writing in man's development, both in contemporary life and in the
history of civilization. Every American school child should have an
opportunity to develop specific related skills in reading, writing, spelling, alphabetizing, playing spelling and word games, working cross-
word puzzles, anagrams, double crostics, rebuses, and so on. Such
an appreciation of alphabets and alphabetical writing, associated
with a variety of skills, is of inestimable educational and cultural
value; acquiring this appreciation and these skills can be an interesting and rewarding experience.

CONCEPTS AND UNDERSTANDINGS TO BE DEVELOPED. 1. Ancient
men used picture writing, other mnemonic devices, and rebuses for
a very long time before they developed alphabets and the alphabetical principle. A few remote peoples today still use picture writing;
many still have no writing system comparable to ours. (A study of
rebuses could be a means of linking picture writing to alphabetical
writing.)

2. Picture writing, rebuses, syllabaries, alphabets, alphabetical writing, and our own (Roman) alphabet, all have rich and interesting developmental histories; a specialist could devote his life to any one of these topics.

3. Today we still have many graphic symbols, whole *systems* of graphic symbols, that do not directly represent speech: musical notation; mathematical "languages"; chemical symbols; weather flags in ports and on ships; traffic signs and symbols; and others associated with various occupations and activities.

4. Alphabetical writing, originally, was invented as a direct representation of speech; it is a system in which both upper and lower case letters may be either handwritten or printed. Alphabetical writing, though different in many ways from speech, still retains its close link with the spoken language.

5. Twenty-six symbols — the letters of our alphabet — can represent all the written and printed words and sentences in English and all its dialects, past, present, future.

6. This same (Roman) alphabet, with only minor variations, does the same thing for other people speaking other languages: Czech, Dutch, Finnish, French, German, Hungarian, Italian, Polish, Portuguese, Spanish, Turkish, Welsh, and others.

7. Other alphabets and other writing systems, and many different hand tools and machines for writing and printing, have been developed in many parts of the world. Some are still in use today; Arabic, Chinese, Hebrew, Greek and Russian alphabets are all different from the Roman; Chinese, strictly speaking, does not have an alphabet; German has a special black-letter script version of Roman.

8. Alphabetical writing — and printing — are of incalculable importance in recording, preserving, and transmitting knowledge, culture, and skills of many kinds: correspondence, diaries, and journals; current books, magazines, newspapers; libraries, general and specialized, where all such items from former times are preserved and available for study. The importance of alphabetical writing and printing can hardly be overemphasized, especially in the age of super-electronic communications media.

9. Alphabetizing is an important system for ordering and arranging items; address books, catalogs, dictionaries, encyclopedias, files of all kinds, indexes, telephone directories, and so on. Alphabetizing is an invaluable tool for the learner; it should be thoroughly taught and thoroughly learned in the middle and upper grades.

TEACHING SUGGESTIONS: Every one of the above topics could be the basis of a major project or unit. Some classes might like to have the opportunity of considering them all. Other classes might do better with a single topic selected by the teacher. Here is God's plenty.

Phonetics, Phonemics, Graphics

Phonetics and **phonemics** deal with the sounds of language in terms of their smallest functional or communicative units; **graphics** deals with visual symbols for transcribing those units. These topics have traditionally been ignored in the preparation of teachers, often to their sorrow. I hope that this presentation will help teachers at all levels to work with greater security in relating spoken English to written English. This section will survey phonetics and phonemics with special attention to information, concepts, and attitudes pertinent to teaching English and the language arts; spelling will be briefly discussed under the last main heading of the chapter, Phoneme-Grapheme Relationships. The remainder of the section is presented in eleven subsections, as follows:

OVERCOMING THE VISUAL BIAS
DIFFERENTIATING PHONETICS AND PHONEMICS
THE TWENTY-FOUR CONSONANTS
THE PHONEME AS A CLASS OF SOUNDS: ALLOPHONES
THE VOICED-VOICELESS CONTRAST
THE NINE SIMPLE VOWELS
THE SEMIVOWELS.
THE THIRTY-SIX VOWEL NUCLEI
SUMMARY OF THE SEGMENTAL PHONEMES OF AMERICAN ENGLISH
SUPRASEGMENTAL PHONEMES
MORPHOPHONEMICS

OVERCOMING THE VISUAL BIAS. The very existence of our alphabet and the alphabetical writing system — books, magazines, newspapers, and all the forms of hand- and typewritten communication — undoubtedly has a pervasive influence on the way we perceive English sounds. The fact that written and printed words are cleanly separated from each other by regular white spaces, and that every letter is also a separate and distinct entity, clearly visible, profoundly influences our auditory impressions of the sounds of the language, which in reality go flowingly as in a continuous stream. Consider, too, our individual acquisition of literacy — the ability to spell, read, and write — dominated as it is by the kind of phonics instruction most of us receive in school, and you begin to understand the sources of the visual bias toward language that we all have to some degree. To appreciate the differences and relationships among phonetics, phonemics, and graphics, it is necessary to make a conscious and determined effort to overcome this powerful visual bias. In addition to this mental effort, it is essential to say aloud the many examples of speech sounds that are represented here by silent graphic symbols; this practice helps to associate vocal symbols with graphic symbols, and both with the underlying articulatory movements that are their common origin. For further discussion of the visual bias, see pp. 228–29.

DIFFERENTIATING PHONETICS AND PHONEMICS. Phonetics is the scientific study of speech sounds; because of its ability to discover and describe precise, verifiable units of data, phonetics is the most rigorous branch of linguistics. There are two main divisions, articulatory and acoustic. **Articulatory phonetics** minutely describes all the movements and positions of the organs used in speech; **acoustic phonetics** describes all the sounds produced by these articulations; both kinds of analysis may be applied to any language in the world. The International Phonetic Alphabet (I.P.A.) has enough symbols and diacritics to enable it to transcribe accurately all the sounds of all languages. *The I.P.A. is designed to transcribe the technical content of all languages viewed narrowly in terms of their articulatory and acoustic properties;* it yields narrow transcriptions of all the variable details of speech sounds without regard to their *communicative function* in any particular language system. The I.P.A. finds very little application in teaching English and the language arts, if any.

Phonemics, on the other hand, is concerned with the *communicative function* of speech sounds in one particular language and with nothing else: phonemics deals with speech units that are distinctive and significant in a single language. While there is some disagreement among linguists on the theory of the phoneme, a large majority are agreed in principle on a definition: *a **phoneme** is the smallest unit* *of speech that distinguishes one utterance from another*. Phonemic transcription represents those and only those units of speech that are distinctive and significant in a given language. The concept of the phoneme finds numerous applications in the teaching of English and the language arts.

The ability of a phoneme to distinguish one utterance from another is well illustrated in the story of a little boy in school who, in his art class, fondly drew a large round pot with a thin line of smoke curling up from it. When his teacher asked him to explain his concept, he said, "That's where the story begins — once a pot a time." The difference between *once a pot a time* and *once upon a time* is precisely a difference of one phoneme. Another child, explaining the prominence of a jolly, rotound character never before seen in the stable scene at the birth of Christ, said it was "round John Virgin." A very close difference marks the single phoneme that differentiates **round John Virgin** from **round yon virgin** in the old song. These children, like pupils the world over, were doing their best to interpret the auditory data they had received.

TEACHING SUGGESTION: Many jokes about children's misunderstandings hinge upon their making the most of language they do not quite understand: in patriotic and religious songs, for example, or the pledge of allegiance to the flag. Often a single phoneme substitution is just what they need to help them to make some kind of sense of an otherwise unintelligible expression. A discussion of examples given by students can be enlightening as well as amusing.

A convenient way to distinguish phonemes is by minimal pairs of words. A minimal pair are identical in all but one phoneme, *pat* and *bat,* for example. The existence of one minimal pair does not establish the initial *p* and *b* sounds as phonemes, but a consideration of all similar pairs in English, such as *pan* and *ban, pin* and *bin,* will reveal the fact that no smaller difference exists. The same is true of the *p* and *b* sounds in final position: *tap* and *tab, nap* and *nab, nip* and *nib.* We conclude that the *p* and *b* sounds are true phonemes, examples of the smallest units of speech that distinguish one utterance from another.

THE TWENTY-FOUR CONSONANTS. A complete examination of American English words will show that we have twenty-four consonant phonemes. Graphic symbols selected to represent them include some letters of the alphabet, plus a few additions to eliminate duplication and overlapping: each phonemic symbol represents one and only one phoneme. It is a linguistic convention that phonemic symbols are enclosed in oblique brackets / / and phonetic symbols in square brackets [ ]. Both oblique and square brackets signify that the enclosed symbol is not to be interpreted as a letter, but as a graphic representation of a sound; square brackets signify the narrow transcription of phonetics, oblique brackets, the broad transcription of phonemics.

In talking about phonemes, or reading phonemic transcriptions aloud, we use the names of the letters of the alphabet that are applicable, plus the names assigned to the few special symbols. For the consonants, the seven special symbols and their names are:

/č/	c check, as in *church*		/ŋ/	eng, as in si*ng*
/ǰ/	j check, as in *judge*		/θ/	theta, as in *thin*
/š/	s check, as in *show*		/ð/	eth, as in *then*
/ž/	z check, as in bei*ge*			

The following display of consonant phonemes shows them in initial and final positions in monosyllabic words, excepting those that do not occur in both positions in American English.

/b/	*bat*	*tab*		/t/	*tan*	*gnat*
/d/	*dill*	*lid*		/v/	*vane*	*knave*
/f/	*fit*	*tiff*		/w/	*was*	*cow*
/g/	*gat*	*tag*		/y/	*yell*	*lay*
/h/	*hat*	*ha*		/z/	*zoo*	*ooze*
/k/	*cat*	*tack*		/č/	*church*	*church*
/l/	*lap*	*pal*		/ǰ/	*judge*	*judge*
/m/	*mat*	*tam*		/š/	*ship*	*pish*
/n/	*nit*	*tin*		/ž/		*beige*
/p/	*pan*	*nap*		/ŋ/		*sing*
/r/	*rip*	*tear*		/θ/	*thin*	*oath*
/s/	*sag*	*gas*		/ð/	*then*	*lathe*

TEACHING SUGGESTION: Without using phonemic symbols, children of nearly all ages can master the concept of the phoneme by producing lists of words that begin or end with the consonants displayed above. They may say, "The first sound of _____" and "The last sound of _____." Try it.

THE PHONEME AS A CLASS OF SOUNDS: ALLOPHONES. So far this discussion of consonant phonemes has been oversimplified; rather than the smallest sound unit, a **phoneme** is more accurately defined as *the smallest class of distinctive and significant speech sounds*. This is true because variations in the phonological environment have a modifying influence on successive phonemes occurring in sequential order; that is, the articulation of the various sounds going before and coming after each sound unit produces articulatory and acoustic modifications of that unit. In fact, it is only a convenient fiction to think of speech in terms of discrete sound units anyway, because speech is much more like a continuous stream of sound, ever changing, than like a sequence of segmented units; in addition to articulatory modifications, variations of stress (loudness, or accent) may also produce modifications in the phonetic properties of phonemes. Some patterns of phoneme modification occur regularly enough to be considered different members of the class, or phoneme; such different members are **allophones.**

Consider /p/, for example. In initial position in English /p/ is aspirated: a distinct puff of air may be felt if you hold your fingers before your mouth as you say *pan;* it may be strong enough to blow out a match or candle held close to your lips. This property of initial /p/, aspiration, is represented phonetically by [p']. Yet following initial /s/ in the consonant cluster /sp/, /p/ is unaspirated. There is no puff of air following /p/ in *span,* and the flame of a match will not flicker or go out as it does before aspirated /p/. The linguistically naive speaker is not likely to be aware of this gross difference in the phonetic properties of [p] and [p'] because they are not functional (phonemic) in English. They never occur in the same environment; thus they do not contrast, and their distribution is said to be **complementary.** They are **allophones** of /p/.

The same kinds of allophonic variations that characterize aspirated and unaspirated /p/ also characterize /t/ and /k/ in the same two positions: (1) initial word position and (2) after /s/ in a consonant cluster before a vowel. Compare and contrast /p/ in *pan* and *span* with /t/ in *tan* and *Stan,* and with /k/ in *can* and *scan;* the three pairs of words are identical to the native ear except for the phonemic contrasts of /p/, /t/, and /k/ in the same environment. In initial position, all three are aspirated, and may be represented phonetically by [p′], [t′], and [k′]; following /s/ in the consonant clusters /sp/, /st/, and /sk/, all three are unaspirated. Note that the aspirated and unaspirated allophones of each phoneme do not occur in the same environment; this kind of allophonic distribution is **complementary.** In summary, then, the three phonemes /p/, /t/, and /k/ do occur in the same environment, where they stand in contrast to each other; but the two allophones of each phoneme — aspirated and unaspirated — occur only in different environments and thus cannot stand in contrast to each other.

There is another allophonic variation of /p/, /t/, and /k/ that should be noted. In final position, they may be audibly released (or "exploded"), or they may be inaudibly released (or "unreleased"). When inaudibly released (unreleased), they may be phonetically represented by [p⁻], [t⁻], and [k⁻]; examples are *nap, gnat,* and *knack.* To the native ear, these three words are identical except for the phonemic contrasts of final /p/, /t/, and /k/; the three phonemes contrast in the same environment, but the allophones of each phoneme do not. The phonetic difference between [p] and [p⁻], [t] and [t⁻], and [k] and [k⁻] is not phonemic: that is, it is not functional in terms of communication in English. This kind of variation of allophones — non-distinctive in the same environment — is called **free variation.**

The two kinds of non-distinctive variation illustrated here — complementary distribution and free variation — account for three allophones each of /p/, /t/, and /k/. This is the kind of objective analysis and data that enable us to define the phoneme accurately as, not a single sound, but the smallest class of distinctive and significant speech sounds. The untrained native speaker of English, however, perceives allophones as the same sound, because their differences have no bearing on communication in English and are therefore not functional; in another language they might be functional, that is, instead of allophones, they would be phonemes.

For our purposes, the consonant phonemes /p/, /t/, and /k/ will serve to illustrate the concept of the phoneme as it is generally understood by linguists. An exhaustive analysis would demonstrate that each English phoneme is a class of different non-distinctive allophones comprising a single distinctive and significant structural unit within the total language system; *the phoneme is the entire set of allophones functioning as a single unit for communication, the smallest unit that distinguishes one utterance from another.*

TEACHING SUGGESTION: Demonstrate aspirated /p/ in initial position by blowing out a match or candle. Then ask your students to hold their fingers before their lips and say *pan*, *span*, and *nap*. They should readily perceive the difference between aspirated and unaspirated /p/. The difference between audibly and inaudibly released /p/ is perhaps less noticeable; sometimes the closure of the lips on inaudibly released /p/ is noticeable.

THE VOICED-VOICELESS CONTRAST. While consonant phonemes contrast in several concurrent features that would be detailed in a complete description, the voiced-voiceless contrast will suffice for our purposes; books carrying complete descriptions of English phonemes are listed in Selected References at the end of the chapter. To persuade yourself of the reality of the voiced-voiceless contrast, cup your hands tightly over both ears and make a loud, prolonged *z* sound; it should sound like a resonant buzz (voiced sound) inside your head. Now alternate the *z* with a prolonged *s* sound; a distinct hiss (voiceless) will issue from your lips, but all will be silent inside your head. The buzz is caused by vibrations of the vocal folds in your larynx when you make the *z* sound; since the *s* sound is voiceless, the vocal folds are still. Another method is to hold your larynx (Adam's apple) lightly between thumb and fingers while producing the *s* and *z* sounds; you should feel a definite vibration in your fingertips on the voiced *z* sound, and no vibration on the voiceless *s* sound. Again, the vocal folds vibrate to produce the *z* sound and remain still on the *s;* the sibilant hiss is part of both sounds, but only the *z* is voiced.

Below is a display of phonemic symbols for the contrasting **voiced** and **voiceless consonants,** with words illustrating the sounds in initial, medial, and final positions.

	INITIAL	MEDIAL	FINAL
VOICED /b/:	bat	labor	tab
VOICELESS /p/:	pat	taper	type
VOICED /d/:	dot	leader	load
VOICELESS /t/:	tong	later	gnat
VOICED /g/:	gate	tiger	plague
VOICELESS /c/:	coat	token	plaque
VOICED /v/:	vote	shriven	give
VOICELESS /f/:	fate	stiffen	laugh
VOICED /z/:	zip	laser	rays
VOICELESS /s/:	sip	lesser	loss
VOICED /ǰ/:	jibe	rigid	badge
VOICELESS /č/:	chip	catsup	patch
VOICED /ð/:	though	either	bathe
VOICELESS /θ/:	thought	ether	bath
VOICED /ž/:	*____	azure	beige
VOICELESS /š/:	shape	usher	lash

* Does not occur initially in English except in imported names like Gigi and Zsa Zsa.

TEACHING SUGGESTION: Children of all ages enjoy the hiss and buzz game described above the display. Many primary children can suggest words showing the contrast of voiced and voiceless consonants in initial position. Older children can illustrate the other positions according to their interest and ability. Try it.

THE NINE SIMPLE VOWELS. In addition to the twenty-four consonant phonemes, American English has nine simple vowel phonemes, which may be represented by five letters of the alphabet and four special symbols. These letters and symbols are displayed below with suggested names and key words for each sound.

/i/	short i	p*i*t
/e/	short e	p*e*t
/æ/	digraph	p*a*t
/i̵/	barred i	r*e*bel, *e*ffect
/ə/	schwa	*a*bout, sof*a*, b*u*t
/a/	ah sound	h*o*t, p*o*t, c*o*t
/u/	uh sound	f*oo*t, c*oo*k, p*u*t
/o/	o sound	**g*o*nna** (/o/ rarely occurs alone)
/ɔ/	open o	c*au*ght, t*au*ght (in my dialect)

These symbols represent the author's Midwestern dialect. Some speakers do not distinguish short *i* (/i/) and short *e* (/e/); some do not have both the barred i (/i̵/) and schwa /e/; and some, especially in New England, have open *o* (/ɔ/) in **hot, pot, cot.**

Both the barred i (/i̵/) and the schwa /ə/ occur frequently but inconsistently throughout American English in *weak-stressed positions in running speech as distinct from single words pronounced in isolation.* Most of my students say, **You** /ji̵st/ **missed it,** but if asked how they pronounce the word spelled j-u-s-t, they will insist upon /**jəst**/ (with the schwa), *even in that sentence.* This is one of the "common errors" harped on by Miss Fidditch, so nearly everyone has been bitten and burned by it; it is a gross example of over-corrective spelling pronunciation.

Teachers should realize that their individual dialects vary not only in the use of the schwa and the barred *i,* but also in the other items displayed above. Words like the following are pronounced quite inconsistently in various dialects: *cog, dog, fog, frog, hog, log, watch, water, swatter.* Similarly, the distinction between short *e* and *i* (/e/ and /i/) does not exist in some dialects; in particular, /i/ is common in such words as *cent, many, men, pen, penny, sent, ten,* and **when.** Teaching based on the mistaken notion that there is only one correct pronunciation of these words can raise particular havoc.

TEACHING SUGGESTION: As a diversion, ask your students to pronounce the words in the two lists above. Note the various ways they group them. If you have tenure, you might try this stunt on your colleagues.

The nine simple vowel phonemes are usually classified according to the relative position of the speaker's tongue that is required to say them in American English. The tongue position in the mouth varies in two principal directions, from front to back and from high to low. These nine relative positions are illustrated in the tabulation below.

	FRONT	CENTRAL	BACK
HIGH	i	ɨ	u
MID	e	ə	o
LOW	æ	a	ɔ

Lip rounding is a third variable in the utterance of the simple vowels, noticeable only in the three back vowels; it is most marked in /u/, less in /o/, and least in /ɔ/. In pronouncing these nine phonemes, note also that the lips are separated least on the high vowels, more on the mid, and most on the low, as the jaw is lowered to form the vowels in order from high to low. (Figure 4.1.)

	FRONT	CENTRAL	BACK
HIGH	bit	rebel	bush
MID	bet	but, banana	boracic
LOW	bat	bottle	bought

Two of these phonemes, /o/ and /ɔ/, occur less frequently and regularly by themselves than the other seven; /o/ usually and /ɔ/ occasionally combine with the semivowels /w/, and /h/, respectively, to make vowel-semivowel sequences, as explained later.

So far we have discussed twenty-four American English consonants and nine simple vowels. We have noted that only a few American speakers have all nine vowels, and that speakers of different standard dialects have different simple vowels. American speakers also differ somewhat in their sets of consonants, but consonant differences are less significant than vowel differences.

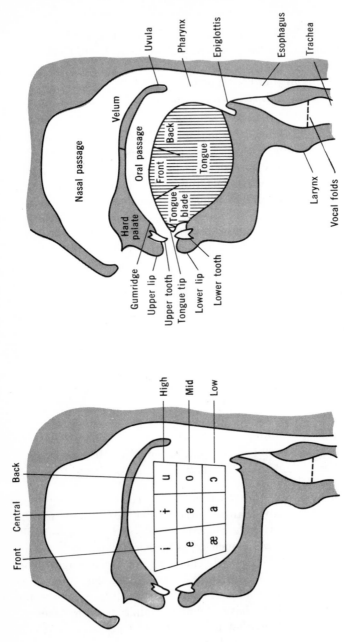

*Figure 4.1 Production of simple vowel phonemes.**

* From *Linguistics and the Teaching of Reading*, by Carl A. Lefevre, McGraw-Hill, 1964. Used with permission of McGraw-Hill Book Company.

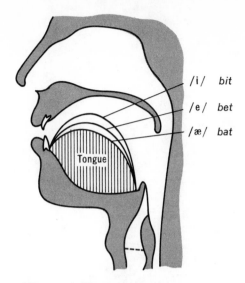

/i/   bit

/e/   bet

/æ/   bat

Tongue

Figure 4.2 Simple front vowels: /i/, /e/, /æ/; as in bit, bet, bat.*

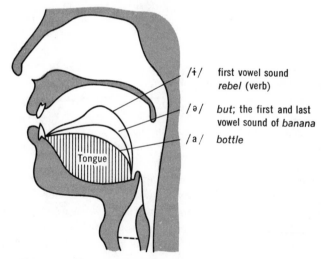

/ɨ/   first vowel sound
rebel (verb)

/ə/   *but;* the first and last
vowel sound of *banana*

/a/   *bottle*

Tongue

Figure 4.3 Simple central vowels: /ɨ/, /ə/, /a/; as in the first syllable of rebel *(verb);* but, *the first and last vowel sound of* banana; *bottle.***

* From *Linguistics and the Teaching of Reading,* by Carl A. Lefevre, Mc-Graw-Hill, 1964. Used with permission of McGraw-Hill Book Company.

** From *Linguistics and the Teaching of Reading,* by Carl A. Lefevre, Mc-Graw-Hill, 1964. Used with permission of McGraw-Hill Book Company.

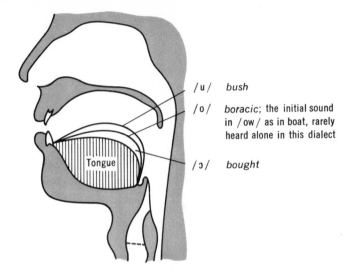

Figure 4.4 Simple back vowels: /u/, /o/, /ɔ/; as in bush; boracic; *the initial sound in* /ow/ *as in* boat, *rarely heard alone in this dialect;* bought.*

THE SEMIVOWELS. We must still discuss a number of vowels, commonly interpreted as single phonemes, that are actually sequences of two very closely related phonemes: a simple vowel immediately followed by a semivowel. The three semivowels are /h/, /w/, and /y/, the phonemes associated with the letters *h, w,* and *y* in some spellings. In initial position, these phonemes resemble consonants, but in the vowel-semivowel sequences they resemble vowels; thus the name **semivowel**. Semivowels are unlike either consonants or vowels in one major property, however. Simple vowels and consonants except /l/ and /r/ are produced while the articulators are momentarily in a required position; but semivowels are produced during rapid gliding movements from one position to another.

THE THIRTY-SIX VOWEL NUCLEI. Often because they are dealing with single dialects of English, linguists differ somewhat in their analyses; they also use different symbols, which may be inconvenient for their readers, but not so serious as different interpretations of data. Although an exhaustive analysis is not attempted here, the

* From *Linguistics and the Teaching of Reading,* by Carl A. Lefevre, Mc-Graw-Hill, 1964. Used with permission of McGraw-Hill Book Company.

presentation of phonemes is of a kind that could account for all English dialects; this kind of inclusive treatment is important for teaching. The vowels, particularly the vowel-semivowel sequences, provide some of the greatest dialectal differences. Taking all dialects into account, the nine simple vowels can combine with the three semivowels to make a total of twenty-seven vowel-semivowel sequences; these, plus the nine simple vowels, give a total of thirty-six possible vowel elements in English words.

A strong visual bias is probably responsible for the general restriction of the term **diphthong** in school usage to mean *vowel sequences spelled with two letters*. Everyone is familiar with *ou* and *ow* in *house* and *howl,* and with *oi* and *oy* in *point* and *oyster*. Again because of a visual bias, these four spellings may be thought of as *four* diphthongs, but they represent only *two* vowel-semivowel sequences. The term **diphthong** has a confusing variety of meanings; here we shall use either **vowel-semivowel sequence** or **compound vowel nucleus,** which are defined below.

Since every speech syllable contains a vowel element, perhaps we can approach vowel-semivowel sequences through a brief discussion of the syllable; so-called syllabic *l* and *n,* as in *apple* and *widen,* are preceded by a weak-stressed vowel, either barred i (/ɨ/) or schwa (/ə/). The English **syllable** is not in itself a structural unit but a phonological unit that usually consists of more than one phoneme — and always carries a degree of stress. No syllable can be uttered without some degree of stress: a literally unaccented syllable would be inaudible.

If we consider the vowel element as the syllable nucleus, we may define a simple vowel phoneme as a **simple vowel nucleus,** and a vowel-semivowel sequence as a **compound vowel nucleus.** A simple vowel nucleus is produced when the tongue and other articulators are momentarily in the position required for that phoneme; a compound vowel nucleus is produced during a rapid glide from a simple vowel position to a semivowel position. Since speech is a continuous stream of variable sound rather than a sequence of discrete segments, any syllable division is arbitrary; it certainly does not correspond to the division of printed words into "syllables" following practices originated by printers in order to adjust spellings to lines of fixed length, where words had to be divided at line ends. The purposes of our analysis will best be served by one-syllable words where the vowel element receives a strong stress.

The vowel nucleus /ay/, generally called "long *i*" in schools, is easily perceived to be a vowel-semivowel sequence. It begins with the low-central vowel /a/; the sequence is produced during a gliding movement as the jaw closes and the tongue moves upward and forward. Try doing it slowly at first, and then gradually increase the speed until the sequence sounds natural: /ay/ begins with /a/, moves through /i/, and ends with the glide /y/. Try it first in word-final position: *buy, cry, dye, my, sigh, tie, try, why.* Then try it in this list of monosyllabic words, all having the compound vowel nucleus /ay/.

aisle	guile	light	right
bite	height	might	sign
cite	isle	night	tile
dine	jive	plight	vine
file	kite	quite	wine

Try it in words of your own choice.

As you study and work on compound vowel nuclei, keep in mind that the common school terms, **long vowel** and **short vowel,** have literally nothing to do with the duration of English vowels. *In this usage,* **long** *and* **short** *are nothing more nor less than conventional misnomers.* For example, the compound nucleus /ay/ — so-called long *i* — is perceptibly longer (1) as the final sound in words like *buy, cry,* and *dye,* than (2) as the medial sound in such words as *height, kite,* and *light.* In the first group, /ay/ trails off or fades away into silence; in the second group, /ay/ is sharply terminated by final /t/, a voiceless consonant stop. Moreover, so-called short *i* in *kin* is of longer duration than so-called long *i* in *kite.* The /i/ of *kin* is longer because it precedes and is terminated by a nasal continuant consonant, /n/; the /ay/ of *kite* is shorter because it precedes and is terminated by a voiceless stop consonant /t/. Such environmental differences as these affect the duration of English vowels quite irrespective of whether they are conventionally called **long** or **short.**

Similarly, "long *a*" (/ey/) is a compound vowel nucleus. It begins with the mid-central vowel /e/; the sequence is produced during a gliding movement as the jaw rises and the tongue moves upward and slightly forward. Try it in words that have the same nucleus, as in *bay, day, gay, say, date, Kate, vane, lane, mane,* and so on. "Long *e*" begins with the high-front vowel /i/ and proceeds through a slightly upward and forward glide to produce /iy/, as in *bee, he, lea, she, three, we, bean, dean, feat, lean, meat, peen,* and so on. The vowel nucleus in *boy, point, soy,* and *oyster* /ɔy/ is produced during a similar glide; it begins with the low-back vowel /ɔ/ in my dialect, and is produced during a marked upward and forward movement of the tongue. Try it in *alloy, annoy, joint, ploy, soy, toy,* and others that occur to you.

"Long *o*" (/ow/) and "long *u*" (/uw/) are both formed by glides terminating in /w/; lip rounding is usually a noticeable feature of /w/ and is thus one means of identifying it by the way it looks and feels. The vowel nucleus /ow/ begins with the mid-back vowel /o/ (which only very rarely occurs except in /oy/ and /ow/); /ow/ is produced during a rapid glide upward and forward, as in *bow, doe, hoe, row, sew, tow, boat, coat, dote, loan, moan,* etc. The vowel nucleus /uw/ begins with the high-back vowel /u/ and is produced through a rapid forward glide, as in *blue, dew, lieu, moo, new, rue, Sue, boot, coot, dune, dupe, loon, moon, moot,* etc. The vowel nucleus in *cute, few,* and similar words is not /uw/ but /yuw/; some speakers have /yuw/ in words where I have /uw/ as in the previous sentence, but where I come from that is an affectation.

The vowel nucleus /aw/ as in *bough, cow, how, now, plow* begins with the low-central vowel /a/ and proceeds through a rapid glide upward and forward. Try it in *bounce, bout, house, hound, louse, mouse,* and other words as they come to you. Some speakers have /æw/ where I have /aw/, and others have /ew/, which I have heard in Philadelphia and all across Canada. These few examples may serve to illustrate how phonemic analysis enables us to represent the various dialects of American English with a phonemic alphabet having only thirty-three symbols. With careful study, patience, and a tape recorder, why not try your luck?

Whereas /w/ and /y/ are relatively easily identified glides, /h/ is a centering glide that merges less perceptibly with other articulatory movements. Compound vowel nuclei with /h/ are by no means so easy to identify, nor so contrastive, as vowel sequences with /w/ and /y/. In my dialect, for example, /ɔh/ occurs finally as in *law* (/lɔh/), and before /l/, as in *call* (/kɔhl/), but rarely before /t/ or /k/, as in *caught* (/kɔt/) and *talk* (/tɔk/). I also have (/æh/) in *can* /kæhn/) used emphatically, but this is rare. Compound vowel nuclei with /h/ vary greatly among American English dialects and within any single dialect.

A final word on the semivowels. Both initially and following in sequence, each semivowel is produced during a glide rather than by the momentary position that characterizes a simple vowel; the principal difference between initial and sequential semivowels is the direction of the glide. For example, the word *say* is like the word *yes* said backward (and vice versa): their phonemic transcriptions are /sey/ and /yes/. A tape recording of the monosyllables *ha, woo,* and *ye,* when played backward, still produces *ha, woo,* and *ye:* /hah/, /wuw/, and /yiy/. I have heard a recording with these syllables paired in sequence, the first member spoken in normal order and the second played backward; here is how they sounded: /hah-hah/, /wuw-wuw/, /yiy-yiy/. This appears to be conclusive proof that initial and final /h/, /w/, and /y/ are, as it were, mirror images of each other.

SUMMARY OF THE SEGMENTAL PHONEMES OF AMERICAN ENGLISH (AUTHOR'S DIALECT)

CONSONANTS

Voiced   (contrasting pairs)   *Voiceless*

/b/	the first sound in *bat*	/p/	the first sound in *pat*
/d/	the first sound in *dot*	/t/	the first sound in *top*
/g/	the first sound in *goat*	/k/	the first sound in *cope*
/v/	the first sound in *van*	/f/	the first sound in *fan*
/z/	the first sound in *zeal*	/s/	the first sound in *seal*
/ǰ/	the first sound in *jewel*	/č/	the first sound in *chew*
/ð/	the first sound in *then*	/θ/	the first sound in *thin*
/ž/	the medial consonant in *azure*	/š/	the first sound in *shape*

/m/	the first sound in *met*
/n/	the first sound in *net*
/ŋ/	the final sound in *song*
/l/	the first sound in *late*
/r/	the first sound in *rate*

SIMPLE VOWELS

/i/	the vowel sound in *bit, kit, hit, pit, sit*
/e/	the vowel sound in *bet, get, let, pet, set*
/æ/	the vowel sound in *bat, cat, hat, pat, sat*

/ɨ/	the first vowel sound in **rebel**, **effect**	(Barred i and schwa occur throughout American English in weak-stressed syllables)
/ə/	the first vowel sound in **about**	

/a/ the vowel sound in **cot, dot, got, hot, lot** (Eastern speakers may have /ɔ/)

/u/ the vowel sound in **book, cook, foot, put**

/o/ the simple vowel in the compound vowel nucleus /ow/ as in **go, dome, poke** (the first sound in **gonna**; rarely heard except in a vowel-semivowel sequence)

/ɔ/ the vowel sound in **caught, chalk, talk, taught** (in the author's dialect)

SEMIVOWELS

/h/ the first sound in **hot**; the first and last sounds in **ha** /hah/

/w/ the first sound in **wound**; the first and last sounds in **woo** /wuw/

/y/ the first sound in **yeast**; the first and last sounds in **ye** /yiy/

COMPOUND VOWEL NUCLEI

/ey/ the vowel nucleus in **fate**

/iy/ the vowel nucleus in **feet**

/ay/ the vowel nucleus in **fight**

/ow/ the vowel nucleus in **vote**

/uw/ the vowel nucleus in **coot**

/aw/ the vowel nucleus in **house, howl** (others have /æw/ or /ew/)

/ɔy/ the vowel nucleus in **point, oyster** (others have /oy/)

/ɔh/ the vowel nucleus in **law, call**

SUPRASEGMENTAL PHONEMES. The foregoing discussion has dealt only with **segmental phonemes** of American English: thirty-three functional classes of consonant and vowel sounds. In addition to segmental phonemes, some linguists treat certain phonological units as suprasegmental phonemes; some do not regard them as phonemes; others consider them separately from segmental phonemes for other reasons. I prefer to include suprasegmental features under intonation, handled by itself as a major topic in Chapter 9 of this book. Twelve **suprasegmental phonemes** often mentioned are: four relative degrees of **stress** on syllables (accent); four relative ranges of voice **pitch;** and four **junctures** and **terminals,** or ways of interrupting or terminating the stream of speech. The total of forty-five American English phonemes sometimes referred to by linguists thus includes four stress phonemes, four pitch phonemes, and four juncture phonemes — twelve suprasegmentals added to thirty-three segmental phonemes.

MORPHOPHONEMICS. Since this term appears in professional discussions of spelling and reading, a brief discussion of it here in relation to phonemes and morphemes may be useful. Just as the phoneme is the smallest class of distinctive and significant speech sounds, the morpheme is the smallest meaning-bearing unit of language; morphemes include word bases, inflections, and derivational prefixes and suffixes. Morphemes are explained in some detail in Chapter 5, Word Classes, and Chapter 6, The Derivational Affixing System. The substance of morphophonemics is dealt with in Chapter 5, though not by name. The basic meaning of **morphophonemics** is the study of the phonemic differences between **allomorphs** of the same morpheme (allomorphs are to morphemes as allophones are to phonemes). For example, the /-s/, /-z/, and /-ɨz or -əz/ allomorphs of the noun plural morpheme, as in *cats* (/kæts/), *dogs* (/dɔgz/), and *houses* (/hawzɨz/). Other common examples are the /-t/, /-d/, and /-ɨd or -əd/ allomorphs of the past verb morpheme, as in *dropped* (/drapt/), *dreamed* (/driymd/, and *regretted* (/rɨgretɨd/). While the substance of these distinctions is important to the teacher of English and the language arts, the term *morphophonemics* has no place in elementary school classrooms and little in secondary. See the displays in this chapter on pp. 108–9.

Phoneme-Grapheme Relationships

The **grapheme** is to written and printed English what the phoneme is to spoken English: it is a graphic representation of a basic sound unit, consisting of one or more letters. The suffix **–eme** is an invention of linguists to mean "a unit of"; a phoneme is an auditory unit, a grapheme, a visual unit. For example, the three letters of *cat* are three graphemes representing three phonemes, /kæt/; *c, a,* and *t,* respectively, represent /k/, /æ/, and /t/. The five letters of *laugh* are also three graphemes representing three phonemes, /læf/, but not by single letters; *l* represents /l/, the digraph *au* represents /æ/, and the digraph *gh* represents /f/. In *though,* six letters represent three phonemes: the digraph *th*, /ð/; and the four-letter grapheme *ough*, /ow/. In *through,* seven letters represent four phonemes: here, the digraph *th* represents /θ/; the letter *r*, /r/; and the grapheme *ough*, /uw/. The digraph *th* almost always represents either /ð/ or /θ/. The *ough* grapheme is an extreme example of the kind of irregularity that makes some people despair altogether of English spelling, but in all fairness *ough* should be recognized as not merely unusual but unique. English has a list of common words that must be learned as a small set of exceptions: *bough, cough, dough, drought, enough, though, thought,* and *through;* less common are the Scot *lough,* and *hiccough,* a variant spelling of *hiccup.*

The material so far presented in this chapter, if mastered, should enable the teacher to make true observations and statements about phoneme-grapheme correspondences in American English, based upon correct phonemic analysis; and also to avoid making the kind of false statements that often characterize phonics instruction. The teacher who has grasped this material should also realize clearly that *dialect* is not a pejorative term, that everybody speaks one dialect or another, and that several standard dialects coexist in North America, along with various divergent dialects. But this is not enough to deal adequately with spelling. We need (a) to reexamine our attitudes toward correct and incorrect spelling; (b) to study carefully the spelling of high-frequency structural elements of English, such as allomorphs; and (c) to consider some of the results of spelling research.

The remainder of this final section is discussed under four subtitles:

CORRECT SPELLING
REGULAR SPELLINGS OF STRUCTURAL ELEMENTS
SPELLING AND READING
SPELLING RESEARCH

CORRECT SPELLING. Attitudes toward correct spelling have varied enormously over the past three hundred or so years. Shakespeare cared so little for the spelling of his own name that he signed it several different ways. English gentlemen of the seventeenth and eighteenth centuries were quite indifferent to consistency in spelling; some may indeed have felt that a healthy variety of spellings displayed their individuality. Apparently a concern with correct spelling began to develop into a shibboleth during the Industrial Revolution, as one ready means of distinguishing the rising middle class from the great unwashed. The condescending laughter that accompanies anecdotes about misspelling (in the teachers' lounge, sometimes) is due in part to the narrator's secure knowledge of how to spell the word in question; it is not a matter of communication failure. Current attitudes toward spelling often have more to do with social superiority than with successful communication.

On the other hand, many educated persons believe that English spelling is so irregular as to preclude any hope of a rational explanation of it. A few languages do have spelling systems that approach a one-to-one correspondence between phonemes and graphemes; Finnish, Hawaiian, Italian, and Turkish have this reputation, though they do not have the same stress system as English, nor the proliferation of dialects. Regardless of its reputation, however, English spelling is based upon the alphabetical principle; that is, English graphemes generally represent phonemes, not syllables or words; some spellings consistently represent high-frequency structural elements, however, as we shall note further in the next section.

REGULAR SPELLINGS OF STRUCTURAL ELEMENTS. Communication is central to all forms of composition and writing; spelling should therefore be viewed in the perspective of communication — especially during the primary and elementary years. If we harbor punitive social attitudes toward misspelling, we should curb them and try to approach spelling problems and spelling instruction inductively; the young learner should be led to discover spelling patterns and regularities for himself. *More important by far is guidance in spelling irregular words, structure words, inflections, and derivational affixes that will occur with high frequency in what he reads and what he writes.* For illustrations, see Word Classes; The Derivational Affixing System; and Chapter 8, Structure Words. The point of this recommendation is that high-frequency *structural* elements as represented in the graphic system are crucial to communication in a sense that phoneme-grapheme correspondences of non-structural elements are not.

Below is a display of the allomorphs for the **noun plural,** the **noun genitives,** and the **third person singular verb:** /-s/, /-z/, and /-iz or -əz/. Please note that we are concerned here only with the phonemic differences required by American English phonology, not with the three grammatical functions, which would require three separate displays, not relevant to our purpose here.

/-s/	after voiceless /p/, /t/, and	*stops, spot's, ticks*
	after voiceless /f/ and /θ/	*muffs, wife's, births*
/-z/	after voiced /b/, /d/, /g/	*knobs, dad's, drugs*
	after voiced /v/ and /ð/	*loaves, wives', breathes*
	after voiced /m/, /n/, and /ŋ/	*slams, man's, sings*
	after voiced /l/ and /r/	*hauls, cars', bars*
	after all simple and compound vowel nuclei	*rays, tree's, says*
/-ɨz or -əz/	after /s/ and /z/	*classes, class's, cruises*
	after /š/ and /ž/	*crushes, garage's, mirages*
	after /č/ and /ǰ/	*matches, watch's, cages*

The following display shows the allomorphs of the past verb morpheme: /-t/, /-d/, and /-ɨd or -əd/.

/-ɨd or -əd/	after /t/ and /d/	*fated, aided*
/-t/	after all voiceless consonants except /t/	
	after /p/ and /k/	*stopped, frocked*
	after /f/ and /θ/	*stuffed, berthed*
	after /s/, /š/, and /č/	*stressed, wished, watched*
/-d/	after all voiced consonants except /d/	
	after /b/ and /g/	*sobbed, bagged*
	after /v/ and /ð/	*saved, writhed*
	after /m/, /n/, and /ŋ/	*skimmed, planned, banged*
	after /l/ and /r/	*bawled, soared*
	after /z/, /ž/, and /ǰ/	*blazed, rouged, judged*
	after all simple and compound vowel nuclei	*said, played, plowed, tried,* etc.

TEACHING SUGGESTION: Many learners will enjoy and profit by oral and written exploration of the sounds and spellings of the structural elements in the above displays.

Since these spellings represent important high-frequency structural elements of standard English — the noun plural and genitive morphemes, the third-person singular present verb morpheme, and the past verb morpheme — they are much more important than spellings that represent non-structural elements. *This part of English spelling appears to be better understood as* **morphemic** *rather than* **phonemic**. In teaching English as a second language, or teaching standard English as a second dialect, this distinction is of crucial importance and should be particularly helpful to the teacher. *What the non-standard speaker lacks in these examples is* **morphemes,** *not* **phonemes:** *his first dialect uses a different inflectional system.*

SPELLING AND READING. Bloomfield over thirty years ago began his work on phoneme-grapheme correspondences in relation to primary reading instruction; his learning program, after inconclusive testing and long delay, was published in 1961, with his statement of theory and some testimonials.[1] Despite the extreme narrowness of phonemics in the broad field of linguistics, a focus on phoneme-grapheme correspondences, or on spelling patterns, is widely regarded as THE linguistic approach to reading. But programs carrying this linguistic label, like phonics programs and basal readers incorporating phonics, suffer the crippling limitation of taking the word to be the most important unit of language and reading.[2] I have consistently been a severe critic of this theoretical and practical limitation; some of my work is listed in Selected References, with other pertinent contributions. In addition to the reading programs based upon phoneme-grapheme correspondences according to traditional English spelling, several approaches have been based upon new sets of graphic symbols.[3] Of these, the Initial Teaching Alphabet (i.t.a.) is closest to traditional orthography and is the most widely known.

The *i.t.a. represents the pronunciation of Received Standard (British), a dialect spoken mainly in the south of England and nowhere in this country.* Users of i.t.a. are not permitted to make any changes, additions, or deletions whatsoever, for any reason; its use under these conditions is free of charge.

Although many of its proponents claim that i.t.a. "encodes the phonemes of English," this claim is not supported by careful phoneme-grapheme analysis. My study of children's writing in i.t.a. revealed that neither the children nor the teachers had developed linguistic skill in transcribing speech sounds, though many of the teachers believed they had; the most successful teachers were quite permissive about the children's spelling. I observed first-grade classrooms where very good work in both reading and writing was done with i.t.a.;

but I also observed that i.t.a. when used as a synthetic phonics system was just as deadly as traditional spelling treated synthetically. None of the children read aloud with good English rhythms and tunes, a fault that betrays word-oriented instruction. But with permissive spelling, the result in some rooms was: no spelling shibboleth, no trauma; the child was freed to write fluently in i.t.a. during his first semester in school. There is no reason, however, why the same results cannot be obtained by a policy of permissive spelling of traditional orthography; many humane teachers have had excellent results in beginning composition simply by not taking correct spelling too seriously.

SPELLING RESEARCH. The bad reputation of the English spelling system is not entirely deserved; our spelling is more regular and consistent than has generally been realized. Research into phoneme-grapheme correspondences tends to show that approximately four-fifths of English words are spelled according to regular and consistent relationships between phonemes and graphemes. This is not to say there is a four-fifths-to-one correspondence between single letters and phonemes, but between all graphemes (both single and multiple letter) and all phonemes (both simple and compound nuclei). These correspondences take into account different positions in syllables, and different patterns of stress (accent); they also take into account numerous spelling conventions, such as consonant doubling to differentiate such pairs as *canning* and *caning* or *supper* and *super;* the final *e* that differentiates pairs like *man* and *mane* or *fat* and *fate;* and other conventions less applicable to school instructional programs.[4]

Selected References — Classified

THE ALPHABET

David Diringer, *The Alphabet: a key to the history of mankind* (New York: The Philosophical Library, 1948).

Ignace J. Gelb, *A Study of Writing: The Foundations of Grammatology* (Chicago: University of Chicago Press, 1952).

Edmund Burke Huey, *The Psychology and Pedagogy of Reading: with a review of the history of reading and writing, and of methods, texts, and hygiene in reading.* First published in 1908 by Macmillan. (Cambridge, Mass.: M.I.T. Press, 1968). Chapters X and XI.

Oscar Ogg, *The Twenty-Six Letters* (New York: Crowell, 1948).

Unesco, *The Art of Writing: An Exhibition of Fifty Panels* (Baden-Baden: Douch and Verlagshaus F. W. Wesel, 1965).

PHONEME-GRAPHEME RELATIONSHIPS

Leonard Bloomfield, "Linguistics and Reading," *Elementary English Review* Vol. 19, 1942, pp. 125–130, 183–186.

Charles C. Fries, *Linguistics and Reading* (New York: Holt, Rinehart and Winston, 1963).

Robert A. Hall, Jr., *Sound and Spelling in English* (Philadelphia: Chilton, 1961).

Paul R. Hanna, Jean S. Hanna, Richard E. Hodges, and Edwin H. Rudorf, *Phoneme-Grapheme Correspondences as Cues to Spelling Improvement* (Washington, D.C.: U.S. Government Printing Office, 1967).

Paul R. Hanna and Richard E. Hodges. "Spelling and Communications Theory: A Model and an Annotated Bibliography," *Elementary English, XL* (May, 1963), pp. 483–505, 528.

Richard E. Hodges, "The Case for Teaching Sound-to-Letter Correspondences in Spelling," *The Elementary School Journal, 66*, No. 6 (March, 1966), pp. 327–336.

Richard E. Hodges and E. Hugh Rudorf, "Searching Linguistics for Cues to the Teaching of Spelling," *Elementary English, XLII* (May, 1965), pp. 527–533.

Ernest Horn, "Phonetics and Spelling," *Elementary School Journal, LVII* (May, 1957), pp. 424–432.

———, "Spelling," *Encyclopedia of Educational Research*, pp. 1337–54. Chester W. Harris (ed.) (New York: Macmillan, 1960).

Carl A. Lefevre, *Linguistics and the Teaching of Reading* (New York: McGraw-Hill, 1964).

———, "The Simplistic Standard Word-Perception Theory of Reading," *Elementary English, 45*, No. 3 (March, 1968), pp. 349–353, 355.

———, "A Longer Look at Let's Read," *Elementary English*, March, 1964, pp. 40–45.

———, "A review of Fries' *Linguistics and Reading*," *The Elementary School Journal*, April, 1964, pp. 398–400.

Walter T. Petty, "Research Critiques," edited by Patrick Groff, *Elementary English, XLII* (May, 1965), pp. 584–587.

"Roundtable Review," *Research in the Teaching of English, 1*, No. 2 (Fall, 1967), pp. 201–223.

Richard L. Venezky, "English Orthography: Its Graphical Structure and Its Relation to Sound," *Reading Research Quarterly, II*, No. 3 (Spring, 1967), pp. 75–105.

———, "Reading: Grapheme-Phoneme Relationship," *Education, 87*, No. 9 (May, 1967), pp. 519–524.

Richard L. Venezky and Ruth H. Weir, *A Study of Selected Spelling to Sound Correspondence Patterns;* Cooperative Research Project No. 3090 (Stanford: Stanford University Press, 1966).

Ruth H. Weir and Richard L. Venezky, *Rules to Aid in the Teaching of Reading,* Cooperative Research Project No. 2584 (Stanford: Stanford University Press, 1965).

PHONETICS AND PHONEMICS

Cynthia D. Buchanan, *A Programmed Introduction to Linguistics* (Boston: D. C. Heath, 1963).

Francis P. Dinneen, *An Introduction to General Linguistics* (New York: Holt, Rinehart and Winston, 1967).

W. Nelson Francis, *The Structure of American English* (New York: Ronald Press, 1958).

Charles C. Fries, *Linguistics and Reading* (New York: Holt, Rinehart and Winston, 1963).

H. A. Gleason, Jr., *An Introduction to Descriptive Linguistics,* rev. ed. (New York: Holt, Rinehart and Winston, 1961).

R. H. Robins, *General Linguistics, An Introductory Survey* (Bloomington: Indiana University Press, 1966).

Norman C. Stageberg, *An Introductory English Grammar* (New York: Holt, Rinehart and Winston, 1965).

PHONEMIC DIFFERENCES AMONG DIALECTS

Hans Kurath, *A Word Geography of the Eastern United States,* second printing (Ann Arbor: University of Michigan Press, 1966).

Raven I. McDavid, Jr., "The Dialects of American English," Chapter 10 in *The Structure of American English,* by W. Nelson Francis (New York: Ronald Press, 1958), pp. 480–533.

Carroll E. Reed, *Dialects in American English,* in the New World Language and Linguistics Series (New York: World, 1967).

Roger W. Shuy, *Discovering American Dialects* (Champaign, Illinois: National Council of Teachers of English, 1967).

Chapter 5

Word Classes:
Nouns, Verbs, Adjectives, Adverbs

For clarity and precision in teaching English and the language arts, it is helpful to distinguish two different categories of English words:

1. **Reference words** (the bulk of vocabulary), well over a half million words.
2. **Structure words** (or function words), about three hundred.

Reference words are verbal symbols for what lies in "the real world" outside the language system itself: objects, actions, qualities, thoughts, feelings, impressions. In the formal analysis of the language system — grammar — reference words are the four word classes generally recognized by English language scholars: nouns, verbs, adjectives, and adverbs. **Structure words** are verbal symbols for patterns and relationships primarily within the language system — grammatical relationships. Many structure words may conveniently be designated as "markers" of various sentence elements, a concept that is clear and useful in classroom instruction. Chapter 8 is devoted exclusively to structure words.

The French linguist de Saussure termed reference words "full words" because of their "real" content, or referential meaning; and structure words "empty words" because of their relative lack of referential meaning. Full words clearly symbolize referents outside

114

verbal structures such as sentences, but structure words have only minimal outside reference; it would not be true, however, to say that they have *none*. Both classes of words have some referential meaning and some grammatical function; reference words have more meaning in the sense of vocabulary items, and structure words have more grammatical function. Yet de Saussure's terms *full* and *empty* may serve a useful purpose in teaching, if only as a suggestive figure of speech.

There is as yet no fully satisfactory system for classifying English words. A complete system would almost certainly be too complex for teaching except in specialized courses in grammar as a formal discipline. The common school grammar method of defining "the parts of speech" — some by meaning and others by function — is unsatisfactory for many reasons, its circularity being perhaps the chief reason. That is, verbal definitions are given that are not consistently applied as a means of classifying words; instead, words tend to be labeled independently and then cited as examples satisfying the definitions. Another difficulty is that combining definitions by meaning with definitions by function does not work out very well. Many students memorize definitions and labels without gaining any grammatical understanding. All this can lead to interminable woolgathering and nit-picking. (For suggested exploratory investigations, refer to the final Teaching Suggestion in this chapter, pp. 137–38.)

And yet we need to find ways of handling word classifications in English and language arts classrooms. One way is to attempt to define the word classes objectively, in terms of structure; this method can give both teacher and student a good footing for exploration and discovery procedures in their study of English words. Two different kinds of structural criteria may be used to define or identify the four word classes; these criteria are helpful but not infallible.

1. Distribution in syntactical patterns — the fundamental criterion, and possibly the more important.
2. Ability to take the word-form changes of the word class; these changes include two subsystems:
   a. grammatical inflections;
   b. derivational prefixes and suffixes.

The present chapter treats all the above except derivational prefixes and suffixes; this large and very important subsystem is treated in

Chapter 6, The Derivational Affixing System: Prefixes and Suffixes (pp. 139–162).

"Words" and word-form changes are the morphemes of linguistic description. A **morpheme** may be defined as the smallest meaning-bearing structural unit of English; morphemes include word bases, grammatical inflections, and derivational prefixes and suffixes. A morpheme that can pattern independently in larger structures is a "free" morpheme, *cat*, for example; a morpheme that cannot pattern independently is a "bound" morpheme, for example /-*s*/ in **cats** and /-*y*/ in **catty**. Generally, **free morphemes** are the structure words and the word bases of the four word classes; conversely, although some bound bases do occur, **bound morphemes** are generally the grammatical inflections and the derivational affixes of the four word classes. A **compound word** is a combination of two or more word bases, **sidewalk,** for example.

TEACHING SUGGESTION: As a basis for open-ended exploration, introduce the morpheme concept to your students, along with the notion of bound and free morphemes. Ask them to give examples of their own. See whether they can inductively arrive at a distinction between grammatical inflections and derivational affixes.

Some words may hold membership in two word classes. In handling word classes, one of the subtlest problems is the ease with which English words seem to slip from one word class or function to another. Such words as **steel** and **stone,** to mention only two, may be distributed in four positions of **noun, verb, adjective** and **adverb**; this is true of many words.

NOUN: *Steel* is an excellent metal.

VERB: You must *steel* your nerves.

ADJECTIVE: The knife has a *steel* blade.

ADVERB: The color of the pony was *steel* gray.

Moreover, **steel** will take the grammatical inflections of both noun and verb classes; NOUN: **steel, steels, steel's;** VERB: **steel, steels, steeling, steeled. Steel** will not, however, take grammatical inflections for adjective or adverb (*-y* is a derivational suffix that converts the noun *steel* to the adjective *steely*).

Many words in English will fill three positions of noun, verb, and adjective, and will also take the grammatical inflections of both noun and verb classes; *barrel, gun,* and *tree,* for example. Any word that can pass both structural tests for two or more word classes is a member of those classes; *steel* and *stone* in the paragraph above, and *barrel, gun,* and *tree,* judged by these two structural tests, are full members of both noun and verb classes. In adjective or adverb positions, they may be regarded as nouns in those functions or uses, rather than members of the adjective or adverb class. There is fertile ground here for students of all ages to discover and explore for themselves.

TEACHING SUGGESTION: Open a class discussion of words that may fill more than one position in good English sentences. See whether or not the students can inductively reach true generalizations about noun distribution and grammatical inflections. (The actual terms are not the important thing, of course.)

The following topics will be introduced and briefly discussed in the remainder of this chapter:

Nouns.
Pronouns.
Verbs.
Adjectives and adverbs.
Objective contrasts of word classes.

Both kinds of structural criteria are used here to describe the four word classes: (1) distribution in sentences, illustrated by slot-and-filler techniques; (2) grammatical inflections, illustrated by examples and word lists. *Both methods exemplify teaching by association of grammatical terms with specific, concrete referents; neither depends upon abstract verbal definitions or rules for defining word classes and their uses.*

Nouns

Words that can fill such slots or frames as those below are nouns as defined by distribution in sentences:

A *car* is expensive.
A (an, the) _____ is expensive (interesting, dull, time-consuming, etc.)

The *car* is in the garage.
A (an, the) _____ is in the garage.

The car is in the *street*.
The car is in the _____ (garage, ditch, field, etc.)

They have a *car*.
They have a (an, the) _____.

Where is the *car?*
Where is a (an, the) _____?

These examples of test slots are offered as suggestive rather than exhaustive; any class of lively students can add many more of their own.

TEACHING SUGGESTION: Open a class discussion of the distribution of nouns in sentences. Ask your students first to give examples of their own to fill slots; then ask them to devise new noun slot tests for themselves.

The remainder of this discussion of **Nouns** is presented under the following eight subtopics:

SUBSTITUTIONS OF ADJECTIVES IN NOUN POSITIONS
THE NOUN INFLECTIONS: SINGULAR, PLURAL, GENITIVE
THREE SOUNDS OF THE NOUN PLURAL AND GENITIVE INFLECTIONS
IRREGULAR NOUN PLURALS
MASS AND COUNT NOUNS
PROPER AND COMMON NOUNS
DISTINCTIONS AMONG NOUN MARKERS (DETERMINERS)

SUBSTITUTIONS OF ADJECTIVES IN NOUN POSITIONS. In contrast to words that may be either noun or verb, we find adjectives that may be substituted in noun positions: examples are *poor, rich; old, young; good, evil.*

> The *poor* get poorer; the *rich* get richer.
> The *old* get older; but so do the *young.*
> One *evil* flows from another. . . . *Good* find *good.*

TEACHING SUGGESTION: Present examples like these to your class. Ask them to give examples of their own. The tentative generalization would have to do with substitutions of adjectives and possibly other words in noun positions in English.

THE NOUN INFLECTIONS: SINGULAR, PLURAL, GENITIVE. Most nouns (but not quite all) have a singular and a plural form: *cat* and *cats,* for example. A simple slot test for singular and plural forms is **one cat, two cats;** but it is so simple that it will not work for all nouns (*one accuracy, two accuracies?*). Some nouns also have a genitive form (the possessive of school grammar): *cat's* for example, as in *the cat's meow;* also a plural genitive, *cats',* as in *the cats' caterwauling.* The four noun inflections may be conveniently summarized in a model:

N	N-s	N-'s	N-s'
cat	cats	cat's	cats'

These four are all the noun inflections, but other distinctions among nouns should be noted: the different sounds of the plural and genitive inflections; irregular plural forms; count and mass nouns; and proper and common nouns.

THREE SOUNDS OF THE NOUN PLURAL AND GENITIVE INFLECTIONS. The plural inflection written -*s* and the genitive singular and plural inflections written -*'s* and -*s'* have three different forms and sounds — /-*s*/, /-*z*/ and /-*iz* or -*əz*/ — determined by the preceding phoneme. Since the genitives follow the same phonological rules as the plurals, it is necessary to deal only with the plural forms to make the point clear.

Following an unvoiced consonant, the plural inflection is usually /-s/, as in *racks, foodstuffs, maps, hats.* Following a voiced consonant, the plural inflection is usually /-z/, as in *cabs, cars, dolls, hams, pans, pads, rags, stores.* Following a vowel, which is a voiced sound, the plural inflection is also /-z/, as in *bananas, fellows, guppies, potatoes, tomatoes.* Following unvoiced /s/ and /č/ and voiced /z/ and /ǰ/, the plural inflection is generally /-iz or -əz/, as in *classes, churches, blazes, judges.* The three forms — /-s/, /-z/, /-iz or -əz/ — are the **allomorphs** of the noun plural morpheme.

TEACHING SUGGESTION: Introduce the three forms and sounds of the noun plural to your class; unless they bring up the genitives, it is better to deal with them in a follow-up lesson. Ask students to give examples orally and to prepare lists for each form. This practice, both oral and written, is especially helpful in early (and remedial) work in spelling and reading, and in work with non-native speakers.

IRREGULAR NOUN PLURALS. In one small set of singular nouns ending in unvoiced /f/, this sound becomes voiced /v/ in the plural: the plural inflection is /-z/, as in *knife, knives; leaf, leaves; life, lives; loaf, loaves; wife, wives.* The plural of *house* is a unique exception, where the final /s/ becomes /z/ and the inflection is /-iz or -əz/ in *houses.*

Some old words have retained irregular plural forms with /-en/: *child, children; man, men; ox, oxen; woman, women;* and while *brothers* is the regular plural of *brother,* the archaic *brethren* is still used in some religious and fraternal contexts. Some other nouns also retain old irregular forms: *foot, feet; goose, geese; tooth, teeth* (three pairs with an identical vowel change); *louse, lice; mouse, mice* (two pairs with the same vowel change). A few nouns have the same form for singular and plural: *deer, sheep, fish* (but also *fishes* in reference to species). In hunting and fishing, the names for the quarry are often singular in form even when the meaning is plural.

TEACHING SUGGESTION: Exploration of irregular noun forms has an intrinsic interest all its own. It can also be helpful in sharpening visual and auditory discrimination, and in improving speech articulation.

MASS AND COUNT NOUNS. Some nouns refer to a mass or quantity that cannot be counted; they are known as **mass nouns.** In this usage they have only a singular form and do not take the article *a* or *an;* examples are *milk, grain, sand, butter, beer, water, gas,* and others like them. We speak of *a cup of milk, a bushel of grain, a load of sand, a pat of butter, a keg of beer, a glass of water, a cubic measure of water.* Other nouns known as **count nouns,** refer to countable items. In their singular form, they take the article *a* or *an;* in their plural form they take noun markers (or determiners) that indicate plural number, such as *few, many,* and the cardinal numbers, that are not generally used with mass nouns. Mass nouns may take such noun markers as *less, little,* or *much.* In a different sense, mass nouns occur in such usages as *a heavy gas* and *heavy gases* or *a dark beer* and *dark beers;* but these usages contrast with *a heavy stone* and *heavy stones,* or *a dark picture* and *dark pictures.* Here the distinction between mass and count nouns is quite apparent; it is the difference between noncountable and countable quantities. It also applies to such abstract nouns as *accuracy, honesty, love, patriotism.*

The distinction between mass and count nouns is a point of usage that characterizes the speaker or writer who is sensitive to the finer points of English; good writers in particular observe it.

PROPER NOUNS AND COMMON NOUNS. The distinction between **proper nouns** and **common nouns** probably is taught largely because capitalization of proper nouns is a convention of written English; such capitalization does not reflect any feature of spoken English. Interestingly, this distinction between two kinds of nouns supports the school grammar definition of a noun as the name of a person, a place (proper nouns), or a thing (common noun).

DISTINCTIONS AMONG NOUN MARKERS (DETERMINERS). In addition to the articles of school grammar — *a, an,* and *the* — many other words can fill the same slots and perform the same general function of noun markers, and thus help to identify nouns by distribution in sentences. The cardinal numbers may be markers of count nouns, as in *one car, two cars, ninety-nine cars, one hundred ninety-nine cars,* and so on. Genitive noun forms may also be noun markers of both mass and count nouns:

> *Man's* work is from sun to sun, but *woman's* work is never done.
> *Goats'* milk is said to be very good for you.
> *Dogs'* voices vary with mood and situation.
> *Maxwellton's* braes are bonny.

The following words, listed alphabetically, may all be used as noun markers, either individually or in combination; some may also be substituted for nouns: *all, another, any, both, either, enough, every, few, her, his, little, many, more, most, much, my, neither, no, other, our, several, some, such, that, their, these, this, those, your.* Note that some are generally used with singular nouns, others with plural nouns, and still others with mass nouns.

TEACHING SUGGESTION: Students of all ages are able to grasp some of the distinctions among noun markers and between count nouns and mass nouns. Open a class discussion with your students and let them explore the subject, giving their own examples orally. When you have discovered their level of understanding, you can follow up with appropriate activities, or drop the subject until a later time.

Pronouns

Pronouns may be considered a word class in themselves, a set of structure words, or a subset of nouns. The eight pronouns are *I, we, you, he, she, it, they,* and *who.* They do not share the plural and genitive inflections of the nouns, but they do have variant forms that will fill the positions of nouns and of noun markers. Thus they fit well here in the discussion of nouns and noun markers. The forms and functions of the pronouns may be shown in a model:

Subject	Object	Noun marker (possessive)	Noun use (possessive)
I	me	my	mine
we	us	our	ours
you [1]	you [1]	your	yours
he	him	his [2]	his [2]
she	her [3]	her [3]	hers
it [4]	it [4]	its [5]	its [5]
they	them	their	theirs
who [6]	who(m) [6]	whose [7]	whose [7]

Who is used to begin a question or a clause, and as an object, but not in the normal subject position; *whom* is used only in quite formal speech and writing nowadays. Please note that while the model is complete, this is only because seven forms are used twice; the pairs of raised numerals indicate the unsystematic distribution. This inconsistency, added to dialectal irregularities, makes the system difficult for many students to master.

TEACHING SUGGESTION: Present the pronoun model to your students in dittoed form or on the board. Invite them to explore it and experiment orally, inventing sentences using pronouns in all the ways indicated. See whether they want to develop some kind of attack that might help them gain mastery of the system.

NOUN AND PRONOUN USAGES AS DIALECT MARKERS. Some features of class or social dialect are in effect dialect markers: the use of such divergent features tends to stigmatize the speaker as ill-educated, illiterate, uncouth. In noun usage, one such dialect marker is lack of the noun plural inflection.[1]

Three *boy* ran down the alley.
Two *lady* came to visit.

Another is the lack of the noun genitive inflection.

This is my *brother* bike.
Mr. *Brown* hat blew off.

Any motivated student can learn standard noun plurals and genitive inflections by doing enough oral and written practice on pattern drills on the standard forms. Any motivated teacher can show him the way, and then he can produce drills of his own. But it will take much practice, patient practice. Needless to say, the student must be ready to volunteer, else the whole project will be abortive.

In pronoun usage, one social dialect marker is the analogous addition of the /-*n*/ of *mine* to *our, your, his, her,* and *their.* The resultant system of dialect-marking forms is *mine, ourn, yourn, hisn, hern,* and *theirn;* perhaps in good standing several generations ago in England but not considered tolerable in America today. Another dialect-marking pronoun usage is *them* instead of *those,* as in *them books, them people, them things.* Still another is compounding, as in *them-there fellows, them-there things;* and *these-here chairs* and *these-here desks.* These stigmata too will yield to pattern practice drills by a motivated student with a motivated teacher to get him started.

TEACHING SUGGESTION: If you have students who want to eliminate these dialect markers from their speech and writing, you can help them to make up pattern drill material. The first work should be oral; then written drills may be prepared for oral practice. It is important to devise practice materials that sound as natural as possible to the student. See the examples below.

Three boys ran down the alley.	Two ladies came to visit.
This is my brother's bike.	Mr. Brown's hat blew off.
This desk is mine.	Mine is clean.
This desk is ours.	Ours is new.
This desk is yours.	Yours is older.
This desk is his.	His is neat.
This desk is hers.	Hers is too.
This desk is theirs.	Theirs is a big one.
I bought these boots.	He bought those boots.

N.B.: For some students, an extra drill item of major importance may be the verb *is,* which commonly is not present in black English equivalents of such sentences as these.

Verbs

In contrast to English **nouns,** which are relatively simple, English **verbs** are extremely complex. Most linguistic descriptions of English include a fairly extensive discussion of our verbs; at least two American linguists and one British have written full-length books on the English verb system.[2] The following exposition introduces points relevant to teaching English and the language arts. Considering the complexity of the English verb system, it is entertaining to see how very simply one linguist has defined **finite verb** (all verbs except the infinitive: *to go, to run, to see,* etc.);

> For our purposes, a finite verb is one that requires a subject and can take a subject chosen from the list *I, we, he, she, they,* or else a verb that is in all other respects similar but has *it* instead: "He looked at them" and "It rained on them." [3]

Words that can fill such slots or frames as those below are verbs as defined by their distribution in sentences.

INTRANSITIVE: The man *walked.*   Did the man *walk?*
                The man _____.   Did the man _____?
                Who _____?

TRANSITIVE: The man *bought* it.   Did the man *buy* it?
                The man _____ it.   Did the man _____ it?
                Who _____ it?

These examples of verb test slots are merely suggestive; livewire students can invent many of their own. Pronouns and personal names may be used in the noun positions, for instance, and the whole system of verb markers for tense and aspect could be used. The point of a slot test, however, is simply to identify the word class, not to ring all the changes.

TEACHING SUGGESTION: Begin a class discussion of the distribution of verbs in sentences. Ask your students first to give examples of verbs to fill the slots above. Then ask them to devise new verb slot tests as a basis for further exploration and discussion of verbs.

With the exception of the verb *be* with eight parts, and the modals with two or even one (*must*), English verbs may be classified as having three, four, or five parts. Some of our most common verbs have five parts that can fill slots in a variety of complex verb groups. But a three-part verb can fill all the same slots by using one of its forms in three ways; and a four-part verb, by using one of its forms in two ways.

The remainder of this discussion of *Verbs* is presented under five subtopics, as follows:

THE VERB INFLECTIONS: THE "IRREGULAR" FIVE-PART VERBS
THE VERB INFLECTIONS: THE "REGULAR" FOUR-PART VERBS
THE VERB INFLECTIONS: THE THREE-PART VERBS
THE MODALS AND THE VERB be
THE VERB be AND DIVERGENT DIALECTS

THE VERB INFLECTIONS: THE "IRREGULAR" FIVE-PART VERBS. The five-part verbs are called "irregular" because their forms are not parallel for all verbs in the class. Below is a model of some common five-part verbs. The sounds of the **V-s** inflection are parallel to those of the noun plural inflections, **N-s**: the same phonological rule gives /-s/, /-z/, or /-iz or -əz/. These three forms are allomorphs of the third-person singular verb morpheme (inflection). For example, *eats* and *writes* have /-s/; *does, draws,* and *goes* have /-z/: *chooses* and *freezes* have /-iz or -əz/. These points of sounds and spellings are pertinent to teaching the regular spellings of verb inflections, and to phonics instruction.

V	V-s	V-ed	V-ing	V-en
choose	chooses	chose	choosing	chosen
do	does	did	doing	done
draw	draws	drew	drawing	drawn
eat	eats	ate	eating	eaten
freeze	freezes	froze	freezing	frozen
go	goes	went	going	gone
write	writes	wrote	writing	written

Five uses of the five verb parts can be shown in simple sentences: Today I *go;* he *goes* with me. Yesterday we both *went*. Before that we had *gone* every day. Today I am *going;* he is *going* with me.

TEACHING SUGGESTION: Expose your class to five-part verbs and their simple functions in sentences; adjust difficulty of verb meanings to class level. Have students extend the list as far as they can; ask them to demonstrate simple functions in sentences.

In the examples above, note that *go* is not accurately described as the present tense or form. In *Today I go, go* expresses future action; in *We go every day, go* expresses a regular and continuing activity that began sometime in the past and will continue into the future — but one thing it does not express is action going on right at this very moment, or present action. *I am going* may express present, continuing, or future action, depending on the entire verbal context and the actual situation to which it refers. Consider the following sentences with **V-ing.**

We are going.	We will have been going.
We have been going.	We were to be going.
We had been going.	We were to have been going.
We will be going.	

Note the effect on each sentence as you add a definite time indicator: *today, every day, tomorrow, next week;* some will also take *yesterday, last week.*

TEACHING SUGGESTION: Introduce the above sentences to your students for comment and discussion. Ask them to invent similar sentences with other verbs. Ingenious students may enjoy writing a paragraph or story using a whole set of such sentences.

Now consider the following sentences with **V-en.**

We have eaten.	We will have eaten.
We had eaten.	We were to have eaten.

Here too note the effect of additions of time indicators: *today, every day, tomorrow, next week.*

THE VERB INFLECTIONS: THE "REGULAR" FOUR-PART VERBS.   All the regular English verbs have four parts. These verbs are "regular" because their parts are parallel in form, and perhaps also because the largest number of English verbs belongs to this class. Each verb has one part that functions as both **V-ed** and **V-en**; note the two categories in the model below, headed **V-ed** and **V-ed/-en**. Note also that the **V-s** inflections have the same three sounds as the **N-s** inflections for nouns and the **V-s** inflections for the five-part verbs: $/-s/$, $/-z/$, and $/-iz$ or $-\partial z/$. Please note further that the **V-ed** forms also have three parallel final sounds: $/-t/$ as in *dropped;* $/-d/$ as in *rolled;* and $/-id$ or $-\partial d/$ in *regretted.* These three forms are allomorphs of the **V-ed** and **V-ed/-en** morphemes (inflections). These precise differences of sounds and spelling are pertinent to teaching the regular spellings of verb inflections, and to phonics instruction.

V	V-s	V-ed	V-ing	V-ed/-en
drop	drops	dropped	dropping	dropped
play	plays	played	playing	played
roll	rolls	rolled	rolling	rolled
regret	regrets	regretted	regretting	regretted

TEACHING SUGGESTION: Use these verbs to start a discussion of regular English verbs, their sounds and their spellings. Students can supply dozens of examples. Help them approach their own generalizations as to why verbs of this particular class are called "regular."

In addition to the very large class of regular four-part verbs, English has several smaller classes of four-part verbs that are irregular. Five are displayed in the model.

V	V-s	V-ed	V-ing	V-ed/-en
sleep	sleeps	slept	sleeping	slept
send	sends	sent	sending	sent
bring	brings	brought	bringing	brought
teach	teaches	taught	teaching	taught
think	thinks	thought	thinking	thought

THE VERB INFLECTIONS: THREE-PART VERBS. A number of common English verbs have only three parts; each verb in this group has one form that serves three functions: **V, V-ed,** and **V-en.** Four are shown in the model.

V	V-s	V-ed	V-ing	V-ed/-en
cut	cuts	cut	cutting	cut
hurt	hurts	hurt	hurting	hurt
put	puts	put	putting	put
set	sets	set	setting	set

Three-part verbs exemplify the principle of redundancy in language, but in reverse. Redundancy simply means that a sentence has more than one signal for singular and plural, for time and aspect, and so on; because there are many signals, an auditor or reader does not have to pick them all up with equal specificity or attention in order to decode the message. Word order and the order of sentence parts are also linguistic signals of great importance in English; three-part verbs work because they can fill all the verb positions that other verbs fill with four or five parts; the other signals in the sentence help carry the message.

TEACHING SUGGESTION: Open a discussion of five-part, four-part, and three-part English verbs. Help students to approach the generalization that the verb system works as a five-part system because some verbs have interchangeable parts that play several verb roles in sentences. A class that shows talent might be ready to think about the principle of redundancy.

THE MODALS AND THE VERB **be.** The modals and the verb *be* are in many ways more like structure words than members of the verb word class; for this reason they will be discussed briefly here and then again in Chapter 7, English Sentences, and in Chapter 8, Structure Words. The present discussion will be a summary one.

The modals in English occur as verb markers (auxiliaries) in combination with other verbs; thus they are treated as structure words in this book. In terms of referential meaning, they express mood, or aspect, more than time. They suggest answers to the question, "What is the appearance (aspect) of the thing under consideration?" *Possible, probable? Real, unreal? Likely, unlikely? Certain, uncertain?* The ten common English modals are: **can, could; may, might; must** (one form); **ought** (followed by an infinitive, **to-V**); **shall, should;** and **will, would.**

The verb **be** is in a class by itself in English, the busiest, most versatile word in the language. It has eight parts, three more than any other verb, and is the most irregular:

am   are   be   been   being   is   was   were

It is used as the only verb (copula) in linking verb sentences: **Kennedy was President;** as the verb marker in passive sentences: **Kennedy was assassinated;** and as a verb marker in active-verb structures with **V-ing:** *I am (was) writing; They are (were) reading; He is (was) studying.* And **be** is possibly the most common relic of the nearly extinct subjunctive: **If I were you. . . .**

THE VERB **be** AND DIVERGENT DIALECTS. Perhaps because of the intricacy of the **be** system, simplification characterizes the social dialects of the uneducated; on the other hand, verbs in some dialects seem to express aspect rather than tense. The difference between *I busy* and *I be busy,* is a difference of aspect: *I busy* means *I'm busy now,* but *I be busy* means *I'm busy all the time.* Parallel examples are *He there* and *He be there; He tired* and *He be tired; He sick* and *He be sick.* Such regular, consistent, systematic distinctions are extremely difficult for a speaker to change, even if he has the desire.

According to McDavid, some speakers of divergent dialects use only one form of **be** instead of the three present forms of standard dialects, **am, is,** and **are;** or the **be** form itself may be used for all three.[4] An individual might use any of four systems shown in this model.

I be (am, is, or are)   We be (am, is, or are)
You be (am, is, or are)   You be (am, is, or are)
He be (am, is, or are)   They be (am, is, or are)

As noted after the suggested practice drills on page 124, some speakers do not have any **be** form in linking verb sentences: *He a* *good player* or *We ready.* Similarly, the **V-ing** verb forms may occur without a form of be as a marker (auxiliary): *She dancing* or *They swimming.*

Before tampering with any of these patterns, a teacher should understand quite precisely what he is doing. Good intentions are not an adequate basis for undertaking to help a student change his dialect, or to learn how to speak two dialects; it is necessary first to know both the divergent speaker's dialect and one's own dialect *as different systems,* and to be able to focus on the points of similarity and contrast between them. It is a profound mistake to diagnose a specific dialect divergence as an "omission" or "dropping" of an orthodox element that simply is not a part of the dialect. How can a speaker "omit" or "drop" a feature that he never had in the first place?

TEACHING SUGGESTION: If you have students who speak a divergent dialect and who are motivated to learn a version of the standard dialect, encourage them to explore points of similarity and contrast with you. This is a difficult and extensive project, but given right attitudes on both sides, it can be constructive and rewarding. See the references at the end of Chapter 7; also Chapter 1, Selected References, American English Dialects: Social, Nonstandard, Disadvantaged, pp. 33–34.

Adjectives and Adverbs

Despite duplication, overlapping, and insufficient information, it may be worthwhile to note some distinctions between two elusive word classes, *adjectives* and *adverbs,* whose general function is *modification.* Perhaps the simplest distinction is that adjectives generally modify nouns:

A *green* apple;   The apple is *green.*

And that adverbs generally modify verbs:

He was *well* coached.   He ran *swiftly.*

But this is not a "rule" because some modify both nouns and verbs:

He went up the *down* stairway.   He fell *down*.

To some extent, the distinction can be made by applying both kinds of structural tests — distribution in sentences and ability to take appropriate word-form changes — but this procedure is far from infallible. The truth is that we have no adequate linguistic description of adjectives and adverbs; of the two, we are much less sure of adverbs, but more study is needed of both, and in relation to each other.

In classroom discussion of adjectives and adverbs, it is desirable to call attention to only the main distinctions, through an inductive, descriptive approach. Beyond that, adjectives and adverbs offer good territory for exploration and discovery by students. It should not take too long to discover, for example, that "the *-ly* ending" is falsely rumored to be a reliable test for adverbs: it fits too many adjectives. While many adverbs do have the *-ly* suffix (**badly, certainly, quickly, suddenly**) so does a whole set of common adjectives (**lovely, manly, sickly, womanly**): others in this set are **beastly, brotherly, cowardly, earthly, fatherly, friendly, gentlemanly, leisurely, masterly, motherly, scholarly, sisterly**. Generally, adverbs with *-ly* are derived by adding the suffix to an adjective base; and adjectives with *-ly*, by adding the suffix to a noun base.

The very common words **hard, fast,** and **slow** pattern as both adjectives and adverbs.

Adjective	Adverb
It's *hard* work.	Go *hard*.
It's *fast* work.	Go *fast*.
It's *slow* work.	Go *slow*.

Slow and *slowly* are used interchangeably as adverbs; so are *quick* and *quickly:*

They said to drive *slow* (*slowly*) down the hill.
They said to come *quick* (*quickly*).

Hornby lists the following words used as adjectives, but also as adverbs, sometimes with and sometimes without the *-ly* suffix: **clean, clear, close, dead, direct, easy, fair, firm, high, large, loud,** *mighty, pretty, quick, right, sharp, slow, soft, sound, sure, tight,* and *wide.* He says that "the use of these words without *-ly* is a matter of usage and cannot be explained by giving rules"; he has an interesting discussion of them, however, with excellent examples.[5] For other references, see the list at the end of the chapter.

TEACHING SUGGESTION: Use the above words to open a discussion of words that may be used as both adjectives and adverbs. Ask students to give examples; discuss the differences of meaning, tone, degree of formality. The sentences below may be used as models, and for further discussion.

Adjective	Adverb
They had an *early* class.	The class met *early*.
They took a *fast* train.	The boys ate too *fast*.
	They were *fast* asleep.
	The stamp was stuck *fast*.
Ask me a *straight* question.	The boys came *straight* home.
I'll give you a *straight* answer.	

Some members of both adjective and adverb classes, but by no means all, take the inflections for degree, /*-er*/ and /*-est*/; others express degree by using the structure words **more** and **most,** or **less** and **least;** still others express degree by changing form completely. Note the following model.

Adjective	Adverb	Adj-er Adv-er	Adj-est Adv-est
good	well	better	best
		better	best
bad	badly	worse	worst
		worse	worst
far	far	farther	farthest
		further	furthest
old		elder	eldest
		older	oldest
little	little	less	least

TEACHING SUGGESTION: Use this model as a basis for an exploratory discussion; only the distinctions between *farther* and *further* and *elder* and *older* should offer difficulty. Ask students to invent sentences exemplifying the various forms; if oral work is successful, a written follow-up may be indicated.

The remainder of this discussion of **Adjectives and Adverbs** is presented under three subtopics:

ADJECTIVE FRAMES
ADVERB FRAMES
VERB-ADVERB UNITS

ADJECTIVE FRAMES. The frames below may be used to test for many adjectives.

They sold the _____ one.   A _____ person arrived.

Even though some adjectives will not fill the slot after the intensifier *very*, the following frame is also useful.

The very _____ (noun) is _____.

In "real life," probably no one would use the same adjective twice in one sentence, but that need not affect the usefulness of the frame; for variety, *extremely* and *rather* may also be used as intensifiers.

ADVERB FRAMES. The frames below may be used to test for many adverbs.

It happened _____.   They came _____.

Adverbs may also be preceded by the intensifiers *very, extremely,* and *rather.*

He ran very *swiftly.*   He was very *well* coached.
He (V-s, V-ed) very _____.   He or it was very _____ (V-ed/-en).

TEACHING SUGGESTION: Use the suggested adjective and adverb test frames as a basis for a class exploration of distinctions between adjectives and adverbs. Ask students to fill the slots orally, in the spirit of a game. Then ask them to devise test frames of their own. Try to interest them in the kinds of generalizations that might hold true of the evidence they find.

VERB-ADVERB UNITS. English has a set of words that combine with verbs to form verb units, as in *break through, put on, set up*. Singly, many of them look like prepositions, and they may function so: *through the looking glass, on the town, up the street*. But when they combine with verbs, their function seems to be adverbial; some grammarians call them fused adverbs, because each two-word unit has a special meaning, often different from that obtained by simply adding the meanings of the separate components. Common words of this set are *away, back, down, in, off, on, out, over, through,* and *up*. The verbs that may combine with these to form verb units are too numerous to be listed except in an exhaustive grammatical investigation; among the more common are the following:

break	break away, break down, break in, break off, break out, break over, break through, break up
come	come back, come off, come on, come out, come through, come up
draw	draw back, draw down, draw in, draw off, draw out, draw up
get	get away, get back, get in, get off, get on, get out, get through, get up
give	give away, give back, give in, give off, give out, give up
hold	hold back, hold down, hold in, hold off, hold on, hold out, hold over, hold up
look	look back, look down (upon), look in (on), look out, look up
mark	mark down, mark off, mark out, mark up
pull	pull back, pull down, pull in, pull off, pull on, pull out, pull over, pull through, pull up
put	put away, put back, put down, put in, put off, put on, put out, put over, put through, put up

In many sentences, the verb and the adverb are separable but indispensable. The police *broke up* the gang; . . *broke* the gang *up*. She *drew back* the blind; . . . the blind *back*. He *got back* his money; . . . his money *back*. They *pulled out* the stopper; . . . the stopper *out*. The supply is virtually inexhaustible.

TEACHING SUGGESTION: Introduce some of these verb-adverb units to your class for discussion and fun. Note the extreme variations of tone and formality; some are slang, others belong to limited speech communities. If enthusiasm continues after the oral work, various written assignments are possible; one is simply to write a narrative in which all the changes are rung on one or more of these units.

Objective Contrasts of Word Classes

Just as students learn and retain new words best in a meaningful context, sometimes they can remember an entire "family" of words more readily than isolated words. The members of a word family are contrasting word forms derived from one base, which may be noun, verb, or adjective. The base forms are underscored in the following model.

Noun	Verb	Adjective	Adverb
act	act	active	actively
	(activate)		
beauty	beautify	beautiful	beautifully
continuation	continue	continual	continually
		continuous	continuously
sadness	sadden	sad	sadly
(strength)	(strengthen)	strong	strongly
stupidity	stupefy	stupid	stupidly
(stupefaction)			

Words in parentheses illustrate special points of interest: *activate* is an *-ate*-suffix derivative of *active; strength* is a *-th*-suffix noun

derivative of **strong,** with a vowel change (parallel with **long, length**)*;*
stupefaction is an *-ation*-suffix noun derivative of **stupefy.**

Other families of contrasting forms may have odd numbers of
members, sometimes in only two word classes.

Noun	Verb	Adjective	Adverb
friend	befriend	friendly	
friendliness			
friendship			
good		good	
goodness		goodly	
indignation		indignant	indignantly
		long	
length	lengthen	lengthy	lengthily
relative	relate	relative	relatively
relation			

TEACHING SUGGESTION: Provide your students with
examples like these of word families as a basis for discussion
and exploration. Ask them to give sentences orally showing
how to use the various words in a single family. Students
may want to discover other families for themselves; given
sufficient interest, this activity can be the beginning of a term
or even a year project of linguistic investigation. (Chapter 6,
The Derivational Affixing System, would also be pertinent to
this work.)

TEACHING SUGGESTION: Any capable, motivated student, beginning about grade seven and including graduate
work, might enjoy doing part or all of the following exercise.

Make an oral or written report explaining the inadequacies
of one or more of the following definitions of word classes:

1. Noun. A noun is the name of a person, place or thing.
2. Verb. A verb expresses action or state of being.
3. Adjective. An adjective modifies a noun. Or, an adjective tells which one, what kind, how much, how many.

4. Adverb. An adverb modifies a verb, adjective, or another adverb. Or, an adverb tells how, when, where, or why.

(Many of the words that are indicated in 3. and 4. above are treated in descriptive grammars as structure words.)

Selected References

For references in addition to those cited in the Notes, see Selected References for Chapter 6, The Derivational Affixing System, and for Chapter 7, English Sentences.

Chapter 6

The Derivational Affixing System:
Prefixes and Suffixes

Consider this categorical syllogism:

a. Students who do well on vocabulary tests also do well in academic work.
b. The derivational affixing system is an important part of English "vocabulary."
c. Therefore, students who want to succeed academically should study a subject called "vocabulary," with special attention to derivational affixes.

No, quite the contrary. Strong control of vocabulary is best acquired by comprehending words in meaningful contexts, with access to a variety of dictionaries; students who do well academically and on vocabulary tests are usually successful readers who have mastered their textbooks and assigned readings and have read widely outside formal courses — *they have also learned how to write academic papers and examinations.* Such students often have educated parents and a home atmosphere conducive to good talk as well as wide reading: their versatile language development comes from a rich soil. It is very doubtful that the best way to duplicate their success is to attack vocabulary head on, as a "subject" in itself.

A study of the English affixing system, however, as a critically important element of the English language system as a whole, related functionally to reading, writing, and the study skills, would no doubt help many students to increase their mastery of the language. But apparently no comprehensive, sequential effort has ever been made to teach this language subsystem in the schools; it tends to be obscured in study of "vocabulary" and "word-attack" skills. And yet what a difference it might make if our students understood the affixing system and attained even a minimal mastery over it.

This chapter attempts to do three main tasks in a short space:

1. to interest teachers and prospective teachers in the principles and some of the fascinating details of the English derivational affixing system (the grammatical inflections are treated in Chapter 5);
2. to combine expository and reference functions by using a classification system that displays a varied wealth of linguistic principles and data relating to derivational prefixes and suffixes;
3. and to provide enough information and teaching suggestions to enable teachers and prospective teachers to motivate their own students to study and explore some of the processes of English derivational word-formation.

The remainder of this presentation appears under the following subdivisions; the classification referred to in item 2 above appears under the main heading: Classification of Derivational Affixes.

The Nature and Importance of the Derivational Affixing System
Bound and Free Morphemes
   THE QUICK AND THE DEAD
   A FEW QUICK ONES
Grade Level and Vocabulary Problems
Dictionaries and the Derivational Affixing System
   ABSTRACT FUNTIONS OF AFFIXING.
Classification of Derivational Affixes
   NOUN CLASS AFFIXING
      Noun-forming suffixes
      Noun suffixes
      Noun prefixes
   VERB CLASS AFFIXING
      Verb-forming suffixes
      Verb-forming prefixes
      Verb prefixes
   ADJECTIVE CLASS AFFIXING
      Adjective-forming suffixes
   ADVERB CLASS AFFIXING

The Nature and Importance of the Derivational Affixing System

The elaborately detailed English affixing system is so large and complex that it could be covered completely only in a full-scale linguistic investigation. Like the grammatical inflections, derivational affixes resemble structure words in their abstractness, or "emptiness" in de Saussure's sense (see pp. 112–13). But whereas the English grammatical inflections are very few, and we have only about three hundred structure words used in relatively limited ways, there are hundreds of derivational affixes used in thousands of ways. The derivational affixing system is fruitful ground for students to discover and explore for themselves.

English derivational prefixes and suffixes comprise an intricate system whereby word bases may be moved from one class to another, and meanings may be changed within classes; one of the many intricacies of this remarkable system is the unsettling fact that "the same suffix" may function in a number of different ways when combined with bases from the four word classes. The *-ant/-ent* pair of suffixes (identical in sound), make adjectives when added to certain verb bases, as in *defiant, observant,* and in *excellent, insistent;* but they also make nouns from other verb bases as in *occupant, servant,* and in *dependent, superintendent.* Similarly, *V-ing* verb forms function generally in adjective positions: *running water, sleeping children, warring factions* (participial adjectives); but certain *V-ing* forms have simply become full nouns (not gerunds): *covering, scaffolding;* and a few have developed special plural meanings: *earnings, makings.* These examples are merely illustrative.

An occasional affix may serve as both prefix and suffix. The common affix *-en* or *en-* can provide a better idea of the intricacy of the English affixing system. The *suffix -en* makes adjectives of nouns: *ashen, golden, woolen;* but it also makes verbs of nouns: *lengthen, heighten, strengthen;* and verbs of adjectives: *sweeten, harden, fasten;* moreover, *-en* is commonly an inflectional verb suffix: *broken, proven, taken;* and an irregular noun plural suffix inflection in *brethren, children, oxen,* with a side glance at *men* and *women.* This versatile bound morpheme also marks a number of diminutive forms of nouns: *maiden, kitten;* and then turns around and functions as a verb prefix in a number of senses: *enact, enable, encamp, encircle, encourage, entangle, entrain, enwrap.*

The *suffix -en,* added to the adjective *light,* forms the verb *lighten;* the *prefix en-,* added to *lighten,* forms another verb, *enlighten* (note also the *-er* suffix nouns of agency, *lightener* and *enlightener*). By further affixing, we form *enlightening, unenlightening,* and *enlightenment.* All these interrelated forms are also historically related to *lightning,* from the Middle English gerund of the verb *lightenen, to lighten* (note the double use of the *-en* suffix); *lightning* distributes in noun, verb, adjective and adverb positions, and takes the regular inflections of both nouns and verbs. Because of its complex system of branching and layering, this family of words is fabulously rich in forms and meanings attached to the base *light.* It is a fair sample of what the affixing system is like when you examine it closely.

TEACHING SUGGESTION: A bright, motivated high school student might enjoy making a report on the uses of the prefix *en-* and the suffix *-en;* or on some other interesting affix.

Bound and Free Morphemes

Bound and free morphemes were defined in Chapter 5, where it was pointed out that grammatical inflections and derivational affixes are all bound forms, and that word bases are generally free forms (see p. 116). Bound bases in English are often found, however, in words borrowed from other languages, Latin and Greek in particular. Examples of bound bases of Latin origin are *-cede* in *concede* and *precede;* or *-duce* in *conduce, deduce, induce, reduce;* these bases would not be used as free morphemes today except in the coinage of a new word or perhaps in a sophisticated wordplay; the same is true of the Greek base *-gram* on *diagram, epigram, program;* or *agon-* in *agony* and *protagonist.* The bound base *litho* (also *lith*) from the Greek *lithos,* meaning *stone,* is the trunk of an extensive family tree of English words. Two well-known members are *multilith* and *lithography,* for two printing processes; less known are *lithology,* the scientific study of stones, and *lithoid,* meaning *stonelike.*

TEACHING SUGGESTION: Some curious student might like to find out why a word base meaning *stone* is used in words designating printing processes. An even more curious student might like to investigate an odd word base that he has found for himself.

THE QUICK AND THE DEAD. As a topic to be taught in English and the language arts, word formation may be conveniently looked at in relation to two kinds of words: (1) words made up of free and bound morphemes that may be naturally manipulated by young native speakers today; and (2) words from ancient languages whose morphemes, generally, are fossilized in modern English; that is, both bases and affixes are bound. These borrowed words are interesting, significant, and altogether worthy of study, especially by volunteers in junior and senior high school; but before investigating these valuable fossils, students should understand the principles of affixing in relation to the common morphemes of the living language. Defined meaningfully for students, a morpheme in speech and writing is a word element that they can understand, use, and manipulate as a morpheme; the grammatical inflections and the common derivational prefixes and suffixes satisfy this definition, and so do the high-frequency bases with which they combine. These morphemes are the live ones; understanding them is the basis of understanding the fossils. *The distinction should be kept clear between the two kinds of morphemes: the quick and the dead.*

A FEW QUICK ONES. Many errors made by children and others learning English involve combining regular inflections as living morphemes with bases that take irregular changes of form. Until such speakers learn the exceptions, they are likely to invent such **V-ed** forms as *cutted, digged, drinked, singed* (*sang*), and *telled.* Similarly, they invent *N-s* forms like *childs, deers, mans, sheeps,* and *womans.* Such "errors" actually demonstrate mastery of important grammatical inflections; youngsters are also able to do much better than combine live inflections with bases that do not take them. Even a preschool child may chant this mischievous doggerel that plays on the noun suffix *-ity:*

> The very ideosity
> Of your curiosity —
> If I were your mother,
> I'd spank your bumbosity!

It also plays on "the very idea" and suggests childish curiosity that is improper to the point of spanking, reflecting more than linguistic sophistication.

We are all fond of the *-er/-or* suffix of agency that converts an action verb into a person (or "thing") that performs the action: *actor, batter, farmer, hunter, opener, pitcher, runner, shutter, swimmer, teacher.* This fondness for actors and action and a lively sense of rhythm and elliptical syntax — along with an acquisitive attitude — are involved in the familiar

Finders keepers, losers weepers.

In the jingle below, note the sharp sense of live morphemes required to enjoy ringing the changes on *-er* in the verb **utter** (**er** is a syllable but not a morpheme); in the noun **shutter** (*a thing that shuts*); in the comparative degree of the adjective, **shutter** (*more shut*); and the pun on the verb **shut** and the adjective **shut.**

> A woman to her son did utter
> Go, my son, and shut the shutter.
> The shutter's shut, the son did utter,
> I cannot shut it any shutter.[1]

Limericks are appealing for many reasons, including their heavily stressed rhyming words, their rambunctious meter, their linguistic tricks. One of my all-time favorites treats of one tutor tutoring two tooters to toot the flute.

> A tutor who tooted the flute
> Tried to tutor two tooters to toot.
> Said the two to the tutor:
> Is it harder to toot, or
> To tutor two tooters to toot?

This limerick just about exhausts the possibilities of the *-er/-or* suffix as a live morpheme, with one pun on *tutor* and *tooter;* another on *tutor* as a noun and as a verb; and a three-way pun on *tutor, tooter,* and *toot, or.* Moreover, there are numerous sight-and-sound gags on *to, two, toot,* and *tut-; to toot, to tutor; one tutor, two tooters; to* as a phrase marker and as an infinitive marker (*to-V*); and *two* as noun marker and as a noun substitute.

A sportsman explaining how he happened to miss, may say, "When he *zigged,* I *zagged.*" This versatile piece of good humor applies to hunting game birds and animals, and to team sports like basketball, football, hockey, lacrosse, and soccer. The linguistic part of the humor involves splitting the verb *zigzag* and treating each half as a verb base having regular **V-ed** forms. Speakers who say this are quite conscious of the living quality of the bound and free morphemes of a rather unlikely verb, zigging and zagging at will.

Some of the wittiest puns depend upon a keen sense of the qualities of live morphemes. A play on the adjective suffixes *-ed* and *-y,* for example, gives the definition of prisoner as "a bird in a *guilty* cage." Awareness of the abstract sense of the suffix *-al,* accompanied by a play on the meanings of bound *-but* in *rebut* and the free form *butt,* gives the definition of *rebuttal* as "being knocked down twice by the same goat." A literal interpretation of the three separate morphemes of *un-utter-able* is the basis for defining *unutterable* as "a thought for which the words haven't been invented yet." The irregular noun plural inflection *-en,* combined with the unique spelling and pronunciation of the bound base *wom-,* enabled a masculine wit to define *women* as the plural of *whim;* this pun also depends on the fact that many speakers have no /h/ represented in *wh-* spellings.[2]

Special speech communities, teenagers and college students, for example, have invented terms using freewheeling bases and affixes. *Bugology* is an ancient play on *biology. Bird-dogging* is a coined *V-ing* form for "masculine reconnaissance and inspection of the feminine population." *Hawking* is a synonym for *bird-dogging; mickeymousing* is a term for juvenile behavior. From *flush* meaning "to cancel a date," *flushogram* is derived, the form of communication often used by a co-ed to announce the cancellation. Such terms vary from campus to campus and from year to year; any investigator is likely to discover new ones.[3]

Interesting boners may be based, innocently or with intent to kill, upon fractured relationships of bound and free morphemes. The free form *true,* for example, combined with the bound suffix *-ancy,* yields "something proved to be true" as the definition of *truancy;* and the combining form *trans-* meaning *cross* gives "a cross father" as the definition of *transparent.* It is not clear to me just what kind of linguistic shenanigans spurred some malefactor to define **union suit** as **under-overalls.** *Monogamy* and *polygamy,* by false analogy with geometrical terms, enabled one errant inventor to define *trigonometry* as "when a lady married three men at the same time." [4] The possibilities for this kind of linguistic play in English are virtually limitless.

TEACHING SUGGESTION: Manipulation of living morphemes can offer many opportunities for linguistic fun having valuable ramifications in language development. Begin a class discussion of this topic with your students and explore it orally with them; fractured French and German might offer a basis for an approach to fractured English; many limericks and nonsense verses involve playing with morphemes. The follow-up might be compiling glossaries, writing compositions, or writing limericks and other nonsense verse for oral presentation; the students themselves may have the best suggestions for your particular class.

Grade Level and Vocabulary Problems

Grade level alone is a very poor indicator of the difficulty of the vocabulary students are asked to handle; a comparison of vocabularies used in textbooks in different subjects for the same grade, or in textbooks in the same subject published by different companies, will show little agreement. My general impression, however, is that textbooks place a heavy burden of vocabulary and concepts on the students' shoulders, in addition to needless syntactical ineptitude and complexity. Listed below are *selected examples of key words used in mathematics and science textbooks for the middle grades;* the meaning and structure of many of these terms could be clarified by some discussion of bases and affixes in meaningful contexts.

TEACHING SUGGESTION: These terms also appear in textbooks used in high school and college; many college students cannot define them and use them in sentences. As a means of opening a class discussion of affixes, present a selection appropriate to your students. Students can group words having some of the same morphemes as an inductive approach to generalizations.

SCIENCE, GRADE THREE: axis, chlorophyll, chemical change, evaporation, carnivore, herbivore, equator, hemisphere, glacier, penicillin, fulcrum, molecule, nocturnal, satellite, telescope, sediment, lubricate, protective coloration, communicate, invisible, radar, sonar, vocal cords.

MATHEMATICS, GRADE THREE: remainder, difference, regroup, fraction, multiplication, division, line segment, triangle, rectangle, square, degree, graph, cube, sphere.

SCIENCE, GRADE FOUR: atmosphere, biosphere, hydrosphere, lithosphere, arteries, bacteria, cohesion, frequency, oxidation, combustion, capillaries, hydroelectric, turbine, refraction, translucent, resource management, visibility, water table, water cycle, wavelength.

MATHEMATICS, GRADE FOUR: sets, parentheses, fractions, fractional numbers, unit of measure, quotient, ray, figure, angle, right triangle, diameter, plane, bar graph, line graph, denominator, numerator.

SCIENCE, GRADE FIVE: electron, neutron, nucleon, proton, atom, molecule, symbol, formula, electrolysis, electrolyte, metamorphic, seismograph, paleontologist, photosynthesis, paper chromatography, inertia, momentum, amplitude, hypersonic, subsonic, ultrasonic, tropism, hydrotropism, phototropism, friction, rolling friction, sliding friction.

MATHEMATICS, GRADE FIVE: inverse, divisor, dividend, pictograph, point of intersection, polygon, quadrilateral, rectangular prism, radius, latitude, longitude, meridian, perimeter, ratio.

SCIENCE, GRADE SIX: atmosphere, convection current, exosphere, ionosphere, mesosphere, stratosphere, troposphere, ozone, ultraviolet rays, cumulonimbus, anemometer, hygrometer, psychrometer, potential energy, motor neuron, sensory neuron, protozoans, fission, diffusion, electric emission, photoelectric emission.

MATHEMATICS, GRADE SIX: digit, cardinal number, ordinal number, exponent, subscript, reciprocals, annexing zeros, vertices, arc, negative numbers, prime number, composite numbers, man-hours, passenger-miles, light-years.

Dictionaries and the Derivational Affixing System

Unless they are carefully guided, many students will never discover that dictionaries carry prefixes and suffixes among their alphabetical entries, using a hyphen to indicate the "bound" nature of each affix: *a hyphen* **before** *a suffix, a hyphen* **after** *a prefix*. Thus, **ability** is a noun and **-ability** a suffix used to form nouns from adjectives ending in **-able: capability** and **dependability** (**ability** in the first place is a noun formed from the adjective **able**). Similarly, **be** is the base form of the most versatile verb in English, and **be-** is a prefix used to form verbs from noun bases: **bedevil** and **bewitch,** for instance.

Dictionaries vary somewhat in their definitions of affixes and greatly in their selection of affixes to define and illustrate in detail; one dictionary may ignore an affix that another defines carefully and illustrates with a goodly list of words. On affixing as well as other questions of definition and examples, students should consult a number of dictionaries, always including Webster's Third New International edition. Teachers can very profitably pursue their own investigations of affixing. Students can be encouraged to explore the resources and operations of English affixing as a regular part of their academic work, with special reference to reading, writing, and formal speaking.

TEACHING SUGGESTION: An interested high school student might enjoy comparing the treatment of selected affixes in Webster's Second and Third New International editions;

many students in lower grades may profit from making comparisons among desk dictionaries at various grade levels.

ABSTRACT FUNCTIONS OF AFFIXING. Definitions of affixes are necessarily abstract because their linguistic functions are abstract. Affixes are commonly defined in such terms as these:

-acy	*— class:*	magistracy
	— state, quality:	accuracy
-cy	*— action, practice:*	mendicancy
-ance	*— amount* or *degree:*	conductance, impedance
	— act or *fact of* _____*ing* (V-ing):	avoidance
	— a thing that _____*s* (V-s):	conveyance
	— state of being _____*ed* (V-ed):	annoyance
	— what is _____*ed* (V-ed):	contrivance
-age	*— aggregate* or *collection:*	stumpage, trackage
	— condition or *status of:*	dotage, peerage
	— cumulative result of:	breakage

Given the taste for it, or sheer ability to handle such verbal abstractions, many students can enjoy playing with such definitions, but play cannot be compulsory. Definitions of affixes serve best as a means to familiarity in practical uses: reading, writing, listening, speaking, thinking. It is far more important for students to acquire a concrete sense of English affixing through exposure, imitation, manipulation, than to memorize any part of an elaborate system of abstract definitions.

Classification of Derivational Affixes

Affixes may be classified in several ways; but for the sake of convenience and uniformity, they are classified here according to the four word classes: noun, verb, adjective, adverb.

Following are examples of "noun-class affixing." Some suffixes combine with a base to form a word of another class: *-age* combines with the verb **break** to make the noun **breakage**; *-dom* combines with the adjective *free* to make the noun *freedom*. Other suffixes combine with a base to affect the meaning of a word that remains a member of the same word class: *-age* combines with the noun *mile* to give the noun *mileage.* Only a few prefixes change a word from one class to another; prefixes generally affect the meaning of a base without affecting the word class as such: *mis-* combines with the noun *adventure* to make the noun *misadventure,* or with the noun *conduct* to make the noun *misconduct; re-* combines with the noun *appearance* to make the noun *reappearance* (*appearance* having been formed by combining the verb *appear* with the suffix *-ance*). This general method of classification will be followed in the presentation of the affixing system for each of the four word classes under the following headings:

NOUN CLASS AFFIXING
  Noun-forming suffixes
  Noun suffixes
  Noun prefixes
VERB CLASS AFFIXING
  Verb-forming suffixes
  Verb-forming prefixes
  Verb prefixes
ADJECTIVE CLASS AFFIXING
  Adjective-forming suffixes
ADVERB CLASS AFFIXING

TEACHING SUGGESTION: In order to help your students with affixing and vocabulary development, it is wise to survey the vocabulary requirements in the texts in all subjects taught at your grade level; some of them will have word lists or glossaries that you can consult; livewire students can also help themselves by helping you in this project. The benefits of such a practical basis for this kind of study should be self-evident to your students. See pp. 146–48.

NOUN CLASS AFFIXING

Noun-forming suffixes

Suffixes added to **verb** bases: *-age, -ance/-ence* (same sound); *-ant/ -ent* (same sound); *-ation/-ion* (choice depends on final sound of verb base); *-er/-or* (same sound); *-ment; -ing, -ory, -th.*

-age:

breakage	leakage	postage

-ance/-ence (same sound, different spelling)

-ance:

acceptance	appearance	attendance	assurance
admittance	compliance	ignorance	reliance
repentance			

-ence:

difference	dependence	emergence	existence

-ant/-ent (same sound, different spelling)

-ant:

accountant	occupant	servant

-ent:

dependent	solvent	superintendent

-ation/-ion (mainly **-tion** endings, the choice depending on the final sound of the verb base)

-ation:

civilization	combination	examination	flirtation
imagination			

-ion:

abdication	anticipation	appreciation	completion
construction	cooperation	correction	discussion
interruption	selection	suggestion	

-er/-or (same sound, different spelling)

-er:

buyer	doer	helper	learner
runner	teacher	worker	

(a very large and important class)

-or:

actor	competitor	creditor	distributor
donor	elevator	grantor	governor
juror	refractor	sailor	survivor

-ment:

adjustment	amusement	assignment	attachment
employment	establishment	excitement	government
management	movement	shipment	treatment

-ing:

covering	doings	earnings	goings on
makings			

-ory:

crematory	directory	dormitory	lavatory
observatory			

-th:

health *	growth	stealth *

Suffixes added to **adjective** bases: *-acy/-cy, -dom, -ery, -hood, -ism, -ist, -ity/-ty, -ness, -ship, -th.*

-acy/-cy:

accuracy	bankruptcy	democracy	expediency
fluency	secrecy	vacancy	

-dom:

freedom	wisdom

-ery:

bravery	drollery	finery

-hood:

falsehood	hardihood	likelihood

-ism:

Americanism	Briticism	nationalism	socialism

-ist:

Alpinist	rationalist	royalist	socialist

-ity/-ty:

actuality	clarity	cruelty	entirety
novelty	safety	versatility	

-ness:

awareness	coolness	darkness	fierceness
gladness	goodness	happiness	kindness
mildness	politeness	promptness	selfishness
sickness	sweetness	tardiness	tiredness
weakness	willingness		

-ship (rare):

hardship

-th:

breadth *	(broad)	dearth *	(dear)
depth *	(deep)	length *	(long)
strength *	(strong)	truth	warmth
width *	(wide)		

* with vowel change

Noun suffixes

Suffixes *affecting the meaning* of **noun** bases: *-age, -hood, -ing, -man, -woman, -ness, -ship.*

-age:

| acreage | cooperage | lineage | mileage |

-hood:

| adulthood | boyhood | brotherhood | childhood |
| girlhood | manhood | womanhood | parenthood |

-ing:

| boating | canoeing | scaffolding | shirting |

-man/-woman

-man:

| anchorman | cattleman | horseman | seaman |
| shipman | workman | | |

-woman:

| horsewoman | cattlewoman |

-ness:

| boatness | dogness | (and like coinages) |

-ship:

| friendship | horsemanship | kingship | seamanship |
| workmanship | marksmanship | | |

Noun prefixes

Prefixes *affecting the meaning* of **noun** bases: *down-, ex-, mis-, out-, over-, pre-, re-, sub-, super-, tele-, trans-, under-, up-.*

down-:

| downbeat | downdraft | downside | downstairs |

ex-:

| ex-boyfriend | ex-girlfriend | ex-champion | ex-husband |
| ex-marine | ex-soldier | ex-teacher | ex-wife |

mis-:

| misadventure | misbehavior | misconduct | misfit |

out-:

| outbox | outcropping | outgrowth |

over-:

| overanxiety | overcoat | overgrowth | overeagerness |

pre-:
| preadulthood | preconcert | precondition | |

re-:
| realignment | reappearance | reconfirmation | rededication |
| redivision | renomination | | |

sub-:
| sub-basement | subclass | subclerk | subfloor |
| subset | | | |

super:
superbelief	superbias	superbomb	supercargo
supercarrier	superhighway	superman	supermarket
(superette)	superpower		

tele-:
| teletype | television | televisor | |

trans-:
| transaction | transcription | transformation | transshipment |
| transfiguration | | | |

under-:
| underachiever | underarm | underbelly | underdog |
| underclothes | | | |

up-:
| upbeat | updraft | upcountry | upland |
| upkeep | upside | upstairs | |

VERB CLASS AFFIXING

Verb-forming suffixes

Suffixes added to **noun** bases: *-ate, -en, -ify/-fy, -ize/-ise* (*-ize* and *-ise* are often alternate spellings, but in some words one is standard).

-ate:
| assassinate | chlorinate | evaporate | refrigerate |
| vaccinate | | | |

-en:
| hearten | heighten | lengthen | strengthen |

-ify/-fy:
| beautify | citify | classify | dandify |
| glorify | liquefy | | |

-ize/-ise:

Americanize	atomize	burglarize	crystallize
galvanize	sympathize		

Suffixes added to **adjective** bases: *-en, -fy/-ify, -ize/-ise.*

-en:

blacken	darken	deepen	harden
roughen	shorten	weaken	whiten

-fy/-ify:

clarify	Frenchify	simplify

-ize/-ise:

finalize	immortalize	realize	sterilize
vitalize			

Verb-forming prefixes

Prefixes added to **noun** bases: *ac-, be-, de-, em-/im-, en-/in-, un-.*
(The *em-/im-,en-/in-* prefixes may be used interchangeably as variants in certain words.)

ac-:

accompany	accustom	acknowledge

be-:

bedevil	bedew	befriend	behead
bejewel	bewitch		

de-:

debunk	deflea	degerm	delouse
deplane	dethrone	derail	

em-/im-:

embark	embody	embosom	embowel
embower	empower		

en-/in-:

encamp	encircle	entrain

un-:

unbelt	unbonnet	unbosom	unbrace
uncap	unchurch	unfrock	unhair
unhorse			

Verb prefixes

Prefixes that *affect the meaning* of **verb** bases: *dis-, de-, en-, mis-, out-, over-, pre-, re-, super-, tele-, trans-, un-, under-, up-.*

dis-:

disabuse	disagree	disappoint	disapprove
disarm	disembowel	disorganize	

de-:

deactivate	debrief	decentralize	decode
desegregate			

en-:

enact	encompass

mis-:

miscopy	misfile	misguess	misguide
mishear	misinform	mislabel	mislay
mislead	misplace	misspeak	misteach
mistreat	misunderstand		

out-:

outbox	outdo	outgun	outplay
outrun	outshoot	outtalk	

over-:

overact	overcook	overeat	overreact
overshoot	overwork		

pre-:

preconfirm	precook	precool	preheat
preregister			

re-:

realign	reappear	reapply	rebuild
recopy	redo	redraw	relearn
reteach	rewrite		

super-:

superintend	supervise

tele-:

telecast	telegraph	telephone	telephotograph (*-y, -ic*)
teletype	teletypewrite	televise	

trans-:

transact	transcribe	transfigure	transfix
transform	transplant	transship	

un-:

unbalance	unbend	unbind	unclasp
unclench	uncoil	undo	unleash
unwind	unwrap	unzip	

under-:

underachieve	underbid	undercut	undergo
underpay			

up-:

update	upend	uphold	uplift
upset	upstage		

ADJECTIVE CLASS AFFIXING *

Adjective-forming suffixes

Suffixes added to **noun** bases: *-able, -al, -an, -ar, -ary, -ate, -ed, -en, -ful, -ic/-ical, -ine, -ish, -less, -like, -ly, -ous, -some, -y.*

-able:

answerable *	comfortable *	knowledgeable *	lovable *
objectionable *	saleable		

-al:

accidental *	continental	departmental *	global *
national *	optional *	regional *	

-an:

American	Australian	Canadian	diocesan
European	Mexican		

-ar:

circular *	consular	linear *	molecular
oracular *	polar	rectangular *	spectacular *

-ary:

customary *	functionary	honorary	visionary

-ate:

collegiate	passionate *	roseate	temperate *

* Denotes availability of *-ly* adverb suffix.

-ed (analagous with **V-ed/en**):

armed	bearded	bellied	bigoted
cultured	eyed	headed	hearted
legged	moneyed	mouthed	sugared
toothed	tongued	versed	

-en:

ashen	earthen	oaken	wooden *
woolen			

-ful:

beautiful *	careful *	harmful *	helpful *
joyful *	masterful *	painful *	playful *
woeful *			

(*-less* often makes antonyms with these, but not invariably.)

-ic/-ical:

allergic	alcoholic	amoebic	angelic
angelical *	Byronic	economic	economical *
historic	historical *	homeric	ironic
ironical *	poetic	poetical *	

(Often an important difference in meaning depends upon the choice of *-ic* or *-ical*; for example, *economic, economical*; *historic, historical*.)

-ine:

adamantine	asinine	crystalline	heroine
leonine	opaline		

(Note also *-ine/-ene,* a feminine combining form in many names: **Adrienne, Angeline, Bernadine, Charlene, Clementine, Georgene, Pauline,** etc.)

-ish:

bookish *	boyish *	devilish *	Finnish
British	Danish	English	Spanish
freakish *	girlish *	mulish *	

and a group having a generally deprecatory sense:

babyish *	childish *	mannish *	womanish *

-less:

armless	childless	motherless	fatherless
deathless *	faithless *	headless	homeless *
hopeless *	lifeless	peerless *	penniless *
pitiless *	valueless	witless *	

* Denotes availability of *-ly* adverb suffix.

-like:

catlike	childlike	doglike	fishlike
lifelike	wavelike		

-ly:

beastly	fatherly	motherly	sisterly
brotherly	daily	hourly	weekly
monthly	yearly	godly	saintly

-ous:

bulbous *	clamorous *	dangerous *	famous *
glamorous *	glorious *	joyous *	nervous *
omnivorous *	poisonous *	sonorous *	wondrous *

-some:

awesome	burdensome	quarrelsome	troublesome

-y:

arty *	beggary	blossomy	chilly
cloudy *	curly	dirty	dusky
healthy *	homey	icy *	muddy
rainy	snowy	stagy *	watery
wavy			

(Note also the *-y* diminutives: **Billy, Bobby, Joany, Tommy, Willy; horsy, kitty, puppy, pussy,** etc.)

Suffixes added to **verb** bases: *-able/-ible, -ant/-ent, -ed, -ful, -ing, -ive, -less, -ory, -some, -y.*

-able/-ible:

adaptable *	breakable	collectible	corruptible *
definable *	drinkable	get-at-able	insurable
learnable	obtainable	perishable	resistible
reversible			

-ant/-ent

-ant:

ambulant *	defiant *	expectorant	observant *
radiant *	reliant *	somnambulant	

-ent:

excellent *	different *	insistent *	provident *
transcendent *			

* Denotes availability of *-ly* adverb suffix.

-ed:
amused *   daunted *   faded *   inflated *

(Mainly the adjective use of **V-ed** forms)

-ful:
forgetful *   harmful *   helpful *   resentful *
wakeful *

-ing: (mainly the adjective use of **V-ing** forms)
doting *   loving *   running *   sleeping *
warring *

-ive:
abusive *   active *   conclusive *   corrective *
creative *   destructive *   disruptive *   permissive *
prohibitive *   sportive *   submissive *

-less:
countless *   dauntless *   fadeless *   relentless *
tireless *

-ory:
congratulatory   contributory   prohibitory

-some:
cuddlesome   cumbersome   loathsome

-y:
chatty *   clingy *   drowsy *   sticky *

ADVERB CLASS AFFIXING

In addition to what has already been said about the availability of the adverbial *-ly* suffix in the foregoing presentation, we should note that some adverbs are made by adding certain suffixes to various bases: *-time/-times; -ward/-wards; -way/-ways/-wise;* and *-where.* Many of these words may also be distributed in adjective positions, and some as nouns.

-time/-times:
anytime   daytime/s   dinnertime/s   mealtime/s
nighttime   sometime/s

* Denotes availability of *-ly* adverb suffix.

DEFINING THE SENTENCE IN THE CLASSROOM. Beginning in the primary years, it is helpful to teach that a written or printed sentence begins with a capital letter and ends with a period, except when it ends with a question mark or exclamation point.

> *I know a bank where the wild thyme blows.*
> *What on earth is thyme?*
> *It's not time!*

It is also helpful to teach that in speech and oral reading a sentence usually ends with a fall in pitch and a fading out of the voice (fade-fall terminal); but lesser structures may also be terminated in the same way, sometimes *within* sentences as spoken by many Americans. And while some questions are terminated by a rise in voice pitch, many end normally with a fade–fall terminal; the following, for example:

> *What is your name?   Where are you going?   What time is it?*

These and related points are discussed in greater detail in Chapter 9, American English Intonation.

Someone may have taught us that every sentence must have a subject and predicate; yet commands and requests — imperatives — notoriously lack visible subjects, which we may have been taught are "understood."

> *Give up.   Drop dead.   Cool it.*

The trouble with understood elements is, the teacher understands them but the students don't. And Miss Fidditch strongly disapproves the innumerable "incomplete sentences" that occur in everyday conversations, and in printed dialogues.

> *Where did you go?   Out.   What did you do?   Nothing.*

DEPENDENT AND INDEPENDENT SENTENCES. The concept of dependent and independent sentences is pertinent here. An independent sentence may (a) initiate discourse or (b) occur in discourse without ambiguity or the need for a defining context. Conversely, a dependent sentence may not (a) initiate discourse or (b) occur in discourse without ambiguity or the need for a defining context. The word *conversely* in the last sentence is an essential link to the previous sentence and thus makes the last sentence dependent; without the word *conversely*, however, it could be independent. This is only one of several types of dependent sentences that have been defined;[3] but for our purposes, only a general definition is needed. Both dependent and independent sentences may be structurally complete or structurally incomplete.

Following are examples of dependent sentences that are structurally incomplete; any of them might be an effective part of a well-written paragraph.

Hardly.	*Out of sight, out of mind.*
The arrogance of it!	*What a man!*
Full circle.	*Without a doubt.*
A poor gamble.	*The sooner the better.*
Not this time.	*No hero he.*

In the next examples, a verb is needed to supply an action referent.

I would.	*You will in time.*
We all do.	*They would if they could.*
He should.	

Competent writers frequently treat expanded noun elements without verbs as sentences; such sentences are structurally incomplete, yet independent.

The sleepy little town of Eggsville, Pennsylvania; one plain dirt street of row houses, with a refrigerated storage building alongside an unused railroad siding on the edge of town.

This is a perfectly good description.

DEFINITION BY ASSOCIATION. So we see it is not helpful to insist, as some teachers still do, that every sentence must have a subject and a predicate, and must also "express a complete thought." Rather than attempt to lay down an abstract verbal prescription that means little or nothing to the learner, it is preferable to allow him, over a generous period of time, to develop his own inductive definition of **sentence** by associating the term with varied examples of sentences with common components. In fact, defining linguistic terms by association with a variety of well-chosen examples is the teaching method of choice — even in courses in linguistics or grammar as formal disciplines, where examples must also be used to flesh out the bare bones of formal definitions.

TEACHING SUGGESTION: Try an inductive method of approaching a definition of a sentence; introduce dependent and independent sentences, structurally complete and structurally incomplete sentences. Depend upon examples rather than verbal definitions. Use examples from the foregoing section, or make up more suitable examples. Begin with oral examples; see how far the students are able to go. One good follow-up would be exploration of the use of such sentences in published writing, including poems; oral or written reports might be shared with classmates.

Forecast: A Summary of Methods

In a textbook like this, the language must be divided into topics treated separately in different chapters; but in teaching English and the language arts, concentration on any single topic for a long period would be ineffectual, and concentration on the formal side of grammar and linguistics inappropriate. We are concerned in the classroom with language study in a broader and deeper sense than that. One of the specific aims of our teaching is to nurture growth toward maturity in the learner's personal handling of English, both spoken and written; lessons should provide many opportunities for oral work, even when the main concern may be a point of grammar or sentence structure. So far as feasible in any given lesson, presentation of sentence patterns should include incidental references to other topics, particularly structure words (Chapter 7), word-form changes (grammatical inflections, Chapter 5), derivational suffixes and prefixes (Chapter 6), and intonation (Chapter 9).

The remainder of this *Summary of Methods* is presented under four subheadings:

THE SIMPLEST BASIC PATTERNS FIRST
EXPANSIONS OF NOUN AND VERB PARTS
REDUCTION OF CLAUSES AND PHRASES
PATTERN VARIATIONS AND TRANSFORMATIONS

THE SIMPLEST BASIC PATTERNS FIRST. A sequential treatment of sentences begins with the simplest basic patterns, using single words at first in each sentence part: *Cats / like / milk* or *Dogs / like / bones;* or sentences with very simple articles and auxiliary verbs: *The cat / is drinking / her milk* or *The dog / is chewing / his bone.* In early pattern work with isolated, single sentences, it is desirable to use simple auxiliary verbs as soon as possible, or past verb forms; in modern American English, present verb forms are rather uncommon, except in defining contexts, perhaps because their meanings tend toward generality and abstraction. As an opening remark, *Cats like milk* sounds more like a philosopher talking than a child speaking spontaneously.

EXPANSIONS OF NOUN AND VERB PARTS. After introductory work with very simple sentence patterns, expansions may be introduced, first the expansion of **Noun part,** or complete subject, with adjectives: *The black cat / . . .* or *The little dog / . . . .* Next, expansions with prepositional phrases: *The cat on the bed / . . .* or *The dog in the manger /. . . .* Then, expansions with simple clauses: *The cat that swallowed the canary / . . .* or *The dog that talks / . . . .* Finally, Noun parts may be expanded with combinations of two or more of these elements: *The little dog in the manger that talks in his sleep / . . . .* Even though it may take a child several years to become fluent in these expansions, they are among the most elementary manipulative operations; such oral and written practice can help very much to develop sentence sense, a feeling for the basic pattern that carries the heart of the message.

The second kind of expansion usually will be of **Verb parts** (verb groups or phrases), not of complete predicates including objects and complements. As with expansion of Noun parts, at first single words will be used — adverbs in Verb parts; next, adverb groups, including prepositional phrases; then simple clauses; and finally combinations of two or more of these elements. Much of this work should be oral as well as written. Examples of expansions of **Verb parts** will be displayed in a later section of this chapter.

REDUCTION OF CLAUSES AND PHRASES. Just as all the foregoing practice may be taught spirally, with returns to the same processes at ever higher levels, so may the more formal and sophisticated aspects of style and rhetoric; much of this latter work will be written, but written compositions can be strengthened and improved as a result of critical oral reading. Most of the foregoing kinds of practice tend to increase the length of sentences, which is desirable up to a point; but it is also desirable to teach processes of reduction of clauses and phrases for revising and rewriting simple patterns, by means other than simple-minded combinations of entire sentences and sentence elements.

For example: *The reading teacher evaluates her students' growth. She gives them a variety of reading tests. She measures their reading speed. She measures their reading comprehension. She measures their vocabulary development.*

Revised by reduction and combination: *The reading teacher evaluates her students' growth by various tests: tests of speed, of comprehension, of vocabulary development.*

This kind of practice tends to produce the shorter and more dense sentences that are characteristic of a mature English writing style; it can also help to develop ability to read more mature books and articles with adequate comprehension.

PATTERN VARIATIONS AND TRANSFORMATIONS. Following work on expansion and reduction of pattern parts, the basic declarative patterns may be varied by pattern inversion, substitution within pattern parts, and active/passive transformations; patterns of requests and commands may also be introduced, and various question patterns. Beyond this imitative and manipulative practice, sequentially and spirally presented at different levels of difficulty at different grade levels, the patterns may be augmented and varied by manipulating movable elements: prepositional phrases, clauses; and compounding and appositive elements in introductory, medial, and final positions. All such elements may be studied, imitated, and consciously manipulated by the learner, both orally and in writing. Increasing maturity in handling sentences will involve more complex **Noun** and **Verb parts**; more sophisticated structure words; and more complex vocabulary, reflecting greater control of derivational prefixes and suffixes, as well as more advanced concepts.

The final section of this chapter, **Techniques of Exposure, Imitation, Practice, Manipulation,** illustrates many of the foregoing topics; for more extended and detailed treatments, refer to items under Lefevre in Selected References at the end of this chapter.

Some Practical First Approaches

Even in primary teaching, it is not only possible but desirable to begin early to work on the whole sentence. In addition to beginning with a capital letter and ending with a period, a handwritten or printed sentence uses many other signals to clue the reader in on its meaning. Probably the most important signal is word order, or the order of main sentence parts. Normal English sentence order is subject-predicate, with the words in the following order.

A bird is singing.

But note the structural features of this sentence that will occur over and over again:

A ____ is ____-ing.

This sentence begins with the noun marker (determiner or article) *A;* it is crucial not to confuse this structure word with the letter *a* or *A* in primary language arts instruction, and also never to study it by itself, but always with a noun. The child should be taught to say it quickly, with a light stress, while giving a main stress to the noun that follows it: *a bird.* This sentence also uses a very common verb group for present action, the *is* form of *be* marking the present participle of a verb; a formula for this verb group might be **is V-ing.**

The child does not need the terminology and apparatus displayed in the foregoing paragraph, at least not at the very first; structural generalizations should be approached inductively, by examples. But attention should be called to the following structural features: the order of *A bird* and *is singing;* the word combinations and stress patterns of *A bird* (above) and of *is singing* (where the main stress is on **sing-,** and **is** receives a light stress); and the verb group pattern, **is** ___-**ing.** Attention should also be called to the rhythm of the whole sentence, with two main stresses on **bird** and **sing-,** and two light stresses on **A** and **is,** followed by a falling or dropping of the voice at the period. Normally the light stress on the -**ing** verb inflection will occur naturally, and can be passed by without comment.

À bírd ìs sínging. ↘

All this can be done very quickly by the oral example of the teacher, which the children can easily imitate. They can then volunteer other nouns and verbs to fill the same positions as **bird** and **sing-.** Using experience chart methods already familiar to the class, the teacher can write the children's examples on the board.

A boy	*is singing.* ↘
A boy	*is running.* ↘
A girl	*is dancing.* ↘
A man	*is talking.* ↘
A teacher	*is reading.* ↘

And so on.

By similar steps and methods, other noun markers, such as **the, my, one** may be introduced; the plural verb marker **are;** and then the tense markers **was** and **were,** along with plural noun inflection, -**s.** For example,

Two girls	*are dancing.* ↘
Two ___-*s*	*are* ___-*ing.* ↘

The children can then give their examples of this sentence pattern orally, and the teacher can write them on the board as before.

The foregoing very simple examples are basic and primary illustrations of readily available means of incorporating learnings pertinent to sentence sense from the very beginning of language arts instruction. The techniques and methods suggested also preview the more detailed materials to follow in this chapter, and show how various structural elements may be introduced incidentally into the study of sentences. These suggestions may be adapted by teachers at any level of primary-elementary language arts instruction, and adapted to remedial work in English wherever it is needed.

TEACHING SUGGESTION: According to your class and its needs, adapt the above lesson and try it out. You may easily substitute more appropriate elements for those presented, as well as expand them if you like, following the suggestions on pp. 181–86.

The remainder of this discussion of **Some Practical First Approaches** is presented under two headings:

A FIRST GRADE CLASSROOM PROJECT
SCRAMBLED SENTENCES

A FIRST GRADE CLASSROOM PROJECT. This section is based on a project report given by one of my graduate students in my course, Linguistics for Classroom Teachers.[4] This project is one of hundreds developed in my classes by experienced teachers; their work supports the statement that many of my recommendations are based upon classroom experience.

The originator of this project had taught primary language arts for many years before attending a two-week summer institute in applied English linguistics. The institute included a series of lectures, daily discussions with other teacher-participants, and study of two textbooks then in trial editions.[5] In a follow-up course, this teacher accepted suggestions about techniques and materials and adapted them to her first grade class. Her approach to the project was one of open-minded interest and good humor, disciplined by hard-boiled scepticism; she closely approximated the ideal investigator.

Before presenting the outline of her oral report, let me quickly call some points of interest to your attention:

1. The clearly stated aim for the project.
2. Introduction of "difficult" concepts in terms suitable for Grade 1.
   a. The concept of patterns in general.
   b. The concept of sentence patterns, at first not differentiating word classes (parts of speech) from the corresponding sentence parts.
   c. Use of the nomenclature of **Noun, Verb, Adjective,** and **Adverb,** with their abbreviated symbols, **N, V, A, Ad** — but with only a few traces of conventional verbalism, rote memorization, or attempted applications of verbal formulations.

3. Correlation of much oral work, manipulations by the children of cards on the peg board, and dittoed handwritten worksheets.
4. Use of the discovery method as the basic technique, with the children themselves as informants, reaching their own generalized conclusions.
5. Encouragement of, and professional exploitation of, the children's natural excitement and enjoyment in exploring language.

The following outline with notes for an oral report is edited only in minor details; the italics for emphasis and comments in brackets are my additions.

First Grade Classroom Project

Aim: *To develop sentence sense* through the concept of basic sentence patterns, in order to improve reading and creative writing at the *First Grade level.*

Methods and Materials

1. **Use of patterns:** I showed the children that we have design patterns in art and rhythm patterns in music. Similarly, there are sentence *patterns in language.*
[She displayed such motifs as the fleur de lis and paisley design; the music illustrations were demonstrated in songs and piano melodies.]

2. **Eliciting oral examples of sentences:** After a simple explanation of a sentence, I tried to draw simple sentences from the children but got such examples as *Come, Tim.. Oh, look. Sometimes when my daddy comes home from work, he plays with me.*
[The first two examples reflect the language of basal pre-primers and primers, and show how insidious its effect can be. The third example is very good as a sentence, but not applicable to introductory work on sentence patterns.]
Therefore I gave *simple illustrations*, which they followed quickly with similar examples, such as *Spot runs. Birds fly. Mother cooks.*

3. **Meaning and function of nouns:** I explained nouns simply, gave some *examples* orally, and asked the children to give their own *examples.* Then I gave *additional examples*, mixing other parts of speech with the nouns. The children raised their hands when the word I said was a noun. *We made a game of this and did much oral work.*

4. **Meaning, function, and "look" of verbs and other word classes:** The same procedure was followed as was used for nouns. I made colored cards and introduced a color code for the four main form classes — nouns on blue cards; verbs on orange cards; adjectives on yellow cards; adverbs on green cards.

   [Some of the lectures featured projectuals showing sentences in a similar color code; many other teachers also found the use of color for grammatical analysis to be interesting to the children, and helpful.]

5. **Developing the N V sentence pattern:** I suggested putting a noun and verb together, using the simple sentences introduced earlier — *Spot runs. Birds fly. Mother cooks. The children discovered a sentence had been formed in this way, and the N V pattern.* We thought of the nouns as the *actors* and the verbs as the *action.*

   [The notion of an English sentence as having an actor first, an action second, and even a consequence or result third, may be helpful in introducing basic sentence patterns. It can be overdone, however, or even misleading if carried too far.]

6. **Considerable oral work:** (a) *The children volunteered sentences,* telling which was the noun and which was the verb. (b) I gave them *new examples of simple sentences,* interspersing sentence fragments. The children tried to decide which ones were and which were not sentences, and *why* — in terms of the **N V** pattern. This was not too successful at first, and required considerable oral work and discussion. (c) I then gave them the incomplete "Dick said . . . ." After much discussion, *the children concluded* that to be an **N V** sentence, it must satisfy these rules:

   1. It must have both a noun and a verb.
   2. It has to make sense.
   3. "The voice has to sound finished."

This was very exciting because I had not said anything about intonation. (d) Children used the colored cards to make up sentences, which they put on a pegboard to demonstrate visually and orally to the class. They loved doing this and were eager to participate. It is interesting to note that in doing this, *they figured out* the inflected form *Jane runs* without any instruction from their teacher. When I then presented the form *Puff is jumping,* etc., *they were very quick to grasp it and form similar sentences on the pegboard.* This was very successful.

7. **Written work:** The above work was followed by a dittoed
worksheet with similar exercises for them to complete; the
results were very good. A second worksheet (on adjectives)
WAS TOO DIFFICULT.
[The adjective exercises were introduced prematurely; the
secret of the success of the first exercise is the thorough
preliminary work, with plenty of oral work originated by
the children.]

8. **Meaning and use of adjectives:** The same procedure was
used as for nouns and verbs. The children picked out
adjectives in *red sweater, frisky kitten, happy pumpkin,*
etc.

9. **Developing the N V A and N Lv A patterns** [Lv means
linking verb]: I introduced this pattern with such examples
as *Puff looked funny. Dick seemed sad. Mother is pretty.
The sky looks dark.* All went well until I showed the
children how adjectives could improve a picture. We
played a game in which they added adjectives to the original sentence *The house is pretty,* until it became *The big
red brick house is pretty.* They enjoyed this activity, but
difficulty arose when they called the pattern of this sentence **A A A N Lv A.**
[Linking verbs other than the forms of *be* are unnecessarily
confusing if the teacher tries to make the distinction between linking verbs and other verbs; in this instance, the
teacher used mainly forms of *be* and had no problem with
that aspect of the pattern. The problem of multiple adjectives arose because the teacher did not differentiate
between word classes and main sentence parts; the **N**
part of the pattern (the complete subject) includes the
noun and all its modifiers.]

I tried to illustrate what is meant by *the basic pattern*
by drawing a simple dress pattern on the board. I then
decorated it with a collar, buttons, trimming, etc. *The
children saw that the basic pattern did not change.* We then
practiced picking out the main thing or noun the sentence
was talking about, but this seemed hard for the children.
[This procedure is abstract verbalism, precisely; the
teacher shifted her own ground here, and reverted from
the inductive discovery procedure used up to this point
to the methods of the past. The children clearly had
an intuitive sense of what the subject was, but they
could not handle the concept in the terms used by the
teacher.]

10. **Developing the N V N sentence pattern:** In giving examples, someone suggested ***Dick plays ball.***   Another child said, "That's two nouns with a verb in the middle." I explained that was another pattern we had not yet studied. *They immediately picked it up, so, unexpectedly, we learned the N V N pattern.* They liked the pattern particularly, because they found it very amusing to change the position of the two nouns, as in ***Mother feeds Spot*** and ***Dick flies the kite.***

[The **N V N** pattern is the most common basic pattern and probably the most easily understood; it may be preferable to begin basic pattern work with this pattern.]

Projected Future Development

I hope to introduce adverbs and the **N V Ad** and **N Lv Ad** patterns, and perhaps do some work with markers, but I do not feel it advisable to go much beyond that at this level.

[The problem here again lies in not distinguishing between word classes and main sentence parts; these two patterns have limited usefulness at best.]

Conclusion

I have been quite surprised and actually amazed that five and six year old children have been able to grasp this material. They consider it a game and enjoy it. At this level and at this stage, it is difficult to judge how much carryover there will be. It has seemed to me, however, that *the sentence structure in their first written stories has been better than in other groups I have had.*

It has been a very exciting experience!

SCRAMBLED SENTENCES. Presenting scrambled sentences to be rearranged in the right order is another good technique for introducing sentence pattern analysis; a combination of oral responses followed by writing is very effective. Students enjoy this method, but the main advantage for teaching is emphasis on the meanings and functions of sentence parts without analytical nomenclature.

The most direct approach is simply to present a list of sentence parts out of order:

me

gave

my father

a puppy

The parts may be written on the chalkboard or duplicated on work sheets; they may also be lettered on cards for use with flannel, peg, or pocket board. The essential activity is rearranging the parts in the right order, both orally and in writing; preferably, the oral response first. Elementary school children enjoy wearing bibs or sandwich boards carrying the various sentence parts; the children arrange themselves in order so that their classmates can read their sentences.

At higher levels, more sophisticated sentences may be presented.

> *Cholmondely*
> *seems to have made*
> *the new leader of the fraternity*
> *what happened that week*

(What happened that week / seems to have made / Cholmondely / the new leader of the fraternity.)

Or, for greater puzzlement, the scrambled sentence parts may be further reduced to scrambled words:

week	*new*	*fraternity*
the	*to*	*that*
made	*Cholmondely*	*happened*
seemed	*have*	*the*
had	*leader*	*of*
what	*have*	

This kind of problem helps teach a fundamental lesson: individual words are of little consequence as individuals; they find their meanings and functions primarily in ordered combinations with other words. This lesson is basic to sentence sense.

Straight and scrambled nonsense sentences can help develop both general sentence sense and a consciousness of some of the ways the smaller parts of the language system work.

Straight nonsense:	*The woople / klarged / a fleeger.*
Scrambled:	*the klarged fleeger woople a*

Nearly everyone enjoys a modicum of this sort of nonsense; young children have been known to try to make it their way of life. It is another good way to motivate exploration, discovery, imitation, and manipulation of language elements.

Techniques of Exposure, Imitation, Practice, and Manipulation

Earlier in this chapter, this section was previewed and illustrated with a few simple examples (pp. 169–172). Recommended techniques for teaching sentence sense — especially the ability to read and write good English sentences — are presented here under the following twelve subheadings.

A SUMMARY OF COMMON SENTENCE PATTERNS
EXPANSIONS OF NOUN PARTS
EXPANSIONS OF VERB PARTS
WHOLE SENTENCE EXPANSIONS
REDUCTION OF CLAUSES AND PHRASES
PATTERN VARIATIONS
QUESTION PATTERNS
SIMPLE PASSIVE TRANSFORMATIONS
PATTERNS OF COMMANDS AND REQUESTS
COMMON PATTERN INVERSIONS
THERE AND IT PATTERNS
SUBSTITUTIONS WITHIN SENTENCE PATTERNS

A SUMMARY OF COMMON SENTENCE PATTERNS. A relatively few structural sentence patterns, with their common inversions and passive transformations, are used with such high frequency that they may be presented even to elementary school children as a means of sharpening sentence sense. The patterns illustrated in the following tabulations have proved useful in the classroom. *They make no pretense of exhausting the possibilities of English syntax;* their rationale is descriptive and structural, with a practical view to teaching. They may be usefully introduced at any grade level.

The symbols **N** for **Noun**, **V** for **Verb**, **A** for **Adjective**, and **Ad** for **Adverb** represent **sentence parts** rather than parts of speech (word classes); each sentence part will usually have a headword of the corresponding word class which may be expanded almost indefinitely by single words, word groups, phrases, and clauses. Children learn to identify sentence patterns and sentence parts in the same way they learn the parts of the body — by association. (***Knee*** means knee; its symbol might be **kn**.) No verbal definitions (abstractions) are needed. Perhaps the best use of such pattern formulas is to motivate children to imitate and manipulate them in their own oral and written language, but they may also be used to analyze sentences in reading. *They should not be misused to process every living sentence and to wrap and ticket its parts for storage in refrigerated categories.*

In the display below, the falling arrows represent the fade–fall voice terminal at the end of each sentence.

Pattern One

N V   The fire / crackled. ↘
N V A   The flowers / arrived / fresh. ↘

Pattern Two

N V N   A tornado / demolished / the village. ↘
             The clown / blew / his whistle. ↘
             His speech / angered / the crowd. ↘

Pattern Three

N V N N   She / knitted / him / a sweater. ↘
N V N N   They / elected / him / captain. ↘
N V N A   Carbohydrates / make / him / fat. ↘

Pattern Four

N Lv N   A nom de plume / is / a pen name. ↘
N Lv A   Some antiques / are / valuable. ↘

In **Pattern Three,** the verb in the first **N V N N** pattern is of the *give* class; in the second, the verb is of the *name* class. Verbs of these two classes lead to different relationships of the **N** parts of the **N N** completers: verbs of the *give* class are completed by an indirect and direct object; verbs of the *name* class (*nominate, appoint,* etc.) are completed by a direct object and an object complement. **Pattern One** is structurally the simplest; **Pattern Two** is the most frequently used, however. The symbol **Lv** represents linking verb; in these examples, the only linking verbs used are forms of *be*.

TEACHING SUGGESTION: Choose examples suitable to your class and introduce one of the basic patterns for oral imitation and practice. *Pattern Two, N V N,* is the most common and possibly the easiest to begin with. Discuss both the structure and the meaning of the examples. Differentiating between sentence parts and the corresponding word classes is extremely important in beginning sentence pattern work; if this distinction is not made clear, students may become permanently confused. Follow-up work may be suggested by any of the following manipulative topics in this section.

EXPANSIONS OF NOUN PARTS. The term **Noun part** covers the simple and complete subjects and objects of school grammar; a **Noun part** generally contains a noun headword, and it may also contain a number of modifiers.

Example: the jolly old *man* in the moon
                              noun
                              headword

Simple subject: *The man* dropped his aitches.
Complete subject: *The jolly old man in the moon* dropped his aitches.
Simple object: Everyone saw *the man.*
Complete object: Everyone saw *the jolly old man in the moon.*

The above example shows that expansions of **Noun parts** are the same in both subjects and objects; we therefore illustrate **Noun part** expansions further by using the simplest pattern, **N V:**

            The man   is snoring.

The following three displays show three kinds of **Noun part** expansion: 1. with adjectives; 2. with prepositional phrases; 3. with clauses.

    1. *The man is snoring.* (adjectives)
       The big man . . .
       The big fat man . . .
       The great big fat man . . .
       The great big fat pink man . . .
       The great big fat round pink man . . .

       The great big fat round pink man is snoring.

2. *The man is snoring.* (prepositional phrases)
   The man in green pajamas . . .
   The man in green pajamas by the palm tree . . .
   The man in green pajamas by the palm tree on the beach . . .

   The great big fat round pink man in green pajamas by the palm tree on the beach is snoring.

3. *The man is snoring.* (clauses)
   The man who came from New York . . .
   The man who came from New York where the weather is cold . . .
   The man who came from New York where the weather is cold when winter comes . . .
   The man who came from New York where the weather is cold when winter comes is snoring.

   The great big fat round pink man in green pajamas by the palm tree on the beach who came from New York where the weather is cold when winter comes is snoring.

TEACHING SUGGESTION: To introduce *Noun part* expansions, choose a simple sentence, suitable to your grade level, for spontaneous oral practice. The order of the above discussion is best for step-by-step work: (1) *adjectives,* (2) *prepositional phrases,* (3) *clauses.* Such oral exercises can be instructive and entertaining, but expansion for its own sweet sake is tolerable only at first. The question of effective style should be discussed also, especially in relation to written sentences.

EXPANSIONS OF VERB PARTS. The term **Verb part** covers the simple and complete verbs of school grammar; a **Verb part** generally contains a verb headword, and it may also contain a number of modifiers. The following displays show three kinds of **Verb part** expansions: 1. with simple adverbs; 2. with prepositional phrases; 3. with clauses.

1. *The man is snoring.* (simple adverbs)
   . . . is gently snoring.
   . . . is gently and quietly snoring.
   . . . is gently and quietly, peacefully snoring.

   The man is gently and quietly, peacefully snoring.

2. *The man is snoring.* (prepositional phrases)
   . . . is snoring in the shade.
   . . . is snoring with the breezes in the shade.
   The man is snoring in harmony with the breezes in the shade.

3. *The man is snoring.* (clauses)
   . . . is snoring while the sun is hot.
   . . . is snoring while the sun is hot before it sets in the sea.
   *. . . is snoring while the sun is hot before it sets in the sea
   and the cool, cool moon comes up.*

   *The man is gently and quietly, peacefully snoring in harmony
   with the breezes in the shade while the sun is hot before it
   sets in the sea and the cool, cool moon comes up.*

TEACHING SUGGESTION: As with *Noun part* expansions,
it is best to begin with one-word modifiers of *Verb parts*, adverbs; and then proceed to prepositional phrases, followed by
clauses. Try adapting the above suggestions to the needs of
your class; combine oral and written work for the best results,
which should appear later in their free compositions.

Here is the complete expansion as we have worked it out for
the simple **N V** sentence, *The man is snoring.*

*The / great / big / fat / round / pink / man / in green pajamas / by
the palm tree / on the beach / who came from New York / where the
weather is cold / when winter comes / is / gently / and quietly, /
peacefully / snoring / in harmony / with the breezes / in the shade /
while the sun is hot / before it sets in the sea / and the cool, cool
moon comes up.*

TEACHING SUGGESTION: If your class profits from this
kind of work, let them try an entire exercise like the one above.
After the students have used up the possibilities, ask them to
try revising their sentences in various ways to obtain the most
effective statement. This work should acquaint them with some
of the ways of getting sentence variety in their writing. The
payoff should come in their free compositions.

Other kinds of verb expansions, using combinations of verb markers (auxiliary verbs), are illustrated in Chapter 8, **Structure Words.**

WHOLE SENTENCE EXPANSIONS. Following are examples of sentences expanded in various ways to achieve a better descriptive style. The basic pattern headwords are shown in bold-face type, the expansion elements in bold-face italic.

A man / entered / *the* shack.
A very old, decrepit man / entered / *the broken-down* shack.

The teacher / changed / *her* attitude.
The calm, soft-spoken young teacher / *suddenly* changed / *her oh-so-sweet* attitude.

The sun / was shining.
The warm summer sun / was shining *on the still blue deep.*

A troop / followed.
A frightened troop *of newly arrived campers, very young, very pink, and very callow,* / followed *nervously, their teeth chattering in the cold.*

The vessel / was / *a* mess.
The wrecked sailing vessel / was / *a tangled* mess *of upended planks, and splintered boards, and smashed woodwork.*

The shadows / were cast.
The long, long shadows *of those weird figures* / were *eerily* cast *along the deserted streets and all up across the town.*

The tree / was / lovely.
The chinaberry tree / was / *as* lovely *as always, as full of sweet flowers, and as perfectly graceful and still.*

TEACHING SUGGESTION: Present your class with some very simple basic patterns like those above; or better, develop them through class discussion. Then have each student write the most effective sentences he can by expanding them in any way he likes. This exercise approaches the conditions of free composition.

Sentence expansions of the kinds illustrated in the previous sections can be of great help in developing sentence sense, the ability to write varied and proper sentences; or as Benny Goodman used to say, "to play correct clarinet." But it was not simply correct clarinet that made Goodman's playing great; it was artistry and musicianship. Similarly, practice on imitation and manipulations of single sentences, like mastery of scales and finger exercises, though essential for quality performance, are but one of many means of achieving the ultimate skills we hope to develop. Work on sentences must never be divorced from the arts and skills of literacy in the sense of reading and writing extended discourse.

REDUCTION OF CLAUSES AND PHRASES. One of the most common faults of ineffective writing is the immature repetition of simple-minded one-clause sentences. In addition to expanding and combining sentences, sometimes writers reduce clauses and phrases so as to get a denser, more mature style. Following is a composition by a youngster well drilled on simple sentence patterns, each with a capital letter to begin with and a period at the end.

My Vacation

Last summer I took a vacation. I went to Camp Potawatami. I stayed there four weeks. I slept in a tent. The tent had a floor made of wood. The tent was made of canvas. The canvas had been waterproofed. It kept the rain out. I never got wet when I was in the tent. It was warm inside the tent during the day. It was cool inside the tent at night. I slept well every night. It was a comfortable way to live. I had a nice vacation.

This composition can be improved somewhat, but not enough, by being rewritten in compound sentences that combine or connect some of its simple clause-sentences; or that reduce some clauses into predicates, all compounded with *and, so,* and *but,* as follows:

For my vacation last summer I went to Camp Potawatami and stayed there four weeks. I slept in a tent that had a wooden floor. The tent was made of canvas that had been waterproofed. It kept the rain out and I never got wet. It was warm inside during the day but it was cool at night, so I slept well and had a nice vacation.

Now this is no earth-shaking topic for a school exercise, but it is far from execrable. Its main trouble remains, simple-minded, dull repetitive sentences; some clauses require further reduction, and a few clauses and phrases can be reduced to adjectives. For example, *The tent was made of canvas that had been waterproofed* can be revised to read more effectively, *a waterproof canvas tent.* Further reductions and a generalizing closing sentence produce a fairly interesting paragraph on the old familiar subject.

> During my four-week vacation last summer at Camp Potawatami, I slept comfortably in a waterproof canvas tent pitched on a wooden platform. It was warm inside during the day, but cool at night for sleeping. Because the rain was kept out, I never got wet. If you like outdoor life as much as I do, you would enjoy a vacation at that camp.

TEACHING SUGGESTION: Use the original paragraph above, or one like it from your own student's papers (by **Anon.**), to open a class discussion of the possibilities of reduction of clauses and phrases. If the above examples are suitable for your class, you might duplicate them on three separate sheets for distribution; then lead your class by easy stages to an approximation of the third phase. Follow-up work might well include class discussion of similar problems in their own compositions.

PATTERN VARIATIONS. In syntactical analysis it is convenient to treat a few patterns of statement as basic and all others as variations or transformations; this is the method of the present discussion. *We must recognize, however, that the actual psychological processes of speakers and writers in creating and responding to sentences may bear little or no relationship to our convenient analysis;* that is another matter altogether. Native speakers simply feel, intuitively, that there is some systematic relationship among such sentences as:

> Wienie is our dachshund.
> Is Wienie our dachshund?
> Whose dachshund is Wienie?
> Has Wienie been inoculated?
> Wienie has been inoculated by the vet.

TEACHING SUGGESTION: A good method of interesting students in sentence patterns and analysis is to introduce a set of related sentences like those above. Most classes can produce their own sets orally much faster than a teacher can write them on the board. Follow-up activities may take a number of forms; the point of this activity is to stimulate curiosity and a readiness to explore.

Regardless of any connection there may or may not be between syntactical analysis and psycholinguistic processes, it is useful in teaching to present sentences in terms of basic patterns, variations, and transformations. The next section introduces common question patterns, considered as variations of basic patterns.

QUESTION PATTERNS. Questions take several common forms: (1) simple inversions with a form of *be* as the only verb; (2) split-verb inversions with forms of *be, have,* and *do* as auxiliaries, as well as the modals; (3) the same inversions as in (1) and (2), but introduced by question markers; and (4) questions in which the question markers themselves occupy the initial position before verbs in inverted patterns.

(1) Simple inversions with forms of *be* as the only verb:

Lv N N?	*Are / you / the Queen of the Nile?*
Lv N A?	*Is / John / old enough?*

TEACHING SUGGESTION: Questions of this kind can provide useful, relatively painless oral practice on the various forms of *be,* and on agreement in number of subjects and verbs.

---

(2) Split-verb inversions with forms of *be, have,* and *do* as auxiliaries; in these formulas, small *v* stands for the auxiliary, or verb marker.

v N V?	*Is / she / coming?*	
v N V N?	*Are / they / bringing / the food?*	(forms of *be*)

v N V?	*Have / you / showered yet?*	(forms of *have*)
v N V N?	*Has / he / locked / the gate?*	

v N V?	*Did / he / win?*	(forms of *do*)
v N V N?	*Do / they / know / the score?*	

All the English modals may also be used in these questions:

can, could, may, might, must, shall, will, would, ought (to)

TEACHING SUGGESTION: In addition to direct oral practice on these questions, working with these auxiliaries can help to develop an awareness of the contrasts of forms in standard and divergent dialects.

---

(3) The same inversions as in (1) and (2) above, but introduced by question markers (**Wh-words,** such as *what, when, where, which, why, who,* and also *how*). These patterns may be represented by the following formulas, in which **QM** represents **Question Marker.**

QM Lv N N?	*When / was / he / a Mystic Knight of the Sea?*
QM Lv N A?	*Why / is / Algernon / so green?*
QM v N V?	*Where / has / that young whippersnapper / gone?*
QM v N V N?	*How / had / Winston / lost / his / bumbershoot?*
QM v N V?	*What / does / Marybeth / mean?*
QM v N V N?	*Where / did / Myrtle / hide / the vinegar cruet?*

TEACHING SUGGESTION: Work on these patterns can reinforce learning of patterns (1) and (2) above, as well as give further practice on standard English forms.

---

(4) Questions in which the question markers themselves occupy the initial position before verbs in inverted patterns; the great variety

of **Wh-word** meanings gives a similar variety of meanings to the questions.

QM V?	*How / come? What / cooks? Who / comes?*
	Who / goes there? Who / supervises?
QM V N?	*What / is making / that infernal noise?*
	Who / broke / the McGillicuddy's window?
QM Lv N?	*Who / is / Sylvia? What / is / she? Where /*
	is / Michiana?
	When / was / breakfast? How / are / you?
	Which / is / the culprit?

TEACHING SUGGESTION: Work with this pattern provides an opportunity to review, compare, and contrast all the questions presented. The purpose of such practice is not memorization of a set of patterns, but increased ease and familiarity with the language.

The foregoing is offered as a suggestive introduction to a few sets of simple question patterns; an interested and alert class can easily add new sets of its own; moreover, questions, like other sentences, can be inverted, expanded in many ways, and provided with attached clauses. Many questions can also be cast in the form of passive transformations, the topic of the next section. The possibilities of exploration, practice, and manipulations are virtually inexhaustible.

SIMPLE PASSIVE TRANSFORMATIONS. Active and passive equivalent sentences like those displayed below have the same meaning and lexical elements, expressed, however, by contrasting structural patterns and different syntactical relationships: the object in the active sentence is the subject in the passive equivalent. In short, subjects and objects switch syntactical roles in active/passive equivalent sentences; the meaning remains the same.

Only **Pattern Two** and **Pattern Three** have common passive equivalents:

Active pattern **N V N** becomes **N vV by N.**
Active pattern **N V N N** becomes **N vV N by N.**
Active pattern **N V N A** becomes **N vV A by N.**

In the pattern formulas, **v** in **vV** is the symbol for the forms of the *be* auxiliary, always used in passive transformations; **by** is a symbol in the formula because it is the only structure word used to express agency (by *what* or *whom* the action is performed). Examples follow.

ACTIVE: **N V N** (Pattern Two)
A driving snowstorm / chilled / our winter cookout.

PASSIVE: **N vV by N**
Our winter cookout / was chilled / by a driving snowstorm.

ACTIVE: **N V N N** (Pattern Three)
His dad / gave / Bob / his first shaver.

PASSIVE: **N vV N by N**
Bob / was given / his first shaver / by his dad.
His first shaver / was given / (to) Bob / by his dad.

ACTIVE: **N V N A** (Pattern Three variant)
Too many carbohydrates / made / Bartholomew / obese.

PASSIVE: **N vV A by N**
Bartholomew / was made / obese / by too many carbohydrates.

TEACHING SUGGESTION: Try giving your class practice in manipulating active/passive equivalents, not only to develop ease and fluency, but to understand that the same meaning is expressed by a clear-cut contrast of patterns having different syntactical relationships.

In English sentences, the **Noun part** in initial position generally receives greater emphasis:

ACTIVE: *The boys down the hall / gave / a party.*
PASSIVE: *A party / was given / by the boys down the hall.*

The active sentence gives priority to *the persons who gave the party;* the passive, to *the giving of the party.* If those who gave the party are of even less interest, the sentence may be merely, *A party was given.*

In technical writing, authors often use passive sentences when the agent, or the function of **agency,** is not important or even very clear.

> *A pulse of current is applied to the drive coils in order to keep the tuning fork vibrating.*

In such sentences, the question of agency (here *who* or *what* applied the current) does not arise; the action occurs mechanically as part of an automated process.

A parting note: the term **transformation** may seem to suggest that all passive sentences are derived from active sentences. This is not true. Quite common passive sentences have no active equivalents; for example:

> *The cattle were drowned in the flood.*
> *Three persons were killed in the collision.*
> *The entire flotilla was lost during the typhoon.*

Such sentences have been called "activeless passives." Note 68 to Chapter 10, pp. 359–360, discusses this point further and refers to other studies.

TEACHING SUGGESTION: Advanced (or just plain curious) students may enjoy exploring the stylistic uses of passive sentences as briefly suggested above, either for emphasis or to express relationships in which agency is not a factor. Such students can be asked to justify their claims and choices.

PATTERNS OF COMMANDS AND REQUESTS. Most of the imperatives of school grammar are either commands or requests. In speech, they are often differentiated only by tone and manner; in writing and speech, *please* and related **starters** and **fillers** function as request markers (though a contrary tone can negate their surface meaning).

The simplest commands are like those mastered in obedience school by all well-behaved dogs.

V   *Come. Fetch. Heel. Sit. Lie. Stay. No.*

Some of these become requests when properly addressed to people.

> *Please come. Do sit down. Please stay. Just fetch my wraps, please.*

In schoolrooms, teachers often use either command or request patterns, as follows.

V N	*Erase / the boards.*	*Please erase / the boards.*
	Clear / your desks.	*Please clear / your desks.*
	Take / paper and pencil.	*Please take / paper and pencil.*
V A	*Look / alive.*	*Please look / alive.*
	Stand / tall.	*Please stand / tall.*
	Sit / still.	*Please sit / still.*
V Ad	*Go / to the chalkboard.*	*Please go / to the chalkboard.*
	Come / here.	*Please come / here.*
	Stay / in your places.	*Please stay / in your places.*

Requests often take the form of questions, spoken in the appropriate tone and manner. The above commands, for example, become requests if they begin with *Will you,* or *Will you please.* These same additions to the requests at the right above would render them even more polite.

TEACHING SUGGESTION: Young children, especially, can practice their manners while playing games with the differences between commands and requests. Let them try role-playing, with appropriate tone of voice and general manner: teacher, parent, minister, school principal, rude or polite child.

COMMON PATTERN INVERSIONS. Recall that the most common English sentence order is subject-predicate; for greater emphasis or other stylistic effect, it is sometimes preferable to invert this order, in whole or in part. All the basic patterns presented in this chapter may be inverted, with varied effects; the context of other sentences generally will determine whether or not inversion is effective: it should not be done for its own sake, but kept in mind as a stylistic possibility. Following are some simple examples.

N V becomes **V N**	*Came / the dawn.*
N V A becomes **A V N**	*Bright and clear / crackled / the fire.*
N V Ad becomes **Ad V N**	*Low / swooped / the fighter plane.*

N V N becomes **N N V**	*One mistake / he / always made.* *That holiday / he / never missed.*
N V N N becomes **N N V N**	*Percy the pain / the students / called / him.* *This pittance / the court / awarded / us.*
N V N A becomes **A N V N**	*Neurotic / they / called / her.*
N Lv A becomes **A Lv N**	*Brighter by far / was / Trombley.* *Utterly revolting / were / his table manners.*
N Lv Ad becomes **Ad Lv N**	*Outside by the door / was / the suspect.* *Everywhere in the woods / were / mortal dangers.*

TEACHING SUGGESTION: Try some oral work with your class on simple patterns and pattern inversions. If it is successful, ask each student to write a paragraph in which a pattern inversion makes for better style. See if they can justify their choices.

There AND **It** PATTERNS. The words **There** and **It** in these special patterns are the expletives of traditional grammar. **There** is not an adverb, nor is **It** a pronoun; they are simply structural devices for beginning certain kinds of sentences.

There Lv N	*There / are / many answers to your question.* *There / had to be / a good reason for his absence.* *There / seem to be / no words to express my feelings.*
It V	*It / is raining* (snowing, blowing, etc.).
It Lv A	*It / is rainy* (snowy, blustery, warm, hot, cool, cold, damp, etc.).

Certain pattern inversions also begin with **There** and **It.**

There V N	*There / came / an urgent telegram from London.* *There / emerged / a sad-eyed monster.*
It Lv A N	*It / was / perfectly clear / that he was lying.* (**N** is a clause.)

It Lv N N   *It / is / common knowledge / that they are lovers.*
(**N** is a clause.)
It / was / the court's ruling / that he was guilty.
(**N** is a clause.)

It Lv Ad N   *It / has been / only since yesterday / that I have
known.* (**N** is a clause.)
It / was / because of your interest / that I returned.
(**N** is a clause.)

TEACHING SUGGESTION: Allow your class to experiment with creating *There* and *It* sentences. Caution: In these patterns, avoid confusing *There* with the adverb *there,* and *It* with the pronoun *it.*

SUBSTITUTIONS WITHIN SENTENCE PATTERNS. The very great ease with which words slip from one form-class to another is part of the genius of the English language; this trait was noted in some detail in Chapter 5, pp. 116–117. To a lesser extent this same trait is exhibited by broad substitutions in main sentence parts, most particularly in **Noun parts.** Following are a few illustrations.

Verbal groups as **Noun parts** (**V-ing** groups):

Swimming across the lake / is / good exercise but hard work.
Loudly ringing the bell at all hours / caused / untold anguish.
Being on time / turned out to be / his best asset.
Hunting upland game birds / is / an excellent fall sport.

Infinitive groups as **Noun parts** (**to-V** groups):

To fly or not to fly / is no longer / a practical choice.
To breathe polluted air all day long / can be / to invite disease.

Clauses as **Noun parts:**

What the Supreme Court decides today / will deeply affect / the lives of all Americans.
Whether or not the weather holds good / has become / the main question now.
The general / did not doubt / that the replacements would arrive on time.

Adjective / adverb groups as **Noun parts** in *be* sentences:

Nearby / will be / close enough.
Over the white line / is / out of bounds.
Once in a while / is / not very often.
Just outside the city / will not be / sufficient.

Various groups as **Verb parts:** It seems possible not only to substitute nouns and adjectives as verb headwords — *The boss made him stop horsing around* or *They are trying to pretty up the place* — but also to substitute almost any kind of word group as a **Verb part** in a sentence pattern. Often these substitutions are spontaneous inventions, in the spirit of fun.

Don't you *I-told-you-so* me!
His partner *behind-the-eight-balled* him once too often.
He can't *golf-every-weekend* forever with her.
See if you can *hole-in-one* it.

This kind of thing could be carried too far, but students deserve to understand that such substitutions are part of the rich expressive capacity of the English language. This is a liberating insight.

TEACHING SUGGESTION: The possibilities of exploration into the broad area of substitutions are practically endless; imitation and practice can loosen up the fixed ideas of many learners, and help them to develop a freer, more communicative style. Especially important are substitutions in *Noun parts* of *V-ing* groups, *to-V* groups, and *clauses*. Students can be encouraged to discover and report on all kinds of substitutions in good literature, including poetry.

Selected References

SCHOOL TEXTS

Harold B. Allen, Verna L. Newsome, Thomas H. Wetmore, Helen J. Throckmorton, Enola Borgh, *New Dimensions in English* (Wichita, Kansas: McCormick-Mathers Publishing Company, 1966).

David A. Conlin, *Grammar for Written English* (Boston: Houghton Mifflin, 1961).

Bernard L. Greenberg and Sara Withers, *Better English Usage: A Guide for the Deaf* (New York: Bobbs-Merrill, 1965).

Helen E. Lefevre and Carl A. Lefevre, *Writing by Patterns, Form A and Form B* (New York: Knopf, 1965, 1968).

———, *English Writing Patterns*, 2–12 (NewYork: L. W. Singer, 1968).

Helen E. Lefevre, Jack A. Minnis, and Carl A. Lefevre, *Oral/Written Practice in Standard English Forms* (New York: Random House, 1969).

Paul Roberts, *English Sentences* (New York: Harcourt, Brace & World, 1962).

———, *Patterns of English: Teacher's Edition* (New York: Harcourt, Brace, 1956).

COLLEGE TEXTS

Margaret M. Bryant, *A Functional English Grammar* (Boston: D. C. Heath, 1945).

———, *Modern English and Its Heritage*, second ed (New York: Macmillan, 1962).

W. Nelson Francis, *The Structure of American English* (New York: Ronald Press, 1958).

H. A. Gleason, Jr., *Linguistics and English Grammar* (New York: Holt, Rinehart and Winston, 1965).

Baxter Hathaway, *A Transformational Syntax: The Grammar of Modern American English* (New York: Ronald Press, 1967).

Archibald A. Hill, *Introduction to Linguistic Structures: From Sound to Sentence in English* (New York: Harcourt, Brace, 1958).

A. S. Hornby, *A Guide to Patterns and Usage in English* (London: Oxford University Press, 1954).

Carl A. Lefevre, *Linguistics and the Teaching of Reading* (New York: McGraw-Hill, 1964).

V. E. Leichty, *Discovering English* (Englewood Cliffs, N.J.: Prentice-Hall, 1964).

Harold Whitehall, *Structural Essentials of English* (New York: Harcourt, Brace, 1955).

Chapter 8

Structure Words

English structure words comprise a subsystem of about three hundred items that mark structural elements within sentences; they also signal relationships between and among sentences in paragraphs and more extended discourse. Sentences linked by structure words are among the dependent sentences briefly discussed in the last chapter, pp. 167–69. Because structure words identify many syntactical elements, and also signal the structural and semantic relationships among these elements, they are both meaningful and rather abstract. They should not be taught singly, as vocabulary items; instead, their functions and uses should be taught in meaning-bearing structures and in context.

A sentence lacking content-bearing words from the four word-classes cannot carry a message: it is only a skeleton of the full form the message may take.

Because _____ _____ _____ many _____ _____,
and also _____ the _____ and _____ _____
among these _____, they ____ both _____ and
rather _____.

The foregoing is the third sentence in the paragraph above with the content-bearing words removed; the structure words are all that remain. The sentence structure is clearly outlined, but the message is not there. In fact, a large number of messages could be written using that structure.

On the other hand, the content words of that same sentence,

without the structure words that delineate its structural pattern, would not be much more than a pointless list of words, vaguely related by their common reference to language.

_____ structure words identify ____ syntactical elements, __ __ signal ____ structural ____ semantic relationships _____ _____ elements, ____ are ____ meaningful ____ _____ abstract.

TEACHING SUGGESTION: At your grade level, find or write your own parallel sentence. Present it to your class in two ways: (1) structure words only; and (2) content words only. Let them fill in the other words orally. Follow up with sentences suggested by students.

Just as structure words are an important subsystem of the language system as a whole, so are they important to the development of a mature writing or speaking style. For simplicity, we may group structure words into five major sets of common markers — sets of words that identify and mark off main syntactical elements — as follows:

1. **Noun markers** (articles and other words that serve a similar function).
2. **Verb markers** (auxiliaries, modals and others that serve a similar function).
3. **Phrase markers** (single prepositions as well as groups).
4. **Clause markers** (all conjunctions, words, and groups that serve similar functions).
5. **Question markers** (words that start questions).

Structure words also include the expletives, *there* and *it* (see pp. 194–95); intensifiers, such as *very, more, most, little, least, less;* and miscellaneous starters and proposers, such as *please, well, if you like, say Mac, oh say,* etc. (this miscellany has little to do with composition except in casual dialogue). The pronouns may also be considered as structure words, or as a subset of nouns (see pp. 122–23).

One difficulty of mastering the system of structure words is the confusion of the categories and terminology of common school grammar; for example:

connectors;
coordinating conjunctions, subordinating conjunctions, conjunctive
adverbs;
relative pronouns, demonstrative pronouns, interrogative pronouns,
reflexive pronouns, reciprocal pronouns, numeral pronouns, in-
definite pronouns, personal pronouns, impersonal pronouns, poses-
sive pronouns;
articles, definite and *indefinite;*
auxiliary verbs, modal auxiliaries;
interjections;

and so on, far, far into the night.

Aside from their overlapping multiplicity, such terms are inconsistent in their bases of classification:

some seem to be objective and structural — **connector, correlative, conjunction, interjection;**

others, subjective, concerned with meaning without regard to structure — **numeral, personal,** and **indefinite pronouns;** still others suggest the fictitious analogy with Latin — **auxiliary verbs, modal auxiliaries, reflexive pronouns.**

Another difficulty of mastering the subsystem of structure words, more real than the confusion presented by the terms and categories of school grammar, is the uncomfortable fact that "the same word," as a structure word, may serve different functions. A few may be distributed in positions and uses of the four word classes.

NOUN:	*Down* is not *out.*
VERB:	They plan to *up* the ante.
	He could not *down* the capsule.
ADJECTIVE:	He went in the *out* door.
ADVERB:	He followed *after.*

Many prepositions serve as clause markers (**after, before, since, until**); as adjectives (the way **out,** the morning **after**) and as adverbs (draw **in,** pull **up,** fall **through**); some clause markers are identical with question markers, and in some sentences may perform both functions simultaneously:

What would he have said if I had not been there?

Moreover, structure word groups frequently pattern the same as single structure words (**as to how, as to why, as far as, inasmuch as,** *on the other hand*). Even the deceptively simple coordinating conjunctions are elusive and inconsistent as a set, as we shall note later (pp. 217–19).

Because the verb *be* is unique, it may be regarded as forming a class by itself; it requires a special statement. *Be* is more irregular and has more forms (eight) than any other English verb: *am, are, be, been, being, is, was, were;* its forms may combine into groups in which one form of *be* serves as a marker in a verb group that has a form of *be* as a headword: *were* to have *been.* As a verb marker *be* has two distinct uses: as marker of active verbs (*is* running, *was* thinking); and as marker of passive verbs (*was* beaten, *had been* hurt).

In linking verb sentences, *be* is so devoid of content, so lacking in reference to the world of reality outside language, as to make it virtually a structure word; in essence it is an equal sign (=), the principal difference being its various forms that enable it to combine into verb groups as well as to signal tense differences.

The strange object *is* a child's toy.
The strange object *was* a child's toy.
The strange object *had been* a child's toy.
The strange object *might have been* a child's toy.

Structure words demand careful consideration both in the analysis and description of the language system, and in applications of the results to a sequential development of language skills. Ranked according to my sense of their increasing complexity, structure words will be presented under the following subheadings in the remainder of this chapter:

Question Markers
Noun Markers
Verb Markers
Phrase Markers
Clause Markers

Question Markers

A question marker typically signals a question by its initial position, preceding an inverted sentence pattern; in handwriting and print, the question mark is an additional signal. The difference between two questions, a simple inversion and the same inversion preceded by a question marker, lies in the specificity expressed by the marker. For example, *Did you lose it?* is a simple question of the fact of loss. But several other, more specific questions may be asked by leading into this same inverted pattern with *how, when, where,* or *why.*

Question markers also enable us to structure other forms of questions, such as: *Why fight it? Where were you? How is she? When was it? How did it happen?* (*Did it happen?* can occur, but with low frequency.)

In all our teaching of questions, we should combat the prevalent school fallacy that all questions end with a rising tone of voice, "a rising inflection." Out of all the questions above, only the simple inversions, *Did you lose it?* and *Did it happen?* would normally end with a fade-rise terminal. All those beginning with markers would normally end with a fade-fall terminal, identical with the terminal that signals the end of a statement. While it is possible to end the other questions with a fade-rise terminal, they become different questions: the fade-rise terminal introduces some form of special intent (irony, disbelief, incredulity) or may simply mean a request that the other person in the conversation repeat what he just said. The *sound* of questions should be covered in all lessons dealing with question patterns (this topic is covered more fully in Chapter 9, pp. 243–4; 249; 251–53).

Grade-level differences in question patterns do not depend heavily upon the markers, most of which are known to preschool children, nor upon the simple operation of pattern inversion, but upon structural and conceptual differences that become increasingly mature in succeeding years.

Questions have various functions in composition and speech. A writer may pose a question just so that he may give his own answer; or he may ask it and deliberately leave it unanswered, with the intent of suggesting that no one can answer it; both these uses of the rhetorical question are also effective in debate. The five questions, **who, when, where, why,** and **how,** are often cited as a formula for a good news story; a series of questions in a speech or article may suggest the complexity, or the sheer weight, of the problems that must be faced. Teachers and other public speakers sometimes use questions to perk up their listeners, or as a check on their attention. The uses of questions, in contrast to their forms, are infinitely varied.

TEACHING SUGGESTION: According to the nature of your class, ask students how questions may be used for other reasons than to require direct answers. See whether they can think of examples in everyday life; or in public speech, such as campaign oratory. See whether they can find examples in their reading. A follow-up assignment might be either a talk or composition in which they demonstrate the use of a question or questions in new or unusual ways.

This brief discussion of questions and question markers is supplementary to the section on QUESTIONS in Chapter 7, pp. 188–190. For more teaching suggestions, please refer to that section.

Noun Markers

For background discussion of nouns, refer to Chapter 5, pp. 118–122.

Either mass or count nouns may occur in ordinary sentences with or without noun markers; for example:

Money is not the root of all evil; the *love* of money is.

In general usage, *money* is a mass noun; in law, the plural *moneys* means sums of money; *moneys* may also refer to different systems of money; a young child may say *moneys* meaning *coins*. In the above sentence and in general use, *love* also is a mass noun. *Money* has no marker; *love* has *the* as its marker.

Following are three sentences containing five count nouns:

Men are always aspiring.
Chairs come in many shapes.
If *wishes* were *horses, beggars* would ride.

None of the five count nouns has a noun marker.

A DEFINITION. **Noun markers** are words that pattern, or distribute, in the **the** position in such sentences as the following:

The cat was asleep.   *The cats* were asleep.

Though some markers may occur with either singular or plural nouns, the singular/plural distinction sometimes makes a crucial difference in the choice of markers. Study the markers suggested below.

SINGULAR: *The cat* was asleep.   (*a, another, each, every, either, neither, this, that*)

PLURAL: *The cats* were asleep.   (*all, few, many, more, most, other, several, two, three,* etc.)

EITHER: (*the, any, some, no, what, whatever; which, whichever, my, your, his, its, our, their, whose; John's, Mary's*)

TEACHING SUGGESTION: After pointing out to your class that the noun marker *the* occurs with both singular and plural nouns, ask them if they think this is true of all noun markers. Ask them to give examples orally of those that occur only with singular nouns, then those that occur only with plural. A follow-up activity might be a composition that deliberately features differences of markers; or a report, written or oral, on the use of singular and plural noun markers in printed matter.

Similarly, though some markers may occur with either mass or count nouns, the mass/count distinction often makes a crucial difference in the choice of markers. Study the markers suggested below:

MASS NOUN: *Most fruit* is sweet.   (*less, little, much*)

COUNT NOUN: But *lemons* are sour.   (*many, several, two, three,* etc.; *few* occurs with count nouns, but it would be slightly absurd in the above sentence)

TEACHING SUGGESTION: Introduce the contrast of mass and count nouns to your students; if the above examples are suitable, try them. Allow the class to explore ramifications of the topic, giving their own examples orally. Discuss differences of meaning expressed by different noun markers. A follow-up assignment might be a talk or composition with special emphasis on the significance of the choices of mass and count nouns and their markers.

Some noun markers (*a, an, the*) are sometimes designated **determiners,** apparently because only a noun may follow them; however, the class of true determiners is only a small fraction of all the words that may occur in the *a, an, the* position. I think the term **noun marker** is preferable for teaching. Sometimes more than one noun marker occurs, as in *a few cats* or *all the cats;* or in *many a cat, not a cat, such a cat, never a cat,* and so on.

TEACHING SUGGESTION: Introduce the above examples of noun marker groups, or phrases. See whether your students can orally construct sentences using them. Ask them to volunteer other examples. Discuss their stylistic effect. A follow-up assignment might be to search for others in reading, including poetry and fiction; an oral or written report might be appropriate.

Following is a tabulation of common noun markers, arranged in groups according to their possible meanings and uses:

a, an	every
the	other, another
all, any, some	no, such
both, each	this, that; these, those
enough	what, whatever
either, neither	which, whichever
few, many, several	my, your, his, her, its, our, their, whose
less, little	Bob's, Carl's, Anne's, Vicky's, etc.
much, more, most	one, two, three (cardinal numbers)

TEACHING SUGGESTION: Write this tabulation on the board, or duplicate it for distribution to your class. Ask them to invent spoken sentences using the markers, group by group. Ask which markers can be used with singular and plural nouns; with mass and count nouns. Discuss how many may be used irrespective of these distinctions. Discuss the stylistic effects of noun markers. See whether the students can add others to the tabulation. Many follow-up activities are possible; perhaps your class can suggest appropriate ones that interest them.

Verb Markers

For background discussion of verbs, refer to Chapter 5, pp. 125–131. **Verb markers** include certain single verbs and marker groups that may accompany various forms of other verbs as headwords in verb groups. Although the term *verb marker* applies primarily to single verb forms, it is applied here to more involved marker groups preceding a headword.

The analytical discovery of and formal practice with single verb markers is a primary or perhaps middle-grade learning process, reviewed later only for review and reinforcement. Discovery and practice involving more complex marker groups is part of mastering more mature sentence patterns in reading, and in formal writing and speaking.

A formal process of analytically discovering and manipulating verb markers logically begins, therefore, with simple markers, followed by the modals. A major purpose is to develop sentence sense and familiarity with the structure of sentence parts, with emphasis on **Verb parts.** In this or any other formal sequencing, however, we expect some children to say and write constructions "above grade level." In lessons on verb markers and verb groups, teachers should be sweetly permissive, never ruling out good English constructions because "we don't get to that until next year." God forbid.

The following presentation is suggestive rather than definitive or exhaustive; this topic provides rich opportunities for joint explorations by teachers and students. Teachers are urged to encourage investigation and experimentation with verb markers at will. The simplest verb markers can be presented successfully in Grade 3 to normal children working at grade level. More advanced children will say and write sentences with **Verb parts** that have complex marker groups.

The simplest and most common verb markers are the auxiliary verbs ("helping verbs" of school grammar): the traditional number, person, and tense forms of *be* and *have* in active sentences:

I   *am* (you, we, they) *are* (*were*) **running the race.**
I   (you, we, they) *have* (*had*) **run the race.**

He (she, it, Carl, the boy) *is* (*was*) running the race.
He (she, it, Carl, the boy) *has* (*had*) run the race.

The above patterns may also incorporate the negatives *not, never, hardly, scarcely.*

TEACHING SUGGESTION: Ask your students to invent sentences using the above verb groups. Discuss the various times of the actions.

It should be pointed out that the above verb markers may also pattern as full verbs; they are markers only when they function as markers and appear in verb marking positions.

I / *am* / hungry. (N Lv A)   You / *have* / the measles. (N V N)
Carl / *is* / a cool cat. (N Lv N)   He / *has* / three guitars.
(N V N)

As soon as children are aware of the contrast of active and passive patterns, the forms of *be* as markers in passive sentences may be noted.

ACTIVE: Bob *is* (*was*) running the race.
PASSIVE: The race *is* (*was*) being run by Bob.
The race *is* (*was*) being run. (Not necessarily by Bob.)

In informal speech, there is a common passive transformation pattern with *get* as the marker. It is sometimes called the *get*-passive. Examples follow, with *be*-passive equivalents in parentheses.

He *got* arrested.   (He *was* arrested.)
The tent *got* put up.   (The tent *was* put up.)
The dish *got* broken.   (The dish *was* broken.)

It is probably better to describe and discuss the *get*-passive than attempt to proscribe it. But alternative sentences can be suggested: they are not quite identical in meaning and tone.

Other common verb markers are the modals: *can, could; may, might; shall, should; will, would;* and *must.*

I   *can*   swim.
N   m   V   (m for modal)

N: *you, he, she, it, Anne, the girl, we, they*
m: *could; may, might; shall, should; will, would; must*

TEACHING SUGGESTION: Use the above patterns for oral/written practice. Many sentences will need explanatory phrases or clauses to give more meaning to the sentences. Discuss with your students the different meanings given by the various modals.

Other possible markers in the above sentences include: *do, does, did; dare, dared; need, needed; dare* and *need* may require the infinitive marker *to* before the verb. If your students did well on the above Teaching Suggestion, they might enjoy working with these.

As a verb marker, *do* often has an intensifying function that differentiates it from the others; *do* may also function as a full verb in some patterns.

INTENSIFIER: I *DO* like bananas.   I *DO* walk when I can.
FULL VERB: I *do* the dishes every night.   I can *do* the work.

Children have their own special *do* intensive with *too:*

I *DO TOO* like bananas.
I *DO TOO* do the dishes every night.

In the last examples, the first *do* is an intensifier, the second a full verb.

Other common markers form verb groups with the marked infinitive, to-V: *be to-V, be going to-V, be about to-V, need to-V, ought to-V, get to-V, have to-V* and *have got to-V;* and *used to-V.*

I   *am   to swim*   in the next race.
N   (x)   to-V   (x for marker)

N: *you, he, she, it, Vicky, the girl; we, they*
(x) to: *be to, be going to, be about to, need to, ought to, get to, have to, have got to, used to*

Corresponding forms of some modals may also be used in the above example; for instance:

> They *might be going* to swim across, or take a boat.
> She *must be about* to swim any minute now.

TEACHING SUGGESTION: The previous teaching suggestion may also be applied to the above markers. Some students might enjoy exploring the use of some of these markers and marker groups in printed material, and report back to the class.

Another group of common verb markers forms verb groups with **V–ing** verb forms: *get, go, keep,* and *start.*

> I (you, he, she, it, Bob, the boy, we, they) *got* going.
> (*Got to go* is possible, but has another sense.)
> I (you, he, she, it, Bob, the boy, we, they) *went* skating.
> I (you, he, she, it, Bob, the boy, we, they) *kept* running.
> I (you, he, she, it, Bob, the boy, we, they) *started* eating.
> > (also **to-V**: *to eat*)

TEACHING SUGGESTION: The above rather simple markers involve interesting questions of meaning, especially when used with modals and other markers. Present these to your class for oral/written work. Ask your students to invent sentences of their own, using the above verbs as markers and as full verbs. Some students might enjoy searching for various uses of these verbs in printed materials and report back to the class on their findings.

Below are a few examples of ***have-been V-ing*** verb groups in active patterns, contrasted with ***have-been V-en*** forms in passives.

ACTIVE: I (you, we, they) *have been running.*
He (she, it, Bob) *has been running.*
I (you, he, she, it, Bob, we, they) *had been running.*

PASSIVE: The race *has (had)* *been run.*
The races *have (had)* *been run.*
He *has (had) got* (himself) *arrested.*
They *have (had) got* (themselves) *arrested.*

TEACHING SUGGESTION: With the exception of *have got*, the above patterns are very good for oral/written work. Ask your students to invent sentences using them. Discuss the times of the actions.

Phrase Markers

Phrase markers are the prepositions of traditional grammar. They include single words and combinations of words that pattern, or distribute, in phrase-marking positions within sentences. Because prepositions have such variety of structure and specificity in expressing relationships, mastery of the system can contribute a great deal to the development of mature style in speech and writing.

A number of prepositions may pattern as clause markers, or as adverbs; they are designated **phrase markers** only when they fill phrase-marking positions.

PREPOSITIONS: The children were not expected *until* five o'clock.
But they came back long *after* dark.
CLAUSE MARKERS: They were not missed *until* we had eaten dinner.
After several hours had passed, we began a search.
PREPOSITIONS: Jack and Jill went *up* the hill.
The hunters ranged *through* the woods.
ADVERBS: The attorney drew *up* the papers.
The whole agreement fell *through.*

Discriminating among these structural positions and functions is a part of mastering not only the system of prepositions, but the other structure-word systems as well.

TEACHING SUGGESTION: As introductory oral work, ask your students to make up sentences using the prepositions, clause markers, and adverbs in the above examples. Have a class discussion of differences of word class and meaning. Then ask them to volunteer similar examples of their own. See if they can suggest follow-up work (for example, investigations and either oral or written reports on uses of phrase markers in everyday speech; on radio or television; in printed matter).

Phrase markers may be classified into four groups according to their structural constituents:

1. **Simple prepositions:** a single free morpheme — *at, by, in, on, through.*
2. **Double, or compound, prepositions:** two prepositions *written* as a single word — *into, throughout, upon.*
3. **Complex prepositions:** two or more morphemes, one of which is bound — *aboard, beneath, concerning.*
4. **Group, or phrasal, prepositions:** two or more words written separately but treated as a single preposition — *according to, along with, away from, in back of, in connection with.*

TEACHING SUGGESTION: For rapid oral work introducing the topic, ask your students to use the above classes of prepositions in phrases of their own. Here are a few examples:

1. *at the time; by the way; in the morning; on the bus; through the window.*
2. *into the soup; throughout the night; upon my soul.*
3. *aboard the ship; beneath contempt; concerning the tureen.*
4. *according to my information; along with the other supplies; away from it all; in back of the building; in connection with the conference.*

After your students have given examples of phrases, ask for oral sentences using their phrases. Open a discussion of both the structural and semantic aspects of prepositions classified by structural constituents. This discussion may lead to follow-up work based on further exploration of the uses of phrase markers.

Phrase markers may also be classified into five groups according to the semantic relationships they signal.

1. Location: *at, aboard, within, on top of.*
2. Direction: *up, under, toward, into.*
3. Association: *with, concerning, of, in addition to.*
4. Agency: *by, out of, by means of.*
5. Time: *from, after, until.*

TEACHING SUGGESTION: Use oral examples to begin a class discussion of the students' acquaintance with prepositions; try to sharpen their sense of the different kinds of relational meanings that may be expressed by phrase markers.

1. *at home; aboard ship; within four walls; on top of the world.*
2. *up the street; under the wheels; toward the city; into the house.*
3. *with us; concerning ourselves; of the class; in addition to our friends.*
4. *by the plumber; out of despair; by means of electricity.*
5. *from now on; after the ball; until morning.*

After examples of phrases have been given orally, ask for oral sentences using those phrases. Have a class discussion of both structural makeup and relational meanings of prepositions of *Location, Direction, Association, Agency,* and *Time.* This discussion could lead to various follow-up investigations into the relational meanings of phrase markers and their uses in speech and writing; one possibility is the development of a glossary.

These two classifications of phrase markers — according to their structural constituents and according to their relational meanings — overlap almost completely. Prepositions expressing **Location, Direction,** and **Association** include examples from all four groups classified above on the basis of structure; those expressing **Agency** and **Time** include examples from three of the four structure groups (all but compound prepositions). Taken together, both classifications can be useful in explaining the structure and meaning of phrases used in sentences — in speech, reading, and writing.

In the following alphabetical listings of phrase markers grouped by structural makeup, letters indicate some of the classifications by relationships:

L, location;   D, direction;   A, association;   Ag, agency;   T, time.

There is considerable overlapping of the relationships that may be expressed by phrase markers; these differences in usage may be of crucial importance in reading and composition.

Numerals suggest grade levels where formal discovery and practice with the markers might be introduced, based intuitively upon educated guesswork (there is no research). Probably not all possible relationships would be treated at the level of introduction; later lessons and work in higher grades can develop more mature meanings and relationships.

SIMPLE PHRASE MARKERS

at	L, D, A, T	3	out	L, D	3
but	A	3	past	L, D, T	4
by	L, D, Ag, T	3	per	A, Ag, T	6
down	L, D	3	round	L, D, T	4
for	D, A	4	since	T	3
from	L, D, Ag, T	3	than	A	6
in	L, D, A	3	through	L, D, Ag, T	3
like	A	4	till	T	3
near	L, A, T	3	to	L, D, A, T	3
of	A, T	3	up	L, D	3
off	L, D	3	via	D, Ag	7–8
on	L, D, A	3	with	A, Ag	3

DOUBLE, OR COMPOUND, PHRASE MARKERS

inside	L, D	3	throughout	L, D, T	3
into	D	3	upon	L, D	4
onto	L, D	3	within	L, D	4
outside	L, D	3	without	L, D, A	4

COMPLEX PHRASE MARKERS

aboard	L, D	3	across	L, D	3
above	L, D	3	after	L, D, T	3

about	D, T	3	against	L, D	3
along	L, D	3	between	L, D	3
alongside	L, D	7–8	beyond	L, D	4
amid	L	7–8	concerning	A	4
amidst	L	9–12	considering	A	9–12
among	L, D	3	despite	A	7–8
around	L, D, T	3	during	T	4
atop	L	7–8	except(ing)	A	3
before	L, D, T	3	opposite	L, D	7–8
behind	L, D	3	pending	A	7–8
below	L, D	3	regarding	A	7–8
beneath	L, D	3	respecting	A	9–12
beside	L, D	3	toward(s)	L, D, T	5
besides	A	3	unlike	A	4
			until	T	3

GROUP PHRASE MARKERS

according to	A	6	by means of	Ag	7–8
ahead of	L, D, T	3	down at	L	3
alongside of	L, D	7–8	down from	L	3
along with	L, A	3	down in	L	3
apart from	L, D, A	4	down on	L	3
aside from	L, D, A	4	due to	A	7–8
as to	A	5	except for	A	6
away from	L, D, A	3	in accordance		
back of	L, D	3	with	A	9–12
because of	A	3	in addition to	A	5
by agency of	Ag	9–12	in back of	A	3
by dint of	Ag	9–12	in (on) behalf of	A	7–8
in consideration			in connection		
of	A	9–12	with	A	9–12
in exchange for	A	5	on board of	L, D	5
in front of	A	3	on either side		
in lieu of	A	9–12	(of)	L, D	5
in place of	A	5	on top of	L, D	3
in regard to	A	9–12	outside of	L, D, A	3
inside of	L, D	3	over at	L, D	3
in spite of	A	5	over to	L, D	3
in view of	A	9–12	owing to	A	9–12
next to	L, D	3	relative to	A	9–12
on account of	A	5	together with	A	9–12
			with regard to	A	9–12
			with respect to	A	9–12

TEACHING SUGGESTION: According to the interests and abilities of individuals in your class, a variety of classroom and outside work can be based upon each of the above four structural categories. Fruitful explorations can be made into speech; casual, informal, formal, dialectal; and into all forms of written and printed literature. Written compositions designed to exploit the possibilities of phrase markers can be educational as well as interesting. A few possible topics follow:

1. Either orally or in writing, develop a good sentence using each of the relational meanings suggested for a single phrase marker. Consider whether contradictory or simply additional meanings can be discovered.

2. Compare and contrast the possible uses of compound phrase markers used both as compound and as separate words: *into, in to; onto, on to; throughout, through out; upon, up on; within, with in; without, with out.*

3. Write sentences using *different* phrase markers that might be effective. Discuss the pros and cons in order to determine which phrase marker is best for a specific purpose or context.

4. Explore the uses of phrase markers in a chosen language setting: everyday speech; the special language of a vocation, or a sport; formal speech on radio or television; various styles and forms of prose, drama, or poetry. These investigations may be small or large; of short or long duration; they may be reported orally or in writing.

5. Look up any phrase marker in a dictionary, preferably *Webster's Third New International; on* is a rewarding one, but all are interesting.

6. Develop an essay or story using some of the techniques and devices of Marion Gleason's article below. Many other topics may occur to you or be suggested by interested students.

Following is a witty and hilarious exploration of the peregrinations of one little two-letter word — *up*. The author revels in the uses of *up* as an adverb, almost "an adjunct to every verb," as a suffix; as a prefix; and even incidentally as a preposition!

Coming up in every conversation, met up with on every street corner, is the most formidable little word in the English language — *up*. It featured recently in the title of a best seller; it has helped to name a popular drink. No longer do we add a column of figures, shake a son, dress a daughter, eat the popcorn. We add them up, shake him up, dress her up, eat it up. Not expressible by a Latinate prefix because the Romans had no word for it, *up* is rapidly becoming in the English language an adjunct to every verb.

Who said *up* was the opposite of *down?* When we tie it up, set it up, drink it up, shake it up, close it up, it is quite possible that at the same time we are tying it down, setting it down, drinking it down, shaking it down, closing it down. Who said *up* means *up* anyway? When we clam up, slip up, fold up, mess up, frame up, there is no sense of an upward direction; in some of them quite the contrary.

Often the *up* makes no difference whether we say it or not. Did you wake this morning or wake up? Did you eat your breakfast or eat it up, wipe the table or wipe it up, make your bed or make it up, lock your apartment or lock it up, start your car or start it up? Did you wrap a package or wrap it up, pay your bills or pay them up?

On the other hand, you did get up, not merely get; you did louse up the big deal, not louse it; the lost paper turned up, it didn't merely turn. Furthermore it makes quite a difference if a girl makes a face or makes up a face, if a man lives his life or lives it up, if I make a defense or make one up, if you bring your children or bring them up, for that matter if they grow up or if they just grow. You know whether you are dressed up or dressed, whether he beat you up or beat you, whether you're done up or done.

When *up* snuggles close to the mother word as a suffix, it may or may not form an entirely new meaning. Thus markup, writeup, and closeup have apparently joined forces merely to create new nouns. Buildup, frameup, cutup, and makeup, on the other hand, adopt metaphorical meanings; makeup may do a lot of things, but that is another story.

When the uppity *up* prefers to become a prefix, it is sometimes upsetting to the meaning. The upset is different from the setup, the upstart from the start up, an upshot from a shot up; upbraiding is quite unlike braiding up. Uplift, uphill, upstairs, upstate, however, all mean just what they should mean, with no adjustment whatsoever. The degree of togetherness of the prefix is sometimes a matter of choice. It makes little difference whether you stand up right or upright. Whether you go up stream, up-stream, or upstream is apparently up to you.

With or without hyphens, there is no end to the flexibility of *up*. Its upper-classmanship, its up-to-dateness, its one-upmanship over objections of linguistic purists give comeuppance to those who prefer a Latinate language to the tough Anglo-Saxon product. Like it or not, we can all see how this upward movement is going to end. To end up, that is.[1]

"On with Up" is a lovely illustration of both the spirit and the learning possibilities of creative explorations of our language. I wish every teacher who reads this concluding section would take it as a broadside Teaching Suggestion.

Clause Markers

Clause markers are words and word groups that *identify clauses*, usually in the starting position; they also *signal specific relationships* between two or more clauses; like phrase markers, clause markers shift rather easily from one structure-word classification to another; they are designated **clause markers** only when they fill the clause marking position and/or function (see p. 210).

Clause markers include three main groups:

1. so-called **coordinating conjunctions,** with *and* as the prototype;
2. so-called **subordinating conjunctions,** with *because* as the prototype;
3. **sentence connectors,** with *therefore* as the prototype.

The terms **coordinating** and **subordinating conjunctions** do not describe the relationships of the clauses marked and connected by these two sets of clause markers; in particular, they do not describe the content or meaning relationships.

In school grammar, by definition, a **complex sentence** contains one **main clause** and one or more **subordinate clauses;** in such a sentence, the clause without a **subordinating conjunction** is defined as the **main** or **independent clause;** an attached clause that is marked by, or contains, a **subordinating conjunction** is defined as a **subordinate clause.** The complex sentences below show that these terms do not reflect the relative importance of the clauses in the statement; that is, one clause is not necessarily of main importance and the other subordinate by virtue of the presence or absence of any kind of conjunction.

SUBORDINATING CONJUNCTION: *Because* **he was seriously ill, he was absent.**

COORDINATING CONJUNCTIONS: He was absent, *for* he was seriously ill.

He was seriously ill, *so* he was absent.

These three sentences all have the same basic meaning; the serious illness seems of greater importance than the absence. Stylistically, they are arranged in the order of descending formality.

In the following complex sentences, *although* may mark either of two clauses, with some difference in emphasis:

Although I must expose him, he is my own brother.
Although he is my own brother, I must expose him.

TEACHING SUGGESTION: Use the above or similar examples to open a class discussion of clause markers. See whether your class can develop the generalization that the terms *coordinating* and *subordinating* are purely technical: in themselves they say nothing about the substantive meanings nor the relationships between clauses. Follow-up work might lead into any of the diverse topics discussed later in this section.

COORDINATING CONJUNCTIONS. Coordinating conjunctions are used in compound sentences to connect two or more main or independent clauses separated by commas, or without commas if the clauses are very short. (*He entered quickly and they all left at once.*) The seven coordinating conjunctions of school grammar are *and, but, for, nor, or, so, yet.* What they have in common is principally their one-syllableness, for they are not an especially logical grouping: their meanings vary considerably, and they may serve a variety of functions. Notice these characteristics:

and is a simple connector of equal elements, a plus sign:

The heavy snow fell for hours, *and* great drifts closed the roads.

but and *yet* signify contrasting basic statements:

The heavy snow fell for hours, *but* the work went on.
The heavy snow fell for hours, *yet* the men kept the road open.

but may double as a preposition:

Everyone came *but* George.

yet may double as an adverb:

> The team is not here *yet* (or *yet* here).

nor and *or* both signify alternative basic statements:

> They would not walk, *nor* would they ride. (*nor* is negative, with *not* or *neither*)
> You must leave at once, *or* I will call for help. (*or* is positive, with or without *either*)

for and *so* may both signify causal relationships between basic statements:

> "Who or whom is in charge here?" asked Cholmondely, *for* he had been studying school grammar.
> He insisted on eating starchy foods, *so* he got fat.

for may double as a preposition:

> That will be all, *for* the nonce.

so may double as an intensifier:

> The entertainment was not *so* hot.

or as a pronoun:

> He was born poor but did not remain *so*.
> It will take two hours or *so*.

or as an adverb:

> You must hold your mouth just *so*.
> *So* you don't believe me.

TEACHING SUGGESTION: According to the interests and abilities of your class, introduce the above examples, or more suitable ones, in order to stimulate class discussion of co-ordinating conjunctions. Before attempting any generalizations, lead them to a full exploration of the specific meanings and uses of this small set of small words; try to get them to differentiate between the loosely defined coordinating functions and the others. A highly motivated junior or senior high school student might write an extensive paper on one or more of the coordinating conjunctions; shorter papers can be based on dictionary study of single items.

Five of the seven coordinating conjunctions — *and, but, nor, or, yet* — often connect single words or word groups, as well as the clauses of compound sentences. These compoundings can provide interest and variety to sentences; below are a few simple illustrations.

NOUNS:

Frankie and Johnny were lovers.
The school colors are *cherry and white.*
I bring *not peace but a sword.*
They did not ask for *bread nor wine.*
Come *hell or high water,* our side must win.

VERBS:

The helpless old man *stormed and ranted and raged.*
The lithe cat *did not walk but ran swiftly.*
Most fish *cannot walk nor fly.*
The condemned man was asked whether he would *stand or sit.*
How do you propose to *go yet stay?*

ADJECTIVES:

Jolly good company indeed was that *fat and sassy* character.
They arrived home past midnight, *bone-weary but satisfied.*
Pert and cheerful, handsome and strong, the young man danced a jig.
He wanted no *red nor yellow* fabrics in his mardi gras costume.
The provost said he was *quite willing yet quite unable.*

ADVERBS:

The chief officer *loudly and angrily* cursed his hapless crew.
The wounded men crawled *painfully but quickly* through the muck.
Sooner or later, they knew they would have to retreat.
The loser kept coming on, *not gaily nor jauntily,* but on he came.
The assassin moved *politely yet remorselessly* among the guests.

TEACHING SUGGESTION: Using the above examples or others of your choosing, introduce compounding of one form class at a time: nouns, verbs, adjectives, adverbs. This work may involve four or more lessons. This is a good opportunity for oral work on sentences. Follow-up work may take a variety of forms: some students may enjoy composition assignments that require various kinds of compounding throughout, as a means of developing variety in their sentences.

SUBORDINATING CONJUNCTIONS. In the **complex sentences** of school grammar, a large and varied group of markers start clauses that are connected in specific ways — by the choice of marker — to other sentence elements: single words, word groups and clusters, entire sentence patterns. Some clause markers may also serve as phrase markers, others as question markers (see p. 210 and p. 217). *Because* may be considered the prototype; other common ones are *if, that, how, when, which, since, why.* Following are colloquial examples of sentences using the listed items:

Grandfather is bedfast *because he is so old and weak.*
If you want us to, we'll all go with you.
Chet said he would go *if Ned did.*
I was sure *that you would buy it.*
Geordie can't see *how you can do it.*
We'll cross that bridge *when we get to it.*
Just tell the man *which one you want.*
Dickie Bird hasn't eaten a seed *since the cat died.*
I don't know *why you say that.*

However, generally a sentence connector, also serves as a clause marker of the above set:

However hard I try, I can't do it right.

TEACHING SUGGESTION: Use colloquial sentences such as the above to introduce a class discussion, with oral examples, of clause markers. Clause markers are common in everyday speech, yet many students are not sufficiently aware to use them effectively in composition, where they can make the difference between mature and immature style. Follow-up work might take the form of written assignments in which the student writes a paragraph in simple sentences first and then translates it into complex sentences; interested students might like to analyze the use of clause markers in something they are reading: a textbook, fiction, a newspaper or magazine article. Skill in the use of clause markers is well worth acquiring.

SENTENCE CONNECTORS. Sentence connectors may be used in compound sentences with two or more basic sentences connected by semicolons; sometimes between two sentences separated by a period (in speech, both would generally be terminated by a fade–fall voice terminal). They have the special trait of signaling quite specific relationships between main clauses; often they mark the beginning of a second or a third clause, but they are also movable within the clause. In meaning, they commonly signify cause, contrast, or addition. We may take *therefore* as the prototype; others are *consequently, furthermore, hence, however, indeed, moreover, nevertheless, otherwise.* These words may also be used within single sentences, but normally with reference to a previous sentence in the discourse.

I think; *therefore I am.*
I am; *therefore I think.*
The expedition soon ran out of funds; *consequently, the explorers had to stop far short of their goal.*
The dean is urging the appointment; *furthermore, the provost is backing the dean.*
The deacon is a modest soul; *hence, he is hesitant to press matters.*
The graduate students seemed indifferent; *the undergraduates, however, were all up in arms.*
The Congress began to oppose the President; *indeed, they delayed action even on routine housekeeping appropriations.*
The Air Force and the Marines are calling up their reserve units; *moreover, the Army is beginning to deploy its strategic forces.*
The royal consort was no longer a young man; *nevertheless, he managed to get in a few chukkers in nearly every match.*
The ceremony should be held very soon now; *otherwise, it will have lost a good deal of its meaning.*

TEACHING SUGGESTION: Sentence connectors can help attain a balanced style in rather formal writing. Students should have an opportunity to read aloud, and to hear, sentences using them in order to associate the sound of the sentence with its printed form. Discuss the meanings of the examples above; ask the students to move connectors within clauses, where suitable. Follow-up work might include compositions in which connectors are used, and exploration of their use in articles and books the students are reading; dictionary study might interest some students, who could make oral or written reports.

Coordinating or subordinating conjunctions that work together in pairs are **correlative conjunctions**. When used well, they produce a feeling of logical balance and maturity of writing style. Correlative conjunctions mark not only clauses, but other syntactic structures as well. Following is a brief illustrative list.

either . . . or	*not only . . . but also*
neither . . . nor	*whether . . . or*
if . . . then	*while . . . still*
when . . . then	*both . . . and*

Either the drain must be cleared *or* the water pipes will freeze.
Neither the man in the moon *nor* the green cheese the moon is said to be made of were of the slightest interest to old Higginbotham.
If you want to dance and sing, my lad, *then* you must pay the piper.
When the birds sing in April, *then* young lovers come to life.

(The first eighteen lines of "The General Prologue" to Chaucer's *Canterbury Tales* is a single *when . . . then* sentence; the *when* part is the first eleven lines, the *then* part the last seven.)

Not only the bright-eyed and bushy-tailed teenagers, *but also* the stolid squares over thirty must try to bridge the generation gap.
Whether he will come at once when called, *or* wait upon his own sweet whim, time alone can tell.
While nearly everyone understood the underlying causes, *still* they were not ready to accept the consequences.
Both the old guard *and* the young turks closed ranks against the common foe.

TEACHING SUGGESTION: Like sentence connectors, correlative conjunctions are perhaps best studied in printed matter first, or in written examples on the board or duplicated for distribution; students should be helped to associate the sound of the sentences with their printed or written forms. Correlatives are a good topic for dictionary study, or for exploration in articles and books the students are reading. Many topics are suitable for oral or written reports.

Clause markers are possibly more important than the system of prepositions for developing a mature speaking and writing style. As a system, clause markers overlap and cross-classify just as prepositions do; and their meanings become richer and more complex, corresponding to more sophisticated concepts and vocabulary as students mature.

TEACHING SUGGESTION: Advanced students who are interested in analyzing writing style, or in acquiring knowledge either for its own sake or for possible application in their own writing, should be encouraged to enrich their understanding of structure words by dictionary study in *Webster's Third New International,* or even the *Oxford English Dictionary.* Some might profit by study of some of the books listed in Selected References. Motivated students may then apply their findings to analysis of literary style, or to deliberate use of new items in their own compositions.

Selected References

See Chapter 7, Selected References.

Chapter 9

American English Intonation

A sentence is a sound in itself on which other sounds called words may be strung. You may string words together without a sentence-sound to string them on, just as you may tie clothes together by the sleeves and stretch them without a clothes line between two trees, but — it is bad for the clothes. The sentence-sounds are very different entities . . . they are as definite as words. It is not impossible that they could be collected in a book. . . .

Robert Frost

A venerable literature exists on English intonation, mainly written before the development of modern linguistics, or without benefit of modern linguistic information and insights. "Oral interpretation" and the familiar school term, "reading with expression," refer to **interpretive intonation.** Some descriptive linguists use the term **paralanguage** for this emotive dimension of language, and refer to it as an **overlay** upon the language structure as such; paralanguage is an individual option, the personal expression of the speaker's attitude or feeling. **Structural intonation,** on the other hand, is part of the language system itself: it is **grammatical;** thus, structural intonation is **obligatory,** in precisely the same way as other parts of grammar are. Linguists are not in complete agreement about the grammatical level of structural intonation; some consider it phonemic or morphemic (at the level of basic sounds or of words), others syntactical (at the level of the sentence) — but there is general agreement that structural intonation is grammatical and obligatory, not optional or interpretive. Within the system of structural intonation, the speaker does make choices, just as he does in lexicon and syntax, but these choices are not merely expressive of the speaker's personal attitude or feeling. In sum, structural intonation is linguistic, not paralinguistic.

Scholarly study of structural intonation in American and British English is of comparatively recent origin. Bloomfield dealt broadly with intonation in *Language* (1933);[1] in 1945 Pike presented detailed analyses of American intonation, with special attention to pitch contours and stress-timed rhythm;[2] in 1951 Trager and Smith published their analysis of English phonology, including twelve "suprasegmental phonemes" (intonation features);[3] the British phonetician Abercrombie has published an interesting view of English stress-timed rhythm;[4] Halliday, a British linguist, has done significant work on intonation as part of the grammar of British English;[5] and Lieberman has studied features that he believes may underlie American English intonation.[6] From quite different theoretical positions, both Halliday and Lieberman argue, as do I, that intonation is central rather than peripheral to the study of language. Most of the foregoing work is either "pure linguistics" or linguistics applied to teaching English as a second language; apparently a chapter of mine has been the principal discussion in print that deals with intonation in relation to reading and language arts instruction for American children.[7]

Intonation plays a systematic role in the overall sound and rhythm of English speech and oral reading; it has a pervasive influence on both writing and silent reading. Intonation patterns combine features of (a) **relative loudness** or **stress,** (b) changes in level of voice **pitch,** and (c) **pauses** that separate or terminate significant segments of speech or oral reading. In successful composing of written work and in silent reading, rhythms and echoes of intonation accompany and reinforce the visual shapes of meaning-bearing language patterns — sentences predominantly. Sentences are the basic building blocks of written English: exposition, fiction, poetry, drama. Intonation patterns help to integrate and coordinate sentences, and to clarify their meaning; this is why intonation is of critical importance to both written composition and reading comprehension.

Intonation is a rich, complex subject, potentially an interdisciplinary study, of profound importance to understanding American English. It has not received the attention its importance demands, either as a technical specialty or an area of applied linguistics. My own work on intonation began with undergraduate study of acting and oral interpretation; it has continued through graduate study, independent study, and teaching of speech, rhetoric, English language, linguistics, and literature. Intonation permeates and informs the spoken language; it is the essence of the auditory and kinesic elements of all forms of written English. Intonation is a fundamental part of English structure, and thus fundamental to English style and rhythm.

The remainder of this chapter is presented under four main topics as follows:

Summary and Forecast
The Fundamental Stress-timed Rhythm of English
Structural Features of Intonation
Prose: Written Sentences and Sentence Intonation

Summary and Forecast

This chapter is a fresh attempt to explain to teachers the relevance of intonation to teaching English and the language arts. Someday, when we understand intonation more fully, we will have drawn upon various disciplines to make applications in teaching — a spectrum ranging from basic sounds and rhythms in kindergarten–primary instruction to acting and artistic interpretation of poetry. Ideally, we will have made a synthesis from our understanding of language — linguistics, grammar, phonetics, phonemics; psychology — learning theory, psychology of language; composition and rhetoric; speech and persuasion; acting and oral interpretation; imaginative literature — style, language, and form in drama, fiction, and poetry; and theory of language and language instruction. We have only begun our exploration of intonation, its applications and implications.

But it is not necessary to be a linguist to begin to enjoy intonation and apply it significantly in the classroom. Any native speaker's consciousness of intonation can be heightened if he will only train his ear to perceive both structural and interpretive features that he already responds to unconsciously. Because he is a native speaker, his control of intonation has become automatic, intuitive, unconscious; as a teacher or performing artist, he must cultivate conscious awareness and control if he hopes to approach professional excellence. Classroom teaching experience is an invaluable basis; simple tape recorders have many pertinent applications, inside and outside the classroom. Oral practice recorded on tape, with repeated playback of "the disembodied voice," provides objective data for both teacher and learner alike to study. Once a teacher has made his first breakthrough in conscious mastery of intonation, new insights and applications will come crowding in upon him.

The remainder of this chapter and part of the next provide a brief survey of intonation in relation to English and language arts instruction; full coverage of all topics would make a sizable book. We begin with the visual bias toward language that afflicts many well-educated persons, and then discuss the interplay of spoken and written English; rhythm and tone of voice; the distinction between structural and interpretive intonation; language structure and its physiological basis; the speaker/writer as the source of language rhythm; the three structural elements of intonation, (a) **stress,** (b) **pitch,** and (c) **voice terminals** and **pauses;** prose sentence patterns and sentence intonation; word-calling; intonation and punctuation; and finally, in Chapter 10, intonational aspects of poetry, fiction, and literary forms in general.

Discussion of voice pitch focuses on voice terminals and associated rises, drops, and pauses. Pitch contours are but lightly treated here because, of all the elements of intonation, they are the most highly technical and the least susceptible of being presented simply yet accurately; the chief teaching application of precise descriptions of pitch contours is in the art of acting and oral interpretation.

Technical terms and notation symbols are used only in so far as they are essential to grasping the rudiments; even so, they have been chosen for teachers, not prescribed for their students. This chapter is aimed at the understanding of the teacher; thus it is largely substantive, with some suggestions of method. The decision to use special terms and symbols with students lies with the teacher. My recommendation is to use them sparingly if at all, especially in elementary grades; direct example and nontechnical explanation are the methods of choice.

The remainder of this *Summary and Forecast* is presented under three subheadings:

THE VISUAL BIAS

RHYTHM AND TONE OF VOICE

A QUALITATIVE DISTINCTION

THE VISUAL BIAS. As a side-effect of "book-larnin'," most of us have acquired a visual bias toward language — a bias severe enough to skew our perception of speech and the speech-related processes of reading and writing. (This is true of linguists as well as ordinary mortals; it is poignantly true of many transformationalists.) We forget that speech is the primary symbol system in language learning, and that handwriting and print comprise a secondary symbol-system, based upon and derived from speech. Handwriting and print are graphic symbols for vocal symbols: thus we have a dual set of symbols; but because of a strong visual bias, many educated but linguistically unsophisticated persons tend to regard the graphic system as normative for both speech and writing.

This visual bias toward language must be overcome if we are to understand the complex interplay between the spoken language and its graphic counterparts, an interplay of crucial importance to language theory and to instruction in composition, literature, speech and oral interpretation.

RHYTHM AND TONE OF VOICE. In our well-meaning approach to intonation, occasionally Americans mingle national chauvinism with linguistic naivete. Oh, a few foreigners have an odd, singsong speech — vaudeville Swedes and comic-strip Chinese. But we Americans speak just plain natural English. No nonsense about us, and no singsong either. Yet we all share the linguistic wisdom of the intonation joke, *He always puts the emphasis on the wrong syllable.* We know that a rule of English intonation requires that the *emphasis* be placed on the right *syllable. This is a structural rule of English rhythm.*

We have a set of intonation jokes based upon the following rhythmic contrast:

(a) *He is a comic-book salesman.*

(b) **He is a comic book-salesman.**

In (a) the *books* are comic; in (b) the *salesman* is comic. (Notice that hyphens may be used to convey the difference in rhythm and stress placement.)

We know too that "tone of voice" can warp the literal meanings of words and sentences, can even turn surface meanings into their opposites. "I like what you say, but I don't like the way you say it" is part of our folklore. So is the melancholy line from the blues song, "I could read her letters, but I sure couldn't read her mind." (What he couldn't read was her tone of voice.) These are matters of paralanguage, or of interpretive intonation.

Rhythm and tone of voice represent two aspects of intonation — *structural* and *interpretive*, respectively — both highly relevant to teaching English and the language arts.

A QUALITATIVE DISTINCTION. English and language arts teachers should grasp the clear distinction between:

(1) structural intonation patterns and features, and

(2) interpretive intonation patterns and features.

Regardless of subtleties and exceptions, and overlapping of the two kinds, this is a qualitative distinction; it has great clarifying power for the study of English intonation, and particularly for its application to English and language arts instruction. It must not be blurred.

Structural intonation patterns and features are grammatical elements of the total language system; they occur with very high frequency, and some choice among features is usually obligatory. **Interpretive intonation** is an expressive dimension of language having great richness and complexity, the ultimate basis for the creative uses of language as art. Both structural and interpretive intonation are important to all the skills of speech and literacy, but for primary and basic instruction in reading and writing, the structural is fundamental, the essential foundation for the interpretive ("with expression").

TEACHING SUGGESTION: As a start on intonation, introduce the joke about placing the emphasis upon the wrong syllable, and the one about the comic-book salesman. See whether your students can contribute others. Try to lead them to understand that these points are structural.

For contrast, introduce tone of voice. Amusing and instructive games include reading from a telephone directory, a grocery list, or other neuter material, using various ludicrous paralinguistic overtones, such as amorousness, anger, boredom, excitement, grief, hunger, thirst.

The Fundamental Stress-timed Rhythm of English

A human being talking (or reading) is a biological organism ruled by the iron necessities of basic metabolism: respiration (the basic stuff of speech), circulation of the blood, digestion. These and related physiological processes are fundamental to his existence; in another sense they are also fundamental to his speech. These underlying physiological functions, breathing especially, determine in basic ways the nature and rhythm of speech sounds.

The innate muscular rhythm of breathing makes possible the organization of two different timing systems for language rhythm: *stressed-timed* and *syllable-timed;* these timing systems are not mechanically physiological, but conditioned and learned. English is a stress-timed language, in contrast to such syllable-timed languages as French and Spanish. Mastery of stressed-timed rhythm eventually becomes automatic to native speakers of English, along with automatic control of the entire language system, but this mastery of stress-timed rhythm in speech does not necessarily transfer to the psycholinguistic processes of writing and reading: the teacher must intervene and teach accurate information about stress. Because ours is a stress-timed language, stress is probably the most important single element of intonation for successful teaching of composition, literature, and oral interpretation. Stress is basic to English rate and rhythm.

The remainder of this discussion of stress-timed rhythm is presented under four subtitles, as follows:

THE SPEAKER/WRITER AS SOURCE OF LANGUAGE RHYTHM
THE NATURE OF STRESS-TIMED RHYTHM
THE RHYTHMIC FOOT
SILENT FEET AND LESSER SILENT STRESSES

THE SPEAKER/WRITER AS SOURCE OF LANGUAGE RHYTHM. We have noted that a human being talking is a biological organism; so is a human being writing or reading. All rhythm perceived by man may ultimately be felt emphathically as bodily (muscular) rhythm. There is no question that speech rhythm originates in the muscular movements within each speaker; the native English speaker has learned to control his breathing musculature so as to impart a pulsating, stress-timed rhythm to the stream of air carrying speech sounds. The auditor does not respond simply to the sounds he hears; he identifies himself with the speaker and picks up the speaker's language rhythms by empathy. The auditor probably identifies with the more specific muscular movements of articulation also, but these are peripheral to rhythm.

Just as the speaker imparts a stress-timed rhythm to his speech, so does the writer impart a corresponding rhythm to the graphic counterparts of speech; stress-timed rhythm is inherent in the English language, both spoken and written. The reader picks up the writer's rhythm by an empathy parallel with that of the auditor and the speaker; that is, the reader identifies with the writer (as speaker) and empathizes with the muscular stress-pulse beat of the language patterns written down by the writer. In short, the reader responds to the rhythm of written and printed language in the same way as the auditor responds to the rhythm of spoken language; the rhythm of written English may indeed be stronger and more regular, because the composing process allows for painstaking construction and revision of wording. Reading can thus go flowingly, like hearing a fluent speaker, but at a much faster rate. Successful reading requires a transfer of muscular empathy from the role of auditor to the role of reader, in both oral and silent reading. This transfer of rhythm does not imply slow visual reading (at the rate of speech) any more than visual perception of words and sentences does. On the contrary: because rhythm is a fundamental part of the language, clear perception of it should contribute to both speed and comprehension.

THE NATURE OF STRESSED-TIMED RHYTHM. English rhythm has a regular beat of *approximately* equally spaced (timed) stress-pulses; the time allotted to all syllables between these major stresses in English tends to be *approximately* equal in any given utterance. A syllable may be defined as a speech unit that includes a vowel sound and carries a degree of stress. In English, syllables carry varying degrees of stress according to their distribution in rhythmic patterns; in syllable-timed languages, all syllables carry *approximately* the same degree of stress. Thus French for example has a rapid metronomic rhythm of *evenly stressed syllables;* but the rhythm of English speech and oral reading is characterized by successive bursts of *unevenly stressed syllables*.

Mixing his French and English, naturellement, the Frenchman says, "Mon accent, it is noticeable, non?" The American replies, "Your accent, it is noticeable, yes!" In the display below, vertical lines mark *all syllables* in the French. French syllable-timed rhythm sounds like a small outboard motor, with fairly even stresses on all ten syllables:

Putt	putt	putt,	putt	putt	putt	putt	putt	putt,	putt?
Mon	ac	cent,	it	is	no	ti	cea	ble,	non?

In contrast, with heavy stresses on only three syllables, and light stresses on seven, English stress-timed rhythm sounds more like a one-cylinder engine that skips and misses:

Pt	PUTT	pt,	pt	pt	PUTT	pt	pt	pt,	PUTT!
Your	AC	cent,	it	is	NO	ti	cea	ble,	YES!

TEACHING SUGGESTION: Introduce your class to this contrast of French and English rhythm; or use a different example, or another language. Students who are familiar with a second language may be interested in developing parallel examples; Mexican and Puerto Rican children (whose languages are syllable-timed) should find this interesting. Try it.

THE RHYTHMIC FOOT. For analysis and notation of the rhythms of English sentences, we may designate as a foot that unit beginning with the first major stress and including all syllables up to but not including the next major stress. A vertical line before each major stress marks off successive feet. Abercrombie cites *This is the house that Jack built* as a sentence having three kinds of feet according to the number of syllables.[8] The four feet, with their syllable counts shown below the text, are as follows:

| |This is the |house that |Jack |built.
| | 3 | 2 | 1 | 1

The English foot as described and illustrated here is a convenient unit for analyzing and notating the basic stress-timed rhythm of speech, prose, and verse. It can be very helpful in determining rhythm and rate of passages to be read aloud.

Below is the powerfully-rhythmed opening paragraph of the Declaration of Independence, divided into rhythmic feet designated by vertical lines. Notice that rhythmic feet are no respecters of word boundaries; a foot may begin or end within a word, as in e | *vents,* dis | *solve, po* | *litical, con* | *nected, an* | *other, as* | *sume, a* | *mong,* en | *title, re* | *spect, o* | *pinions, man* | *kind, re* | *quires, de* | *clare,* im | *pel,* and *sepa* | *ration.* The dotted vertical lines below suggest optional or additional rhythmic feet, depending upon desired emphases and rate of delivery; these optional feet are well within the constraints of English stress-timed rhythm, which is structural. One important feature of English rhythm — silent stresses and silent feet — is ignored in this passage; the silent foot is illustrated and explained in the paragraph below the Teaching Suggestion, and silent stresses are developed later in this chapter.

| *When, in the* | *course of* | *human e* | *vents, it be* ⁞ *comes* | *neces-sary for* | *one* ⁞ *people to dis* | *solve the po* | *litical* | *bonds which have con* | *nected* ⁞ *them with an* | *other, and to as* | *sume a* ⁞ *mong the* | *Powers of the* | *earth, the* | *separate and* | *equal* | *station to* ⁞ *which the* | *Laws of* | *Nature and of* | *Nature's* | *God en* | *title them, a* | *decent re* | *spect to the o* | *pinions of* ⁞ *man* | *kind re* | *quires that* ⁞ *they should de* | *clare the* |*causes* ⁞ *which im* | *pel them to the sepa* | *ration.*

TEACHING SUGGESTION: The student's first objective is to acquire a degree of conscious perception and control of a fundamental feature of English intonation: stress-timed rhythm. Experience shows that inexperienced native speakers have difficulty perceiving rhythm accurately and in notating it. The visual bias probably contributes to their difficulty; young children understand rhythm more readily and spontaneously than older ones.

Choral work with prose having a strong rhythm is a good way to begin; for many reasons, poetry should not be used to introduce this topic. For best results, reading should be deliberate but not unnaturally slow; avoid dramatic readings and all histrionics, especially at first.

After successful choral work, carefully directed by the teacher, individual oral work may be introduced, preferably using a tape recorder for critical playback. As a follow-up, ask individual students to select, analyze, and notate a short passage, and then rehearse it for oral presentation and for taping. Don't expect brilliant results the first time.

SILENT FEET AND LESSER SILENT STRESSES. One other feature of English stress-timed rhythm must be noted: silent stresses, often entire silent feet, occur as integral parts of rhythm patterns. Abercrombie cites the first line of Hamlet's famous soliloquy as an example, and uses a caret ∧ to mark the silent foot.[9]

To | *be or* | *not to be* | ∧ | *that is the* | *question*

Even though the middle foot is silent — that is, contains no speech syllable — it is nevertheless *felt* as a strong beat of approximately the same length as the other feet. This is true as we have seen because the stress-pulse beat originates in the English speaker's controlled movements of the chest musculature, not in the vocal folds. The rhythmic beat is muscular rather than vocal: the auditor responds by empathy with this basic rhythm. Silent beats and stresses occur frequently in English prose as well as verse; throughout our discussion entire silent feet will be marked with a large caret ∧, and lesser silent stresses with a small caret ∧.

The pauses in the music are not music,
Although they make the music what it is.[10]

Structural Features of Intonation

So far we have been considering only stress, because stress is the most readily accessible feature and probably the most decisive single element of English intonation. As used here, the term **intonation** includes not only **stress,** but two other features, **voice pitch** and **voice terminals** with their associated pauses. For clarity and specificity of analysis, it is possible to describe the separate features of stress, pitch, and terminals, but in meaning-bearing sentence structures they normally occur together in overall configurations.[11]

In discursive speech and writing — prose — the sentence is the basic meaning-bearing pattern, not the word; this is a point of major importance in teaching. Structural features of stress, pitch, voice terminal and pauses, as revealed by a deliberate but fluent reading in a neutral tone of voice, are closely associated with the syntactical pattern of each sentence. Features of intonation combine in patterns that limit and delineate meaning-bearing-patterns of English; these intonation patterns have a qualitative effect on the message as sent by the speaker/writer and received by the auditor/reader.

Following are the structural features of English intonation, commonly designated **suprasegmentals.**

   a. **Stress or loudness** — four relative degrees of stress on syllables.
   b. **Voice pitch** — four relative levels or ranges of pitch.
   c. **Voice terminals and pauses** — four ways of separating or terminating significant segments of speech or oral reading.

Below, these structural features are explained in some detail.

The remainder of this discussion of structural features of intonation is presented under three subtitles:

   STRESS OR LOUDNESS.
   VOICE PITCH.
   VOICE TERMINALS AND PAUSES.

STRESS OR LOUDNESS. Stress may be defined as relative loudness; it is a measure of the varying relative strength of muscular pulses imparted to exhaled air in the speech stream. English has many silent stresses, but there is no such thing as an "unstressed" syllable; without some degree of stress there can be no syllable. The four stresses described by many linguists include only one more than are recognized by dictionaries that notate primary and secondary accents (stresses) while silently assuming a tertiary ("unaccented"). The four stresses may be described as **heavy, medium, light,** and **weak.** Following are the common stress symbols:

╱ heavy   ∧ medium   ╲ light   ◡ weak

The basic English stress-pulse beat usually takes the form of either a heavy or a medium stress, according to the patterning of beats in the whole utterance. If we apply the rhythm unit of the foot as described here to a classical example of all four stresses, we find two feet, each with four syllables:

| elevator | operator
4   4

If we apply the common stress symbols, we have

| élevàtor | operàtor
4   4

Two other examples illustrating all four stresses are:

|télĕphòne |biî   and |báskĕtbàll |gâme

On p. 229, without marking all four stresses, we cited the joke based on the difference between

|cómĭc |bòok sâlesmăn   (funny man)
|còmĭc bóok |sâlesmăn   (funny books)

Similar examples, not quite so laughable, are

a |Spánĭsh |têachĕr   (a teacher of Spanish)
a |Spânĭsh |téachĕr   (teacher is a Spanish national)

Children have pairs of riddling questions in which contrasting stress patterns differentiate a compound noun from a noun-verb group; the meaning differences are amusingly incongruous. For example:

Did you ever see a hôrse flý?   (noun-verb group)
Did you ever see a hórseflỳ?   (compound noun)
Did you ever see a cât níp?   (noun-verb group)
Did you ever see cátnìp?   (compound noun)

Parallel examples are *boardwalk* and *board walk; cakewalk* and *cake walk; cloudburst* and *cloud burst; cowslip* and *cow slip; house fly* and *housefly.*

As a matter of curiosity, the verbs in these riddles are unmarked infinitives (the **to-V** form without **to**). The spelling of the contrasting pairs follows a common writing practice: the noun-verb group is written as two words, the compound noun as one; thus we have graphic signals for the contrasting stress patterns. Though not without exceptions, this practice is worth noting and calling to the attention of students; it is further illustrated in other contrasting pairs discussed on pp. 238–39.

TEACHING SUGGESTION: The above examples, especially the jokes and riddles, are on the order of parlor tricks, yet playing them can sharpen the perception of stress. Interested students might enjoy exploring some of these possibilities for themselves and reporting to the class. A good source of data is comedy routines on radio and television, especially those of dialect comedians. Students who are native speakers of American English will have greater success in this research if they approach it through meaning first and stress second; if English is their second language, they will be more preoccupied with stress itself.

In speech and oral reading, the heavy and medium stresses are the most significant, because they coincide with the stress-pulse beat and begin each rhythmic foot. In English rhythm, successive feet are of approximately equal length, and the varying numbers of syllables, including all silent stresses, are spoken (or read) in recurrent bursts beginning with each beat; following the major stress, all syllables in each foot receive reduced stresses roughly in proportion to their number. Here for example is an old familiar saying, notated to show seven rhythmic feet that include two lesser silent stresses; the rhythmic identity of the seven feet is a powerful mnemonic device.

|*Now is the* |*time* ∧ *for* |*every good* |*man* ∧ *to* |*come to the*
|*aid of his* |*party.*

Stress-timed rhythm is fundamental to both structural and interpretive intonation, whether the reading is silent or oral.

English has three sets of contrasting word pairs or word groups in which stress placement is the primary signal for a structural contrast. For example:

(1) *cóntest* and *contést* are a pair consisting of a **noun** and **verb** differentiated primarily by the contrast of a heavy stress on the first syllable of the noun but on the second syllable of the verb.

(2) *blácksnake* (a species of snake) and *black snáke* (any snake that is black) consists of a **compound noun** and a **noun group** differentiated primarily by the contrast of a heavy stress on the first syllable of

the compound noun but on the second syllable ("word") of the noun group.

(3) *trýout* and *try oút* are a **compound noun** and a **verb-adverb** group differentiated primarily by the contrast of a heavy stress on the first syllable of the compound noun but on the second syllable ("word") of the verb-adverb group.*

In speech and oral reading of such items, **use,** and **position** or **distribution** in sentences, are the only means of knowing which stress placement is structural and obligatory. In writing and reading, as noted earlier, the convention of white space between words is a visual clue that further signals the contrast. In both oral and silent reading, however, the obligatory stress pattern in words like *abstract, contest, contract, convert, present, progress, project, rebel, record, reject,* is determined solely by their distribution in larger meaning-bearing patterns. There is no single way of pronouncing them correctly in isolation; there are two ways.

TEACHING SUGGESTION: Close work on these three sets of contrasting items is excellent for sharpening the students' sense of grammatical functions as well as their perception of stress patterns. Ask them to discover their own examples of the three sets. They should report their findings both orally and in writing, using pairs of contrasting sentences, or single sentences with both items in contrast. Oral work on this material is particularly important; it is the only check on the students' actual perception of stress, because written examples can be imitated strictly on the visual level.

VOICE PITCH. Pitch may be defined as frequency of vibrations produced in the voice stream by the vocal folds; but this definition has greater relevance to music than to speech. Speech tones are not held "on pitch" as song notes are (relatively); a tone that is held on pitch

* An interesting side issue here is that the compound nouns in the second and third contrasting pairs derive their form and meaning from the original word groups: *blacksnake* represents the adoption of a common description as a name for a particular species (from *blacksnake* in this sense we have a figurative extension to mean a kind of whip); *tryout* is a simple substitution of a verb-adverb group in a noun use and position, making a new noun. A similar linguistic operation may also account for the development of the contrasting noun-verb pairs.

is either a song note, or a tone suitable for recitative or chanting. In contrast, speech tones in American English vary up and down within four significant relative pitch levels (or ranges) for each speaker; significant levels of pitch in speech vary on a relative scale, not an absolute. A bass and a soprano speaker of English may be octaves apart on the absolute scale, but they both follow the same system of four relative pitch levels, each within his own voice range; they can communicate with each other with the greatest of ease.

Numerals may be used to designate the four levels of pitch; **1, 2, 3, 4;** but the terms **low, normal, high,** and **extra high** are more descriptive. A step arrangement helps to visualize the four ranges, or levels, of pitch.

extra high (**4**)

high (**3**)

normal (**2**)

low (**1**)

Normal is the level where the speaker usually begins, the range within which the main part of an utterance is often pitched. In ordinary conversation, and calm, matter-of-fact reading, Americans may use only the three levels: normal, high, and low. For example, "Tomorrow is another day."

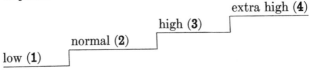

HIGH (**3**) mor oth
NORMAL (**2**) To row is an er
LOW (**1**) day.

Rises in pitch level to high or extra high may occur at certain points for several reasons, but some rises are structural; the same may be said for drops to low. For example, a question expressing surprise or incredulity: "Is this a zither?"

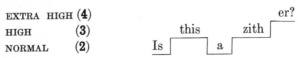

EXTRA HIGH (**4**) er?
HIGH (**3**) this zith
NORMAL (**2**) Is a

We can observe examples of a few of these rises and drops in relation to structural terminals and associated pauses.

VOICE TERMINALS AND PAUSES. The term **pause,** useful as it seems intuitively, is not precise enough for accurate analysis and notation except as it can be related to English stress-timed rhythm; as I perceive them, structural pauses occur with and depend upon silent feet and lesser silent stresses within an utterance. There are four significant (structural) ways of terminating the voice stream: **open** or **minimal juncture; fade-fall terminal; fade-rise terminal;** and **fade-level terminal.** Perhaps all these terminals are normally followed by structural pauses that coincide with silent stresses: it might be possible to differentiate four degrees of silent stress as well as four stresses on syllables. In this discussion, however, no finer distinction is attempted than that between entire silent feet ∧ and lesser silent stresses ᴧ.

Open or **minimal juncture** is a sharp, quick "cut" in the stream of vocal sound — perceived as a split-second silence. An open juncture, marked with a plus sign (+), differentiates such contrasting pairs as:

great + rain	*gray + train*
flight + rack	*fly + track*
fly + trap	*flight + wrap*
needed + rain	*need + a + drain*
night + rate	*nitrate*
night + ride	*nitride*

Other features occur in the immediate environment of this contrast: different stress patterns on the syllables separated by the juncture, perhaps related to a silent stress coinciding with the short silence; also phonetic or allophonic differences, particularly the fricative quality of voiceless /r/ in the /tr/ cluster in **nitrate, nitride,** and **track.**

The more careful the speaker's articulation, the more open junctures in his speech — but too much careful articulation can be too much. In oral reading, for example, open junctures sometimes separate the printed words as indicated by white spaces, but a deliberate effort to use open junctures to separate "words" in any such way must end in a travesty of English rate and rhythm. Instead, a general sharpening of articulation is recommended, with attention to sentences as meaning-bearing patterns, and to structural features of intonation. Of the four structural English terminals, open juncture is perhaps the least significant; it appears to be phonemic or morphemic, the other three syntactical.

TEACHING SUGGESTION: American students usually profit from trying to improve their articulation. Oral/written work with open junctures can both amuse and instruct. Try the above examples on your class.

Some related problems of articulation involve using one of two identical contiguous phonemes; for example, *good + deal* and *good + eel;* or *time + me* and *tie + me.* Similar are shifting or elisions of final or initial phonemes from one word to another:

> *an + ape* and *a + nape*
> *an + ice + truck* and *a + nice + truck*
> *ice + cream* and *I + scream*
> *illegal* and *ill + eagle*
> *inclined* and *ink + lined*
> *knee + towel* and *neat + owl*
> *neat + trick* and *knee + trick*
> *seem + able* and *see + Mabel*
> *slope + up* and *slow + pup*
> *that + sardine* and *that's + ar + dean*

Oral/written work on such examples can make students aware of articulation, and of these particular aspects of the speech/writing relationship. Follow-up work might involve individual explorations, later shared with the class, orally and in writing.

The **fade-fall terminal** is symbolized here by a falling arrow ⤵ As the term suggests, it is a fading, falling termination of the stream of speech, often preceded by a one-level drop in pitch to low and followed by a silent stress that coincides with a structural pause. Its structural significance is finality, the completion of an utterance. In the many fits and starts of casual conversations, however, and in ineffectual formal speech and reading aloud, fade-fall terminals may occur with no linguistic significance whatsoever. But because the fade-fall is a structural intonation signal for termination of an utterance, it should generally be reserved for that function in public speaking and oral reading. Children doing primary work in composition and reading can learn not to use fade-falls within sentences, where they tend to fragment the total meaning-bearing pattern and make it more difficult to comprehend. In teaching good structural use of the fade-fall terminal, emphasis upon sentences rather than words is crucial.

In successful oral reading, and in the psycholinguistic processes of writing and silent reading, fade-fall terminals occur with very high frequency at points marked by semicolons and periods.

His playing was excellent. ↘

His playing was excellent; ↘ *however, it was not superior.*

The Declaration of Independence was written in 1776. ↘

Germany first attacked Poland; ↘*then England attacked Germany.* ↘

It does not seem possible to limit the national debt. ↘

The fade-fall terminal also occurs with frequency to mark the completion of such questions as:

Where is the library? ↘

Who is the author of this book? ↘

Where is he living now? ↘

These terminals will be discussed further in the section on punctuation later in this chapter.

The **fade-rise terminal** is symbolized here by a rising arrow ↗. As the term implies, it is a rising, fading termination of the voice stream; its structural significance seems to be that something more follows or is expected, either in response to a question, or in the continuing utterance of the speaker.

The fade-rise terminal, when preceded by a one-level rise in pitch, often marks the completion of a question that requires a *yes-or-no* answer:

Have you received your orders? ↗

Did they come today? ↗

Are you ready to go? ↗

But such direct *yes-or-no* questions can be converted to ironical statements if the speaker uses a drop in pitch instead of a rise on the last word, and a fade-fall instead of a fade-rise terminal; an appropriate tone of voice may enrich the message.

Aren't you ready yet? ↘

Did you tell me you are ready? ↘*Yes or no?* ↘

The fade-rise terminal preceded by a one-level rise in pitch is also the structural intonation signal that a statement in syntactical form is actually a question:

> *You think this is a joke.* ⬂   (statement)
> *You think this is a joke?* ⬀   (question)

In writing, the question mark is the only clue, and a bit tardy; the reader must understand that the question mark in itself signals neither a fade-rise nor a fade-fall terminal. The question mark is neutral with respect to intonation.

A different use of the fade-rise terminal occurs within sentences; it is usually not preceded by a one-level rise in pitch, but is followed by a silent stress or structural pause; the voice stream ends by fading up and out within the pitch range where it begins:

> *He waited two* ⬀ ˄ *three* ⬀ ˄ *four* ⬀ ˄ *five years before he finally employed an attorney and instituted court action.*

Fade-level terminals also occur with high frequency in these positions. The fade-level terminal is symbolized here by a level arrow ⟶ In level terminal, the voice neither rises nor drops in pitch but cuts off or fades out within the pitch range of the preceding segment of speech, which is usually somewhat lengthened, or sustained; level terminal is often followed by a lesser silent stress, or structural pause. In careful, deliberate speech and oral reading, level terminal frequently marks off syntactical elements such as noun and verb groups; followed by a slight pause, it is an integral part of the structural and rhythmic flow of the utterance. For example:

> *The boy who won the race* ⟶˄ *is an excellent athlete.* ⬂

Analyzed to show its rhythm in feet, the sentence might be marked this way:

> *The | boy who won the | race* ⟶˄ *is an | excellent | athlete.* ⬂

These notations are not intended to be either prescriptive or interpretive. But since they represent fluent readings in a neutral tone of voice, they probably indicate high-frequency structural features.

As noted above, level terminals may occur within a sentence where fade-rise terminals would also be appropriate.

> *He waited two* ⟶˄ *three* ⟶˄ *four* ⟶˄ *five years before he finally employed an attorney and instituted court action.*

Level terminals may also occur within a sentence between two clauses that are closely connected, but punctuated with a semicolon.

*Germany attacked Poland;—→*ʌ *then England attacked Germany.*

Prose: Written Sentences and Sentence Intonation

Let us begin by noting the importance of high-frequency structural intonation features. Despite the reality of structural intonation and the well-known fact that intonation, of all signaling systems in English, most mercilessly separates the native speaker from the non-native, it is virtually impossible to make generalizations about intonation that have the uniform validity of rules. This is true because every individual native speaker, having developed an intuitive, automatic control of English intonation may — actuated by his specific attitude and intent, affected by any of an infinite variety of emotional states, and in his particular circumstances at the moment of utterance — vary his speech from any norm. Indeed, deliberate variation from a structural norm is often used for a special effect.

Nevertheless, high-frequency structural intonation features do exist in English; knowledge of them can be of great utility when applied intelligently to English and language arts instruction. This knowledge has various potential applications from the rudiments of kindergarten–primary instruction to the fancier flights of acting and oral interpretation. But it is essential to note a basic difference between the role of the speaker/writer and that of the reader. The reader — who receives communications in graphic form — does not have anything approaching the almost limitless options available to the spontaneous speaker, or to the writer — who originates and sends the communication. *Every reader is obligated to deal with the language and its structural features, including intonation, as presented on the printed page.* On this structural basis the reader sensitive to language picks up a range of interpretive intonation features corresponding to the intentions of the writer, supported by the general tenor of the passage and of the whole work, and limited by the immediate context. To read a worthwhile piece of writing in any other spirit would be irresponsible as well as inefficient; a completely "free" reading, that is, without regard to the actual language used by the author, would be sheer undisciplined chaos.[12]

The remainder of this discussion of written sentences and sentence intonation is presented under two subtitles:

A DEFINITION OF PROSE

INTONATION AND PUNCTUATION

A DEFINITION OF PROSE. Even though handwriting and print are graphic systems ultimately derived from speech, Abercrombie is probably correct in saying that *writing is a system for recording prose*, not conversation,[13] and consequently that "prose is essentially language organized for *visual* presentation." [14] His further statement, "The sentence as traditionally defined is really a unit of prose, not of conversation," applies brilliantly to instruction in both reading and writing.[15] The writing amateur who says, "I write just like I talk," is mistaken. That would be not only impossible but intolerable.

It is true that the spoken sound of prose is the essence of effective style, but neither amateurs nor professionals write as they talk; even when writing in a colloquial style, they succeed only by giving an illusory impression. No, the relation of speech to writing and writing to speech is subtle and profound; the two language systems richly interact, affecting each other in complex ways, far beyond the visual bias. The common terms, "reading aloud" and "reading silently" are wise terms: *oral reading is written language extraverted; silent reading is written language introverted — but it is language.* Written composition and oral reading must be thoroughly learned and carefully taught, as separate and distinct arts and skills, yet in close relation to one another. It would be a sad outcome for most students if they truly read orally "just like they talk."

TEACHING SUGGESTION: There are various ways to introduce your students to the sound of their own writing, with salutary effects. One way is to ask each student to tape record a reading of one of his compositions; the recording may be made by the writer or by a classmate or friend, but the writer should follow the text with his eyes as he listens to the recording; often more than one such playback is needed for effective revision. Another way is to ask students to work together, reading each other's papers aloud and criticizing them for revision.

Students may be helped to associate the sound of good prose style with a text by listening carefully to high-quality professional recordings as they read the passages silently; or to well-prepared readings by a teacher. Such listening and reading experiences can contribute much to both oral reading and writing skills.

In primary instruction, the children's own spoken sentences can be made available to them in graphic form through experience charts and related methods, as an immediate bridge to writing and reading. But so can common "prose" sentence patterns that never, or only rarely, occur in conversation; these could be sequentially taught as a basic part of reading and language arts instruction. It is very important that children associate the sound of these sentences, well spoken, with their graphic forms. Many cannot begin to handle "reading with expression" (interpretive intonation) until they have grasped both syntactical patterns and associated structural intonation features of common prose sentences. Sentence rhythms and tunes they have never heard should be audibly presented to children, in association with the corresponding gross features of syntax. Every learner needs the authentic sound in his ear, whether he is working in his primer or making his first approach to the poetry of John Donne.

Here is one of my own expository paragraphs written for both oral delivery and publication.

What must inevitably come, in my opinion, is a synthesis of linguistic approaches to reading; a synthesis developed, controlled, and corrected by means of an interdisciplinary attack on reading problems, bringing to bear all pertinent knowledge; a synthesis in line with the best experience of teachers of reading and the English language arts, and in line with the best experimentation these teachers are capable of. Such a synthesis must move far beyond spelling and word attack and into reading processes at the sentence level *even in beginning reading;* eventually it should range into problems of reading extended discourse, not only of exposition but the many forms of literature. This is something of what is meant by "a comprehensive linguistic approach to reading."[16]

On page 248 is the same paragraph with suggested notations for rhythm, including structural terminals and associated pauses. Rhyth-

mic feet are set off between vertical lines, each line coming before
a major stress; entire silent feet are indicated by a heavy caret ∧,
lesser silent stresses by a light caret ∧. Arrows mark terminals:⟶
fade-level terminal; ↗ fade-rise terminal; ↘ fade-fall terminal.
Pitch contours are not suggested; they are implied only in so far
as pitch characteristics are associated structurally with other intonation features. The reading suggested by these notations is meant
to be mainly structural and minimally interpretive.

You are invited to read the following passage aloud, deliberately
but fluently, in an emotionally neutral tone of voice, and to compare the notations with your own inclinations; if possible, make a
tape recording of your reading. This oral reading should be as natural
as possible, and above all should not attempt to follow the notations
prescriptively; only a highly skilled oral reader can "read score"
in that way.

What | must in | evitably | come ↗ | ∧ in my o | pinion ↗ | ∧ is a
| synthesis of lin | guistic ap | proaches to | reading↘| ∧ a | synthesis
de | veloped↘| ∧ con | trolled ↘| ∧ and cor | rected⟶| ∧ by | means
of an | inter | disciplinary at | tack on | reading problems⟶∧| bringing
to | bear ∧ all | pertinent | knowledge↘| ∧ a | synthesis in | line with
the | best ex | perience of| teachers of | reading and the | English | lan-
guage | arts⟶| ∧ and in | line with the | best experimen | tation⟶∧ these
| teachers are | capable of↘| ∧ | Such a | synthesis⟶| ∧ must | move
⟶∧ | far be | yond | spelling and | word attack⟶| ∧ and into | read-
ing | processes at the | sentence | level⟶| ∧ | *even in be | ginning | read-*
ing ↘ | ∧ e | ventually⟶| ∧ it should | range into | problems of
| reading ex | tended | discourse⟶| ∧ not | only of expo | sition⟶| ∧ but
the | many | forms of | literature ↘ | ∧ | This is | something of what
is | meant by "a compre | hensive ∧ lin | quistic ap | proach to | reading."↘

TEACHING SUGGESTION: Students who have analyzed a
passage for rhythmic feet as suggested on p. 234 — if they
have had additional instruction and practice since — might
be able to add appropriate notations for voice terminals and
pauses to their original analysis.

This is a rather difficult exercise, but within the capacities
of attentive students if they will submit to the discipline of
tape recording their reading, followed by serious self-criticism
and constructive criticism from others.

In English, a word spoken in isolation normally carries the intonation pattern of a completed sentence: (a) a heavy stress, (b) a falling pitch, and (c) a fade-fall terminal.

NORMAL (2) Týpe   Fóot   Tá

LOW (3)   writer. ↘   ball. ↘   ble. ↘

As answers to conversational questions, all are proper sentences. They can be converted to questions by using (a) a heavy stress, (b) a rising pitch, and (c) a fade-rise terminal.

HIGH (3)   writer? ↗   ball? ↗   ble? ↗

NORMAL (2) Týpe   Fóot   Tá

Word-naming, or word-by-word reading, gives each word a sentence intonation. Nothing could be more damaging to the natural sense of English rhythm: word-naming completely disrupts the regular beat of the basic stress-pulse rhythm of English prose, and by giving a sentence intonation to each word, shatters the meaning-bearing pattern. The oral teaching of isolated words in primary grades can have this effect unless teachers take pains to prevent it. A number of so-called remedial reading devices now in use contribute to this pattern breaking by presenting single lines of text and fragments of lines, to be read without regard to meaning-bearing patterns.

A heart-breaking little classroom episode dramatizes the evil of word-naming. Poor Johnny read the sentence aloud in this way.

| *This* ↘| ∧ | *is* ↘| ∧ | *a* ↘| ∧ | *warm* ↘| *doughnut.* ↘| ∧ |
| *Step* ↘| ∧ *on* ↘| *it.*| ∧ |

But this is what the text actually said.

|*This is a* | *worm.* ↘| ∧ *Do not* | *step on it.* ↘| ∧ |[17]

An elementary sentence such as **This man is John's teacher,** when read word by word, is contorted into ten feet, five spoken and five silent, each spoken foot ending with a fade-fall terminal. It becomes a meaningless sequence of five unintelligible sentence-like utterances:

| *This* ↘ ∧ | *man* ↘ ∧ | *is* ↘ ∧ | *John's* ↘ ∧ | *teacher* ↘.∧ |
| 1 | 2 | 3 | 4 | 5 | 6 | 7 | 8 | 9 | 10 |

The same sentence, read fluently but with no effort at specific interpretation, might have two feet, as follows:

This | man is John's | teacher. ⭢↘

Adding a fade-level after *man* and a fade-fall marker at the end, the sentence appears this way (a high-frequency reading):

This | man⭢⅄ *is John's | teacher.* ↘

At least four distinct emphases can be indicated by saying the sentence four times in normal English rhythm, each time placing an extra heavy stress on a different word; this is the **structural intonation** option of **prominence.**

THIS man is John's teacher.	(This particular man, no other)
This man IS John's teacher.	(Emphasis on *is;* possibly a contradiction)
This man is JOHN'S teacher.	(John's teacher, not Helen's, or yours, or mine)
This man is John's TEACHER.	(Not his uncle, for example)

Word-naming and its related disability, reading by pattern-fragments, are the most crippling of "normal" reading disabilities (excluding the clinical). If such disabilities develop and are allowed to go unchecked in oral reading, they will probably be matched by parallel disabilities in silent reading, with a consequent loss of sentence sense and reading comprehension. Elementary instruction in the structural intonation features of English prose that are closely related to high-frequency sentence patterns can help greatly to preclude such crippling losses. A teacher's experience reported in *Elementary English* gives substantial support to this view.[18]

TEACHING SUGGESTION: To bring out the differences between normal structural intonation and structural prominence, introduce the *John's teacher* sentence to your class for oral practice. Ask them to give similar examples orally. If their interest and progress suggest further work, duplicate the exercise below or make up one of your own.

Such exercises can be varied by adding work on interpretive intonation; after having students read sentences with little if any paralanguage, ask them to read the same sentences intensely, with overtones of boredom, delight, disgust, fatigue, sorrow, etc. These overtones should not affect the underlying structural intonation or emphasis indicated by structural prominence.

1. Models showing normal structural intonation and structural prominence.

    a. Normal structural intonation

        (1) *He's not my friend.* ↘   *John is.* ↘

        (2) *He's not my friend.* ↘   *Don't say he is.* ↘

        (3) *He's not my friend.* ↘   *He's John's friend.* ↘

        (4) *He's not my friend.* ↘   *He's my enemy.* ↘

    b. Structural prominence.

        (1) *HE'S not my friend.* ↘   *JOHN is.* ↘

        (2) *He's NOT my friend.* ↘   *Don't say he IS.* ↘

        (3) *He's not MY friend.* ↘   *He's JOHN'S friend.* ↘

        (4) *He's not my FRIEND.* ↘   *He's my ENEMY.* ↘

2. Imitate the models above.

    a. Normal structural intonation

        John's not walking home with me.

    b. Structural prominence

        Write logical follow-up sentences showing four emphases on

        JOHN, WALKING, HOME, and ME.

INTONATION AND PUNCTUATION. We have noted that the **question mark** is neutral with respect to intonation; both the fade-fall and fade-rise terminals are high-frequency structural terminals for questions. Thus the teacher's ancient saw, "Always raise your voice at the end of a question," is false. A great many questions end with the fade-fall terminal, usually preceded by a one-level drop in pitch. These two features generally signify finality, or the end of an utterance.

    Who killed cock robin? ↘ *Why did he do it?* ↘ *When did it happen?*
    Where is the passenger depot? ↘ *What time is it now?* ↘
    What did the accused have to say for himself? ↘ *How did he testify?* ↘

The length and structural complexity of a question may affect the speaker's choice of a final terminal. Note that the above questions are short, and all begin with question markers having the first sound of /h/, /hw/, or /w/ (spelled *wh*); these are sometimes referred to as "wh" questions (see pp. 189–190).

The above questions and others like them may end with a fade-rise instead of a fade-fall terminal if the speaker is (a) repeating his question, (b) requesting a repetition of the answer given or (c) asking with a special intent or attitude (surprise, incredulity, disbelief, anger, grief, amusement, condescension, for example). Special intent or attitude may also be expressed more specifically by an appropriate tone of voice, but the fade-rise terminal is the high-frequency structural feature.

> *Who killed cock robin?* ↗ *Why did he do it?* ↗ *When did it happen?* ↗
> *Where is the passenger depot?* ↗ *What time is it now?* ↗
> *What did the accused have to say for himself?* ↗ *How did he testify?* ↗

Again, there is no flat rule in English for question terminals. Every speaker has the option of asking any question as a question of special intent, and of choosing the fade-rise terminal as the structural signal of his intent.

"You think this is a joke?" was cited earlier as an example of a statement converted to a question solely by the substitution of a fade-rise for the usual fade-fall terminal. The fade-rise terminal is used for this purpose with very high frequency. Like the question of special intent, this kind of question may be asked in a tone of voice that adds specificity to the speaker's meaning. A few examples follow.

> *This is a ball game?* ↗ *This is a clean bench?*
> *You think you are generous?* ↗ *She believes everything he says?* ↗
> *His name is Cholmondely McGillicuddy?* ↗

To sum up, the question mark is not in itself a reliable guide to the use of the fade-rise or the fade-fall terminal. Contrary to classroom superstition, possibly more questions end with the fade-fall than with the fade-rise terminal; certainly a large number end with the fade-fall. And, like all other syntactical structures, questions may carry a high level of interpretive intonation.

TEACHING SUGGESTION: The following exercises and others like them can be used as a basis for oral/written work; or they can be varied for use either as oral or written tests. Normal, neutral readings in good English rhythm are assumed, at a normal rate. In an actual test, no symbols would be shown; here they provide a teacher's key.

As suggested for the previous exercises, interpretive intonation can be added for interest and variety.

Sentence terminals: In each of the following sets of five, one item has a different sentence terminal from the others. Select that item and write the corresponding letter.

1. a. *What floor do you want?* ↘
   b. *Second.* ↘
   c. *Let me off at third.* ↘
   d. *Third?* ↗
   e. *Yes, third.* ↘

2. a. *Who likes pizza?* ↘
   b. *I like pizza.* ↘
   c. *You like pizza?* ↗
   d. *Pizza is delicious.* ↘
   e. *Give me a no-cal pizza.* ↘

3. a. *How was the movie?* ↘
   b. *They went to the show?* ↗
   c. *You bought popcorn?* ↗
   d. *You call that a tragedy?* ↗
   e. *What are you, crazy?* ↗

4. a. *Where?* ↘
   b. *Why?* ↘
   c. *Last night.* ↘
   d. *You saw the game?* ↗
   e. *Why?* ↘

5. a. *Her cheeks paled.* ↘
   b. *Her cheeks paled!* ↘
   c. *Her cheeks paled?* ↗
   d. *Her cheeks paled at the thought.* ↘
   e. *Her cheeks became pale.* ↘

The **period, semicolon,** and **exclamation point** normally mark completed syntactical structures: sentences and sentence-like elements. So-called fragmentary sentences, felt by an author to be complete, occur naturally as utterances in fictional conversation or dramatic dialogue; good prose stylists occasionally present "fragmentary" structures with the graphic signs for sentences: capital letter to start, and a period, semicolon, question mark, or exclamation point to end. Effectiveness depends on the context and the author's style; such syntactic structures are part of the standard written English of effective writers (see pp. 167–68).

With very high frequency, the semicolon and the period correspond to the fade-fall terminal ↘ in oral reading; but the semicolon often, the period less so, may correspond to the fade-level terminal →. Choice of terminal is affected by immediate context and general rhythmic and tonal aspects of the whole passage. The exclamation point is an optional interpretive signal, a crude indicator of the author's intended tone of voice; the corresponding terminal may be fade-fall ↘ , fade-rise ↗ , or fade-level →, accompanied by and part of a broad spectrum of interpretive features.

> *They're all gone!* ↘
> *They're all gone?* ↗
> *Yes, they're all gone!* →

The comma may correspond to either the fade-level → or the fade-rise ↗ within a single pitch level, followed by a structural pause coinciding with a lesser silent stress. In both reading and writing instruction, students can be encouraged to use only these two terminals within sentences and sentence-like structures.

> *Theophilus Thistle,* ↗ ∧ *the successful thistle sifter,* ↗ ∧
> *thrust three thousand thistles through the thick of his thumb.*

> *Theophilus Thistle,* → ∧ *the successful thistle sifter,* → ∧
> *thrust three thousand thistles through the thick of his thumb.*

Because the fade-fall terminal ↘, generally followed by a major silent stress, is a structural intonation signal for completion of an utterance, English and language arts instruction should encourage its use for that purpose only. Here is a sentence with notations showing the effect of a fade-fall terminal within it: it sounds like two sentences.

> | *After the* | *party,* ↘ | ∧ *they* | *went for a* | *drive.* ↘

Either a fade-level or fade-rise would be better after *party;* but some students will use fade-falls within sentences in formal speech and oral reading if they are not reminded. Such encouragement, incorporated into instruction as a regular feature, can do much to develop sentence sense and appreciation of the sound of good English style.

Below are sentences in which either fade-level or fade-rise terminals within a single pitch level would correspond appropriately to the commas. A two-pronged arrow symbolizes this choice of terminals ⤳.

I know him very well, ⤳ *for we are old friends.* ↘

When the bad weather worsened, ⤳ *he came home again.* ↘

They all knew, ⤳ *we presumed,* ⤳ *that we were not buy-ing.* ↘

John Donne, ⤳ *the seventeenth-century metaphysical poet,* ⤳ *wrote that very famous poem,* ⤳ *"The Flea."* ↘

The assassin shot President Lincoln, ⤳ *who had signed the Emancipation Proclamation.* ↘

The class picnic was scheduled for July 4, ⤳ *1918,* ⤳ *in Memorial Park.* ↘

TEACHING SUGGESTION: Use the above sentences, or sentences like them, to introduce the use of fade-level or fade-rise terminals at the points marked by commas. The basic aim of such oral/written work is to strengthen the students in reading sentences with good English intonation; above all, they should use fade-fall terminals only at the end of each sentence.

Follow-up work might require the students to bring to class their own sentence examples for more oral/written practice.

In such sentences as the following, according to rate and tone, either a fade-rise, or a fade-level terminal may correspond to the comma after an introductory phrase or clause. It is helpful to encourage the use of the fade-rise terminal however, because it so clearly signals expectation of another syntactical structure within the sentence; but above all, oral reading should have a native English ring to it.

| *After the* | *storm,* ↗ | ∧ *the* | *sky* | *cleared and* | *brightened.* ↘

In the | *morning,* ↗ | ∧ *the* | *harrowing e* | *vents of* | *midnight were for* | *gotten.* ↘

When the | *party was* | *over,* ↗ | ∧ *the* | *children* | *left for* | *home.* ↘

| *After he had told* | *his side of it,* ↗ | ∧ *there was* | *little* | *else to* | *say.* ↘

Similarly, the first clause of a compound sentence, especially if it is a short clause, may be structurally linked to the second clause by a fade-rise terminal.

| *I went* | *swimming,* ↗ | ∧ *but my* | *brother took a* | *nap.* ↘

We | *ordered* | *early,* ↗| ∧ *and our* | *tickets* | *came on* | *time.* ↘

My | *sister got a* | *kitten,* ↗ | ∧ *and* | *I got a* | *puppy.* ↘

Fade-rise terminals are also appropriately encouraged in reading instruction to link members of series of various kinds; lists; compound sentences with three or more clauses; series of three or more compound subjects or predicates; as well as series of other structural patterns within sentences. Below are a few examples.

We bought | *apples,* ↗ ∧ | *pumpkins,* ↗ ∧ | *potatoes,* ↗ ∧ | *squash,* ↗∧ | *and gourds.* ↘

| *Chickens* | *squawked,* ↗ ∧ | *turkeys* | *gobbled,* ↗ ∧ | *cows* | *mooed,* ↗ ∧ | *calves bawled,* ↗ | ∧ *and the* | *donkey* | *said* | *hee-haw.* ↘

| *Chickens,* ↗∧ | *turkeys,* ↗ ∧ | *cows,* ↗ ∧ | *calves,* ↗ ∧ | *and* | *the donkey* → | *raised quite a* | *rumpus.*

In | *fact,* ↗ | ∧ *the* | *barnyard* | *denizens made a* | *hullaba* | *loo,* ↗ ∧ | *woke the whole* | *family,* ↗ ∧ | *routed the* | *thieves,* ↗ |∧ *and* | *then went* | *back to* | *sleep.* ↘

In the | *meantime,* ↗ | ∧ *the* | *farmer* | *searched in the* | *milk-house,* ↗ | ∧ *be* | *hind the* | *woodpile,* ↗ ∧ | *under the* | *hay-stack* ↗ | ∧ *and in the* | *chicken coop.* ↘

The foregoing sentences are illustrative rather than prescriptive; they suggest one way of developing language sense and sentence intonation. Level terminals might also be used, or a combination of fade-level and fade-rise terminals.

Although fade-level terminals sometimes correspond to syntactical points marked in prose by commas, they frequently serve to mark sentence elements such as noun and verb parts, or subjects and predicates, where no comma would be used in writing. The syllable before the level terminal is usually sustained, or lengthened slightly, before the voice fades out; the terminal is generally followed by a pause coincident with a degree of silent stress. For example:

The boy who won the race →∧ *is an excellent athlete.*

The clause *who won the race,* if not set off by structural terminals and significant pauses, is "restrictive," as in the example above. If set off by fade-rise or fade-level terminals, however, followed by strong silent stresses, we would have a different sentence, differently punctuated, with a different sound and meaning:

The boy, ↗ ∧ *who won the race,* ↗ ∧ *is an excellent athlete.*

A non-restrictive clause is clearly set off by structural terminals and structural pauses working together; a restrictive clause is closely connected to the word it modifies by rhythm and rate and is not separated by structural terminals and pauses — though it may be followed by a level terminal and a light silent stress, as in the first example above. In writing, a non-restrictive clause is set off or enclosed by commas, as in the second example above; a restrictive clause is not punctuated. A good test of restrictive and non-restrictive clauses is intonation (terminals, pauses, rate, rhythm).

In some sentences, a clause may be either restrictive or non-restrictive; the speaker has two structural intonation options, according to his intended meaning; the writer has corresponding options, to punctuate or not, according to his meaning; the reader, however, has no option: he must supply the structural intonation that goes with the given punctuation.

Here are a few examples of optional restrictive/non-restrictive clauses (either two commas or none):

The vase	*which was to have been my gift*	was smashed.
The old man	*who suddenly collapsed*	was my grandfather.
The jeweler	*who examined the watch*	remained silent.
My brother	*who goes to Yale*	will graduate soon.
The referee	*who is wearing red pants*	is quite permissive.

On the other hand, in some sentences a clause is simply non-restrictive (two commas):

Kent,	*who enjoys outdoor life,*	wants to live in Idaho.
Mother's ring,	*which I carelessly lost,*	was not of great value.
Her father,	*who was an octogenarian,*	died last night in his sleep.

Likewise, in some sentences, a clause is simply restrictive (no commas):

The candidate *that the party must have* has not yet been found.
The library has the book *that I ordered.*
The fact *that you are overweight* should not discourage you.
Will the person *who called a doctor* please stand up?

TEACHING SUGGESTION: Unless the teacher is very clear in his own mind, class discussions of restrictive and non-restrictive modifiers can be a waste of time. On the other hand, sentences like those above can provide excellent opportunities for oral/written practice leading toward language sense and good sentence intonation. When you have mastered them yourself, introduce them, or others like them, to your class. Let the class give their own examples orally.

Follow-up work might be an oral/written assignment to be shared at a later class meeting. Curious students might like to explore the use of restrictive and non-restrictive clauses in books, magazines and newspapers, and report back on their findings.

Adverbial elements in inverted sentence order are commonly marked by level terminals in speech and oral reading, but unpunctuated in writing:

A | cross the | prairie—→ₐ | raged the | blizzard.↘
Wi | thin the dark | tomb—→ₐ | lay the three | brothers.↘

For determining punctuation, oral reading should be neither stilted nor impassioned; punctuation marks are crude signals for certain intonation features as suggested above, but the proof of the pudding is a good natural English rate and rhythm, with appropriate pitch contours. Voice terminal markers cannot show pitch contours; they indicate only the direction in which the pitch is going when the voice cuts off or fades out: their structural significance lies in that direction. In the stress-timed rhythm of English, voice terminals are commonly reinforced by silent stresses underlying significant pauses — structural pauses.

TEACHING SUGGESTION: Below are three different presentations of materials on punctuation related to structural terminals, arranged in order of increasing difficulty; these models may be used as a basis either for oral/written practice or for testing. These three models are in the form of objective tests with teacher's keys built in: the test information is incorporated into the presentation; in forms 1 and 2, structural terminal symbols have also been added. In classroom use, these items would not be included.

1. In this form, an underscore (____) indicates where punctuation marks go.

———————

Punctuation (graphic clues to structural terminals)

Key: A. Ambiguous (may be spoken, and therefore also punctuated, either of two ways)
　　 B. No punctuation
　　 C. Comma(s)
　　 D. Question mark
　　 E. Semicolon or period

(A)　11. They called John ____ their leader (↗ or none)

(C)　12. The student was unprepared ____ a common situation for him. (↗)

(D)　13. Is this a private conversation ____ (↗)

(C)　14. Theirs was a good marriage ____ a true love match (↗)

(D)　15. Is this a private conversation ____ (special emphasis) (↗)

(E)　16. They were married secretly ____ somehow they felt guilty (↘ or ↗)

(C)　17. They would not go ____ however much we entreated them (↗)

(C)　18. Agnes ____ who didn't want to go at all ____ sat perfectly still (↗ and ↗)

(B)　19. That man ____ has the lost dog ____ that I am looking for (none)

(C)　20. Mr. Brown ____ who introduced himself to you ____ is a friend of mine (↗ and ↗)

2. In this form, no indication is given as to where punctuation marks might go. Terminal symbols are suggested here to guide the teacher; they would not be included in materials for classroom use.

———————

Punctuation related to structural terminals. Supply the necessary punctuation according to the following key:

Key: A. One comma
      B. Semicolon
      C. Two commas
      D. No further punctuation required

(A) 41. Although England is much farther north (⤴↘∧) Chicago has a less temperate climate.

(A) 42. The summers in England are not as warm as ours (⤴↘∧) nor the winters so cold.

(B) 43. I have never been to South America (↘∧) I hope to go there some day.

(A) 44. One of the reasons for England's warm winters is the gulf stream (⤴↘∧) a deep current of water that warms the island.

(C) 45. For several miles the road runs along the river (⤴↘∧) turns left into the hills (⤴↘∧) and then spills headlong into the expressway.

(C) 46. The man *who discovered Greenland* was Leif Ericson. (restrictive clause)

(D) 47. Orville Wright (⤴↗ ∧) *who was born in Ohio* (⤴↗ ∧) invented the airplane. (non-restrictive clause)

(D) 48. Trees *that lose their leaves in winter* are called deciduous. (non-restrictive)

(C) 49. Since you are not ready to begin (⤴↗ ∧) your act can come later (⤴↗ ∧) unless you feel strongly about it.

(A) 50. Alice (⤴↗ ∧) did you meet my sister at the game?

3. In this form, five sentences from an extended discourse are presented in their original order. No indication is given as to where punctuation marks might go. Punctuation is shown here for the teacher's information only; it would not appear in materials given to students.

Punctuation related to structural terminals. Indicate the number of sentences according to this key:

      (A) One sentence
      (B) Two sentences
      (C) Three sentences
      (D) Four sentences or more
      (E) Sentence not complete; a fragment

(B) With the coming of spring (,) hysteria creeps across the campus (,) tension mounts steadily (,) and even when it does not erupt in some overt form (,) it still disturbs the last two months of the college year (.) now is the time when the steadily growing psychiatric staffs come into their own (.)

(C) The young people who brood in their rooms (,) who forget to come to the dining hall (,) and who burst into fits of irrationality (,) are not worrying about who will win the great game (,) or who will come to the dance or be tapped for the fraternity (.) Joe College is dead (,) and his little anxieties are unrecognizably antique (.) his successors are immersed in their books and laboratories (,) and their concern is for the grade that an incomprehensible marking system will grind out for them (.)

(D) The trouble is that the students themselves do not know it (.) this generation has been so thoroughly harnessed to the treadmill of the examination that it accepts its servitude as a normal (,) if strenuous (,) condition of life (.) all the external pressures of society encourage that belief (.) since education has become a national emergency (,) it is a patriotic duty to do well in algebra (.)

(A or B) The solicitous letters and the regular phone calls impress upon the student the fact that it is not he alone who is being tested (,) but the whole family (; or .) how proud they are when the stock rises (,) how concerned when it falls (.)

(E) Since the measured blocks and units of formal instruction have clearly defined weight (,) to expend precious energies upon activities to which no immediate reward is attached

Selected References

INTRODUCTORY

David A. Conlin, *Grammar for Written English* (Boston: Houghton Mifflin, 1961).

Kenneth Croft, *A Practice Book on English Stress and Intonation for Students of English as a Second Language* (Washington, D.C.: English Language Services, 1961).

Carl A. Lefevre, *Linguistics and the Teaching of Reading* (New York: McGraw-Hill, 1964).

Jean Pival, "Stress, Pitch, and Juncture in the Diagnosis and Treatment of Reading Ills," *Elementary English*, April, 1968, pp. 458–63, 67.

Paul Roberts, *Patterns of English*, Teachers Edition (New York: Harcourt, Brace, 1956).

Harold Whitehall, *Structural Essentials of English* (New York: Harcourt, Brace, 1955).

ADVANCED AND TECHNICAL

David Abercrombie, *Studies in Phonetics and Linguistics* (*Language and Language Learning, No. 10*) (London: Oxford University Press, 1965).

M. A. K. Halliday, *Intonation and Grammar in British English* (The Hague: Mouton, 1967).

Philip Lieberman, *Intonation, Perception, and Language* (Cambridge, Mass.: M.I.T. Press, 1967).

Kenneth L. Pike, *The Intonation of American English* (Ann Arbor: The University of Michigan Press, 1945).

George L. Trager and Henry Lee Smith, Jr., *An Outline of English Structure* (*Studies in Linguistics, Occasional Papers, No. 3*) (Norman, Oklahoma: Battenburg Press, 1951; reprinted, Washington, D.C., American Council of Learned Societies, 1957).

Chapter 10

Literature: Language and Form

If it is not the aim of language study in the schools to turn students into junior linguists or grammarians, neither is it the aim of reading literature to develop premature literary critics or historians. These are essential basic understandings, because language and literature are forever wedded and bonded together; what is good for one is good for the other. Study of literature must be based upon language because literature is written in language: without language, there would be no literature. Just as stone is the medium of sculpture, paint of art, and sound of music, so is language the medium of literature. But literature is written in a special language, the language of human experience; that is the real point of literature. *The immediate aim of reading literature is to experience it directly,* beginning with intimate acquaintance with the actual language in which it is written; this direct, immediate experience with literature as language is the only means to whatever ultimate ends there may be of reading and studying literature.

ORAL PRESENTATION OF LITERATURE. Most young children can learn to listen perceptively to speech and oral reading, and can respond orally to what they hear, to a degree far outreaching their ability to read and write independently about the same experiences. Selection of literature limited by the children's ability to read it on their own fills their school time with busywork and denies them their literary birthright. For many years this charge has been leveled, justly, at reading materials whose language is dwarfed by slavish dependence upon word counts; more recently, a "linguistic" dwarfing of language has been perpetrated by overdependence on phoneme-grapheme correspondences.

An excellent alternative, as one strand of a varied program, is to select literature and plan experiences so that the teacher reads aloud to the children; sometimes the children should follow the text with their eyes while the teacher reads it aloud. If the teacher is skilled in oral interpretation, well and good, but the teacher's enjoyment and sense of sharing experience with the children is even more important. In this way — perhaps only in this way — can we be sure that most of the children in our schools will ever hear the sound, the actual language, of some of the best literature written for their ears. Such early auditory experiences, moreover, can lay a firm foundation for ongoing language arts activities and later developmental reading of literature. Appreciation of the sound of the English language — its rhythms, tunes, and patterns — is the key to enjoyment of literature.

SUMMARY AND FORECAST. In this exploration of teaching literature as language and form, language is viewed as a dual symbol system in which speech is the basic and primary system, writing a secondary system, separate from but closely related to speech. Written language is a system of fabulous value, a brilliant device for remembering, and for evoking memories: through the eye, writing reminds the inner ear of the sound and sounds of spoken language. Written forms — patterns of letters, words, sentences, paragraphs, the longer forms of discourse and of imaginative literature, including drama — all have subtle interweavings and interlinkages with spoken forms; and they all have complete spoken counterparts; that is, they can be read aloud, and with greater impact. The great body of literature includes a variety of literary forms, large and small; many styles and modes of language; various dialects; sentence elements and sentence constructions, invented in endless variety, yet ultimately traceable to a few basic patterns; and a complex system of rhythms and melodies, both structural and interpretive. These are some of the main elements of teaching literature as language and form. Some of the particulars are presented in the remainder of this chapter under three subtitles:

Literature as Syntax
Intonation in Oral Reading and Interpretation
A Note on Literary Forms and Musical Compositions

Literature as Syntax

No one really reads literature as syntax, but literature is written in syntactic structures which must be grasped as a *basis* for understanding and appreciation. Structural resources such as we have been considering so far in this book lend themselves admirably to imaginative writing. Creative writers are fertile in their production of structural inventions and manipulations of language patterns; an extended treatment would require detailed discussion of many points of linguistic interest in literature that we can only describe generally here, with a few illustrations. An interested teacher can make further explorations for herself, and can lead her students in literary-linguistic explorations. *This is one important aspect of literary study.*

For example: what I call structural puns, the unconventional substitution of a member of one word class for another, such as a noun for a verb, and then the use of verb inflections on the noun base; unusually long, involved sentences running to many lines; extended syntactical constructions that are fragments according to school grammar, treated as sentences; myriad special sentence patterns, apostrophes, commands, inversions, prayers, wishes, and appositions, compounding of all elements, ellipses, parallelism of ellipses, parallelism of certain word forms, and of word groups and clusters, phrases and clauses. Many of these are explained and illustrated in this section.

The point is that for full comprehension of literary passages, especially those having unusual or as often as not unique structure, the reader must respond to entire meaning-bearing patterns as wholes. He may do this either by an automatic, unconscious, intuitive process that is the harvest of long tilling, or he may do it by a direct analysis of each author's peculiar and characteristic uses of language resources. Direct linguistic analysis of language patterns is an excellent means of breaking an author's code and so involving children in an appreciative study of literature in their early and formative years. In time, and with success, they may learn to respond automatically to meaning-bearing patterns as wholes, each having its overriding intonation pattern, or tune, in which literary passages are comparable to the phrasing of music, building toward ever larger movements. This is an important dimension of literature.

The remainder of this section, *Literature as Syntax*, is presented under three subtitles, as follows:

STRUCTURAL PUNS
INVERSIONS
SOME INTERESTING SYNTACTICAL PATTERNS IN POEMS

STRUCTURAL PUNS. In the first six lines of "Christmas Greetings to the American Dream," John Ciardi uses fifteen nouns as verbs with the **V-ed/en** inflection, all in one sentence. These nouns are the names of the gifts children of affluence take for granted. This opening sentence is a conventional well-wishing pattern, turned to satirical purposes. The effect of these structural puns depends, first, on the success of a straight pun on the **V-ed/en** verb *lit* in the first half-line: "May your tree be lit" (lighted/drunk), followed by a straight use of the **V-ed/en** verb *spiked,* parallel with *lit.* The **V-ed/en** form *petted* is at once a structural pun on *pet* as a noun, parallel with all the others, and a straight pun on the verb *pet* meaning fondled, made much of, perhaps spoiled. Several other nouns in this accumulation of structural puns also have verb meanings and uses, but they are quite different from their punning verb meanings in the poem: *skated, biked, railroaded, gunned, holstered,* and *bugled.* Both semantically and structurally, these puns are more rich and complex than they seem at first glance.

> May your tree be lit, your eggnog spiked.
> May all the kids be *skated* and *biked,*
> *Dolled, railroaded, chemistry-setted,*
> *Gamed, gunned, holstered, model-jetted,*
> *Bongoed, bugled,* or *clarinetted,*
> And generally aided and abetted
> To warm your hearts with their happy riot.[1]

In the final stanza of "The Eve of St. Agnes," Keats used the noun *nightmare* as the base of a **V-ed/en** verb form, and gave it greater impact by using the old intensifying prefix, *be-;* aside from its semantic suggestions, *be-nightmared* contributes significantly to the rhythmic effect. The sentence is compound, with an active first and a passive second clause; the passive clause is an unusual inversion, and employs *with* rather than *by* as a structure word of agency.

That night the Baron dreamt of many a woe,
And all his warrior-guests, with shade and form
Of witch, and demon, and large coffin-worm,
    Were long *be-nightmared.* . . .

Blake uses other kinds of puns in the bitter opening lines of "London"; his inventive use of **chartered** has overtones of quasi-legal private control of public thoroughfares, perhaps the entire city of London; his use of **mark** as a verb meaning observe and **marks** as a noun meaning scars is a brilliant pun, evocative of the mood Blake feels.

I wander through each *chartered* street,
Near where the *chartered* Thames does flow,
And *mark* in every face I meet
Marks of weakness, marks of woe.

TEACHING SUGGESTION: The above puns, structural and otherwise, are a sampling of the linguistic inventions that can be found in poems. According to the interests and abilities of your class, introduce some of these, or find others in materials you or your students are reading. This is a good opportunity to explore the subject of puns of all kinds. Follow-up work might be investigations of structural puns in literature, television shows, movies, and advertising; oral/written reports could be rewarding to individuals and to the class.

INVERSIONS. Since inversions occur so often in verse and so seldom in familiar talk, teachers might well call structural pattern inversion to the attention of students trying to penetrate the hard shell of poetry. If line 24 of Browning's "Rabbi Ben Ezra" is not his greatest, perhaps it merits citation for its notoriety.

Irks care the crop-full bird, frets doubt
    the maw-crammed beast?

Inversion is not the only problem in this line, but it is basic; the parallel verbs **irks** and **frets,** and the parallel adjectives **crop-full** and *maw-crammed* also help to make it a conundrum. A loose translation might be: *Does care bother the well-fed bird? Does doubt worry the animal with a full belly?* Browning's poems were once celebrated for their difficulty; they would still repay investigation of their syntactic structures.

Wordsworth's poems contain many inverted structures, some quite effective, others not so effective; the first problem with any inversion, though, is to read it intelligently. The opening line of "Strange fits of passion have I known" is regular inversion of the **N V N** pattern; the fourth line of the stanza is also an inversion, loosely describable as **N N V**, though the good gray poet has used poetic license there.

> Strange fits of passion have I known:
> And I will dare to tell,
> But in the lover's ear alone,
> What once to me befell.

"Lucy Gray" opens with a split-verb inversion; the first line of the second stanza is an **N N V** inversion; and the final stanza is a compound sentence in which the first clause is active, the second a passive inversion.

> Oft had I heard of Lucy Gray:
>
> No mate, no comrade, Lucy knew;
>
> You yet may spy the fawn at play,
> The hare upon the green;
> But the sweet face of Lucy Gray
> Will never more be seen.

The first two lines of Coleridge's "Kubla Khan" embody a statement with two major problems for the unwary: it is a split-verb inversion, with the unusual verb marker *did;* it begins with the movable phrase "in Xanadu," and also uses compression instead of complete statement.

> In Xanadu did Kubla Khan
> A stately pleasure dome decree:
> Where Alph, the sacred river, ran
> Through caverns measureless to man
> Down to a sunless sea.

If we are prepared to destroy the poetry completely, we may translate the opening two lines as follows: *Kubla Khan ordered a palace built for his pleasure in Xanadu.* What a bringdown! But is it often essential to find out what the literal statement of a poem is before it can be experienced as a poem. Aside from its striking syntax and diction, this famous passage is remarkable for its rhythm.

One final illustration of inversion. In his opening stanza of "The Eve of St. Agnes," Keats uses three inversions, one **A It Lv** pattern and two **A Lv N**: . . . *bitter chill it was!* . . . *silent was the flock;* and *Numb were the Beadsman's fingers* . . . ; the final clause is an **N N V** inversion: . . . *his prayer he saith.* This celebrated passage has many fascinating elements, but the reader who is not aware of the basic statement will never be fascinated by them.

> St. Agnes' Eve — Ah, bitter chill it was!
> The owl, for all his feathers, was a-cold;
> The hare limped trembling through the frozen grass,
> And silent was the flock in woolly fold:
> Numb were the Beadsman's fingers, while he told
> His rosary, and while his frosted breath,
> Like pious incense from a censer old,
> Seemed taking flight for heaven, without a death,
> Past the sweet Virgin's picture, while his prayer he saith.

TEACHING SUGGESTION: Without suggesting that syntactical analysis is poetic experience, introduce some of the above, or similar examples of inversion to your class. Allow them to discuss freely the use of inversions and other linguistic inventions in poetry; see whether they can approach the generalization that language is the medium of poetry, and that poets handle language the way sculptors handle stone; artists paint; and musicians sound. As a follow-up, encourage motivated students to make their own explorations of the language of poetry and report to the class.

SOME INTERESTING SYNTACTICAL PATTERNS IN POEMS. Nearly every poem worthy of the name of poetry will repay some of the kind of linguistic analysis illustrated in this section; sometimes it can touch the quick of the poet's inventive language of experience. *Neither linguistic nor any other analysis, however, can be a substitute for the direct, immediate, live experiencing of the poetry itself.* But if used intelligently, such analysis can be enlightening and enriching; it can be especially valuable as a means of entry into the often mysterious realm of poetry. The following sketches suggest points of linguistic interest in selected poems that are familiar to many teachers; *these limited observations are by no means intended to be full critical commentaries.*

In poetic form, Shelley's "Dirge" is an apostrophe to the grieving elements of Nature; their grief seems to give voice to the poet's own disenchantment with the governments and social organization of his time. The syntax is unfamiliar but simple. The poem is a single sentence in eight lines, seven lines of direct address to the elements, followed by one line that includes an imperative verb and a clause. A noun group that includes a clause modifier is the syntactical form used to address each of four elements in turn; two more are addressed in a compound noun construction; the final line includes the single imperative verb — **wail** — followed by an explanatory clause. Each of the first two noun groups comprises two short lines that must be read as one for rhythm and sense: each is a linguistically indivisible unit. Note that the noun groups become shorter and shorter as the poem approaches its climax in the final line.

	Rough wind, / that moanest loud	
	Grief too sad for song;	
	Wild wind / when sullen cloud	Noun groups
Apostrophe	Knells all the night long;	with clauses
	Sad storm, / whose tears are vain, 5	
	Bare woods, / whose branches strain,	
	Deep caves and dreary main, —	Compound noun group
Imperative	Wail, / for the world's wrong!	Verb; explanatory clause

"Meeting at Night" and "Parting at Morning," Browning's sequence of poems for lovers, evokes the urgency of a sailor's poignant rendezvous with his sweetheart. The first poem has two six-line stanzas; the sequel, a single four-line stanza. By the narrow criteria of grammatical sentences, all three stanzas are sentence fragments; Browning's impressionistic style tells the story swiftly, with great economy of language. (In stanza II, line 2, the term *farm* means *farmyard* or *farmhouse*.)

Meeting at Night

I

The gray sea / and the long black land;	Noun group + Noun group
/ And the yellow half-moon large and low;	+ Noun group
/ And the startled little waves / that leap In fiery ringlets from their sleep,	+ Noun group with clauses (that . . . / as . . .)
/ As I gain the cove with pushing prow. 5	
And quench its speed i' the slushy sand.	

II

Then / a mile of warm sea-scented beach;	Noun group
/ Three fields to cross / till a farm appears;	Noun group with clause
/ A tap at the pane, / the quick sharp scratch	Noun group/ Noun group
And blue spurt of a lighted match.	+ Noun group
/ And a voice less loud, thro' its joys and tears, 5	+ Noun group
Than the two hearts beating each to each!	

Stanza I has three noun groups in the first two lines, followed by a rather complex noun element containing two clauses as modifiers; stanza II has, in order, a noun group, a noun element with a clause, and four more noun elements of varying syntactical complexity. This is not the occasion to praise the diction, imagery, and rhythm of this poem, the author's success with an intricate rhyme scheme for both stanzas (*a b c c b a*), nor the exceptionally fine impression made by the poem as a whole. It is simply a small masterpiece.

Parting at Morning

<u>Round the cape of a sudden</u> / <u>came</u> / <u>the sea,</u>	Ad group V N
And <u>the sun</u> / <u>looked over</u> / <u>the mountain's rim</u>;	+ N V N
And / <u>straight</u> / <u>was</u> / <u>a path of gold for him,</u>	+ A Lv N group
And / <u>the need of a world of men for me.</u>	+ N group

Except for some ambiguity in line 3, "Parting at Morning," is a nice little sequel; if *him* refers to the rising sun, laying down *a path of gold* on the water, then the story line is fairly clear. As to syntax, the four-line stanza has two compound sentences of two lines each. The first line contains a **V N** inversion, *came / the sea,* introduced by an adverbial modifier of two linked prepositional phrases. The second line is a straightforward **N V N** sentence. Lines 3 and 4 are made up of an **A Lv N** inversion, with a compound noun element. The two poems taken together make a moving little drama, compact and parsimonious of language.

Before we comment on the opening stanza of Keats' ode "To Autumn," here it is just to read. The rhyme scheme is noted line by line at the right.

Season of mists and mellow fruitfulness,	*a*
Close bosom friend of the maturing sun,	*b*
Conspiring with him how to load and bless	*a*
With fruit the vines that round the thatch-eves run;	*b*
To bend with apples the mossed cottage-trees,	*c*
And fill all fruit with ripeness to the core;	*d*
To swell the gourd, and plump the hazel shells	*e*
With a sweet kernel; to set budding more	*d*
And still more, later flowers for the bees,	*c*
Until they think warm days will never cease,	*c*
For summer has o'er-brimmed their clammy cells.	*e*

Formally addressed to "Season of mists and mellow fruitfulness," this stanza evokes an autumnal mood for many readers through its diction, linguistic inventions, richness of detail, sensuous imagery, and varied rhythms. It also has a rather intricate rhyme scheme as shown above. The prose message of the stanza is that autumn and the autumn sun conspire to bring about a variety of seasonable ripening activities.

Viewed as syntax, this stanza is an eleven-line "sentence fragment," a complex noun element whose intricate verbal webwork tends to elude any simple syntactical analysis. Salient elements may be noted, however, that show in part how poetic language works; most of these are indicated below the lines in the display below. The first line is a noun group descriptive of autumn; the second line is a noun appositive that includes the prepositional phrase *of the maturing sun,* antecedent of *him* in the third line. The main activities of the stanza are stated in terms of the season and the sun *conspiring* (V-ing) *how* to V; there are seven parallel to V actions in lines 3–8, two of them unmarked infinitives, shown below as (to) V; all the to V forms have objects, the seventh a V-ing form (line 8); five of the to V forms are modified by *with* phrases. Except for a few prepositional phrases and four clauses, these seem to be the essential syntactical clues.

Season of mists and mellow fruitfulness,
Noun group

Close bosom friend of the maturing sun,
Noun group appositive

Conspiring with him / how to load and bless
V-ing   how to V (1)   (to) V (2)

With fruit / the vines / that round the thatch-eves run;
           object +   clause modifier

To bend with apples / the mossed cottage-trees,   5
to V (3)   object

And fill / all fruit   with ripeness to the core;
(to) V (4)   object + linked prepositional phrases

To swell / the gourd, and plump the hazel shells
to V (5)   object   (to) V (6)   object

With a sweet kernel; to set budding / more
             to V (7) (V-ing)

And still more, later flowers for the bees,
object of to set budding

Until they / think / warm days / will never cease,   10
clause modifier   unmarked clause as object

For summer has o'er-brimmed their clammy cells.
clause modifier

TEACHING SUGGESTION: To open up class discussion of sentence patterning in poems, introduce one of the poems analyzed in the foregoing section, or choose another poem better suited to your class. Some of your students may recall poems that have baffled them, and bring them into the discussion.

Young children, or students who are uninterested in poetry, may enjoy unscrambling short poems presented to them with the lines out of order. This is the technique of scrambled sentences applied to studying poetry; it has worked well with certain students. It can be another way of getting into a discussion of sentence patterning in poems.

Follow-up work might include individual investigations of sentences in poetry. If fruitful, these investigations might provide an excellent basis for oral/written work on poetry. *These discussions, like all others on poetry, should have as their ultimate focus the direct experiencing of poetry.*

Intonation in Oral Reading and Interpretation

Some linguists designate all that we call "tone of voice" as **paralanguage**: it includes such effects as whining, laughing or crying while talking, or talking with overtones suggestive of these; talking with relish or gusto; talking with distaste or disgust; using rasping, whispering, oversoft, or overloud tones; and all like effects. Paralanguage is often referred to as an "overlay" of subjective interpretive characteristics on the basic language structure required for communication; the point is that every speaker must use the required structural features of the language, but he may exercise various intonational options, both structural and interpretive. His options must never violate the code, however, except for a deliberate communicative purpose.

Some linguists designate as **kinesics** all those non-lingual actions that accompany speech, often more important in communication than all that could possibly be communicated by the bare linguistic structures themselves. **Kinesics** includes all bodily gestures, nudges, nods, finger, hand, and arm signals, shrugs, and facial gestures such as winks, smiles, sneers and leers — the whole gamut of expressive actions, so important in acting and interpretation, and in the small events of daily life.

All these rich resources of human communication should be brought to bear on the oral reading of literature, for the sheer joy of it, but also in order to develop associations that may carry over into the individual student's visual or silent reading of literature.

Professional readings, movie, television, and radio presentations, are all excellent sources of enrichment, but the audio-visual device of choice is the classroom teacher, or a parent, in everyday, seemingly casual interpretive readings. No one loves literature because he was assigned to love it; no one can possibly feel in his heart that it is great, just on his teacher's say-so. *The best approach, not only to drama and fiction, but above all to poetry, is to hear it live and flowing sweetly on the tongue.* A parent at home or a teacher in your schoolroom is not an artist way off on a high pedestal somewhere, but someone you know and can touch.

The remainder of *Intonation in Oral Reading and Interpretation* is discussed in two subsections:

POETRY: SOME FEATURES OF INTONATION AND SYNTAX

FICTION: SOME STRUCTURAL ELEMENTS OF SYNTAX AND INTONATION

POETRY: SOME FEATURES OF INTONATION AND SYNTAX. The arbitrary division of poems into lines, and rigid notions of meter, present problems that often baffle and finally discourage the young hopeful trying to appreciate poetry. The line of verse is generally a visual rather than an auditory unit; even when an elaborate rhyme scheme is followed, the echoing of the rhyme often is contained within longer meaning-bearing structures than the line. Stanzas and other verse forms are overlaid, often very skillfully, on patterns of English syntax.

The stress-timed rhythm of English is fundamental to English metrics and prosody; automated reading of poems in rigid iambic feet or in any meter interpreted as having identical stresses and a dull, repetitive beat, imposes a metronomic rhythm, false to our language, fatal to the sound of poetry. Nothing is more destructive of good verse than such a ding-dong metrical reading, line by line, with a fade-fall terminal at the end of every line. (A mechanically repeated fade-rise terminal would be no better.) English poems are written in sentences or in various syntactical elements; as we have seen, many poems or parts of poems are in fact sentence "fragments." The line of verse may or may not coincide with a meaning-bearing structure and its structural intonation pattern; the line is a visual unit, often visibly and audibly embellished by end rhyme that contributes to an echoing sound pattern within the whole sound of the poem. Rhymes should be perceived as visible and audible references to each other, and as echoes; they may be "internal" rhymes as well as "end" rhymes, and their sounds may be perfectly consonant, assonant, or even dissonant. Rhyme and rhythm are not obvious but subtle elements of poetry.

Stevenson's "Requiem" is an interesting little poem with a tight rhyme scheme and regular meter; its two stanzas are interconnected by their similar rhyme patterns and an identical b rhyme ending each stanza: $a\,a\,a\,b$ and $c\,c\,c\,b$; the three a and three c lines have four spoken beats each, followed by a silent stress at the end, making the first two a and c lines five beats long; the final silent stress of the third a and c line marks a rhythmic foot that carries over and is completed by two weak-stressed syllables beginning the final b line of each stanza. Below is the poem with vertical lines marking rhythmic feet, including silent feet; the rhyme scheme is shown at the right.

Requiem

| Under the | wide and | starry | sky, | ∧ |	*a*
| Dig the | grave and | let me | lie. | ∧ |	*a*
| Glad did I | live ∧ and | gladly | die, | ∧	*a*
And I | laid me | down with a | will. | ∧ |	*b*
5 | This be the | verse you | grave for | me: | ∧ |	*c*
| Here he | lies ∧ where he | longed to | be; | ∧ |	*c*
| Home is the | sailor ∧ | home from the | sea, | ∧	*c*
And the | hunter ∧ | home ∧ from the | hill.	*b*

The poem is written in four sentences, each stanza having two sentences, lines 1–2 and 3–4, and lines 5–6 and 7–8. The deceptively simple syntax involves inversions, structural imperatives used to make requests, and varied ellipses. The second stanza is a requisition for an epitaph to be inscribed on a grave marker; the last three lines are the epitaph itself.

Despite the regularity of the meter, a varied and interesting basic reading can be suggested by notations for structural terminals, combined with either heavy, medium, and occasionally light stresses on the stress-pulse beats; this provides a solid basis for an imaginative interpretive oral reading of the poem. Stresses are marked ′ for heavy, ∧ for medium, ‵ for light; weak stresses are unmarked. (Refer to Chapter 9 for an explanation of these notations.)

Requiem

| Under the | wide and | starry | sky,—→| ∧ |

| Dig the | grave and | let me | lie. ⭦| ∧ |

| Glad did I | live ∧ and | gladly | die, ⭦| ∧

And I | laid me | down with a | will. ⭦| ∧ |

5 | This be the | verse you | grave for | me:—→| ∧ |

| Here he | lies ∧ where he | longed to | be; ⭦| ∧ |

| Home is the | sailor—→∧ | home from the | sea,—→| ∧

And the | hunter ∧ | home ∧ from the | hill. ⭦

The interpretive possibilities of rate, pause, pitch contour, and voice quality are very rich.

Lewis Carroll's "Jabberwocky," aside from its incomparable interest for its own sake, provides entertaining examples of stress-timed rhythm, syntactical patterns, structure words, and word-form changes. In the following display, rhythmic feet and major and minor pauses are notated; but unlike the notation of "Requiem," no differentiation of degrees of stress on the rhythmic beats is shown.

Italicized portions denote structural elements: grammatical inflections and derivational affixes such as **out*grabe*** and **frab*jous;*** and structure words, including all forms of **be, went** as a verb marker, and the pronouns. ***'Twas*** is **N Lv** (for **it was**). Since **brillig** strikes me as a Germanic adjective, I am tempted to show **-ig** as a suffix; but this is a debatable point. Simple, basic sentence patterns are indicated line by line to the right of the text; several carry over from one line to the next. Plus marks (+) here denote **and** in both compound verbs and compound sentences. These notations are broad rather than fine; interpretation and appreciation are left to the reader.

Jabberwocky

'*T*was | brillig |,ʌ *and the* | slithy | toves   N Lv A + N

Did | gyre *and* | gimble *in the* | wabe: | ʌ | V

All | mimsy *were the* | boro | goves, | ʌ   A Lv N

And the | mome | raths *out* | grabe.   + N V

5 "Be | ware *the* | Jabberwock |, ʌ *my* | son! | ʌ | V N/N (of
                   address)

 The | jaws *that* | bite |, ʌ *the* | claws *that* | catch! | ʌ | N N

Be | ware *the* | Jubjub bird |, ʌ *and* | shun   V N + V

 The | frum*ious* | Bander | snatch!"   N

He | took *his* | vorp*al* | sword *in* | hand: | ʌ | N V N

10 | Long | time *the* | manx*ome* | foe *he* | sought – | ʌ | Ad N V

So | rested | *he by the* | Tumtum | tree, | ʌ   V N

And | stood a | while *in* | thought.   + V

                Sentence mod-

And | as in | uff*ish* thought | *he* | stood, | ʌ ifier Ad N V

 The | Jabberwock |, ʌ *with* | eyes *of* | flame, | ʌ N

15 *Came* | whiffl*ing* | *through the* | tul*gey* | wood, | ʌ V

 And | burbled | *as it* | came | !   + V

| *One,*ʌ | *two!*ʌ | *One,*ʌ | *two!* ʌ *And* | *through and*
 | *through* ʌ   Ad

 The | vorp*al* | blade *went* | snicker- | snack! | ʌ | N V A

| *He left it* | dead |, ʌ *and* | *with its* | head N V N A

20 | *He* | went gal | umph*ing* | back | . + N V

| "*And* | hast *thou* | slain *the* | Jabber | wock? | ʌ | + V N N

 | Come *to my* | arms, ʌ *my* | beam*ish* | boy! | ʌ | V Ad/N (of
                  address)

O | frab*jous* | day! Cal | looh! | Callay!" | ʌ N V

He | chortled | *in his* | joy |.

25 *'Twas* | brillig | ,ʌ *and the* | slith*y* | tove*s*

   Did | gyre *and* | gimble *in the* | wabe: | ʌ |

   All | mimsy | *were the* | boro | gove*s*, | ʌ

   | *And the* | mome | rath*s out* | *grabe.*

TEACHING SUGGESTION: Students of all ages find "Jabberwocky" interesting. Even children in middle grades can enjoy pointing out the structural elements that hold the nonsense together. The poem lends itself very well to oral interpretation, either individual or choral.

   T. S. Eliot's contradiction of Chaucer's opening of the Prologue to *The Canterbury Tales* presents interesting features of syntax and intonation. The passage consists of two sentences: the first is an **N Lv N** sentence of four lines, with three parallel sentence modifiers using participles (**V-ing** forms) as adjectives retaining the verb function of having objects (for example, *breeding lilacs*); the contrasting second sentence is an **N V N A** sentence of three lines with two parallel modifiers as in the preceding sentence. These five **V-ing** modifiers are structurally parallel, and at the same time provide an interlacing pattern of "weak" rhymes throughout the seven lines (the **-ing** syllables receive weak stresses at the line-ends). All lines up to the periods in both sentences must be "read on"; each line ends with a **V-ing** form completed by an object in the next line.

   Here are the first seven lines of "The Burial of the Dead" from *The Wasteland*,[2] with notations for syntax and sentence modifiers; the main sentence parts and the **V-ing** modifiers are underscored.

      N Lv N (first sentence)
      N V N A (second sentence)

      N   Lv   N
      April / is / the cruelest month, / breeding   V-ing N
      Lilacs out of the dead land, / mixing   V-ing N
      Memory and desire, / stirring   V-ing N
      Dull roots with spring rain.

```
        N     V    N     A
5    Winter / kept / us / warm, / covering        V-ing N
     Earth in forgetful snow, / feeding           V-ing N
     A little life with dried tubers.
```

The strong rhythm of this passage requires notations for a variety of feet: one, two, three, four and five syllables, and a few silent feet of one full beat. Below is the passage with suggested notations for structural rhythm, including terminals. No attempt is made to suggest the rich possibilities of interpretive variations of rate, pause, pitch contour, and voice quality.

```
        | April is the | cruelest | month, ↘ | ∧ | breeding
             4             3                           2
        Lilacs out of the | dead | land, ↘ | ∧ | mixing
             5               1      1                   2
        | Memory and de | sire, ↘ | ∧ | stirring
             5                              2
        | Dull | roots → ∧ with | spring | rain. ↘ | ∧ |
          1       2                1        1

5       | Winter kept us | warm, ↘ | ∧ | covering
             4              1                 3
        | Earth in for | getful | snow, ↘ | ∧ | feeding
             3             2                       3
        A | little | life → ∧ with | dried | tubers. ↘
          2            2               1       2
```

The syntactical and intonational features suggested above point up the poet's free manipulation of English structures to sharpen the contrast of the birth-shock and womb-comfort imagery of the two successive, juxtaposed sentences; these features help make effective poetry.

Of all creative writers, poets are the most inventive in their abundant manipulations of English language structures. We have examined some of these elements in two quite different poems by Stevenson and Eliot. The possibilities of extending our sampling indefinitely is tempting, but perhaps we can conclude with an entirely different selection from Whitman, the second stanza of "Out of the Cradle, Endlessly Rocking." These three selections illustrate the seemingly infinite structural variety of language to be found in poems written in our language.

Despite its action and movement, this entire nine-line stanza from Whitman is what is commonly called a "sentence fragment," because it does not have conventional sentence structure; instead, the first three lines are adverbial sentence modifiers, followed by a string of noun elements. Paumanok is an Indian name for Long Island; *Once Paumanok* is an elliptical prepositional phrase telling when and where the action occurred. Below, the poem is shown with notations for its syntactical structure; the main structural features are underscored.

/ Once Paumanok,	Ad group
/ When the lilac-scent was in the air and / fifth-month grass was growing,	Ad clause
/ Up this seashore / in some briars,	Ad phrases
/ Two feather'd guests from Alabama, / two together,	N groups
5 / And their nest, / and four light-green eggs spotted with brown,	+ N groups
/ And every day the he-bird to and fro near at hand,	+ N group (adverbial)
/ And every day the she-bird crouch'd on her nest, silent, with bright eyes,	+ N group (adverbial)
/ And every day I, a curious boy, never too close, / never disturbing them,	+ N group and V-ing structures
/ Cautiously peering, / absorbing, / translating.	

In line six, *to and fro* has the effect of a verb, just as in the next line the adjective crouch'd (**V-ed/en** or past participle) does; the "incomplete" **V-ing** structures are also full of action.

This stanza-long sentence of diverse elements achieves its breathless sense of the wondrous partly by its loose structure, its freedom from all tight linkages. The rhythmic bursts vary from one to seven syllables per foot, including a number of silent stresses. Fade-level terminals or fade-rise terminals with no significant change of pitch enhance the excitement and expectation, suggesting more and ever more to come; the entire stanza can be read without a fade-fall terminal, even at the final period. Below, the stanza is shown with suggested notations for structural rhythm; no attempt is made to suggest intepretive variations of rate, pause, pitch contour, and voice quality. The syllable counts include silent stresses as syllables.

| Once Pau | manok ⬈ | ∧
    2   2

When the | lilac-scent was in the air ⬈ | ∧ and | fifth-month
   2   7   2   2

   | grass was | growing ⬈ | ∧
     2   2

Up this | seashore ⬈ | ∧ in some | briars ⬈ | ∧ |
  3   2   3   2

| Two | feather'd | guests from | Ala | bama ⬈ ∧ | two to
  1   2   2   2   3   2

   | gether ⬈ | ∧
     2

And their | nest ⬈ | ∧ and four | light-green | eggs ⬈ ∧
  3   1   3   2   2

   | spotted with | brown ⬈ | ∧   5
     3   1

And | every day the | he-bird to and fro ⬈ ∧ | near at hand ⬈ | ∧
  2   4   5   3

And | every day the | she-bird ∧ | crouch'd on her | nest ⬈ ∧
  2   4   2   3   2

   | silent ⬈ | ∧ with | bright | eyes ⬈ | ∧
     2   2   1   1

And | every day | I ⬈ | ∧ a | curious | boy ⬈ ∧ | never too
  2   3   1   2   3   2   3

   | close ⬈ ∧ | never dis | turbing them ⬈ ∧
     2   3   4

| Cautiously | peering ⬈ | ∧ ab | sorbing ⬈ | ∧ trans
  3   2   2   2   2

   | lating ⬈
     2

TEACHING SUGGESTION: The analytical techniques and notations illustrated above require too much experience to be applicable in most classrooms. Their main application is in helping teachers prepare themselves for effective oral reading to their students, with help, aid, and possibly comfort from a tape recorder.

Such preparation can be a sound basis for choral reading, with careful direction by the teacher. Choral reading, in turn, can provide a sound basis for individual oral reading and interpretation.

FICTION: SOME STRUCTURAL ELEMENTS OF SYNTAX AND INTONATION. The rhythm of poetry is more compelling than that of prose fiction, and therefore more readily notated. Nevertheless, fiction writers also manipulate language to create their effects, and so the structural rhythm and terminals of fiction are of considerable significance. The passage selected for discussion here consists of three paragraphs following the opening exposition of Dickens' *Great Expectations:* the scene and action in the church graveyard where young Pip gains his "first most vivid and memorable impression of the identity of things." The first paragraph contains three sentences; first, an **N Lv N** sentence, with an adverbial sentence modifier longer than the main statement; second, an **N V** sentence with greatly expanded **N** and **V** parts; third, an **N V N** sentence with seven **Noun parts** (clauses) as the completer of the sentence (**N V N + N + N + N + N + N + N**). The dramatic second paragraph is a sudden, frightening command to Pip by Magwitch, the escaped convict, followed by a description of his actions and another command. The third paragraph consists entirely of three "sentence fragments": noun elements descriptive of Magwitch, expanded with prepositional phrases and clauses. This entire passage is shown below with notations for gross sentence patterns.

     N   Lv   N   Adverbial

1. Ours / was / the marsh country, / down by the river, within,

        modifier
as the river wound, twenty miles of the sea. / My first most vivid

                         N
and broad impression of the identity of things, / seems to me to

                 V
have been gained on a memorable raw afternoon towards evening.

Ad modifier   N   V   N (1)
At such a time / I / found out for certain that this bleak place

                          +   N (2)
overgrown with nettles was the churchyard; and / that Philip,

late of this parish, and also Georgiana wife of the above, were

                 +   N (3)
dead and buried; and / that Alexander, Bartholomew, Abraham,

Tobias, and Roger, infant children of the aforesaid, were also

+   N (4)

dead and buried; and / that the dark flat wilderness beyond the churchyard, intersected with dykes and mounds and gates, with

+   N (5)

scattered cattle feeding on it, was the marshes; and / that the low

+   N (6)

leaden line beyond was the river; and / that the distant savage

+   N (7)

lair from which the wind was rushing was the sea; and / that the small bundle of shivers growing afraid of it all and beginning to cry, was Pip.

V   N   V   N   Ad modifier
2. "Hold / your noise!" / cried / a terrible voice, / as a man started

V   A
up from the graves at the side of the church porch. / "Keep / still, /

Appositive   N   V   N
you little devil, / or I / 'll cut / your throat!"

N   prepositional phrases
3. A fearful man, / all in coarse grey, / with a great iron / on his leg.

N + prepositional   +   phrases   +
A man / with no hat, / and with broken shoes, / and with an old

N   passive clauses NvV
rag tied round his head. A man who / had been soaked in water,

+   V   +   V by   N + V by   N
and smothered in mud, and / lamed by stones, and / cut by flints,

+   V   by   N + V   by   N   3 active clauses +
and / stung by nettles, and / torn by briars; / who / limped and

+   +
glared and growled; and whose teeth chattered in his head / as he

seized me by the chin.

    This passage is the work of a great literary artist. It is creative prose, "simple, sensuous, and passionate"; the rate and rhythm of the language brings it closer to poetry than to exposition. Below it is displayed with suggested notations for rhythm, including terminals and silent stresses. Here too, as in the previous displays, the suggestions are largely structural. Pitch contours, voice qualities, variations of rate, gestures and bodily actions of all kinds — these are left to the imagination of the interpreter.

| Ours was the | marsh country ↗ ∧ | down by the | river ↗ | ∧ with | in ↗ | ∧ as the | river | wound ↗ | ∧ | twenty | miles of the | sea ↘ | ∧ My | first most | vivid and | broad im | pression of the i | dentity of | things ↗ | ∧ seems to | me to have been | gained on a | memorable | raw after | noon towards | evening ↘ | ∧ At | such a | time ↗ | ∧ I found | out for | certain ↗ | ∧ that | this | bleak | place ↗ | ∧ over | grown with | nettles ↗ | ∧ was the | churchyard ↗ | ∧ and that | Philip ↗ ∧ | late of | this | parish ↗ | ∧ and also Geor | giana ↗ ∧ | wife of the a | bove ↗ | ∧ were | dead and | bur- ied ↗ | ∧ and that Alex | ander ↗ | ∧ Bar | tholomew ↗ ∧ | Abraham ↗ | ∧ To | bias ↗ | ∧ and | Roger ↗ | ∧ | infant | children of the a | foresaid ↗ | ∧ were | also | dead and | buried ↘ | ∧ and that the | dark | flat | wilderness be | yond the | churchyard ↗ | ∧ inter | sected with | dykes and | mounds and | gates ↗ | ∧ with | scattered | cattle | feeding on it ↗ | ∧ was the | marshes ↗ | ∧ and that the | low | leaden | line be | yond was the | river ↗ | ∧ and that the | distant | savage | lair ↗ | ∧ from which the | wind was | rushing ↗ | ∧ was the | sea ↘ | ∧ and that the | small | bundle of shivers ↗ | ∧ | growing a | fraid of it all ↗ | ∧ and be | ginning to | cry ↗ | ∧ was | Pip | ∧ |

| Hold your | noise ↘ | ∧ cried a | terrible | voice ↗ | ∧ as a | man started | up from the | graves at the | side of the | church | porch ↘ | ∧ | Keep | still ↗ | ∧ you little | devil ↗ | ∧ or | I'll | cut your throat ↘ | ∧ |

A | fearful man ↘ | ∧ all in | coarse | grey ↗ | ∧ with a | great | iron on his | leg ↘ | ∧ A | man with no | hat ↗ | ∧ and with | broken shoes ↗ | ∧ and with an | old | rag tied a | round his | head ↘ | ∧ A | man who had been | soaked in | water ↘ | ∧ and | smothered in mud ↘ | ∧ and | lamed by | stones ↘ | ∧ and | cut by | flints ↘ | ∧ and | stung by | nettles ↘ | ∧ and | torn by | briars ↘ | ∧ who | limped ↗ and | glared ↗ and | growled ↘ | ∧ and whose | teeth | chattered in his | head | ↗ | ∧ as he | seized me | by the | chin ↘

TEACHING SUGGESTION: Just as with the analysis of verse, the main application of the above analysis of fiction is in helping teachers prepare themselves for effective oral reading to their students, with prior assistance from a tape recorder. Students may learn from choral reading, under careful direction of the teacher.

A Note on Literary Forms and Musical Compositions

In literature, as in music, the whole may be equal to infinitely more than the sum of the parts. A sonata or a symphony, a sonnet or a drama — though written down as texts or scores with specific notations for their "parts" — cannot be perceived as static wholes but must be experienced as dynamic processes occurring in time. Both literary and musical compositions are best comprehended when they are skillfully performed for auditors; both, but literature better than music, may also be comprehended by qualified readers skilled in "silent" reading. And just as there may be varied interpretations of music, so there may be of literature; but responsible artistic interpretations are governed by the requirements of each specific piece, its form and style, and by the intent of the creator. It is essential that the performing artist have mastered the structural elements and features of the art as a basis for his interpretation.

A subtle difficulty of learning to interpret literature, orally or silently, is the necessity of "internalizing" new and strange intonation patterns as well as syntactical patterns encountered only in print. Especially in poetry, these are often the author's unique inventions for a single work. The reader must somehow respond to each meaning-bearing pattern as a whole, each sentence and its accompanying intonation, as an approach to the entire piece. After long and successful experience, he may have learned to respond by an unconscious, intuitive process; or he may be competent to analyze each author's unique manipulations of English structural features directly. For the teacher, direct analysis is an excellent means of breaking the author's code and involving children during their formative years in an appreciative response to literature.

Oral reading "with expression" is interpretive reading that builds upon but also soars above structural intonation features and patterns; with practice and enjoyment, oral reading can be developed into a fine art, closely akin to acting. Keen interest in silent reading and written composition can be stimulated by skillfully engaging the student's creative imagination and natural vivacity in oral interpretations. This oral reading is the ideal basis for "silent" appreciation of literature throughout life. So long as the reader or interpreter attends to the structural requirements of English syntax and intonation, he is limited only by dictates of judgment and taste.

Sensitivity to the subtle nuances of language, appreciation of the richness of English dialects, access to poetry, responsiveness to the experience embodied in the varied forms of literature — all can best be cultivated by experiencing the whole sound and shape of a piece excellently read aloud. Every learner should have many opportunities to attend to and enjoy good oral interpretations of literature. *If he has the authentic sound in his ear, in silent reading his eye helps his inner ear tune in on the mnemonic sound track by association with the sounds and tunes of other pieces; but if the reader has never experienced the authentic sound to begin with, then his inner ear may be deaf to the printed presentation, no matter how beautifully done.*

Shorter literary forms resemble songs or sonatas; longer works resemble concertos, symphonies, operas. This is not mere imagery; and it is more than analogy. Musical notation and all the forms and modes of music have developed within cultures of men who speak; no people ever sang who did not first have language. The interrelationships of speech and song, of larger language constructs and the longer forms of music, are a challenge to our research and our imagination.

Why did Poe recommend that a short story be of a length suitable to be read at one sitting? Possibly because such forms as short stories, poems, essays — all those literary forms that can be read in one sitting — have comprehensive melodic and rhythmic designs, embracing all components in an organic form so as to create a sense of completion when the piece has run its course, like an inner rhythmic dance. The various forms of writing, creative writing in particular — poetry, drama, fiction — are not static "forms," but intricate psycholinguistic processes, events patterned through time.

The evocation of a feeling of completion, of finish, in sound and rhythm, is one of the finest attainments of creative writing; an approach to teaching it can be made through interpretive oral readings, which can in turn contribute to appreciation of literary form in silent reading. John Steinbeck quite deliberately wrote musically in the intercalary chapters of *The Grapes of Wrath*, and created prose compositions resembling musical forms. It was the poet John Ciardi who wrote, "The supreme art of poetry is not to *assert* meaning, but to release it by juxtaposition of poetic elements. Form, in its inter-relations, is the most speaking element." [3]

The graphic form, then, is the permanently organized embodiment of the writer's original creative experience: psycholinguistic process in time is the underlying reality expressed in literary form, freshly reenacted with each new reading. Viewed as written communication, the graphic form is the author's letter to the reader; the reader's response is an act of reception. In performing the piece, either silently or orally, the reader recreates for himself the author's experience in the form he shaped it to, with appropriate nuances and overtones from the reader's unique experience.

Selected References

Introductory

John Ciardi, *How Does a Poem Mean?* (Boston: Houghton Mifflin, 1959).
Louise M. Rosenblatt, *Literature as Exploration*, rev. ed. (New York: Noble and Noble, 1968).

Advanced

Northrop Frye, ed., *Sound and Poetry: English Institute Essays* (New York: Columbia University Press, 1957).
Ian A. Gordon, *The Movement of English Prose*, Foreword by Randolph Quirk (Bloomington: Indiana University Press, 1966).

Technical

"Linguistics and the Study of Literature," Part VII in *Readings in Applied English Linguistics* (second ed.), ed. Harold B. Allen (New York: Appleton-Century-Crofts, 1964).
Seymour Chatman and Samuel R. Levin, eds., *Essays on the Language of Literature* (Boston: Houghton Mifflin, 1967).

Part Three

A Broad View
of Teaching Applications

Chapter 11

English Grammars
as Teaching Devices

We who teach grammar must keep ourselves sensitive to the actual quality of the learner's experience with grammar. He probably does not intend to follow in our footsteps, nor to prepare himself for gramary or linguistics; it is all too easy for us to turn him against our discipline — against us. Sometimes a year's residence with a prescriptive teacher is all it takes.

The great lesson I have learned as a teacher of English and of English teachers is that, for countless learners, prescriptivism is daily death by inches in the English classroom. Prescriptivism — the method, the literal verbal prescriptions themselves, above all the very state of mind of it — prescriptivism engenders malformations of learning and appreciation. An inductive, exploratory, discovering approach is incomparably more effective. A teacher's ingrained prescriptivism can embitter the study of the best of grammars, yet a descriptive approach can offset the disadvantages of even a poor grammar. We all need the best grammar we can get: it will not be a Draconian code.

The unlucky student who *hates grammar* has not had the same experience as that other unlucky one who *just loves it*. But both are in trouble. The hater simply hates the whole kit and kaboodle of it —

rule after rule for usage (some plainly absurd); the crazy patchwork verbal nomenclature for everything; verbal definitions of "the eight (or nine) parts of speech"; rules for sentence structure; rules for parsing and diagraming, indentation, punctuation, capitalization, spelling, hyphenation and syllabication; neat handwriting in either blue or black ink on approved theme paper with a red margin on the left — then copying it all over again until it is letter perfect. He hates the whole endless list of prescriptions he associates, for better or for worse, with English. His opposite number, the grammar lover, is often teacher's pet, a proper parrot who never swears but can repeat-after-me to the end of time, and enjoys a decent ego unction associated with the observance of so many nice little English proprieties. Here is a twofold tragedy: as students, neither grammar lover nor grammar hater has a healthy approach to composition; as human beings, both are miserable, preoccupied with English, dwarfish.

This chapter briefly surveys English grammars and theories underlying them, with sharp attention to prescriptivism as a method in relation to grammars. For this purpose, we may initially define a grammar as a set of statements about the patterns and processes of the language system. I prefer the term *statements* to *rules* because *statements* is descriptive and *rules* is prescriptive; the term *rules* cannot be disassociated from the generations-long connotation it has acquired in school grammar, where it means a rigid set of laws, rigidly applied. Descriptive statements about the language system are assumed to have implications for teaching the arts and skills of English — writing and reading in particular; here, *grammar* will mean English grammars regarded mainly as teaching devices. Some applications in textbooks and learning materials will be discussed, but no attempt will be made at a complete survey.

Following are the main topics:

American School Grammar
Twentieth Century Traditional, or Classical, Grammar
Descriptive and Structural Grammar
Tagmemic Grammar
Relationships among Sentences without Explicit Rules
Generative-Transformational Grammar
Stratificational Grammar
Toward a Synthesis of Grammars

American School Grammar

During all the time I was a schoolboy, a college student, a graduate student, and a fledgling English teacher, the atmosphere was subtly permeated by an erroneous English-teaching dogma: The Latin English grammar fallacy. Some teachers were only mild about it, but the high proportion of Fidditch-Pringles who espoused the faith was significant; it gave them a catechism and a mystique with which to alienate themselves from the mere flesh and blood of their students and lesser colleagues. To the innocent young teacher with no better information, this fallacy made just enough sense to appear plausible. *It still has not died out in the schools; far from it.*

The remainder of this topic is presented under the following subheadings:

THE LATIN ENGLISH GRAMMAR FALLACY
THREE COUNTERING BELIEFS, CLOSER TO THE TRUTH
THE ANCIENT ORIGINS OF SCHOOL GRAMMAR
VERBAL PRESCRIPTIVISM AS A METHOD OF TEACHING GRAMMAR
WHAT IS GRAMMAR?
TOPICS OF SCHOOL GRAMMAR
REED AND KELLOGG SENTENCE DIAGRAMS
A SAMPLING OF REED AND KELLOGG DIAGRAMS
SCHOOL GRAMMAR — HAIL AND FAREWELL!

THE LATIN ENGLISH GRAMMAR FALLACY. The Latin English grammar fallacy is compounded largely of three notions — at best dangerous half-truths, at worst unfounded myths.

1. The notion that modern English is somehow like Latin; and the corollary, that a study of Latin grammar is a good means if not the best means of leading an American student to an understanding of English grammar.

2. The notion that a high proportion of modern English words are "descended from" Latin words; and the corollary, that a study of Latin vocabulary is a good means if not the best means of helping an American student to understand English words so as to develop a good English vocabulary. Hidden here is the silent, simplistic

conviction that a language is defined by its vocabulary, rather than by its system for ordering and arranging words in sentences and longer constructs.

3. The notion that the so-called rules of English propounded in common school grammar are soundly based upon Latin rules, in league with logic, reason, and "the laws of thought"; and the corollary, that these rules, or laws, provide an accurate and absolute measuring rod for chastising errors in both speech and writing, and for rejecting out of hand all usages that do not conform. They are "not grammatical," or "not acceptable."

THREE COUNTERING BELIEFS, CLOSER TO THE TRUTH. These are verifiable beliefs based upon historical fact or replicable modern investigations.

1. Modern English and Latin are fundamentally different languages: Modern English is an *analytic* language, one whose structure depends primarily on word order and structure words; while Latin is a *synthetic* language, one whose structure depends primarily on grammatical inflections. Even Old English, the great-grandparent of Modern English and itself a synthetic language, was unlike Latin in the specifics of its structure. *The best way to understand English is to study English directly.* The increased understanding of English that often accompanies study of another language results from sharpened awareness of the comparative-contrastive features of the two languages.

2. A language and its vocabulary are far from identical; a language can be understood only as a complete structural system for communication, not merely as a dictionary, or vocabulary.

Moreover, borrowing words from other languages all over the world is characteristic of English; our modern English dictionary may include derivatives of as many as one-fourth of all the Latin words we know of, but many words of ultimate Latin origin came directly into English from Norman French.

3. Modern linguistics presents a growing body of descriptive data about English that provides a basis for a much truer view of English language structure than common school grammar does, or any previous grammar.

THE ANCIENT ORIGINS OF SCHOOL GRAMMAR. The ultimate origin of the so-called rules of school grammar is the ancient Greek school of grammarians associated with the University of Alexandria, who called themselves analogists. They sought to discover and describe the structural regularities of the Greek language, and began the discussion of most of the topics still considered by linguists and grammarians; the authoritative expression of this grammar was written by Dionysius Thrax about 100 B.C. While hardly scientific by modern standards, the analogists did search, with some success, for regularity and system within the total structure of Greek. Even that long ago, another school, the anomalists, opposed the attempts of the analogists to describe Greek structure objectively and empirically — in somewhat the same way as the traditional and transformational grammarians of our time oppose the methods and results of descriptive linguists.

A difficulty with the work of Thrax, however, is that although some of his attitudes and methods are applicable to the study of other languages, his specifics apply to Greek. Nevertheless, the rules of the analogists became the basis of Latin grammars of the early Christian era, from which the Latin and Greek grammars of Medieval and Modern Europe were developed. These grammars in turn became the basis of English grammars, first developed in England before Shakespeare's time, and later imitated in England and America. In various simplistic forms, they are alive and kicking today in American school programs; perhaps the chief name associated with this grammar today is that of Warriner.[1]

VERBAL PRESCRIPTIVISM AS A METHOD OF TEACHING GRAMMAR. The essence of the rules of school grammar is a verbal prescriptivism based upon the authority of the teacher and the school, and often backed by the community. In another form, and from a different origin, a new verbal prescriptivism for school consumption has been developed, based upon one school of transformational grammar. Old prescriptivism was *the method* of a school grammar based on Latin grammar; New prescriptivism is *the method* of a peculiar transformational grammar with a very much larger number of rules; it is the same old stuff in a complicated new package.

WHAT IS GRAMMAR? Students who hate or love grammar, or who couldn't care less, are reacting in part to popular confusion about what grammar is, or about what some people think it should be. In an influential article, Francis defined three common ways in which people use the term *grammar*.[2]

1. Grammar is "the set of formal patterns in which the words of a language are arranged in order to convey larger meanings." As soon as the native speaker has completed the process of acquiring his language, this kind of grammar works automatically for him; it is often said to be "out of awareness."

This grammar is an unconscious, automatic form of human behavior; it is the operational system of the language.

2. Grammar is "the branch of linguistic science which is concerned with the description, analysis, and formulization of formal language patterns."

This kind of grammar can be reduced to a set of statements about the operational system of the language. Several for English are sketched in this chapter.

3. Grammar is "linguistic etiquette." That epithet of damnation, "bad grammar," is applied to sins in this little universe. Linguistic etiquette at its worst embalms crotchety, antiquated rules, many of them purely imaginary, even in their origin (the elaborate catechism for *shall* and *will*, for example).

In its best sense, however, linguistic etiquette keeps alive many worthy traditional practices of speakers and writers of effective English.

TEACHING SUGGESTION: Ask the question, "What is grammar?" Help your students to explore the possible answers in an open-ended discussion. (Such a discussion is possible at nearly any grade level above primary.)

TOPICS OF SCHOOL GRAMMAR. The three main topics of school grammar texts *as grammars* are (1) sentence construction and analysis, (2) the parts of speech, and (3) spelling. Despite a strong tendency to treat the word as the basic unit of language, the central preoccupation is with the sentence; elaborate systems of diagraming have been devised to show the grammatical relationships of words within sentences. When I was a boy in the eighth grade, we were given almost daily assignments in both parsing and diagraming of sentences. For parsing, we drew vertical lines on our paper to mark off book-keeper's columns for the eight parts of speech: noun, pronoun, verb, adjective, adverb, preposition, conjunction, interjection. Then we tried to figure out which column was right for each word in each sentence; twenty to fifty sentences were commonly assigned for one day's work. We felt mighty uneasy about words that seemed to shift from one part of speech to another in various sentences. For example, the word *tree:*

A *tree* stands in the front yard.   (noun)
A tiny *tree* toad sings there at night.   (adjective)
Our dog likes to *tree* the neighbor's cat in it.   (verb)

Such words seemed to us like fugitives from the system.

TEACHING SUGGESTION: Explore with students the question of words shifting from one part of speech to another. Invite them to suggest examples.

Study of the parts of speech, outside of parsing or some equivalent, generally includes: usage problems; etymology, with some casual attention to derivational prefixes and suffixes; and the grammatical inflections (nouns, pronouns, verbs, adjectives, adverbs). Spelling may be treated along with parts of speech in conjugations and de-clensions; in a separate section of the textbook; or even in a small book by itself, unrelated to anything. The principal shortcomings of school grammars are in the relationships between word-form classes (parts of speech) and sentence structure, two topics that become blended and confused; and in phonology (the sound system), which is badly neglected.

REED AND KELLOGG SENTENCE DIAGRAMS. Many school grammar texts present sentence diagrams that are ultimately based upon the Reed and Kellogg system. These presentations vary substantially in the quantity and complexity of the diagrams shown; few if any give an adequate explanation of their rationale. An enthusiastic discussion by a linguist may be found in *Linguistics and English Grammar*, by H. A. Gleason, Jr.; [3] a college text by Pence and Emery, *A Grammar of Present-Day English*,[4] offers an extensive presentation of diagrams, with only minimal explanation, however.

The real function of Reed and Kellogg diagrams is to symbolize abstract relationships among the words in each sentence; they are not much concerned with word order, which is clearly shown only in the simplest diagrams. They fail to exhibit the basic patterns of sentences; they neither reveal nor clarify the basic sentence constituents, their order and syntactical relationships. This indifference to pattern and order, despite the fact that pattern and order are fundamental to English sentence structure and meaning, may be the chief reason why these diagrams are not appreciated by many teachers and students — or perhaps why they are simply not understood by them.

In my first year of teaching, in order to teach what the textbook required, I quickly relearned sentence diagraming, but I was disappointed with the results. Students who had trouble with sentence structure had trouble with diagraming; those who understood sentence structure had no trouble with diagraming. In other words, students who began with one problem ended up with two; those who had no problem to begin with had no problem in the end. It didn't seem fair. My own further experience bore this out; it has been corroborated by many teachers of English and the language arts. Sentence diagrams of this type are fun for linguists, grammarians, and the like-minded. But many students (and some teachers) are confused and intimidated by them.

A SAMPLING OF REED AND KELLOGG DIAGRAMS. The diagram below of a sentence with only a simple subject and a simple predicate — *Birds sing* — illustrates the heavy base line and the vertical line across the base line separating these elements.

Modifiers are shown by slant lines attached to the words modified. Note that even in a short sentence, word order is distorted.

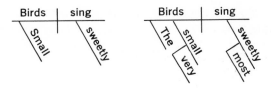

Prepositional phrases are divided and displayed as in the following diagram, with even greater distortion of word order.

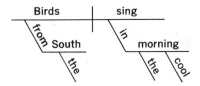

A direct object is indicated by a vertical line extending upward from the base line; order is clearly shown here.

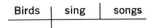

Compound elements are written on forked lines as follows.

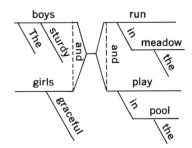

A variety of complements are indicated with a line slanting backward from the base line, between the verb and the complement.

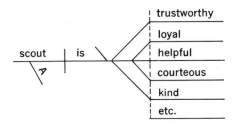

A backward-slanting line is also used between an object and an object complement.

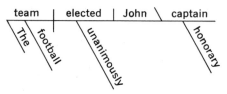

Indifference to word order and order of sentence parts is starkly clear in diagrams of questions. For example, *How many reserved seats does your party need?* For classroom teaching, the words are often first translocated into diagram order, like this: *Your party does need how many reserved seats?* This does not help a confused learner.

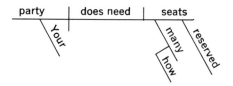

Here is a diagram of *Whom do you want to room with?*

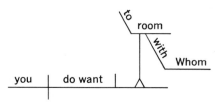

A final example of a simple sentence using the expletive *there,* and with *that* understood. *I think there is to be a formal dance.* With words translocated: (*there*) *I think that a formal dance is to be.*

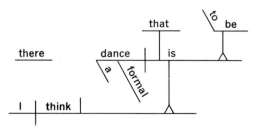

Reed and Kellogg diagrams are better as pleasant games for people who enjoy them than as teaching devices for students who don't.

TEACHING SUGGESTION: Display a few Reed and Kellogg sentence diagrams on the chalkboard. Open a free discussion with your students about their reactions to them.

SCHOOL GRAMMAR — HAIL AND FAREWELL! Much of the grammar taught in American schools does not deserve the reputable name of traditional grammar. To many students, school grammar is more an unhappy state of mind than an explanation of English. Altogether too much so-called grammar has been passed along by word of mouth, without benefit of book, supported by some strong gestures and an enforcing tone of voice from the teacher. Programs of teacher education, not to mention liberal arts English departments, have long neglected professional instruction in linguistics and English grammar; consequently, teachers have had little recourse except to recall a dubious mixture of half-assimilated bits of their own past school experience of grammar, seasoned with Fidditch-Pringlism. Sometimes all that remains is an unholy zeal for castigating human error, with no vision of anyone's hope of grace.

Twentieth Century Traditional, or Classical, Grammar

This discussion of twentieth century traditional, or classical, grammar deals briefly and broadly with the generally neglected work of four important men. Several interesting and historically important earlier works, such as those of Noah Webster,[5] Robert Lowth,[6] and Lindley Murray,[7] are merely mentioned here in passing. One main point must be emphasized: American school grammar, even as represented in leading textbooks rather than in an oral tradition based on hearsay, is generally a rigid, constricted subject, whereas traditional grammar, which developed out of classical European linguistics, is comprehensive, varied, and flexible.

It may surprise many Americans that of four major English grammarians of this century, three are European scholars. In 1909, Etsko Kruisinga's *A Handbook of Present-Day English* [8] was published; also in 1909, the first volume of Otto Jespersen's *A Modern English Grammar on Historical Principles;* the seventh and last came in 1949.[9] In 1914 Henrik Poutsma published *A Grammar of Late Modern English;* [10] a second edition followed in 1926. The American Curme brought out *Syntax* in 1931 and *Parts of Speech and Accidence* in 1935,[11] the two parts he completed of his projected three-volume work, *A Grammar of the English Language.*

Although diverse in many ways, the kind of grammar embodied in the works of these four men and their followers has three distinguishing characteristics:

1. It tends to be conservative in three important respects:
   (a) it looks backward to previously recorded literary sources for examples;
   (b) it is generally indifferent to non-literary and current sources (newspapers and periodicals);
   (c) it tends to ignore English as a spoken language. (Jespersen, however, is interested in phonetics.)

2. With the exception of Jespersen's work, this traditional grammar is not interested in theory of structure and has no adequate view of syntax; it tends to regard the word as the basic unit of language and indeed the key to it; consequently, relationships between sentence structure and word-form classes are never made clear. (But of course language scholars are still studying these problems.)

3. Scholarly and historical, this traditional, or classical, grammar relies upon a great volume of citations from English literature, including poetry; the search for variety and perhaps peculiarity led to the collection of a multitude of curious examples, many of them probably unique. These books are storehouses of specific examples of structure culled from literary English.

Everyone who is seriously interested in English and the language arts should take time for at least a short excursion into this neglected but substantial grammar. For this purpose, you could hardly improve upon Jespersen's *Essentials of English Grammar*, first published in 1933, a condensation of his seven-volume work.[12]

Descriptive and Structural Grammar

Much of the work in applied English linguistics that is called structural is based on elements from two books: *The Structure of English* (1952) by Fries,[13] and *An Outline of English Structure* (1951), by Trager and Smith.[14] These and other important works listed at the end of this chapter are part of the great tradition of American descriptive linguistics, brought to a synthesis in Bloomfield's *Language* (1933).[15] An earlier classic of this same tradition is Sapir's *Language* (1921),[16] a small book available in paperback that should be in the library of every teacher of English and the language arts; it is a highly readable, serious introduction to the broad horizons and humane sympathies of the descriptive linguistics that emerged from anthropology (see Chapter 3, pp. 61–62).

Descriptive linguistics aims to produce a rigorous, objective description of the actual structure of language, focusing attention on its system of overt, physical forms — its basic sounds, its words, its sentences. Speech is regarded as the primary form of language in two senses of *primary:* (1) speech comes first both in man's history and in the development of each individual; some languages do not have writing systems, and some individual speakers are illiterate; (2) speech is the symbol-system represented in the writing system, which is thus a secondary symbol system. The concept of pattern and patterning in language is a structural concept.

Concurrently with an emphasis on overt patterns, structural grammar regards meaning as a subjective rather than objective entity; therefore, objective language analysis cannot *begin* with meaning and is constrained *to minimize (but not reject) meaning as a guide to structure.* This procedure of carefully limiting the role of meaning in the determination of language structure is based upon an empirical theory; it does not reject meaning, but considers meaning unreliable as the sole or primary basis for objective analysis of language structure.

Apparently some well-intentioned people have been genuinely confused over the role of meaning in descriptive linguistic analysis; their confusion has not been clarified by the obfuscations of polemicists who have misrepresented the position. Leaving polemics aside, there is at bottom a profound dichotomy between the objective, empirical position of scientific linguistics, and the subjective, intuitive position of speculative philosophical linguistics; perhaps never the twain shall meet. Fries has clearly discussed the uses of meaning in descriptive linguistic analysis in two scholarly articles,[17] and most other descriptive linguists have had something to say about this critical question. For the Trager-Smith position, see pp. 305–06. Anyone who is seriously interested in this question does not have to rest content with hearsay or misinterpretation.

The remainder of this topic is presented under the following subheadings:

> THE CONTRIBUTION OF FRIES in *The Structure of English*
> THE CONTRIBUTION OF TRAGER AND SMITH.
> *An explicit theory of language and culture*
> *Trager-Smith "microlinguistics"*
> THE IMPACT OF DESCRIPTIVE AND STRUCTURAL LINGUISTICS
> SENTENCE DIAGRAMS, STRUCTURAL STYLES

THE CONTRIBUTION OF FRIES IN *The Structure of English.* "The grammar of a language consists of the devices that signal structural meanings," wrote Fries.[18] This statement indicates further what structural meaning is: "The signals of these syntactical groupings are therefore not the meaning themselves. On the contrary it is the features of correlation of forms and of order that convey the meaning." Fries believed that the native speaker can receive messages because of his automatic grasp of the sharp, precise syntactical constituents that convey meanings.[19] As a descriptive linguist, Fries considered it his business to deal concretely and specifically with the actual language structures before him, as objectively as possible; nevertheless, extensive passages of this book deal with meaning in relation to language structure.

Particularly in Fries' work, the descriptive and structural focus on objective language constituents of sentences was intended to counteract the circular, subjective processes of school grammar, in which analysis begins with the total meaning of a sentence (automatically grasped by the native speaker or reader), and proceeds to assign names to the various parts of the sentence. This naming procedure is often purely verbal in the sense that the student parrots the designations without attaching grammatical meaning to them;

for example, "A noun is the name of a person, place or thing." Fries reported that approximately seventy items of terminology have been commonly used in the schools for labeling individual words and larger sentence elements as a means of demonstrating that the student "knows grammar." [20]

In this study, Fries used his own original, rather complex system of numbers and other designations for sentence analysis; it has not been widely followed, but many of his concepts have been. My own feeling is that he did not succeed in clearly showing the relations and distinctions between sentence structure and word-form classes; in short, that this valuable study is weakened by more than a trace of a basic word-orientation.

THE CONTRIBUTION OF TRAGER AND SMITH. The Trager-Smith approach to syntax proceeded by synthesis (1) from the smallest sound units of language, the phonemes, (2) up through the next larger units, words and parts of words, (3) to sentences and sentence elements; this is the order of *phonology, morphology,* and *syntax.* Following is a summary statement of theory underlying this method:

> It is emphasized that all this is done without the use of "meaning": it is formal analysis of formal units. In fact, it becomes evident that any real approach to meaning must be based upon the existence of such an objective syntax.[21]

Far from excluding meaning from the field of linguistic interest, however, the position is that an objective description of syntactical structure is the required basis for a "real approach to meaning." While this is debatable, the argument against it should not proceed by misrepresentation.

An explicit theory of language and culture. Although it is not elaborated in detail, an explicit theory of language and culture provides the larger framework of the Trager-Smith *Outline.* In essence, the theory holds that language analysis must proceed according to carefully defined levels, beginning with the smallest units and dealing successively with "ascending levels of complexity of organization" *of the language itself and of the culture to which language is the key.* Micro-linguistics deals with the levels of phonology, morphology, and syntax; after that analysis is complete, the area of metalinguistics may be explored. Metalinguistics includes "the overall relation of the linguistic system to the other systems of the cultural totality." [22] Closely associated with the formal language system — in most human communicative situations — are meaningful variations of tone of voice (paralanguage), and meaningful variations of gestures, faces, and bodily movements (kinesics). Some research has been done on paralanguage and kinesics, but much remains to be done.

Following is a concise summary of the position:

> Linguistic behavior is, by definition, part of the overt culture, but the study of it as metalinguistics shows it to be not only a guide to the covert culture but, in large part, the structural framework itself of the covert culture or sentiment-structure.[23]

Surely no one can read in this a denial that language has an inner and an outer aspect; but how much richer this cultural conception of language than a medieval dichotomy of mind and matter.

Trager-Smith "microlinguistics." The empirical aims of *An Outline of English Structure* are explicitly stated in the first paragraph of the Introduction.

> This Outline is intended to serve a two-fold purpose. It exemplifies a methodology of analysis and presentation that we believe to be representative of the scientific method as applied to a social science — linguistics; and it sets forth a series of conclusions about English structure that constitute, in our opinion, *the basis for further study and discussion* (italics added).[24]

This microlinguistic analysis of English assumes a hierarchy of three successive levels of structural patterns:

1. **Phonemes,** the smallest classes of significant sounds, do not occur singly but combine into patterns at the next higher level.
2. **Morphemes,** word bases (roots) and affixes, generally combine into patterns at the next higher level.
3. **Syntax,** language patterns up to and including sentences analyzed in terms of their **immediate constituents** (abbreviated **ICs**). See pp. 307–10.

This microlinguistic analysis from one hierarchical level to the next is more rigid and constrictive than seems necessary today, but *in its time* it was pioneering, ground-breaking work; it was a forward step in the study of language structure.

Trager and Smith presented an English phonemic alphabet of forty-five symbols that is widely used for notation and transcription (see Chapter 4, pp. 104–05). This alphabet provides symbols for thirty-three segmental phonemes (the consonant and vowel sounds of English); and symbols for twelve supra-segmental phonemes: four for relative degrees of stress (accent); four for relative ranges of voice pitch, and four for junctures and terminals (pauses associated with interruptions or terminations of the speech stream). This description of English phonology has been used all over the world. It is widely used in teaching English as a second language, for example; and it provides a basic tool for research on English spelling.

THE IMPACT OF DESCRIPTIVE AND STRUCTURAL LINGUISTICS. This impact has been felt throughout the English profession, at first in the colleges and universities and eventually throughout the entire N–12 curriculum. The evidence abounds in books of linguistic theory and application, articles and entire special issues of professional periodicals, and in revisions of courses and curricula at all levels from preschool through graduate school. Textbooks and multi-media learning materials have incorporated various structural features, from phonemics applied to reading and spelling, to sentence patterns for reading and writing practice. Basic theoretical work and research are constantly in progress; articles, books, and collections are published continually, embodying criticism, revision, and enrichment of theory and practice.

Early in the 1960s, two university professors of Education broke new ground in applying structural linguistic analyses to English teaching problems: Strickland published two studies based on analyses of the language of elementary school children and the teaching of the English language arts; [25] the initial part of Loban's longitudinal study of a carefully selected group of children through twelve grades was the first in a series of research reports published by the National Council of Teachers of English Committee on Research.[26] Loban has continued his work, and many other investigators have contributed research from a descriptive linguistic point of view. Selected references are listed at the end of the chapter.

SENTENCE DIAGRAMS, STRUCTURAL STYLES. **Immediate constituents** **(ICs)** provide the basis for several kinds of structural diagrams. Fries and others have used the concept of layers of structure, beginning with the whole sentence, each layer being divisible into two ICs. A whole sentence is thus thought of as one layer with two ICs, the subject and predicate.

Fries used the method of diagraming shown in Figure 11.1: [27]

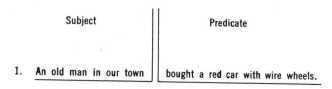

Figure 11.1 First-level immediate constituent diagram, showing first binary "cut."

The space between the vertical lines represents the "cut" that separates the two ICs; the horizontal lines represent the ICs themselves. These constituents may be further cut by binary division, as in Figure 11.2.

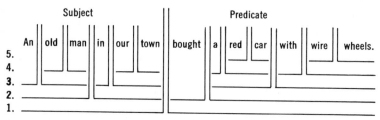

Figure 11.2 Five-level IC diagram, showing five successive binary cuts.

Shown in Figure 11.3 is an IC tree diagram of the same sentence.

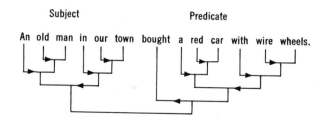

Figure 11.3 IC tree diagram, with arrows showing directions of modification.

In such a tree diagram, the vertical lines designate ICs, and the horizontal lines, structures; arrows show directions of modification. The base line represents the sentence as a whole.

Whitehall presents a variant of the Fries IC diagram that has some advantages for classroom teaching (Figure 11.4). It leaves the sentence undisturbed on the line of print for normal reading; clearly preserves the order of sentence parts and normal word order within parts; displays the ICs on each level; and identifies the constructions by word-groups.[28]

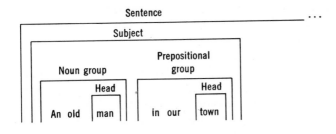

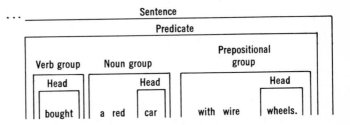

Figure 11.4 Word-group constituent diagram.

There are other IC diagrams for special purposes; they may be more or less schematic, like those shown here, or they may be fully explicit in designating all ICs and all constructions by name. Gleason's book, already cited (note 3), has an extended discussion of all kinds of diagrams; in *The Structure of American English;* Francis presents a set of "Chinese boxes" for IC analysis.[29] Such diagrams are necessary in formal courses in grammar as a discipline, but generally should be used sparingly in school classrooms.

TEACHING SUGGESTION: In a high school class, display three types of diagrams. Open a discussion with your students about them. It might be interesting to use a Reed and Kellogg diagram for comparison and contrast.

Tagmemic Grammar

The work of Kenneth Pike is a substantial linguistic study in itself. Although it is in the mainstream of the descriptive linguistic tradition characterized by the work of such men as Sapir, Bloomfield, and Fries, his contribution is in many respects original. Pike is generally known for *The Intonation of American English* (1945),[30] and has written many other articles and books. His main work is the three-volume *Language in Relation to a Unified Theory of the Structure of Human Behavior*, originally published as follows: Part I, 1954; Part II, 1955; Part III, 1960.[31]

In *Language*, Pike elaborates his theory of "tagmemics." The name derives from *tagmeme*, a unit of grammatical analysis that is defined in terms of both structure and meaning. The term *tagmeme* is coined from the Greek base *tagma*, meaning *arrangement, order, row*, with the added linguistic suffix *–eme*, meaning a unit of significant linguistic structure. Thus a tagmeme is a meaning-bearing unit of language structure that relates to an arrangement, an order, or a string of linguistic items. The central part of a good formal definition of *tagmeme* is "a constituent of a meaningful grammatical relation"; it may also mean "a class of grammatical forms that function in a particular grammatical relation." [32]

The remainder of this topic is discussed under two subheadings:
Applications of tagmemics.
Pike's views on composition, language, and thought.

Applications of tagmemics. Unlike most terms used in linguistics (*phoneme* and *morpheme*, for example), *tagmeme* is not fixed in meaning but flexible. The slot-and-filler technique, often used in tagmemic grammatical analysis, has a number of classroom applications. A slot is a place or position where a choice of alternatives must be made;

a filler is a specific choice from a class of language units that can fill the slot. The tagmeme is the combination: the slot plus the class of language units that can fill it meaningfully.

For example, *An old man in our town* may be defined as a tagmeme in the sentence, *An old man in our town bought a red car with wire wheels.* Any meaningful language unit of the same class can fill the slot (active subject of transitive verb).

____ ____ ____ ____ ____ ____ **bought a red car with wire wheels.**

Bought may also be a tagmeme: a combination of the slot and the transitive verb function. Any meaningful language unit of the same class can fill the slot.

An old man in our town _____ a red car with wire wheels.

The direct object may also be a tagmeme. It is identical in structure with the active subject, but is a different tagmeme because it (1) fills a different slot and (2) has a different grammatical function and meaning.

An old man in our town bought ____ ____ ____ ____ ____ ____.

The slot-and-filler technique can also be applied to sentence constituents at various levels. For example, *man* in *an old man* may be a tagmeme; so may *an* and *old*.

an old ____   ____ old man   an ____ man

The same technique can be applied to other constituents.

The foregoing examples are only a beginning in tagmemics; the full scope of the theory includes applications and interpretations across the whole spectrum of human culture, behavior, and experience.

TEACHING SUGGESTION: Design slot-and-filler grammatical analyses suitable for the students you teach. Introduce them in class for oral and written exploration of sentence structure.

Robert Allen has written a teacher's reference text explaining his own tagmemic approach to the grammar of written English.[33]

He and associates have also produced workbooks that apply certain slot-and-filler techniques to written English sentences; in both content and methodology, these workbooks are concerned with grammatical analysis of sentences already written rather than the production of new sentences or with the larger creative processes of composition.[34]

Pike has made his principal applications of his theory in the analysis of little-known languages and in training young linguists. Some applications of tagmemics to the teaching of composition and literature have been made, however, and Pike himself has published articles on the composing process; two of these, taken together, (a) summarize tagmemic theory with special reference to teaching composition and literature, (b) cite references for further study, and (c) suggest a number of ingenious writing exercises, adaptable to various grade levels.[35]

TEACHING SUGGESTION: Select one of the exercises suggested in the May, 1964, issue of *College Composition and Communication*. Adapt it to the needs of your students and try it out.

PIKE'S VIEWS ON COMPOSITION, LANGUAGE, AND THOUGHT. Following is a basic theoretical assumption that is highly suggestive for the process of composing:

> If one assumes that thought itself is not fully structured until it is articulated through language — a view which I would personally hold — then an analysis of language forms would feed back on an analysis of thought structure.[36] (Cf. Chapter 3, Sapir, pp. 61–62, and Vygotsky, pp. 62–63.)

From this assumption, Pike develops a theoretical view of the relationship between language form in writing and underlying thought processes that shape language and are in turn shaped by language.

> . . . since language and thought are intimately structured together, sloppy rhetoric implies sloppy thought; the careful analysis of the rhetoric of a paragraph implies an analysis of the thought structure underlying it. *This view is empirically supported* (italics added). Fre-

quently when one queries an inadequate sentence one finds that a deeper conceptual difficulty prevents adequate rewriting until the analysis itself is clarified. Therefore training in detecting lack of clarity in mechanical expression has some useful transfer to creative thought.[37]

This is an extremely valuable insight to anyone interested in the composing process as teacher, as writer, or as both; it is pertinent to finer points of style — order, rhythm, diction — as well as to interactions of conceptual adequacy and adequate statement.

TEACHING SUGGESTION: Develop a definition or other statement on the chalkboard, based on class discussion of a key concept in any subject at any grade level. See whether this exercise leads your class inductively to this insight into the interrelationships of language and thought.

Pike is keenly interested in analysis of language structures much larger and more complex than single sentences; structures that are in fact composed of related sequential sentences that interact and interlock with each other and are bonded to the thought they express. His concept of the interaction of language and thought is like that of Sapir: "Language, as a structure, is on its inner face the mold of thought." (Chapter 3, p. 62)

Relationships among Sentences without Explicit Rules

Good English teachers have always been interested in having students compare and contrast related sentences; in having them practice variations and manipulations emphasizing appropriate elements, for rhetorical effect, or for achieving fluency or good style. Such practice has little to do with a complete set of fully explicit rules.

For example, a distinction may be made between passive sentences:

(a) **Hiram Jones was awarded the athletic scholarship by his school.**
(b) **The athletic scholarship was awarded (to) Hiram Jones.** (*to* optional)

According to a common understanding of normal sentence order, the first sentence emphasizes the name of the winner, the second the scholarship itself.

Such passive sentences can be recast in various active forms.

(c) **They awarded Hiram Jones the athletic scholarship.**
(d) **They awarded the athletic scholarship to Hiram Jones.**

Also:

(e) **Hiram Jones received the athletic scholarship (award).** (*award* optional)
(f) **Hiram Jones was the recipient of the athletic scholarship (award).**

But many other sentences are related to these in other ways. Questions, for example, including negations (with a choice of at least two positions):

(a) **Was Hiram Jones not . . . ? Was not Hiram Jones . . . ?**
(b) **Was the athletic scholarship not . . . ? Was not the . . . ?**
(c) **Did they not award Hiram Jones . . . ? Did not they award . . . ?**
(d) **Did they not award the athletic scholarship . . . ? Did not they award . . . ?**
(e) **Did Hiram Jones not receive . . . ? Did not Hiram Jones . . . ?**
(f) **Was Hiram Jones not the recipient . . . ? Was not Hiram Jones . . . ?**

New questions may also begin with *Why, How, When, Where.* In addition to simple negations with *not* in two optional positions, a different negation may be made with *never;* and *ever* may fill the place of *never* to give another emphasis.

Or the original sentences may be recast as requests, or commands.

(a) **Award the athletic scholarship to Hiram Jones.**
(b) **Award Hiram Jones the athletic scholarship.**
(c) **Let Hiram Jones be awarded the athletic scholarship.**
(d) **Let the athletic scholarship be awarded (to) Hiram Jones.** (*to* optional)
(e) **Let them award Hiram Jones the athletic scholarship.**
(f) **Let Hiram Jones be awarded the athletic scholarship.**

These requests can also be recast with *receive* and *be the recipient of:* and all can be made negative with *Do not, Never, Do not ever.*

And then both negative and positive requests can be recast as questions, with *Why, Why not, Why do you not, Why not let them,* and so on *ad infinitum*. These suggestions by no means exhaust the possibilities of varying and manipulating the original sentences.

The good English teachers mentioned at the outset of this discussion would never have allowed anything like this to be run into the ground in the first place. A few non-prescriptive transformational techniques might help students develop fresh insights into the processes of sentence variation and manipulation.

TEACHING SUGGESTION: Open a discussion of relationships among sentences without explicit rules. Have the students volunteer examples of their own. See whether they can suggest any regularities in the processes they discuss.

A practical question is whether it will ever be possible to formulate explicit rules that will generate all such sentences. Suppose such a complete and fully explicit generative-transformational grammar could be developed. Would it be more useful in the classroom than the kind of procedure we have just romped through without reciting a series of rules to derive and justify each new sentence type? These considerations bear on the topic of the next section of this chapter.

Generative-Transformational Grammar

Let's begin by defining generative-transformational grammar ("g-t," to the initiate); citing its principal aims; and referring briefly to four leading models; then we can discuss, as the only one enjoying an appreciable influence in the schools, the Chomsky model. For brevity and the convenience of popular usage, generative-transformational grammar will be called simply transformational.

The remainder of this topic is presented under the following subheadings:

A DEFINITION
FOUR MODELS OF TRANSFORMATIONAL GRAMMAR
CHOMSKY'S WORK

A DEFINITION. Transformational grammar regards the native speaker (or writer) as a sentence-making machine, actuated by internalized rules for generating (or producing) grammatical sentences. These sentences are all considered to be either:

(a) Simple basic sentences (kernels; propositions), or
(b) Variations of basic sentences (transformations; transforms).

Transformations are produced by application to the basic sentences of explicit rules, many obligatory, some optional.

A grammar may be generative without being transformational, but a complete g-t grammar will have three interdependent subdivisions:

1. Phrase-structure rules for generating basic sentences;
2. Transformational rules for producing transformations of basic sentences;
3. Phonological rules for "pronouncing" sentences; and graphological rules for writing sentences.

Transformational grammar thus incorporates rules purporting to account for abstract syntactical relationships throughout the language system; while some transformational grammars have limited objectives, others seek to formulate fully explicit rules for generating all the grammatical and none of the ungrammatical sentences of the language. Since the potential number of sentences is infinite, and since even a single sentence may (in g-t theory) be infinitely long, transformational grammar faces the insurmountable obstacle of reducing its system of rules to manageable size. It is doubtful that any computer in existence could do it.

FOUR MODELS OF TRANSFORMATIONAL GRAMMAR. Some idea of the interest generated by transformational grammar can be gathered from a bibliography published in 1965. It lists four models, identified by the names of their originators, each heading a group of investigators. The compiler emphasizes that *"while these models may resemble one another superficially, they differ fundamentally"* (italics added). The four chief investigators are: Chomsky, Massachusetts Institute of Technology; Harris, University of Pennsylvania; Longacre, Summer Institute of Linguistics; and Shaumyan, Russian Language Institute. The bibliography contains entries for 962 books, articles, and conference papers.[38]

CHOMSKY'S WORK. His principal work is published in five books and numerous articles in periodicals and collections. The books are *Syntactic Structures* (1957), *Current Issues in Linguistics* (1964), *Aspects of the Theory of Syntax* (1965), and *Cartesian Linguistics* (1966); Chomsky and a collaborator, Halle, have written a transformational phonology, *Sound Patterns of English*.[39] He considers that his province includes psychology and philosophy, in addition to linguistics. *Anyone interested in the Chomsky model of transformational grammar would do well to consider carefully his repeated assertions of the consequences of his theory in terms of philosophy and psychology.*

At this point we briefly note Chomsky's speculations (a) that his phrase-structure rules generate basic sentences in "the deep structure"; and (b) that from the deep structure his transformational rules then transform basic sentences into "the surface structure," the name he assigns to spoken or written sentences. He further speculates (c) that the ultimate source of basic sentences (kernels, or propositions) is "the mind." These speculations are part of a complete metaphysical system, derived from intuition and introspection, and unrelated to empirical data. For a more detailed discussion, see pp. 325–30; p. 349, Note 8.

CHOMSKY AND "RULES." There is much confusion over the term *rule* as used in transformational grammar. In Chomsky's work, and in derivative usage pertaining to schools and instruction, *rule* means what it does in common school grammar: a rigid law prescribing (also proscribing) linguistic behavior. Transformational rules are in reality no more than speculative statements about conditions, processes, and relationships. In contrast to the objective approach of descriptive grammar, which carefully limits the role of meaning as a guide to grammatical structure, transformational grammar makes the subjective interpretation of meaning the chief criterion of structural analysis.

Transformational and generative rules may be legitimately regarded as laws only within their own closed system, not outside it. The invention of a scheme of grammar formulized in such rules does not establish any relationship between the rules and the way a native speaker actually creates sentences when he talks or writes — much less the way he acquired his language in the first place. In the present state of the art, contentious certitudes on these topics can only be based on speculation.

Statements of transformational rules combine notation features from mathematics and symbolic logic in formulas that look quite mathematical. For example,

$$NP_1 - Aux + be + en - V - by + NP_2.$$

Actually, understanding such formulizations is not very difficult, as we shall see in a moment; what is difficult is swallowing the rules, which strongly resemble the ancient "laws of thought" once believed to have been embalmed in the rules of Latin grammar.

GRAMMATICALITY. Grammatical sentences are simply those that conform to the rules devised for generating grammatical sentences; ungrammatical sentences would be any that do not conform. A simpler and truer statement is that grammatical sentences are all the sentences generated by the grammar; all other sentences must be ungrammatical. (With respect to instruction, the doctrine of grammaticality is the same as the common notion of correctness.) Grammaticality is concerned only with the system of standard English, principally *written* English, as it pertains to syntax — not with logic, style, or rhetoric. Discussions of grammaticality tend to ignore the grammar of divergent dialects; or to brush divergent dialects aside with the speculation that they incorporate transformations of structures from standard English.

SIMPLE GENERATIVE RULES. Transformational grammar postulates simple rules for generating certain kinds of noun groups. Such formulations may look forbidding at first, but in themselves they are quite simple. They consist mainly of acronyms and abbreviations of common grammatical terms, many of them familiar in school grammar. For example, the rule:

$$\textbf{NP} \rightarrow \textbf{Det} + \textbf{Adj} + \textbf{Noun.}$$

NP is an acronym for **Noun Phrase;** the arrow means "may be rewritten as," or "equals"; **Det** is an abbreviation of **Determiner,** which is often the article of school grammar (noun determiner); **Adj** is an abbreviation of **Adjective;** the plus (+) signs signify simple addition of words to form the string; and **Noun** means **Noun.** All that is needed to apply such a rule is a list of words in each category: **Det, Adj,** and **Noun.** The rule will then generate all such noun groups (NPs) as *the tall boy, a fat cat, an ardent follower.*

An **NP** may appear in any grammatical distribution in a sentence: subject, object, object of a preposition. Such simple generative rules are obvious and transparent; their formulas become more complicated as provisions are added for tense, number, verb-form changes, etc. Transformation rules and rules for derivations, however, are not obvious and transparent; they are arbitrary and prescriptive.

For example, a seemingly simple transformational rule is **T adj,** where **T** means **Transformation.** This is a rule for transforming kernels of the **Det N is Adj** form in **NPs** of the kind described in the paragraph above. Under this rule, *The boy is tall* (Det N is Adj) becomes *the tall boy* (Det Adj Noun). Chomsky has stated this as an unexceptionable rule, but for a scholarly rebuttal, see pp. 359–60.

It is a small step from these simple rules to rules for generating a subject-verb-object sentence. Let's begin with a simple example, apply the required terms to its parts, and derive the acronyms and abbreviations needed as symbols. Following is such a sentence: **Sentence → S.**

The aardvark will devour the ants.

The subject is the **Noun Phrase,** *the aardvark,* designated **NP.** The predicate is *will devour the ants,* designated **VP;** it is made up of the **Verb,** *will devour,* designated **V;** and the **Noun Phrase,** *the ants,* designated **NP.**

This procedure yields symbols for formulizing the rules needed to generate this sentence and all sentences of the same construction.

Following are the rules:

S → NP + VP
NP → Det + N (where **Det** means **Determiner,** or **Article**)
N → Noun
VP → V + NP
V → Aux + V (where **Aux** means **Auxiliary**)
Aux → modal (in this sentence)
V → Verb

These rules may now be represented by the formula we began with:

S → NP + VP

The aardvark will devour the ants.

In this sentence, **Det** represents *the* (used twice); **N,** *aardvark* and *ants;* **Aux,** *will;* and **V,** *devour.*

A branching tree diagram of this sentence appears in Figure 11.5.

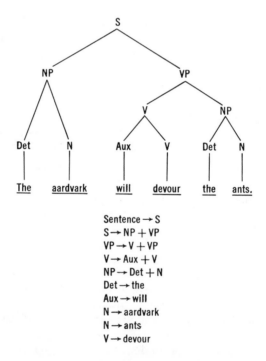

Sentence → S
S → NP + VP
VP → V + VP
V → Aux + V
NP → Det + N
Det → the
Aux → will
N → aardvark
N → ants
V → devour

Figure 11.5 Branching tree diagram.

TEACHING SUGGESTION: In a high school class, or in any class using a transformational text, demonstrate the writing of a sentence by transformational rules. Illustrate it with a tree diagram. Ask for comments and discussion.

All that is needed to generate other sentences of this type is a list of words in each category required by the rules.

The antibiotic should cure his illness.
The children would like the hamburger.
The weight could strain the rafters.
The team might win the championship.

It is also possible to write rules for generating sentences without determiners, or with different determiners; without auxiliaries, or with different auxiliaries; without objects, or with different complements. There is no difficulty in postulating new rules to fit new and different elements and structures; the only difficulty is that there seems to be no end of proliferating rules to account for all contingencies.

Two SIMPLE SENTENCE EQUIVALENTS. While the transformational rules designed to generate surface structures from the deep structure are difficult to explicate if you don't believe in them, the gross relationships presumed to exist between deep and surface structures can be displayed as simple equivalents. For example, between the deep-structure active sentence and the surface-structure passive transformation of it (see Figure 11.6, p. 322).

Deep structure: **The aardvark will devour the ants.**
Surface structure: **The ants will be devoured by the aardvark.**
                    The ants will be devoured.

Like the **T adj** transformational rule, Chomsky has stated his rule for passive transformations as an unexceptionable one; for a scholarly rebuttal, however, see pp. 357–58.

There are also said to be question-transformation rules capable of generating surface structure questions from the deep structure (Figure 11.7).

Surface structure: **Will the aardvark devour the ants?**
Will the ants be devoured by the aardvark?
Will the ants be devoured?

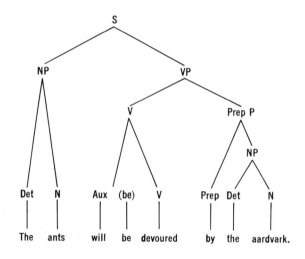

Figure 11.6 The passive transformation — tree diagram.

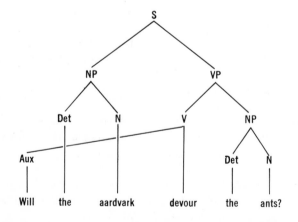

Figure 11.7 The question transformation — tree diagram.

PRESCRIPTIVISM. For improving skills of literacy, it hardly seems necessary to codify native linguistic intuition, as Chomskyan transformational grammar presumes to do — even if you assume the codifier's intuitions are universal and his introspection infallible. There is no evidence that memorization of such rules would help the native speaker to improve *his acquired capacity to invent and interpret new sentences without recourse to book-learned rules.* Such a prescriptive requirement might even undermine the student's *creative* use of introspection in language study and deprive him of this natural birthright.

THE CHOMSKY MODEL IN TEXTBOOKS. Rather than attempt a detailed survey, this section will outline salient developments in the textbook field.

Two authors, Roberts and Thomas, have written textbooks for teachers and college students that closely follow the Chomsky model of transformational grammar. Robert's *English Sentences* (1962) [40] is something less than a halfway stage between his structural *Patterns of English* (1955) [41] and his thoroughgoing transformational *English Syntax* (1964).[42] Carrying a laudatory "Introduction" by Chomsky himself, *English Syntax* is an inch-by-inch transduction of the Chomsky model into a linear-program workbook; it is thoroughly prescriptive from beginning to end, and relies heavily on rote memorization of rules, the more so because of internal inconsistencies in the program.

Thomas' *Transformational Grammar and the Teacher of English* (1966) [43] follows much of the format of *Syntactic Structures*, including formulas and tree diagrams; it too suffers from internal inconsistencies, and is inaccurate on intonation. This text is quite dogmatic and prescriptive, leaving little room for induction, exploration, discovery, levity, or mirth. Thomas says bluntly, "Discovery procedures are difficult to develop, and they seem to have no practical place in a pedagogical transformational grammar." [44]

Hathaway's *A Transformational Syntax* is partially based on Chomsky's work, but differs from it in important ways. He surrenders "the pretense to the writing of precise rules for the generation of all grammatical sentences in English and the elimination of all sentences that are not grammatical," and "is content to suppose that complex structures are generated out of basic structures in terms of a relatively small number of transformational principles." He also acknowledges a deep debt to the structural linguists and calls for "a synthesis of the widely divergent approaches of the last thirty years." [45]

Hathaway's theoretical statements are expressed in plain English rather than Chomskyan acronyms and abbreviations; and he avoids both transformational tree diagrams and the misleading appearance of mathematical formulas. This is an original and valuable book, closer in content to classical grammar than to school grammar, and in spirit more descriptive than prescriptive. Hathaway presents a wealth of excellent examples, many of them from English and American literature, culled from many years of teaching; they are far more interesting and instructive than such matters as the distinction between *John is easy to please* and *John is eager to please*.

Roberts also served as senior author of an elementary English series that begins with simplistic transformational procedures in grade three and develops them toward a complex catechism in grade nine.[46] A somewhat similar beginning was made in another series, initially for grades four through six, and later expanded to cover kindergarten through grade eight.[47] Still another publisher has introduced a transformational series for grades seven through twelve,[48] and the grapevine says others are yet to come. The grapevine also says that the results of school instruction in transformational grammar have not lived up to the advance billing.

If a small transformational bandwagon developed in our schools during the later 1960s, perhaps the chief reason is the close affinity, in both content and spirit, between transformational grammar and school grammar. It is no accident that a large suburban school system near a major city braved all linguistic winds through 1966, then switched from Warriner to Roberts. As the French say, "The more it changes, the more it remains the same."

No one speaks with greater authority on the nature of a Chomskyan pedagogical grammar and its expectations of the teacher than Roberts. Here is a central quotation from a brochure distributed by his publisher.

> *What is required of the teacher at this point is chiefly faith.* The teacher must believe that if one goes along with a particular program, taking each point as it comes and making it clear in the terms of the

text, everything will finally work out satisfactorily. *The teacher must above all resist the temptation to correct or change the materials* — unless, of course, the teacher happens also to be a grammarian.

Perhaps the most significant change of procedure required of a teacher using materials of the sort under discussion is to use them in the order presented. Heretofore, the teacher in the language area has been allowed, or even expected, to make up the course of study. Teachers have prided themselves on, and been praised by their superiors for, not "following the book." One wouldn't normally depart from the order of the book in mathematics or science, but in the somewhat shapeless state of English and social studies, such "creativity" seemed indicated. *It can't be done, however, in the kind of grammar teaching we have here in view.* It won't be much of a temptation, because *it just can't be done* [49] (emphasis added).

There is no need to embroider that.

Without referring to any specific program, one of our leading linguists, speaking on the program of a national convention of English teachers, said that widespread use in the schools of a simplistic transformational grammar would be a national disaster. With a wordplay on the arrows used in transformational formulas, he declared, "Miss Fidditch, armed with arrows, would be a formidable foe." [50]

Hunt has made the most helpful applications of transformational grammar in elementary and secondary school that I know of. His *Grammatical Structures Written at Three Grade Levels* is a model of English research, combining linguistic rigor with kindliness, humor, and perspective, in a delightful and enlightening study; he has also written several helpful articles. [51]

CHOMSKYAN PSYCHO-PHILOSOPHICAL LINGUISTICS. American descriptive linguistics has traditionally shown a close affinity for social and cultural anthropology. It typically views man as a socially and culturally conditioned being, whose incomparably distinguishing feature is his language — language as a vehicle of full-bodied human experience, and the medium of poetry and literature, not the merest utensil of bodiless mind.

As a broad field, descriptive linguistics is ultimately concerned with man's social and cultural heritage, his values and beliefs, and all his characteristic creative achievements; it deals with both the language of intellect and the language of experience. The great descriptive linguists of our time have all addressed themselves to these subjects. In the specific study of language structure, however, descriptive linguistics aims to be as objective and scientific as the study of language permits; so far as possible, it seeks empirical data by empirical means, as a sound basis for sound conclusions. In the sense outlined here, the science of language can be, like all great sciences, a member of the humanities. The descriptive study of language belongs in this broad, humanistic tradition.

This tradition Chomsky holds in contempt; his rejection of all modern linguistics has become increasingly explicit in his successive major publications. In *Cartesian Linguistics, modern linguistics* and *descriptive linguistics* are terms of opprobrium, signifying dismissal out of hand. In "Language and Mind," an article written for popular consumption, he states his anti-empiricist position in simplistic terms.[52] In place of scientific method, he would substitute neo-Platonic and speculative philosophy — in place of empircal data, introspection and intuition. He had previously published this open declaration: "The psychology that develops in this way [rationalist psycho-philosophy] is a kind of Platonism without preexistence." [53]

Chomsky's theory of language directly reflects his philosophical and psychological view of body and mind as separate entities: "Pursuing the fundamental distinction between body and mind, [Chomskyan] linguistics characteristically assumes that language has two aspects . . . an inner and an outer aspect." [54] Correspondingly, his theory of syntax assumes two qualitatively different kinds of sentence structures: deep structure and surface structure. Deep structure is purely mental: it is the semantic component of sentences; deep structure can be explained by phrase-structure rules that generate propositions in the mind (sentences and sentence-like structures, formerly called kernels). Surface structures are the physical shapes of sentences (that is, sentences spoken or pronounced); surface structures are generated by the operation of transformational rules on propositions in the deep structure. Syntax can therefore be described "in terms of two systems of rules: a base system that generates deep structures and a transformational system that maps these into surface structures." [55]

Following is a more explicit definition of this dichotomy:

The deep structure of a sentence is the abstract underlying form which determines the meaning of the sentence; it is present in the mind but not necessarily represented directly in the physical signal. The surface

structure of a sentence is the actual organization into phrases of varying size, into words of various categories, with certain particles, inflection, arrangement, and so on.[56]

His work, Chomsky writes, "attempts to formulate precisely
the processes of sentence formation and interpretation that underlie
the actual uses of language." [57] He then asserts, "the normal sentences of everyday life are formed, characteristically, by a complex
series of transformations underlying structures." [58] Despite repeated
protestations to the effect that grammar is autonomous and independent of meaning, the plain fact is that meaning, known intuitively
or discovered by introspection, is the only basis for identifying
sentence-like propositions and all the rules for strings of transformations. Which is the proposition, which the transformation? This decision is purely arbitrary, and characteristically is offered with no
pretense of proof. The declaration that speakers and auditors, and
also presumably writers and readers, actually go through these "complex series of transformations" is also purely arbitrary. The whole
scheme rests on speculation.

The Chomsky model of transformational grammar aims to formulate all the rules according to which it is assumed a native speaker
invents new sentences of his own and interprets new sentences invented by others. Both systems of rules — the base rules and the
transformational rules — are purely subjective in that they are derived from their creator's introspection into his own mind, intuitions,
and internalized "rules." The entire system is rigidly prescriptive,
because rule depends upon rule like steps in the proof of a Euclidean
theorem: in the resultant chains of propositions and rules, link must
follow link in prescribed order, and every link is crucial to every
other.

Not one iota of objective evidence has ever to my knowledge
been offered in support of this Euclidan set of psycholinguistic
assertions. Instead of evidence, the terms *obvious* and *obviously* are
applied to what it is mandatory to believe; *trivial* and *uninteresting*
are applied to what is unworthy of notice. This is a technique of
persuasion by fiat. Another kind of proof is attempted in *Cartesian
Linguistics:* a selection of opinions of like-minded psycho-philosophers
from days of yore. These citations prove that oblivion has not altered
their views.

This purely speculative position, however, is evidently Chomsky's rationale for routinely dismissing the scholarly tradition of

modern descriptive linguistics. Throughout his extended discussion of linguistics and psychology, he does not mention the world-renowned works of Sapir and Vigotsky (see pp. 61–63); nor does he mention the well-known and respected work of Brown, Bruner, Carroll, Osgood, Sebeok, Whorf, and other modern investigators in psycholinguistics. Chomsky makes no attempt to refute their views; he simply does not recognize their existence. Such wholesale omissions call for a scholarly explanation, not a mere dismissal out of hand.

LANGUAGE COMPETENCE AND LANGUAGE PERFORMANCE. Chomskyan theory speculates a good deal about an elusive distinction between language competence and language performance. "We make a fundamental distinction between *competence* (the speaker-hearer's knowledge of his language) and *performance* (the actual use of language in a concrete situation)." [59] Like the theory of recursive functions, which Chomsky believes accounts for many of his transformational rules,[60] the theory of competence derives from mathematics; the whole discussion would be more clear and open if this derivation were explicitly stated in his argument. No proof exists that such mathematical concepts as recursive functions or competence are applicable to language analysis, or more particularly to language learning — two topics that Chomsky tends to equate. Nor is there any data to support the transformational notion that detailed analogies may be drawn between mathematical languages and natural languages; there is in fact evidence to the contrary.[61] Once more we enter the realm of pure speculation.

The theory of language competence was invented to account for the fact that only a non-existent Ideal speaker could have perfect (that is *abstract*) language competence; real speakers are human beings whose language performance cannot match Ideal competence. (Nevertheless, Chomsky does assume the "underlying" competence of the speaker-hearer).[62] Competence, presumably, is the theory of the abstract language system itself, and performance the complementary theory of actual language behavior. The trouble is that all along Chomsky has insisted that his rules are simply explicit statements of what native speakers know and do intuitively; if so, there can be no sharp or qualitative distinction between competence and performance, because competence is merely an explicit, systematic statement of the native speaker's intuition, which somehow underlies his performance. We come full circle.

The question has often been asked: If native speakers perform all these operations intuitively, why do they need a complicated book of rules to help them do what comes naturally? In other words, does such an analysis, assuming for the moment that it is valid in some sense, have any bearing at all on pedagogy?

THE SHOOTING OF THE HUNTERS. A widely advertised virtue of the system is its alleged capacity to clear up meanings — usually of short strings of words having no context — that are said to be ambiguous. A celebrated instance of ambiguity, much quoted, is supposed to be embedded in the isolated phrase, "the shooting of the hunters." This ambiguity is said to be cleared up if we derive the phrase from the two possible underlying sentences: "the hunters shoot" and "they shoot the hunters." Here is Chomsky's rationale: "The ambiguity of the grammatical relation . . . is a consequence of the fact that the relation of *shoot* to *hunters* differs in the two underlying kernel sentences." [63] One of his adherents extended the discussion of this ambiguity in a professional journal.[64]

Now, the intuitive knowledge of a native English speaker in a speech community of hunters would not permit him to use the phrase, "the shooting of the hunters," in either of the senses cited — because it is not part of the language of that speech community. If a foreigner invented the phrase, probably the immediate context would make its meaning obvious. This is a characteristic transformation of a non-existent problem into a linguistic *cause célèbre*.

Chomsky's theory, for all its claims of "deep insights into intellectual capacity and mental processes," [65] is meager in concept and scope. It is a theory limited to the structure of sentences; it stipulates, in compensation, that sentences may be infinitely long and complex, at least in theory.[66] What a prospect.

Ramsay MacDonald once warned against "an attempt to clothe unreality in the garb of mathematical reality." [67] This warning might well be applied to Chomskyan psycho-philosophical linguistics.

SOME PROFESSIONAL SYNTACTIC STRICTURES. Because Chomsky has been hailed as the founder of a school of linguistics that makes all other linguistics obsolete, readers of this book may not be aware of professional scholarship in linguistics, mathematics, psychology, and the teaching of English that criticizes him sharply on the following main points:

1. His reliance on personal intuition, introspection, and the methods of speculative philosophy in a field where scientific method and empirical data are more appropriate.
2. His disregard for empirical data presented by others, and his failure to present systematic empirical data in his own expositions.
3. His dogmatism, and an apparent effort to brush aside disagreement by using a contentious tone.
4. His failure to develop clear and stable definitions of terms capable of discriminating such pairs of key concepts as *competence* and *performance; grammaticality* and *acceptability; generation* and *production.*
5. His arbitrary assertions about the way his rules supposedly operate within the native speaker to generate and transform sentences.
6. His arbitrary statements concerning language universals presumably applicable to all natural languages.
7. His publication of mistakes that go unacknowledged after they have been pointed out.

Such serious strictures from competent scholars cannot be answered by silence, or simply by labeling them confused, trivial, or uninteresting. For documentation, see Note 68, pp. 357–61.

Stratificational Grammar

Linguists are in general agreement that a complete and satisfactory model of English remains to be written. Most models are rigorous only with respect to language structures no larger than the sentence, and there is dissatisfaction with these; we do not have a fully adequate syntax, or explanation of English sentences, yet the sentence is no more than the basic structural component of longer passages and language constructs. All native speakers, including very young children, easily compose narratives and explanations many sentences long; moreover, the sequences and interrelationships of the component sentences are often complex and intricate. Many linguists have felt that only an adequate syntax could provide a basis for a rigorous understanding of morphology (word formation and analysis) and phonology (basic sound units). Somewhat similarly, some linguists now believe that a model of English that can explain language compositions well beyond the sentence is needed as a prerequisite for an adequate explanation of sentences and structural elements below the level of sentences. Stratificational grammar aims to do that as well as provide a framework for relating and possibly reconciling other grammars.

Stratificational grammar views language comprehensively as the means by which a speaker as sender or encoder relates sounds to an impression of an experience, or to a meaning he wishes to communicate; conversely, as the means by which an auditor as receiver or decoder constructs his version of the speaker's impression or meaning. To explain language, this grammar postulates three major components, for English at least, interconnected by inner strata: (1) semology (relates to meaning); (2) grammar (relates to intermediate patterns and rules linking the other two major components); and (3) phonology (relates to the sounds of speech). To account for reading/writing as well as speaking/auditing, phonology would have to be represented by a graphology. Since each of the three major components is viewed as having two strata, one interconnecting with the component above or below, English is said to consist of six strata; thus the term *stratificational grammar*.

Stratificational grammar aims to discover and describe the elements within each stratum, to formulate precisely the relationships within and between strata, and to develop basic terminology that may be used at all levels of language analysis. A complete stratificational model would be a multidimensional network, showing all the complex elements, relationships, and processes of the language system as nearly as possibly simultaneously. In pure form, with the requisite notation system, stratificational grammar will no doubt be the linguist's linguistics. But if its results are as significant as they hold promise of being, their practical consequences may in due time be made accessible to teachers of English and the language arts.[69]

Toward a Synthesis of Grammars

Although our common school grammar is inadequate and misleading in some respects, there is no question of chucking it all and starting from scratch; the fundamental fault of the teaching of English and the language arts is *prescriptivism*, which can negate the best of grammars, and indeed the teaching of any subject. We need to take a look at many grammars. School grammar can provide useful and familiar terminology. Grammar in the scholarly tradition, especially its varied display of examples, deserves careful study by everyone professionally interested in English. Descriptive grammar, emulating the empirical methods of science, aims to provide an objective account of language patterns and structures based upon verifiable information and replicable investigations; although some critics have charged this approach with indifference to meaning in language study, or to English standards, neither charge holds true. Some of the concepts of generative-transformational grammars may illuminate sentence-making processes and help to relate meaning and structure. Pike's tagmemic grammar, applying analogues of particle, wave and field concepts to linguistic problems, is attempting to develop new insights into language patterns and constructs at higher levels than the sentence. It is possible that stratificational grammar may provide the framework for a comprehensive view of language that can help us meet the requirements of school curricula in English and the language arts.

The main point for us is that language and linguistics are open-ended studies; our present knowledge is so far from closed that it may truly be said to be exploding. In no age has progress been achieved through blind or myopic clinging to what has already been done. Quite the contrary. Modern linguistics is both a revolution in and a continuation of the study of language. When we break eggs to make our omelet, we do not throw away the eggs; a good omelet is more than the sum of its parts. Ultimately we must have a broad view of language, and a new grammar — possibly a flexible new synthesis of grammars.

PEDAGOGICAL UTILITY AND LINGUISTIC RESPECTABILITY. Since it is not an objective of school instruction in English and the language arts to make grammarians out of our students, we must choose elements from the several grammars now at hand that will yield a synthesis capable of meeting two criteria: (1) pedagogical utility in developing the arts and skills of literacy; and (2) linguistic respectability. In the classroom the individual student should be helped to explore inductively and make discoveries for himself that will contribute to his language growth in both theory and practice.

Traditional school grammar provides useful terminology that should be retained: *noun, verb, adjective, adverb, preposition, pronoun, subject, predicate, complement, clause, phrase, modifier* and *modifica-*

tion; statement (active and *passive), question, request, command, negation.* Descriptive and structural grammar provides basic sentence patterns for repeated exposure and imitation, discussion and manipulation by the students: pattern variations, inversions, expansions, transformations; objective ways of identifying word-form classes, grammatical inflections and derivational affixes; objective information about structure words; a widely adopted description of the sound system, from the smallest units to sentence intonation; and an objective view toward language structure; moreover, *the affinity of descriptive linguistics for cultural anthropology is conducive to deepening and humanizing language study.*

Concepts from generative and transformational grammars, if they could be purged of the prescriptivism attached to them by some leading proponents, might help to make individual exploration and introspection into language and language processes a delight to the student; but it is not necessary for him to codify his native linguistic intuitions, especially not by memorizing someone else's introspectively determined rules. English language instruction should encourage the student to exercise his native linguistic abilities fully, freely, creatively, rather than to analyze them too self-consciously.

Functional concepts can illuminate the various processes of composing sentences. Four of these processes are: vary, variation (transform and transformation); shift (relocate and relocation); cut (eliminate and elimination); add (expand and expansion). But it is important to encourage the student to generate his own sentences, creatively, rather than produce them by rules, mechanically; to encourage him to recast or revise his sentences, not transform them by rote. Creative language processes should be nurtured and developed; the mechanical should be minimized and controlled. Motivated and encouraged students can probably do more to develop their language by and for themselves than prescriptive teachers can do for them by the book.

An operational synthesis of grammars for classroom teaching might well focus on successful oral and written practice — in the student's own language — with sentences, paragraphs and longer compositions. Success is the great objective of the student's practice; if his practice is not successful, then he is practicing ways to fail. An excellent road to success is reinforcement of closely related skills by coordinated practice: coordination of oral and written work; of written work and oral reading; of both oral and silent reading with writing. The student can be successful if no wrong examples in print are presented to confuse him; if, instead of abstract verbal rules and definitions, he can learn to associate the essential terminology with specific, concrete examples; if he can practice writing by using his own language to imitate good examples, his own language to manipulate, expand, reduce, combine, and revise what he has written.[70]

In English, as elsewhere, nothing succeeds like success.

Selected References — Classified

Many of the works cited in the text are suitable for further reading or special study projects; a few of the most significant are also mentioned here.

APPLIED ENGLISH LINGUISTICS — COLLECTIONS OF ARTICLES

Harold B. Allen, ed., *Readings in Applied English Linguistics*, second ed. (New York: Appleton-Century-Crofts, 1964).

Alexander Frazier, ed., *New Directions in Elementary English: Papers Collected from the Spring Institutes of the Elementary Language Arts of the National Council of Teachers of English* (Champaign, Illinois: National Council of Teachers of English, 1967).

Robert F. Hogan, ed., *The English Language in the School Program* (Champaign, Illinois: National Council of Teachers of English, 1966).

APPLIED ENGLISH LINGUISTICS — COMPOSITION

David A. Conlin, *Grammar for Written English* (Boston: Houghton Mifflin, 1961).

Charlton Laird and Robert M. Gorrel, *English as Language: Backgrounds, Development, Usage* (New York: Harcourt, Brace, and World, 1961).

Harold Whitehall, *Structural Essentials of English* (New York: Harcourt, Brace, 1956).

LANGUAGE AND LINGUISTICS — COLLECTIONS OF ARTICLES

Wallace L. Anderson and Norman C. Stageberg, *Introductory Readings on Language*, rev. ed. (New York: Holt, Rinehart and Winston, 1962).

Leonard F. Dean and Kenneth G. Wilson, *Essays on Language and Usage*, second ed. (New York: Oxford University Press, 1963).

Elizabeth M. Kerr and Ralph M. Aderman, *Aspects of American English* (New York: Harcourt, Brace and World, 1963).

Donald W. Lee, *English Language Reader: Introductory Essays and Exercises* (New York: Dodd, Mead and Company, 1963).

Albert H. Marckwardt, ed., *Studies in Languages and Linguistics in Honor of Charles C. Fries* (Ann Arbor: English Language Institute, University of Michigan, 1964).

Christine Mohrmann, Alf Sommerfelt, and Joshua Whatmough, eds., *Trends in European and American Linguistics: 1930–1960* (Utrecht: Spectrum, 1961).

Graham Wilson, ed., *A Linguistics Reader*, intro. Paul Roberts (New York: Harper and Row, 1967).

DESCRIPTIVE AND STRUCTURAL LINGUISTICS

W. Nelson Francis, *The Structure of American English* (New York: Ronald Press, 1958).

Joseph H. Friend, *An Introduction to English Linguistics* (New York: World, 1967).

Charles C. Fries, *American English Grammar* (New York: Appleton-Century-Crofts, 1940).

Charles F. Hockett, *The State of the Art* (The Hague: Mouton, 1968).

W. E. Leichty, *Discovering English* (Englewood Cliffs, N.J.: Prentice-Hall, 1964).

William G. Moulton, *A Linguistic Guide to Language Learning* (New York: The Modern Language Association of America, 1966).

William C. Stokoe, Jr., *The Calculus of Structure: A Manual for College Students of English* (Washington, D.C.: Gallaudet College, 1960).

George L. Trager, *Language and Languages* (San Francisco: Chandler, 1969).

Harry R. Warfel, *Language: A Science of Human Behavior* (Cleveland: Howard Allen, 1962).

TRADITIONAL GRAMMAR — COMPREHENSIVE BOOKS

Otto Jespersen, *Essentials of English Grammar* (University, Alabama: University of Alabama Press, 1964).

Ralph B. Long, *The Sentence and its Parts: A Grammar of Contemporary English* (Chicago: University of Chicago Press, 1961).

TRADITIONAL GRAMMAR — OCCASIONAL SOURCES

A. S. Hornby, *A Guide to Patterns and Usage in English* (London: Oxford University Press, 1954).

Noah Webster, *Dissertations on the English Language*, intro. Harry R. Warfel (Gainesville, Florida: Scholar's Facsimilies and Reprints, 1951).

Transformational Syntax

Noam Chomsky, *Syntactic Structures* (The Hague: Mouton, 1957).

Baxter Hathaway, *A Transformational Syntax: The Grammar of Modern American English* (New York: Ronald Press, 1967).

Owen Thomas, *Transformational Grammar and the Teacher of English* (New York: Holt, Rinehart, and Winston, 1965).

Psycholinguistics — Collections of Articles

John P. DeCecco, *The Psychology of Language, Thought, and Instruction: Readings* (New York: Holt, Rinehart, and Winston, 1967).

Eric H. Lenneberg, ed., *New Directions in the Study of Language* (Cambridge, Mass.: M.I.T. Press, 1964).

Charles E. Osgood and Thomas Sebeok, *Psycholinguistics: A Survey of Theory and Research Problems: with a Survey of Psycholinguistic Research, 1954–1964*, by A. Richard Diebold, Jr. (Bloomington: Indiana University Press, 1965).

Sol Saporta, ed., assisted by Jarvis R. Bastian, *Psycholinguistics: A Book of Readings* (New York: Holt, Rinehart, and Winston, 1961).

Benjamin Lee Whorf, *Language, Thought, and Reality: Selected Writings of Benjamin Whorf*, ed. with intro. by John B. Carroll (New York: John Wiley, 1959).

Psycholinguistics — Comprehensive Books

Roger Brown, *Words and Things* (Glencoe, Illinois: The Free Press, 1968).

John B. Carroll, *Language and Thought* (Englewood Cliffs, N.J.: Prentice-Hall, 1964).

Edwin A. Sapir, *Language: An Introduction to the Study of Speech* (New York: Harcourt, Brace, 1921, 1949).

Lev Semenovich Vygotsky, *Thought and Language* ed. and trans. by Eugenia Hanfmann and Gertrude Vakar (Cambridge, Mass.: M.I.T. Press, 1962).

Language and Culture

Edward T. Hall, *The Silent Language*, a Premier Book (New York: Fawcett, 1965).

Herbert Landar, *Language and Culture* (New York: Oxford University Press, 1966).

Jean Malmstrom, *Language in Society* (New York: Hayden, 1965).

Chapter 12

N-12 Perspective: Linguistics and the English Language Arts

It is not the intent of this chapter either to recapitulate the previous eleven chapters or to attempt to write a curriculum for the English language arts. Rather, it has four other purposes: (1) to state briefly the broad teaching and learning objectives implicit in this book; (2) to cite for your consideration some specific questions about the handling of language in the curriculum; (3) to suggest succinctly some of the applications of the language analysis presented in Part Two to the four commonly named communication skills: speaking, listening, reading, writing; and (4) to conclude with a humanistic statement reminding us all of the role of the English teacher and the nature of the human being he deals with in the classroom. The discussion is presented under four corresponding subtitles:

> Broad Teaching Objectives
> Some Questions on Language in the Curriculum
> Applying Linguistic Knowledge to Teaching Communication Skills
> The Role of the English Teacher and the Nature of the Learner

Broad Teaching Objectives

1. Through a continuous spiral program, N–12, to develop the student's ability — and his confidence in his ability — to use his native tongue, American English, in speaking, listening (defined as compre-

hending and responding appropriately to speech), writing, and reading, and in related cognitive, reflective, and conceptual thought.

2. To develop the student's conscious knowledge of and insight into the systematic structure of American English, both as a communicative code and as the medium of literary art; and as group and individual behavior involving a number of dialects.

3. Through clarification of the profound and complex nature of language, to develop the student's understanding of the web of interconnections and the subtle interplay of the primary oral and the derivative written language systems.

4. By means of a broad, deep, interdisciplinary approach to the study of language, to cultivate the understanding that language and the related arts and skills of communication are coordinated strands in a unified field of English and the language arts.

5. Through planned successful experiences, to encourage and develop the student's capacity for independent inquiry and independent study of language and literature, and of related forms of communication (oral interpretation and acting, for example).

6. On the basis of these developing abilities, and in coordination with them, to facilitate the student's access to all areas of study and all human concerns and activities, including study of non-English languages and cultures.

Some Questions on Language in the Curriculum

The following questions focus attention on teaching attitudes as well as on information taught in English language arts programs. They were prepared by the Commission of the Curriculum of the National Council of Teachers of English.

1. Is study of the English language included in the curriculum because of its cultural value as well as its practical usefulness?
   a. Is the realization clearly expressed that language is a uniquely human possession and that study of man's developing use of language sheds light upon man himself?
   b. Are the practical applications of language taught as positive principles rather than negative prohibitions?

2. Is room provided in the curriculum for presentation of basic linguistic knowledge according to the ability of individual pupils to profit from such instruction?

   a. Are students familiarized with the role of language in modern life?

   b. Do students learn, through study of the history of the English language and study of current usage, that language is constantly changing and that "right" and "wrong," with reference to language, are only relative terms? Do they learn that "wrong" means either unclear or out of harmony with current practice of educated Americans?

   c. Do students learn the particular types of symbols that English uses, including the sentence patterns, form classes, function words, and patterns of intonation characteristic of our language? Is such instruction constantly adjusted to the known ability of individual pupils?

   d. Do students learn something about the backgrounds of many words and about the changes in meaning that words may undergo? Do they recognize the extensive use of metaphor in daily language?

3. Does the curriculum reveal the influence of twentieth-century studies of the language and of the ways in which language is learned?

   a. Does the program in grammar recognize the most pertinent and generally accepted findings of modern grammarians so as to avoid such old misconceptions as "A sentence is a group of words expressing a complete thought," stressing rather the use of modification in the expression of increasingly complex ideas as maturity in thinking develops?

   b. Is the study of grammar never permitted to degenerate into exercises in identification and terminology?

   c. Is inductive rather than deductive presentation of grammatical principles recommended? Are "parts of speech" or "form classes," for instance, taught mainly through specific and tangible illustrations rather than through abstract definitions?

   d. Does the curriculum emphasize sentence building rather than concentration on sentence analysis?

   e. Are truths of modern usage taught rather than such untruths or half-truths as those about splitting infinitives, ending sentences with prepositions, and using *shall* and *will?*

    f. Do students learn how punctuation is related to both grammar and intonation?

    g. Do students learn such basic principles of semantics as these: a word is not a thing; meanings of words change with time (democracy 1800 is not the same as democracy 1962) and with place (democracy USA is not the same as democracy USSR); "loaded," or emotional, words are likely to affect a reader or listener differently from unemotional words?

4. Instead of attempting to offer a complete and repetitive course in grammar each year, do teachers concentrate on selected trouble spots?

    a. Does the curriculum designate certain areas for major concentration each year and grant individual teachers freedom to alter the emphasis and make additions or deletions as need arises in their classes?

    b. Is there constant differentiation of program and of levels of abstraction suitable for pupils of different levels of ability?

    c. Is there a consistent program for improvement of spelling? of pronunciation? of usage? [1]

Applying Linguistic Knowledge to Teaching Communication Skills

The five subsystems of American English as explained in Part Two of this book are presented here in descending order of relative importance, according to my sense of it, within the system as a whole; this order reverses the more conventional order of chapters in Part Two. Obviously, all the systems operate simultaneously in language use; what we are doing, then, is setting up an artificial hierarchical arrangement for convenience of discussion. The method of the discussion is to make a brief statement about each subsystem, followed by a summary of applications to teaching speaking, listening, writing, and reading. The discussion is presented under five subsection titles, each corresponding to one of the subsystems.

    INTONATION: STRUCTURAL AND INTERPRETIVE

    SENTENCE PATTERNS (SYNTAX)

    STRUCTURE WORDS

    WORD CLASSES AND WORD-FORM CHANGES (MORPHEMES)

    SOUNDS AND LETTERS (PHONEMES AND GRAPHEMES)

INTONATION: STRUCTURAL AND INTERPRETIVE. Structural intonation includes all the obligatory features and patterns of English intonation; this category provides choices of items, just as we have choices of sentence patterns and of words. Some linguists refer to the structural intonation features of pitch, stress, and juncture as "suprasegmental phonemes," but here they are treated as a separate system; the stress-timed rhythm of English is considered to be fundamental to the language structure and to the intonation system. Interpretive intonation is personal and subjective; it includes what some linguists call "paralanguage," and what many teachers mean by speaking or reading "with expression."

Classrooms should be sparkling with bright talk, instead of standing silent as so many do; this situation is strictly within the province of each individual teacher. Carefully planned, critical use of the tape recorder, with playback for evaluation, can be an excellent supportive technique for effective speech.

Structural intonation, especially stress-timed rhythm, can be taught incidentally as part of lively, effective talk: conversations, reports, reading aloud, oral interpretation. Stress-timed rhythm, with due attention to silent feet and silent stresses, can counteract the dingdong metrical readings of verse so commonly heard in classrooms, knelling the doom of poetry in the schools.

Encouraging the use of the fade-rise and fade-level terminals within sentences in oral/written work can help develop sentence sense. The use of the fade-fall terminal should generally be encouraged where a sense of completion is appropriate, at the end of a sentence or a question. Aside from questions of special intent, the question-ending fade-rise terminal should be reserved mainly for short **wh-**questions and short questions requiring a **yes-or-no** answer; voice terminals may vary considerably in longer, more involved questions. It is better not to try to lay down a single rule governing question terminals.

Interpretive intonation (accompanied by appropriate facial expressions, gestures, and bodily action) is basic to oral interpretive reading and acting, and to reading aloud with expression. Internalized, the elements of interpretation and acting can contribute to developing a strong basis of appreciation of literature. If students are not made conscious of these elements through instruction, however, they may never be able to internalize them.

In addition to hearing the teacher as a model of structural and interpretive intonation, students should have many opportunities to hear good intonation on tapes, records, and films. Discussion and analysis of intonation can help students evaluate these experiences, and later apply their observations to their own tape recordings and to the oral interpretations of their classmates.

In oral/written work, intonation can be an invaluable guide, both in oral reading of sentences, paragraphs, and entire compositions, and in the silent, creative writing stage, when internalized intonation patterns, rhythm in particular, can become a silent monitor, testing the sound of the writing. Again, instruction is needed to make students conscious of these features before they can internalize them. Study of the relationships between voice terminals and punctuation can be very helpful in place of elaborate rules, or in support of simpler rules; this is very true of punctuating restrictive and non-restrictive clauses. The fade-fall terminal generally corresponds to the period or question mark; the fade-rise or fade-level terminals *when followed by structural pauses*, to commas; and the question-ending fade rise to certain question marks only. The question mark is neutral with respect to intonation.

Intonation is of rock-bottom importance in primary reading instruction, where oral reading lays a foundation, good or bad, for all later reading. Stress-timed rhythm, with appropriate voice terminals, defines the sound of a sentence as it should be defined for the child; this rhythm, internalized, helps him read sentences as meaning-bearing patterns. Word-naming, the result of teaching isolated words, destroys the sense of English rhythm by placing a sentence terminal on every single word in succession. The crucial importance of intonation in early reading experience should not obscure its very great value in all later stages of reading for meaning and reading for experience, a value hard to overestimate. Intonation is the basis for that auditory element in silent reading that gives the sense of style.

SENTENCE PATTERNS (SYNTAX). About ten sentence patterns (four basic types and their variants), described in terms of subject, verb, and various completers, provide an objective basis for teaching a great deal about English sentences. The four basic patterns are **N V**; **N V N**; **N V N N**; and **N Lv N**. This description makes no pretense of describing all the grammatical sentences of English; but through calling attention to expansions, inversions, combinations, variations, transformations, and reductions, it can make objective reference to a great number and variety of oral and written sentences.

The introduction of sentence patterns in oral/written work is a means of introducing students to standard English forms without threatening them, and of providing oral practice without self-consciousness or embarrassment. Exposure to and oral practice with a variety of sentences and syntactic operations can lead to conscious sentence sense in casual conversations, group discussions, and reports.

The concept of the sentence as the basic meaning-bearing unit, enriched by familiarity with many kinds of sentences, can help the student learn what to listen for in terms of language structure. In oral/written practice, listening for definite patterns can make him aware of standard English forms; he acquires the priceless advantage of the authentic sound in his ear, available for reference in writing and reading.

It is perhaps in writing that the value of work with sentence patterns shows up most clearly. Students can learn to write a variety of sentences, expansions of all sentence parts, compounding and apposition of sentence elements, inversions, variations, transformations; they can also learn the important skill of reduction of clauses and phrases, essential to a mature writing style.

Reading comprehension can be greatly improved with increased emphasis upon the sentence as the basic meaning-bearing unit instead of the word; such an emphasis should be one strand of reading instruction from the very beginning. In later years, a relatively simple analytical sentence approach to reading can reduce the difficulty of literature of all kinds, as well as of textbooks, reference books, newspapers, and magazines; in such analysis it is helpful to emphasize the interconnections among sentences in discourse, and the nature of dependent and independent sentences.

STRUCTURE WORDS. This is a small but complex system of about three hundred words whose function as markers of various syntactical elements make many of them easy to identify: noun markers, verb markers, clause markers, phrase markers, and question markers. Other structure words are intensifiers, starters, and words having special uses in particular syntactical patterns. Many structure words function in more than one way, and so they cross-classify; this chameleon characteristic must be explained in the process of teaching them.

Unless their attention is called to the wealth and variety of structure words we have in English, students tend to use only a very few over and over again, especially in speech. A varied selection of structure words of all kinds can add interest to conversations, group discussions, and reports. Structure words also have the capacity to produce varied and more interesting sentences, and to help the speaker say exactly what he means by expressing precise relationships or sentence elements. Oral/written practice based on prepared models is a good means of exposing students to new structure words with little or no pain.

In listening to a speaker, structure words are often major clues to sentence structure and meaning. The difference between quick understanding and bewilderment is often the difference between knowing or not knowing a specific structure word used by a speaker. Oral/written practice is one good means of reducing such difficulties.

If the value of work with sentence patterns is clearly reflected in writing, so is work with structure words, especially clause markers and phrase markers. Many writers as well as speakers make use of too few structure words. A course of study that offered a sequential presentation of structure words would give students extremely important tools for effective writing. Oral/written practice in a variety of sentences would be a good first step toward getting these critical items into the students' writing repertoire. Such practice can help develop a varied, interesting, and effective writing style.

A misunderstood structure word can cause just as much difficulty in reading as in listening; in fact, some structure words that occur frequently in printed matter are rare in the speech the student hears, and so do not turn up in his own speech or writing either. He is at a loss when he meets them in print. In reading instruction, structure words should be dealt with in terms of their specific functions, never as mere vocabulary items. In their very first oral reading instruction, students must be taught to read structure words lightly and quickly, with reduced stress; this applies especially to the noun markers, *a, and,* and *the;* to the forms of *be* and *have* as verb markers, and to many prepositions. A vocabulary approach to structure words can undermine reading comprehension by neglecting their specific syntactic functions and by destroying the natural stress-timed rhythm of English.

WORD CLASSES AND WORD-FORM CHANGES (MORPHEMES). The four word classes are noun, verb, adjective, and adverb; they can be defined objectively and non-verbally by (a) their distribution in sentences and (b) their ability to take the word-form changes of their class. There are two kinds of word-form changes: (a) the grammatical inflections of nouns, verbs, adjectives, and adverbs, which are relatively few in modern English; and (b) derivational prefixes and suffixes, a remarkable system whereby hundreds of affixes alter the meaning of word bases, or shift a word from one word class to another.

Grammatical inflections in modern English are a small set of forms, but because their presence or absence is a function of dialect differences in grammar, they are a stubborn set to change; control of grammatical inflections is a part of mastery of standard English, spoken and written. Such mastery has more to do with social acceptance than with successful communication; we all understand each other pretty well. On the other hand, mastery of derivational prefixes and suffixes means, in essence, control of a large and varied vocabulary, usually reflecting rich language experience and wide reading. The affixing system is akin to the system of structure words in richness and complexity; it demands detailed and sequential teaching, related especially to writing and reading.

Some of the most outstanding differences between standard and divergent dialects are in their grammatical inflections, especially noun and verb inflections. As a basis for reading and writing standard English, oral/written practice, beginning with prepared materials incorporating standard inflections, is a good method. Such oral/written practice may eventually open the way to everyday use of standard inflections in speech, but the teacher should expect this to take time.

When students fail to hear or speak standard grammatical inflections, it is not generally because of inattention, orneriness, or poor auditory acuity; it is because the grammar of the speech they are accustomed to hear is a different grammar, often lacking these standard forms. Oral/written practice may help, but the focus must be upon the grammatical differences, not the student's attention or hearing.

In beginning or remedial reading instruction, the divergent speaker will have deep trouble in reading standard English if his teacher tries to force him to read aloud grammatical inflections that he does not possess because they are simply not part of his dialect. This problem has so far not been satisfactorily solved, but the teacher can help by not compounding the student's difficulties. Probably he should either be permitted to read his own forms aloud, regardless of what is printed on the page, so long as he gets the message; or he should be presented with materials written especially for him, with the grammatical features of his dialect. Either of these methods would seem more likely to help him build a bridge to literacy, than any attempt, no matter how well intended, to teach him standard English under the guise of teaching him to read. It seems sensible, as well as merciful, to guide him in learning to read his own dialect from the printed page.

In writing, the use of standard inflections can sometimes be developed through oral/written practice, as with speaking; but in the long run the outcome will be determined by whether or not the divergent speaker has decided to master them.

SOUNDS AND LETTERS (PHONEMES AND GRAPHEMES). The basic sound units of a language are its phonemes; letters and combinations of letters that represent these sounds are graphemes, or writing units. A phonemic alphabet, widely used for phonemic transcription, can approximately represent the basic sounds of the great range of English dialects.

Everyone, beginning with the nursery child, is entitled to know that speech comes first in language learning, and that it is a quite respectable system of communication, used much more in everyday life than writing is. While most students do not need to know as much as their teachers do about phonemic analysis, the concept of basic sounds can reinforce the instinctive knowledge that language is first of all speech. This concept, along with the concept that letters generally represent sounds in alphabetical writing, can help the learner keep sounds and letters apart. He will not prattle about "the sounds the letters make" unless someone teaches him to.

The principal applications of phonemics in school instruction are three: in spelling programs; in reading, where principles of phoneme-grapheme correspondences seem to clear up some of the difficulties of phonics; and in teaching English as a second language, especially in comparative/contrastive techniques of teaching phonemic differences.

The Role of the English Teacher and the Nature of the Learner

No area of instruction is more important than English and the language arts. We tend to forget, though we shouldn't, that language and language study have an immeasurable potential of transforming, humanizing power. This side of heaven, at least, language is really all that marks man off from beast. It is largely through language that we occasionally reach that wonderful and paradoxical condition of man: unique individual identity and a secure social role, first in our immediate circles, ultimately in the greater society of man. Whether or not young people are guided in that direction is governed to an uncomfortable degree by teachers of English and the language arts.

Today, people who have developed the essential skills of communication are finding more and more doors opening to let them in. But if they are seriously lacking in these essential skills, they are likely to become linguistic cripples, hunchbacks and spastics, in the world of fluent communication. They may suffer an irretrievable loss of their potential humanity, a tragedy that often begins before the nursery years.

English teachers are not just teaching English. They are building human beings through the medium of a great instrument, the English language. They have at their command a powerful resource, for language is deeply rooted in personality development, in shaping the image a human being has of himself and others.

Every child possesses a window on the world. Through this window he learns to find himself as he grows toward maturity, to seek for the answers to unasked questions that all men have sought from the beginning of time. Who am I? How did I come to be? What is the meaning of life? What of the past and of the future? What eternal wisdom guides the universe? And what of death? Is it the climax, the commencement, or the termination of life? Stefan Zweig has written that, "Only he who learns early in life to spread his soul out wide, may later hold the whole world within himself." Children are seeking, ever seeking, to encompass the world within themselves.

From the moment of birth to the moment of death, each child looks upon the world through his own unique window. What he sees is determined by many intermeshing forces at work, his own inner resources of mind, spirit, and emotions, the family customs and mores, its language and values, the physical world of silence and sound, beauty and ugliness, shapes and patterns, heat and cold, and the people who impinge upon his daily life. All of these forces make the child what he will become. For one child, the view from the window may become distorted early in life. What he sees is unbearable and the window becomes opaque, blocking out a world from which the child, in his vulnerability, must withdraw. For another child, the view from the window presents delightful vistas of discovery ahead. This is the child who becomes a part of his world. In growing toward maturity, he has incorporated the world within himself. The complete fruition of this process has been described by Rilke, who wrote of a friend, "His face is a love letter to all mankind." [2]

No teacher in the world has a more sensitive task, involving more human values — greater potential for magnificent successes or for degrading failures — than the teacher of our language and literature in American schools.

Chapter Notes

Chapter 2

[1] M. M. Lewis, *Infant Speech: A Study of the Beginnings of Language*, 2nd revised edition (New York: Humanities Press, 1951).

[2] F. Grewel, "How Do Children Acquire the Use of Language?" *Phonetica*, *3*, No. 4, 1959, pages 193–202.

[3] Ruth Weir, *Language in the Crib* (The Hague: Mouton, 1962). (Contains an excellent bibliography.)

[4] Martin D. S. Braine, "Grammatical Structure in the Speech of a Two-Year-Old," *Proceedings of the Washington Linguistic Club, I*, No. 1, Fall, 1963, pages 11–16.

[5] Janellen Huttenlocher, "Children's Language: Word-Phrase Relationships," *Science*, January 17, 1964, pages 264–65.

[6] Philip Lieberman, *Intonation, Perception and Language* (Cambridge, Mass.: M.I.T. Press, 1967).

[7] *Ibid.*, pages 38–41.

[8] Noam Chomsky, *Cartesian Linguistics: A Chapter in the History of Rational Thought* (New York: Harper and Row, 1966).

The following points are all cited from this book; page references are in parentheses.

[a] *The orientation of linguistics should be changed.* Chomsky is concerned with "the problem of changing the orientation of linguistics from 'natural history' to 'natural philosophy'" (p. 59). These are quaint old terms. Chomsky evidently interprets *natural history* to mean *natural science*, or *empirical science*, which is the philosophical basis of modern descriptive linguistics; and *natural philosophy* to mean *philosophical introspection*.

[b] *Language universals are properties of the human mind.* Writing under "The Acquisition of Language," he proclaims some of his universal doctrines. "The general features of grammatical structure are common to all languages and reflect certain fundamental properties of the mind"; these are "language universals that prescribe the form of any human language" (p. 59).

[c] *Language is innate, not learned.* Please note carefully: "Such universal conditions [as in point [b] above] are not learned. . . . By attributing such principles to the mind, as an innate property, it becomes possible to account for the quite obvious fact that the speaker of a language knows a great deal that he has not learned" (pp. 59–60).

Admitting that this psychology is "a kind of Platonism without pre-existence," Chomsky credits a seventeenth-century neo-Platonist, Herbert of Cherbury, with expressing much of the psychological theory underlying Chomskyan linguistics. Three hundred fifty years ago, Herbert knew that these principles of the mind are "a direct gift of Nature . . . imprinted on the soul by the dictates of Nature itself." It follows then, in Chomsky's interpretation, "that these interpretive principles cannot be learned by experience in their entirety, and they may be *independent of experience altogether*" (emphasis added). It is a short step from "may be" to "are," as in Chomsky's first statement above (pp. 60–63).

^d *Innate mental structure eliminates need for learning theory.* If we have been concerned to improve instruction by developing a viable learning theory, we need no longer be: these "strong assumptions about innate mental structure" eliminate the need for "any sharp distinction between a theory of perception and a theory of learning." In both perception and learning, "a store of latent principles is brought to the interpretation of the data of sense" (p. 65). Apparently you either have "the direct gift of Nature" or you don't.

Chapter 3

¹ Joseph Vendryes, *Language: A Linguistic Introduction to History*, translated by Paul Rodin (London: Routledge and Kegan Paul, 1925), page 11.

² Edwin A. Sapir, *Language: An Introduction to the Study of Speech* (New York: Harcourt, Brace, 1921). See A Harvest Book, 1949, page 15.

³ *Loc. cit.*

⁴ *Ibid.*, page 17.

⁵ *Ibid.*, page 18.

⁶ *Ibid.*, page 21.

⁷ *Ibid.*, page 22.

⁸ L. S. Vigotsky, "Thought and Speech," Chapter VII of *Language and Thought*, tr. Helen Kogan, Eugenia Hanfmann, and Jacob Kasanin, in *Psycholinguistics: a Book of Readings*, ed. Sol Saporta (New York: Holt, Rinehart, and Winston, 1961), p. 514.

⁹ *Ibid.*, page 515.

¹⁰ *Ibid.*, pages 510–11.

¹¹ *Ibid.*, pages 534–35.

¹² *Loc. cit.*

¹³ *Op. cit.*, pages 19–20.

Chapter 4

¹ Leonard Bloomfield and Clarence Barnhart, *Let's Read: A Linguistic Approach* (Detroit: Wayne State University Press, 1961).

² Charles C. Fries, Rosemary G. Wilson, and Mildred K. Rudolph, *The Merrill Linguistic Readers* (Columbus, Ohio: Merrill, 1966). Donald Rasmussen, and Lynn Goldberg, *A Hen in a Fox's Den* (Chicago: Science Research Associates, 1964). Pauline M. Rojas, Ralph F. Robinett, Paul W. Bell, and others, *Miami Linguistic Readers*, rev. experimental ed. (Boston: D. C. Heath, 1965). Henry Lee Smith, Jr., and others, *The Linguistic Readers* (Chicago: Harper and Row, 1965). Glenn McCracken, Charles C. Walcott and others, *Basic Reading* (Philadelphia: Lippincott, 1964).

³ George J. Hecht, "English Needs a Phonetic Alphabet," *Parents' Magazine*, Special Education Issue, February, 1962, pp. 55–56, 121–22. The author does not mean *phonetic*, but possibly something like *phonemic*. This is far from a sound or scholarly article; it is cited here solely for its clear visual presentation of three

modified alphabets: augmented Roman (i.t.a.), single sound (Unifon), and the World English spelling alphabet (Shaw-Malone). The underlying doctrine is naive and simplistic.

⁴ Two spelling research programs using computer technology provided new data about the relationships of sounds and letters in English spelling during the mid-1960's. Hanna and several collaborators had been actively engaged in spelling research at Stanford since the early 1950s; in 1967 a detailed summary of the culminating project was published by the Government Printing Office. Another line of investigation was begun at Cornell in 1961 by Venezky, working with Weir; this work was continued at Stanford, and the results have been reported by the University. Both studies support the thesis that English spelling is (a) more regular and (b) more complex than has been generally known. Horn, a spelling expert, has been a severe critic of Hanna's work; so far as I know, neither project has been evaluated by linguists in order to incorporate the findings into a description of English phonemics and graphemics.

The Hanna research focuses on spelling as spelling; its practical outcome is a set of recommendations for sequential spelling instruction and a fully developed instructional program for the elementary school published by Houghton Mifflin. The Weir-Venezky research at first focused on spelling, but a substantial part of it relates to reading, apparently on the assumption that comprehensive spelling rules should be incorporated into primary reading instruction; regardless of the sophistication of this study in some respects, the assumption that reading is primarily a spelling problem strikes me as simplistic. These investigators are not alone in this assumption, however; it is akin to the simplistic standard word-perception theory of language and reading, which I have criticized elsewhere. This article of mine, the other studies mentioned in this note, and additional pertinent books and articles are listed in the Selected References for this chapter.

Chapter 5

¹ Raven I. McDavid, Jr., "A Checklist of Significant Features for Discriminating Social Dialects," *Dimensions of Dialect*, Eldonna L. Evertts, ed. (Champaign, Ill.: National Council of Teachers of English, 1967), page 9.

² Robert L. Allen, *The Verb System of Present-Day American English* (New York: Humanities Press, 1966). Martin Joos, *The English Verb: Form and Meaning* (Madison: University of Wisconsin Press, 1964). F. R. Palmer, *A Linguistic Study of the English Verb*, in Longmans' Linguistics Library (London: Longmans, Green, 1965).

³ Joos, *op. cit.*, page 14.

⁴ *Loc. cit.*

⁵ A. S. Hornby, *A Guide to Patterns and Usage in English* (London: Oxford University Press, 1961), page 195.

Chapter 6

¹ Iona and Peter Opie, *The Lore and Language of Schoolchildren* (London: Oxford University Press, 1959), page 30.

² Leonard L. Levinson, *The Left Handed Dictionary* (New York: Collier Books, Macmillan, 1963).

[3] "New American Dictionary of Colleges," *Chicago Tribune Magazine*, Sept. 29, 1963, pp. 14ff.

[4] Levinson, *op. cit.*

Chapter 7

[1] Leonard Bloomfield, *Language* (New York: Holt, Rinehart and Winston, 1933), p. 170.

[2] Donald Bateman and Frank Zidonis, *The Effect of a Study of Transformational Grammar on the Writing of Ninth and Tenth Graders*, Research Report No. 6, National Council of Teachers of English, 508 South Sixth Street, Champaign, Illinois, 1966. Kellogg W. Hunt, *Grammatical Structures Written at Three Grade Levels*, Research Report No. 3, National Council of Teachers of English, 508 South Sixth Street, Champaign, Illinois, 1965. Walter D. Loban, *The Language of Elementary School Children*, Research Report No. 1, National Council of Teachers of English, 508 South Sixth Street, Champaign, Illinois, 1963. Roy C. O'Donnell, William J. Griffin, Raymond C. Norris, *Syntax of Kindergarten and Elementary School Children: A Transformational Analysis*, Research Report No. 8, National Council of Teachers of English, 508 South Sixth Street, Champaign, Illinois, 1967.

[3] Viola Waterhouse, "Independent and Dependent Sentences," *International Journal of American Linguistics, XXIX*, No. 1, pp. 45–54.

[4] Mrs. Bernice Gilbert, a teacher at North School in Glencoe, Illinois, a suburb of Chicago.

[5] Carl A. Lefevre, *Linguistics and the Teaching of Reading* (New York: McGraw-Hill, 1964).

Helen E. Lefevre and Carl A. Lefevre, *Writing by Patterns, Form A and Form B* (New York: Knopf, 1965, 1969).

Chapter 8

[1] Marian Gleason, "On With Up," *English Journal, 55*, No. 8, November 1966, pp. 1087–88. Reprinted with the permission of the National Council of Teachers of English and Marian Gleason.

Chapter 9

[1] Leonard Bloomfield, *Language* (New York: Holt, Rinehart and Winston, 1933).

[2] Kenneth Pike, *The Intonation of American English* (Ann Arbor, Michigan: University of Michigan Press, 1945).

[3] George L. Trager and Henry Lee Smith, Jr., *An Outline of English Structure (Studies in Linguistics, Occasional Papers, No. 3)* (Norman, Oklahoma: Battenburg Press, 1951; reprinted, Washington, D.C., American Council of Learned Societies, 1957).

[4] David Abercrombie, *Studies in Phonetics and Linguistics (Language and Language Learning, No. 10)* (London: Oxford University Press, 1965).

⁵ M. A. K. Halliday, *Intonation and Grammar in British English* (The Hague: Mouton, 1967).

⁶ Philip Lieberman, *Intonation, Perception, and Language* (Cambridge, Mass.: M.I.T. Press, 1967).

⁷ Carl A. Lefevre, Chapter Four, "Intonation: The Melodies of the Printed Page," in *Linguistics and the Teaching of Reading* (New York: McGraw Hill, 1964), pp. 41–75.

⁸ *Op. cit.*, p. 28.

⁹ *Ibid.*, p. 22.

¹⁰ Conrad Aiken, "Prelude," in *Modern American Poetry; Modern British Poetry, Combined Edition*, Louis Untermeyer, ed. (New York: Harcourt, Brace, 1930), p. 608.

¹¹ Kenneth Pike was well aware of the basic significance of the stress-timed rhythm of English in the early 1940's (*op. cit.*, pp. 34–35), the more so because while he was studying English intonation he began to work on the intonation of Portuguese and Spanish, both syllable-timed languages. He made this categorical statement about stress in relation to English pitch contours: "A stressed syllable constitutes the BEGINNING POINT for every primary contour; there is no primary contour without a stressed syllable, and every stressed syllable begins a new contour" (*ibid.*, p. 27). He also says further: "Intonation contours are intimately related to pauses and to rhythm. . . . Nevertheless, intonation [pitch] must be kept distinct from these latter speech characteristics, since in many respects they are independent of one another. Pause and rhythm are closely dependent upon one another in some of their elements and usage, but in other ways are independent, and so must be handled as separate significant entities (that is, as different types of phonemes or morphemes) . . ." (*ibid.*, p. 30). Here Pike uses the term *intonation* to mean *pitch contour*, and tries to separate it entirely from the other features; this reflects his preoccupation with pitch at the expense of more comprehensive intonation patterns. It is significant that while insisting that pause and rhythm should be kept separate from pitch contours, he also states that *pause and rhythm are types of phonemes or morphemes* — in other words, structural elements of English. The need for more research on English intonation is clear, especially on the relationship of stress to pitch and pause and of their reciprocal effects upon each other.

¹² At this point, it may be useful to consider Pike's position that any *pitch contour* may be used with any utterance provided the speaker [not the reader] has the requisite attitude. In the passage below, he is writing only of pitch contours, for which he used three terms interchangeably: *English contours, intonation contours,* and *intonation curves;* elsewhere he uses *intonation* in the same sense. In reading Pike's brilliant analyses, it is necessary to keep his preoccupation with *pitch contours* firmly in mind, and not confuse them with *large, overriding intonation patterns*, as I am using the term, to include structural combinations of features of *stress, pitch,* and *terminal.*

The utilization of any specific contour is not determined by the structure of the sentence upon which it is to fall, but by the attitude of the speaker utilizing that construction. Any specific construction may have superimposed upon it any of the English contours, provided the speaker has the requisite attitude when he does so; this holds true even when the meaning of the words conflicts with the meaning of the intonation — but irony, or jest, or some special innuendo results from such conflicts. . . . Intonation contours cannot be defined in terms of the grammatical constructions with which they occur.

As a corollary of the previous principle, it follows that there is no 'question pitch' as such, nor any 'statement pitch' as such. Questions may be found with all intonation curves. Statements, likewise, may be found with all intonation curves (*ibid.*, p. 163).

Despite his belief that rhythm and pauses are like phonemes and morphemes (see footnote 11), Pike does not differentiate clearly between *structural* and *interpretive* intonation. More to the immediate point, he does not attempt to apply his findings to composition at all, and only superficially to reading; his references to reading are quite casual and have to do with individual variations in oral renditions — in other words, with interpretive features. Reading and reading instruction must invert Pike's conception of *requisite attitude* — which is that of a spontaneous speaker; but not at all *the requisite attitude of the reader* — a receptive and sensitive auditor, attending to the author's general purpose and specific intent, and above all to the nuances of his language.

[13] *Op. cit.*, p. 6.

[14] *Ibid.*, p. 3.

[15] *Ibid.*, p. 8.

[16] "A Comprehensive Linguistic View of Reading," *Elementary English*, October 1965, pp. 651–59.

[17] I am indebted to Mr. Norman Gottschalk, a Chicago friend, for this little tragedy.

[18] Jean G. Pival, "Stress, Pitch, and Juncture: Tools in the Diagnosis and Treatment of Reading Ills," *Elementary English*, April, 1968, pp. 458–63, 467.

Chapter 10

[1] John Ciardi, "Christmas Greetings to the American Dream," *Saturday Review*, December 23, 1961.

[2] T. S. Eliot, "The Burial of the Dead" in *The Waste Land* (New York: Harcourt, Brace and World, 1936).

[3] John Ciardi, "How to Read Dante," *Saturday Review*, June 3, 1961, p. 54.

Chapter 11

[1] John E. Warriner, *English Grammar and Composition* (New York: Harcourt, Brace and World, 1958).

[2] W. Nelson Francis, "Revolution in Grammar," *Quarterly Journal of Speech*, *40*, pp. 299–312 (October, 1954). Reprinted in *Readings in Applied Linguistics*, ed. Harold B. Allen (New York: Appleton-Century-Crofts, 1964), pp. 69–85.

[3] H. A. Gleason, Jr., *Linguistics and English Grammar* (New York: Holt, Rinehart and Winston, 1965).

[4] R. W. Pence and D. W. Emery, *A Grammar of Present-Day English* (New York: Macmillan, 1963).

[5] Noah Webster, *Dissertations on the English Language* (Boston: 1789), intro. Harry R. Warfel (Gainesville, Florida: Scholars' Facsimiles and Reprints: 1951).

[6] Robert Lowth, *A Short Introduction to English Grammar* (London: 1762). Reprinted: Menston, England: Scolar Press, 1967.

[7] Lindley Murray, *English Grammar Adapted to the Different Classes of Learners* (London: 1795). Reprinted: Menston, England: Scolar Press, 1967.

[8] Etsko Kruisinga, *A Handbook of Present-Day English* (Utrecht: Kemink en Zoon, 1909).

[9] Jens Otto Harry Jespersen, *A Modern English Grammar on Historical Principles* (Copenhagen: Ejnar Munksgaard, 1909–49).

[10] Henrik Poutsma, *A Grammar of Late Modern English* (Groningen: P. Noordhoff, 1914–1929).

[11] George Oliver Curme, *Syntax* (*A Grammar of the English Language*, Vol. 3) (Boston: D. C. Heath, 1931).

———, *Parts of Speech and Accidence* (*A Grammar of the English Language*, Vol. 2) (Boston: D. C. Heath, 1935).

[12] Otto Jespersen, *Essentials of English Grammar* (University, Alabama: University of Alabama Press, 1964).

[13] Charles Carpenter Fries, *The Structure of English: An Introduction to the Construction of English Sentences* (New York: Harcourt, Brace, 1952).

[14] George L. Trager and Henry Lee Smith, Jr., *An Outline of English Structure* (*Studies in Linguistics: Occasional Papers*, 1951), 2nd ed. (Washington, D.C.: American Council of Learned Societies, 1957).

[15] Leonard Bloomfield, *Language* (New York: Holt, Rinehart and Winston, 1933), 2nd printing, 1961.

[16] Edwin A. Sapir, *Language: An Introduction to the Study of Speech* (New York: Harcourt, Brace, 1921, 1949).

[17] Charles C. Fries, "The Bloomfield School," *Trends in European and American Linguistics*, 1930–1960, (Utrecht: Spectrum, 1961), pp. 196–224. See subsection, "The Uses of Meaning," pp. 212–17.

———, "Meaning and Linguistic Analysis," *Language*, XXX (1954) pp. 57–68; reprinted in H. B. Allen, *Readings in Applied English Linguistics* (New York: Appleton-Century-Crofts, 1964), pp. 110 ff.

[18] Fries, *The Structure of English*, p. 56.

[19] *Op. cit.*, pp. 272–73.

[20] *Op. cit.*, p. 55.

[21] *Op. cit.*, p. 68.

[22] *Op. cit.*, pp. 81–82.

[23] *Loc. cit.*

[24] *Op. cit.*, p. 7.

[25] Ruth Strickland, *The Language of Elementary School Children: Its Relationship to the Language of Reading Textbooks and the Quality of Reading of Selected Children* (Bloomington: Indiana University *Bulletin* of the School of Education, July, 1962), *38*, No. 4.

———, *The Contribution of Structural Linguistics to the Teaching of Reading, Writing, and Grammar in the Elementary School* (Bloomington: Indiana University *Bulletin* of the School of Education, January 1964), *40*, No. 1.

[26] Walter Loban, *The Language of Elementary School Children: A Study of the Use and Control of Language Effectiveness in Communication, and the Relations Among Speaking, Reading, Writing, and Listening* (No. 1 in a series of research reports sponsored by the NCTE Committee on Research) (Champaign, Illinois: National Council of Teachers of English, 1963).

[27] *Op. cit.*, Chapter XII, pp. 256 ff.

[28] Harold Whitehall, *The Structural Essentials of English* (New York: Harcourt, Brace, 1956), p. 19.

[29] W. Nelson Francis, *The Structure of American English* (New York: Ronald Press, 1958).

[30] Kenneth L. Pike, *The Intonation of American English*, University of Michigan Publication, Linguistics, Vol. 1 (Ann Arbor: University of Michigan Press, 1945).

[31] Kenneth L. Pike, *Language in Relation to a Unified Theory of the Structure of Human Behavior* (New York: Humanities Press, 1964).

[32] *Webster's Third International Dictionary.*

[33] Robert L. Allen, *The Structure of the English Sentence* (New York: Noble and Noble, in prep.).

[34] Robert L. Allen (and others), *A Linguistic Approach to Writing: Discovery 1 and 2 (Experimental Edition)* (New York: Noble and Noble, 1967).

[35] Kenneth L. Pike, "A Linguistic Contribution to Composition: A Hypothesis," *College Composition and Communication*, May, 1964, pp. 82–88.

——, "Beyond the Sentence," *CCC*, October, 1964, pp. 129–35.

[36] *College Composition and Communication*, May, 1964, p. 83.

[37] *Loc. cit.*

[38] William Orr Dingwall, *Generative Transformational Grammar: A Bibliography* (Washington, D.C.: Center for Applied Linguistics, 1965), p. v.

[39] Noam Chomsky, *Syntatical Structures* (The Hague: Mouton, 1957).

——, *Current Issues in Linguistic Theory* (The Hague: Mouton, 1964).

——, *Aspects of the Theory of Syntax* (Cambridge, Mass.: M.I.T. Press, 1965).

——, *Cartesian Linguistics: A Chapter in the History of Rationalist Thought* (New York: Harper and Row, 1966).

—— (with Morris Halle), *Sound Patterns of American English* (New York: Harper and Row, 1968).

[40] Paul Roberts, *English Sentences* (New York: Harcourt, Brace and World, 1962).

[41] Paul Roberts, *Patterns of English* (New York: Harcourt, Brace and World, 1955).

[42] Paul Roberts, *English Syntax* (New York: Harcourt, Brace and World, 1964).

[43] Owen Thomas, *Transformational Grammar and the Teacher of English* (New York: Holt, Rinehart and Winston, 1966).

[44] *Ibid.*, pp. 54–55.

[45] Baxter Hathaway, *A Transformational Syntax: The Grammar of Modern American English* (New York: Ronald Press, 1967), p. v.

[46] *The Roberts English Series: A Linguistics Program* (New York: Harcourt, Brace and World, 1964–67).

[47] Anne Kirby and Craig Vittetoe, consultant, *Elementary School English* (Palo Alto: Addison-Wesley, 1967).

[48] William West and others, *Language and Composition* (Boston: Ginn and Company, 1968).

[49] "An Interview with Paul Roberts" (New York: Harcourt, Brace and World, 1967), unnumbered pages.

[50] H. A. Gleason, Jr., in a paper read at the annual convention of the National Council of Teachers of English, Houston, Texas, November 28, 1966.

[51] Kellogg W. Hunt, *Grammatical Structures Written at Three Grade Levels* (No. 3 in a series of research reports sponsored by the NCTE Committee on Research) (Champaign, Illinois: *National Council of Teachers of English*, 1965), pp. 110–24.

"How Little Sentences Grow into Big Ones," *New Directions in Elementary English*, ed. Alexander Frazier (Champaign, Illinois: National Council of Teachers of English, 1967), pp. 110–24. "Recent Measures in Syntactic Development," *Elementary English*, November, 1966, pp. 732–39.

⁵² Noam Chomsky, "Language and the Mind," *Psychology Today*, February, 1968, pp. 48–51, 66–68.
⁵³ Chomsky, *Cartesian Linguistics*, p. 63.
⁵⁴ *Op. cit.*, p. 32.
⁵⁵ *Op. cit.*, p. 42.
⁵⁶ Noam Chomsky, "The Current Scene in Linguistics," *College English*, May, 1966, p. 588.
⁵⁷ Noam Chomsky, "Introduction," Paul Roberts, *English Syntax* (alternate edition) (New York: Harcourt, Brace and World, 1964), p. xi.
⁵⁸ *Ibid.*, p. xiii.
⁵⁹ Chomsky, *Aspects of the Theory of Syntax*, p. 4 and *passim*.
⁶⁰ John Viertel, "Generative Grammars," *College Composition and Communication*, May, 1964, pp. 65–81, p. 68.
⁶¹ Edward Crothers and Patrick Suppes, *Experiments in Second-Language Learning* (New York and London: Academic Press, 1967), pp. 9–14.
⁶² *Loc. cit.*
⁶³ *Syntactic Structures*, pp. 88–89.
⁶⁴ Viertel, *op. cit.*, pp. 79–80.
⁶⁵ Chomsky, "Introduction," *English Syntax*, p. xiv.
⁶⁶ Viertel, *op. cit.*, p. 68.
⁶⁷ Quoted in David Sarnoff, "No Life Untouched," *Saturday Review*, July 23, 1964, p. 22.
⁶⁸ *Some Professional Syntactic Strictures.* Because Chomsky has been hailed as the founder of a school of linguistics that makes all other linguistics obsolete, readers of this book may not be aware of professional scholarship in linguistics, mathematics, psychology, and the teaching of English that criticizes him sharply on the following main points:

1. His reliance on personal intuition, introspection, and the methods of speculative philosophy in a field where scientific method and empirical data are more appropriate.

2. His disregard for empirical data presented by others, and his failure to present systematic empirical data in his own expositions.

3. His dogmatism, and an apparent effort to brush aside disagreement by using a contentious tone.

4. His failure to develop clear and stable definitions of terms capable of discriminating such pairs of key concepts as *competence* and *performance; grammaticality* and *acceptability; generation* and *production.*

5. His arbitrary assertions about the way his rules supposedly operate within the native speaker to generate and transform sentences.

6. His arbitrary statements concerning language universals presumably applicable to all natural languages.

7. His publication of mistakes that go unacknowledged after they have been pointed out.

Such serious strictures from competent scholars cannot be answered by silence, or simply by labeling them confused, trivial, or uninteresting. The points cited above have been vigorously pressed against Chomsky in American and British linguistic journals, American professional periodicals in English, and a book on second-language learning co-authored by two psychologists and published in New York and London; notes are at the end of this discussion. These selections are representative of a larger body of criticism; no attempt has been made at an exhaustive survey.

The linguist Winter, while agreeing that in English, statements and elements of statements may have a transformational "correspondence," or "equivalence," strongly insists that one is not derived from the other. Winter thus refuses to recognize the use of arrows in transformational rules, or to use them himself to show the presumed direction of any variation. His choice of a graphic device is the colon. For example, *The boy is tall: the tall boy.*

With convincing evidence, Winter disproves Chomsky's rule that a noun group like *the tall boy* is necessarily a transformation of a kernel like *The boy is tall.* Winter cites many noun groups that do not have any such equivalents; for example,

the lower depths	but not	The depths are lower.
the right side	but not	The side is right.
a criminal court	but not	The court is criminal.
civil rights	but not	Rights are civil.
a second Chomsky	but not	Chomsky is second.

Werner likewise cites kernel statements that do not have noun group transformations, or equivalents; for example,

The Frenchman is last	but not	the last Frenchman
(as in a game or race)		
The girl is right	but not	the right girl
("right" in what she says) [a]		

In the same article, following Quirk,[b] Winter also demonstrates that English has activeless passives, and so disproves Chomsky's assertion that passive constructions are invariably transformations of active propositions (kernels). He cites *I was born in Germany* as a passive construction that has no active equivalent in English. He argues that *to be born* is not the passive equivalent of *to bear* in modern usage: "witness the non-equivalence of *A child is being born* and *She is bearing a child."*

After his convincing presentation of data tending to invalidate two of Chomsky's rules, Winter goes on to this conclusion:

> There is no absolute protection against remaining unaware of matters of detail. I wish that certain safeguards were used more often; it seems better to rely on the inspection of large bodies of text and on the compilations of others (as for instance reflected in major handbooks) than on introspection and a native speaker's intuition. True, the drudgery of painstaking collection of data before developing theories is a major obstacle to the erection of imposing edifices, but at least one has a certain assurance that what one builds is not merely a house of cards. There is need for revision of basic work techniques if one finds that virtually every published paper concerned with the production of sequences of rules contains some outright mistakes which evidently are there because the author just did not happen to think of the right thing at the right moment. It makes criticism easy, and a little cheap, if all a reader has to do is to out-introspect the author. . . .[c]

Another linguist, Householder, denies the psychological reality of Chomsky's strings of rules for English speakers; quite aside from the psychological reality of the rules, he denies their universality in describing the structure of other languages.

---

[a] Werner Winter, "Transforms without Kernels?" *Language, 41*, No. 3, Part 1 (July–September, 1965), pp. 484–89.

[b] Randolph Quirk, "Descriptive Statement and Serial Relationship," *Language, 41*, No. 2 (April–June, 1965), pp. 205–17.

[c] *Op. cit.*, p. 489.

While languages like English may use long series of ordered rules (which are, to me, a nice convenient trick bearing no relation — or very little — to what goes on in a speaker's brain) others, such as Polynesian ones, need very few rules. . . .[d]

Householder writes bluntly of Chomsky's dogmatism; he faults his "God's truth" style in general and in particular. In one of his articles he objects as follows:

> I . . . do not like the use of such God's truth language, saying always "such and such is X" instead of "such and such may be conveniently described or looked at as X." And even if I believed their assertions (Chomsky's and Halle's) were as securely based as those a physicist may make about atomic nuclei, I would say that this makes no difference, and that a physicist who says what an atom IS must be speaking in some sort of figurative language.

Respecting a point of phonology, Householder says simply that he is unable to believe the "God's truth arguments offered in support of it." [e]

In another article, Householder notes that while "Chomsky vehemently rejects the charge of dogmatism, it remains a fact that he KNOWS certain things for sure that I do not know and appear incapable of learning; this knowledge enables him to say what linguists must do to remain linguists (or become linguists)." [f] Referring to Chomsky's authority among his followers and their uncritical acceptance of that authority, Householder notes that some of them "have a practical test for explanatory adequacy," as follows: "(1) If an explanation is not from MIT, it's wrong; (2) of two from MIT, the one O.K.'d by Chomsky or Halle is correct. On many points they must remain in suspense for a time, of course. Nothing ever needs retraction; only exegesis." [g]

McDavid, a linguist and dialectologist, writes as follows of his difficulties with "chomskemics":

> I find that by the time I have read six illustrative sentences in Chromsky's *Syntactic Structures*, I have two disagreements on grammaticality: at least one sentence that he characterizes as grammatical I would reject in my normal discourse; one of those he rejects as ungrammatical would seem acceptable to me in some contexts. To accommodate our differences would require a far more intricate set of formulae, or "rules" than has yet been offered.[h]

In a careful statement of language learning theory, two psychologists, Crothers and Suppes, make the following points in their discussion of current linguistic arguments, notably those of Chomsky and his co-workers. At present, they note, there is no theory in either psychology or linguistics that can explain any substantial part of the systematic details of language learning. Two main objections they raise to transformational discussions of language learning are the contentious philosophical tone of the argument and the indifference to presentation or analysis of any systematic empirical data. These points are especially

---

[d] F. W. Householder, Jr., "Phonological theory: A brief comment," *Journal of Linguistics*, *2*, No. 1 (April, 1966), pp. 99–100.

[e] *Op. cit.*, p. 100.

[f] Householder, "On some recent claims in phonological theory," *Journal of Linguistics*, *1*, No. 1 (April, 1965), p. 33, note 17.

[g] *Op. cit.*, p. 16, note 3.

[h] Raven I. McDavid, Jr., "System and Variety in American English," in *New Directions in Elementary English*, ed. Alexander Frazier (Champaign, Illinois: National Council of Teachers of English, 1967), p. 130.

serious because language learning is a subject that is inherently scientific and empirical in character, as they point out, and does not respond appropriately to classical philosophical methods of reasoning. Possibly the most telling point raised by Crothers and Suppes is that "the existence of formal grammars for characterizing a natural language grammar hardly guarantees that subjects do in fact employ these particular generative rules, or that the rules even have substantial relevance to the actual method of learning.[i]

Some of the most effective criticism of Chromsky's influence on English teaching has appeared in articles by two English professors who combine their knowledge of linguistics with excellent prose style. Myers and DeCamp, sometimes serious, sometimes tongue in cheek, appreciably reduce the solemnity of transformational grammar while scoring points similar to those already noted, and applying their own sharp nips and fillips.

In "Generation and Deviation,"[j] his quips and jests flicking among solid blows, Myers raises fundamental doubts about some of the claims and pretensions of Chomskyan theory, including the ambiguously shifting meanings of terms that have remained the same. He credits structuralism with several positive influences on the teaching of English grammar, and points out that structuralism is by no means dead. Myers declares that the Chomskyan transformational school bases its work on "convenient but improbable assumptions," and that "they are attempting something basically impossible." He simply does not believe Chomsky's assertions about the child's acquisition of language; he is particularly sharp on the tedious preoccupation with language as a species-specific capacity of human beings, and with that "most wonderful of all human accomplishments," our ability to produce and understand new sentences every day.

> The obvious reason that a bird can learn to fly is that a bird has wings to fly with; and the obvious reason that a child can learn to talk is that he has an innate capacity for language . . . But I don't know just how specific, or how nearly uniform; and I see no reason to believe that it is systematically logical. . . . When he reaches a certain point in his schooling, we may, if we like, try to teach him a more unified system. But if we do, *we should not pretend that we are making his own intuitive system explicit* (italics added).[k]

Myers' term *deviation* in his title refers to "a sentence involving any metaphor that hasn't been frozen"; this is his opening into the question of the impossibility of "including the lexicon in the grammar, and of basing many syntactic decisions on unacknowledged semantic grounds." This is a fundamental criticism. The essay as a whole is solid, sophisticated, and delightful to mull over.

In "Sequence of Tenses, or Was James Thurber the First Transformational Grammarian?"[l] DeCamp describes the current scene in linguistics as it has never been described before, scores fencer's points against exposed surfaces of transformationalism, and laces his excellent prose with witty sallies and nimble counter-thrusts. Despite a superficial appearance of lighthearted satire, however, this is a serious article that touches several of the most vulnerable points of Chomskyan theory. The indirectly stated thesis is that Chomsky's "new gram-

[i] Crothers and Suppes, *op. cit.*, pp. 4, 8, 11.

[j] L. M. Myers, "Generation and Deviation," *College Composition and Communication*, XVIII, No. 5 (December, 1967), pp. 214–20.

[k] *Op. cit.*, p. 218.

[l] David DeCamp, "Sequence of Tenses, or Was James Thurber the First Transformational Grammarian?" *College Composition and Communication*, XVIII, No. 1 (February, 1967), pp. 7–13.

mar," in both spirit and form, is really very old, very unscientific, and very prescriptive.

DeCamp opens his study on a note of transformational gloom and doom.

> I think that most linguists, especially recently, are like James Thurber and me: Calvinist to the core, confident that the world is doomed to grammatical perdition, knawed by the agenbite of inwit; and inwardly doubtful of our own state of grace, we whistle and parse in the dark, and try to act like members of the grammatically elect.[m]

After a satirical exposition of the chief speculations of Chomskyan theory and their various changing forms and emphases, DeCamp relates them deftly to the prescriptive mood of school grammar.

> I think we are coming back to the healthy old idea that grammar is basically a negative operation. We all want to communicate, and the grammar is a filter which ensures that only the permissible forms of communication will get through. Grammar is primarily a series of thou-shalt-nots.[n]

But he also knows how to make his point with hilariously pertinent examples.

> In case your student ever produces a flagrantly intolerable sequence of tenses like *He arrived twenty minutes after I will milk the mongoose,* you can "transform" his sentence into two separate sentences: *I will milk the mongoose. Twenty minutes later he arrived.* Point out that these two sentences, though each impeccably grammatical when considered in isolation, have very little coherent connection.[o]

Throughout the essay runs the more-than-half-serious pretense that Thurber's humorously prescriptive school grammar (about 1930), full of witty non sequiturs, and written as only Thurber could have written it, is the direct antecedent of the Chomsky canon.

> Unfortunately, Thurber didn't have quite all the answers. He never thought of putting arrows in his rules, thereby making Chomsky and MIT unnecessary. Therefore he was only the first transformational grammarian, and *Aspects of the Theory of Syntax* is now the grammatical best seller instead of the *Ladies and Gentlemen's Guide to Modern English Usage.* Still, credit must be given where credit is due, and Thurber did come first.[p]

Since the foregoing was written, two other noteworthy antagonists of Chomsky have come to my attention. Gerdan, a productive scholar in statistical linguistics and a competent philosopher in the technical sense, has published a closely reasoned, vigorous polemic against Chomsky *as a modern thinker.* The main thrust of his argument is that it is absurd at this point in the twentieth century to resurrect "innate ideas" from medieval religious philosophy, in the name of any kind of science, linguistic or otherwise.[q] Hockett, author of a standard

---

[m] *Op. cit.,* p. 7.

[n] *Op. cit.,* p. 12.

[o] *Op. cit.,* p. 10.

[p] *Op. cit.,* p. 13.

[q] G. Herdan, "The Crisis in General Linguistics," *La Linguistique,* Vol. 1, pp. 27–37, 1967.

advanced text in linguistics,[r] has published an extended "critical review of current American linguistic theory, directed principally — indeed, almost but not quite exclusively — towards the views of Noam Chomsky."[s] Hockett's argument is cogent, well organized, and detailed; the gist of it is that Chomsky's assumption that languages are well-ordered systems like logic and mathematics is patently false. Readers interested in this topic will want to study this book carefully, in its entirety.

[69] H. A. Gleason, Jr., "The Organization of Language; A Stratificational View," *Report of the Fifteenth Annual (First International) Round Table Meeting on Linguistics and Language Studies,* ed. C. I. J. M. Stuart (Washington, D.C.: Georgetown University Press, 1964). Sydney M. Lamb, *Outline of Stratificational Grammar* (Washington, D.C.: Georgetown University Press, 1966).

[70] Such an operational synthesis of grammars has been implemented in practice-oriented writing programs by Carl and Helen Lefevre, with collaborating classroom teachers, in *English Writing Patterns,* grades 2–12 (New York: Random House-Singer, 1968): eleven upgraded supplementary workbooks, with two program guides for teachers (grades 2–6, and 7–12). This program somewhat follows the authors' *Writing by Patterns,* Forms A and B (New York: Random House-Knopf, 1965, 1968). A fuller implementation is in preparation: *The Lefevre Language Program,* grades K–8, with several classroom teachers as collaborating authors, William H. Sadlier, New York.

Chapter 12

[1] "Language." Excerpt from "A Check List for Evaluating the English Program in the Junior and Senior High School," prepared by the Commission on the Curriculum of the National Council of Teachers of English, April, 1962.

[2] Muriel Crosby, NCTE Presidential address: "Of the Times and the Language," *English Journal,* February, 1967, pp. 206–07.

---

[r] Charles F. Hockett, *A Course in Modern Linguistics* (New York: Macmillan, 1958).

[s] ———, *The State of the Art* (The Hague: Mouton, 1968).

Index